THE GREAT WEALTH TRANSFER SERIES

LEVELING THE SEVEN MOUNTAINS & THE RED SEA MOMENT

by

Jacqueline Towell

Published and distributed by:
Digital Dollars Now
www.DigitalDollarsNow.com

Cover design: Jacqueline Towell
Interior design: Jacqueline Towell
Printed in the United States of America

While efforts have been made to verify information contained in this publication, neither the author nor the publisher assumes any responsibility for errors, inaccuracies, or omissions. While this publication is chock-full of useful, practical information; it is not intended to be business, legal, investment, financial, regulatory, accounting or similar advice. All readers are advised to seek competent lawyers, financial advisors, and accountants to follow laws and regulations that may apply to specific situations, before making any investment decisions. The author of this publication is not a professional advisor in the areas involving finance, cryptocurrency, taxation, securities and commodities trading. The content provided in this publication is intended for informational and educational purposes only; and is premised upon subjective opinions pertaining to currently existing facts readily available, research readily available or personal experience in these areas. No content in this publication is a recommendation or solicitation to buy or sell any securities or digital assets, (e.g., cryptocurrencies). The reader of this publication assumes responsibility for the use of the information. The author and publisher assume no responsibility or liability whatsoever on the behalf of the reader of this publication.

ISBN (paperback): 9798895905586
ISBN (eBook): 9798895903063

1st Edition

TABLE OF CONTENTS

TABLE OF CONTENTS

1ST EDITION

THE GREAT WEALTH TRANSFER SERIES

by
Jacqueline Towell

Book One:	Leveling The Seven Mountains & The Red Sea Moment
Book Two:	Claiming Your Inheritance & Taking The Promise Land
Book Three:	Rebuilding The Seven Mountains of Influence
Book Four:	The Great Harvest
Book Five:	The Fall Of Babylon

Hello!

Welcome and congratulations on taking your first steps in this journey towards personal development, mindset shift, personal growth and knowledge about The Great Wealth Transfer. This is a very exciting time for those who are spiritually awake and willing to put in the work to prepare for building and managing your future wealth.

A little about me, I graduated from California State University, Long Beach with a B.S. in Business Management. Started my career in financial services, helping people plan for retirement and their family through financial planning, Life Insurance, Annuities, and 401k/IRAs. Since 2012, I have been in Sales & Business Development for the Life Sciences Industry. However, it was my passion for cryptocurrencies and investment planning that has brought me to create my company Digital Dollars Now and to publishing this book series on the wealth transfer. In addition, I am currently working to create a corresponding Digital Dollars Now Academy. It's my hope that this academy will aid people and students that are taking part in this book series as well as provide education through step-by-step e-courses on everything you need to know to get started investing in cryptocurrency.

God bless you and your family,

Jacqueline Towell

www.digitaldollarsnow.com

ACKNOWLEDGMENTS

There are special people in my life whose encouragement and assistance have made this book possible:

To my beautiful daughter, Jocelyn:

Words cannot fully express the depth of love, gratitude, and admiration I have for you. You have been an inspiration, a source of strength, and a driving force behind my success and personal growth. Your presence in my life has given me purpose, motivation, and a deeper sense of fulfillment that I could never have imagined.

Through every challenge and triumph, you have been my constant source of encouragement and joy. Your resilience, kindness, and unwavering belief in me have pushed me to pursue my dreams and strive for excellence in all that I do. Knowing that you are watching, learning, and growing alongside me fuels my determination to create a legacy that you can be proud of.

I am beyond grateful to have you in my life, and I cherish every moment we share. You are not just my daughter; you are my greatest blessing and my heart's deepest joy. Thank you for being the incredible person that you are and for inspiring me every day. I love you more than words can express.

—Jacqueline Towell

To my dear friend, Heather North:

Having a friend who is like-minded and shares similar spiritual giftings is truly a gift from God. In recent years my journey of faith and spiritual growth, I consider your friendship invaluable, creating a strong spiritual support system that has fostered mutual encouragement, accountability, and confirmation of God's direction. This friendship goes beyond mere companionship; and I consider to be a God-ordained partnerships that is intended to navigate life's challenges with wisdom, faith, and discernment. You have been a pillar of strength, a source of encouragement, and a faithful companion, walking alongside me with unwavering support. Your spiritual insight, discernment, and prophetic giftings have been a profound blessing, allowing us to align in faith and sensitivity to the Holy Spirit, discerning and interpreting divine messages together. Time and again, God has used you to confirm His revelations and instructions in my life, bringing clarity and reassurance in moments of doubt and uncertainty.

One of the greatest blessings of our friendship has been witnessing how God speaks through you to affirm His plans. There have been times when I have received dreams or visions about significant financial decisions, and without me mentioning them, you have later shared a similar message from the Lord, confirming the steps I needed to take. This alignment has been a beautiful testament to God's faithfulness, showing that He works through His people to guide and encourage us on the right path.

Having a trusted friend who understands the spiritual realm and operates in similar giftings allows for deeper discussions, strengthened faith, and a heightened awareness of God's voice. In seasons of uncertainty, your friendship has been a beacon of wisdom and reassurance, reminding me that I am never alone in this journey. Your unwavering faith, compassion, and obedience to the Holy Spirit have been an inspiration to me and so many others. I thank God for the divine connection He has given us and for the role you have played in shaping my faith and this journey.

May the Lord continue to bless you abundantly, guiding you in His purpose and granting you even greater wisdom, revelation, and spiritual insight. With deep gratitude and appreciation, I honor you in this acknowledgment, knowing that your friendship has been a reflection of God's love and faithfulness.

—Jacqueline Towell

DEDICATION

I dedicate this book to the Lord Jesus Christ, my Savior, my Redeemer, and the divine source of inspiration behind every revelation and insight contained within these pages. It is through His wisdom, guidance, and unfailing love that this book has come to life. He has walked with me through every season, teaching, refining, and preparing me for this moment.

The journey He has led me on over the past few decades has been one of faith, growth, and divine transformation—one that has shaped not only my understanding but also my purpose. I stand in awe of His grace, knowing that without Him, this book would not exist. His divine revelation has illuminated my path, and His presence has been my constant source of strength and encouragement.

It is my sincere hope and prayer that the lessons, knowledge, and wisdom shared in these pages will bless, inspire, and equip others just as they have profoundly impacted my own life. May this book serve as a vessel of His truth, bringing hope, clarity, and revelation to all who read it.

I am eternally grateful and humbled that the Lord has chosen me for this mission and calling. To Him be all the glory, honor, and praise—forever and ever. Amen.

INTRODUCTION

For many years leading up to 2020, my prayers were often directed toward finding strategies to get ahead, pay off debt, and earn additional income to alleviate financial struggles. Despite occasional breakthroughs and moments of relief, my life was frequently marked by unforeseen expenses or events that wiped out my savings or added to financial burdens. This struggle to survive has been the one constant for all of my life. There have been seasons of relief and blessings, don't get me wrong, but the one constant that has remained was the struggle to make ends meet.

This cycle of striving and setbacks seemed unrelenting, a challenge shared by countless others working tirelessly in 9-to-5 jobs or juggling multiple jobs to support their families. Hope for a breakthrough—a better job, a side business, or even to win the lottery—often fueled my dreams of a brighter future. However, I have seen how the weight of generational financial struggles can erode that hope over time, leaving a sense of resignation. Observations of these struggles reveal that a person's mindset often plays a critical role in either blocking or enabling financial breakthroughs.

This book explores the importance of mindset in achieving financial freedom, the knowledge and wisdom necessary to succeed, and how to adopt strategies used by the rich and wealthy. It delves into financial planning, time management, and goal-setting while discussing how money can be leveraged to work for an individual rather than the other way around. Additionally, it examines the great wealth transfer currently underway, offering guidelines for protecting, managing, and growing financial assets. Written from a Christian perspective, this book aims to equip readers with practical and spiritual insights to navigate these transitions.

A Catalyst for Change

To give some additional context to this time in my life, between 2015-2019 I had decided to go back to school and finish my degree (deciding to major in Business Management). One of my main motivations for going back to school was because my lack of degree was preventing me from moving up to the next level of my career and making more money. So, for four and half years I juggled being a wife, mother, full-time student, and working a full-time job which required me to travel (at times about 20-30% of the month). Needless to say, this was the most extreme and stressful time in my life because during this time I never had a day off and between all of my responsibilities I was putting in more than 120 hours of work a week. I believe it was the grace of God that I got through that time in my life without having a mental or physical breakdown.

May of 2019 was the last month of my last semester before I graduated. I was taking five classes and preparing for finals and team projects while trying to balance my work commitments. That month I had to travel every week for my sales job, to either the east coast, where my company was located, or to the mid-west where my company was having a grand opening for a new location. This required taking red-eye flights during the week, allowing time, to return to California in time to complete my school finals and projects before flying back to fulfill work obligations. Balancing these responsibilities demanded careful planning and relentless effort. Thankfully, I passed my classes and graduated in June 2019.

The pandemic and lockdowns of 2020 became a turning point for me. After years of balancing a full-time job, school, family, and marriage, completing my degree marked the first significant financial breakthrough. In January 2020, my degree opened the door to a better-paying job with a lucrative compensation plan, increasing my annual earnings from ~$80,000 in 2019 to ~$180,000 in 2020.

Like millions of people that were affected by these lockdowns, I was faced with similar life events that would force me to make the changes I needed to overcome significant financial instability. My husband's Land Surveying business was affected in a huge way. At this point we only had the income from my base salary to depend on, as it would still be a few months until I received my first commission check. Overnight, my husband's business just seemed to grind to a screeching halt, calls stopped coming in for new jobs and it was obvious that if business did not pick up again soon things were going to get difficult really quick. At this time, my husband had been the bread winner of our household and brought in around 65-70% of our income, and when that income stopped coming in it hurt.

I would say it was during this month that The Lord had strongly dealt with me in the areas of our finances and where I could have been doing a better job of managing things. It was made abundantly clear that while I had surrendered many areas of my life to The Lord, the one area that I had not fully surrendered was my finances. I thought I had, but now looking back on this, I know I was not being honest with myself. So, the first thing that I did during this time of intense prayer was fully surrender our finances to the Lord. Because let's be honest, I needed a miracle here!

"And the peace of God, which transcends all understanding, will guard your hearts and your minds in Christ Jesus"
— Philippians 4:7 (NIV)

Immediately after saying this prayer, I felt this indescribable peace come over me. It was just like described in the bible and it is this peace that is still with me to this day. Up to this point I had not realized how much fear I had allowed to consume my thoughts or influence my decision making. I then started to get to work, making calls and trying to refinance anything and everything that I could. This resulted in some creative financing on my part that was able to reduce our overall expenses just enough for us to get by with the income I was now bringing in. Not only that but within about a week after praying and taking action, my husband started to get calls again for his business (another answer to prayer). Slow at first but over the next couple of months more and more work started to come back in.

I took all of my high interest credit card debt and consolidated it into a zero-interest credit card for the next 12 months. I refinanced the house during this time to combine the main mortgage and the second mortgage that we had taken out a few years earlier to make needed repairs on the house, and this allowed us to lock in a lower interest rate and reduce the overall mortgage payment. I purchased a new car in 2018, a Chevy Tahoe, because my previous vehicle, a 2002 Suburban, had just been totaled in a pretty serious car accident. It made sense at the time to invest in a newer more reliable vehicle, as I was driving a lot more to visit my clients between San Diego to Los Angeles. The car payment (even with $10,000 down) was very high, around ~$1,200 a month, but I had been making additional payments towards the principle for the last two years to pay it off as quickly as we could. With the reduced principle on the loan, I was then able to refinance the car payment to around $300 a month and was able to pay it off completely using my commission checks by the end of the year. With just these few simple actions, I was able to reduce our overall expenses just enough for us to make it through until we were able to get back on our feet financially. And I give all glory and honor to The Lord Jesus Christ for leading and guiding me through this time in my life.

This life-altering experience inspired a determination to never face such financial vulnerability again. The desire for financial freedom sparked a deep dive into learning about investments and long-term planning. Limited resources meant exploring affordable and accessible opportunities, ultimately leading to cryptocurrency and other key investments. This journey, fueled by the need for resilience and adaptability, laid the foundation for a portfolio that continues to grow today.

Current Challenges and Faith

Fast forward to July of 2024, and my circumstances are eerily similar to 2020 with some slight differences: divorced, unemployed, recently moved into a rental, finalizing the sale of a long-time home, and financial uncertainty. Despite these challenges, my faith remains unwavering, and the peace of The Lord is still with me amidst all this uncertainty. In the middle of May, I had moved into a 3-bed, 2-bath house (rental) with my daughter as I worked to put my house on the market to sell. The last asset of my divorce that needed to be liquidated and split. My company had been experiencing financial hardships, prompting me to begin seeking other employment months ago but in my industry, things rarely move fast, and I received the lay-off notice at the end of June. This was a blow for me, because there have been very few times in my career for this to happen. What I did not know at the time was that my company was in the process of being purchased, and the buying company already had a sales force, therefore making my position obsolete.

Now while this was a highly stressful time due to many factors, I was not afraid, the way I had been prior to March-2020, which had in past experiences lead to anxiety and depression. Instead, I felt at peace, motivated to get things completed as quickly and efficiently as possible. Which lead to me doing 90% of the repairs and interior painting of the house on my own, I spent my evenings often working till midnight and on weekends for 8 weeks straight. My ex-husband focused on cleaning and clearing junk out of the covered patio, garage, and fixing up the backyard.

Financially, things would soon become difficult if I was not able to secure new employment, having just used a considerable amount of my savings a month earlier to rent a new place, hire movers to help in that process, make repairs and repaint the entire interior of the house so it could be put on the market. My severance package was only enough to get me through to the end of July. Having divorced my husband in 2022 means I am now the sole bread winner of the household, there is no support, there is no safety net (beside what the Lord provides). I did not ask for alimony in our divorce (I did not want anything else from him), only child support until our daughter turned 18, which was in June of 2024. There are no family or friends that I could ask for help or a loan if I needed it. I had always been that person for others, but not the other way around. I was grateful to have built up a portfolio of various assets over the last four years but am determined not to use them to offset expenses, unless absolutely necessary. Instead, I focused on selling my house, continued interviews with three companies I was considering and seeking guidance from The Lord in prayer.

Now at this point, it would be very easy for me to focus on everything in my life that I don't have or isn't going right and probably obsess about all the things that happened that have led me to this point. Things that may seem unfair. But none of that would make any difference or change my present state of circumstances. So, instead I chose to focus on those things in my life that I did have control over and the things that were within my power to influence. What I find most interesting about that time period of circumstances and the perspective that I am now writing from, is a question that I recently asked someone while doing research for this book.

"If something were to happen causing you to lose your primary source of income and you were unable to work, would your lifestyle significantly change over the next 2 months?"

For the average working American, the answer to this question would undoubtable be, "*yes*". There may be some people that have a safety net of one month income set aside in a rainy-day account. But ultimately, very few people have more than two months of income set aside in cash or liquid assets that can easily be accessed should they need it.

Let's break this down a little further shall we, if a person was making about $150,000 a year, after taxes, health insurance and retirement, they would probably bring home around $91,500 a year (~61% of your gross income). That provides approximately $7,625 a month in take home income, therefore, in order to have a 3-month safety net a person should have savings of at least $23,000. However, surveys show that 69% of Americans have less than $1,000 in savings, underscoring the urgent need for financial education and planning. This highlights the precarious financial state of many households, where the loss of a primary income source could quickly lead to financial strain.

In August 2024, I successfully sold my house, receiving a generous offer on the very day it hit the market. Around the same time, I accepted a new job with a company based in Scotland—a place I've always dreamed of visiting, as my mother's family originally immigrated from there. The sale of my home yielded a substantial profit, nearly doubling in value over the ten years I had co-owned it. This financial windfall allowed me to purchase new furniture for my home, pay off all my credit card debt, supplement my income while waiting for paychecks from my new position, and continue building my investment portfolio. The timing of these events aligned perfectly, providing a much-needed sense of stability and progress.

The Importance of Mindset

The struggle to provide for basic needs often leaves little room to think beyond the immediate. Yet, lasting change requires a shift in mindset. Many individuals operate with a "*now mindset*", prioritizing present concerns over future opportunities. This perspective hinders long-term growth, as short-term thinking often leads to procrastination, avoidance, or fear of taking risks.

Changing one's mindset often requires a significant life event, such as job loss, divorce, bankruptcy or health scares. For many, the pandemic served as that catalyst. It created an opportunity to acquire the knowledge and skills needed to move toward financial freedom.

The Path Forward

The journey toward financial freedom starts with leveraging what one already has. Even with limited resources, small investments can yield significant long-term benefits. Learning how to make money work for an individual, rather than them having to constantly struggle to earn money and identifying opportunities to build wealth are vital steps. The rich and wealthy often utilize the strategy of having their money work for them, rather than trading their time for money—why shouldn't everyone?

Imagining a life free from financial constraints allows for clarity in setting goals and aspirations. Whether pursuing hobbies, owning property, or building businesses, it begins with dreaming big and taking actionable steps to achieve those dreams. Writing down goals and visualizing success can reignite hope and set the foundation for growth.

The Great Wealth Transfer

This book is part of a series exploring the impending wealth transfer resulting from technological revolutions and shifts in global financial systems. Each installment addresses strategies for individuals across various wealth tiers, from modest beginnings to billionaire status. The transition from fiat currencies to digital assets presents opportunities for those prepared to invest, adapt, and thrive during this monumental shift.

The evolution of currency—from bartering and commodities to paper money, credit cards, and digital transactions—reflects humanity's constant adaptation to meet societal needs. Cryptocurrency represents the next step in this progression, offering a decentralized and innovative approach to financial systems. Understanding and engaging with this technology positions individuals to benefit from this wealth transfer and secure their financial future.

This book aims to empower readers with knowledge, tools, and strategies to navigate the changing financial landscape. By embracing a mindset of growth, resilience, and faith, individuals can position themselves to thrive during one of the most significant wealth transitions in history. The journey begins now.

CHAPTER 1

THE 7 KEY FUNDAMENTALS

The first important step to be successful at anything is to identify, learn and apply several key fundamentals. So, what are fundamentals and how do they work? Fundamentals serve as the primary rule or foundation for which something is based.

One of my favorite motivational authors, Jim Rohn writes in his book called The Art of Exceptional Living, that "*Fundamentals are the basics that build the foundation for accomplishment, productivity, success, and lifestyle.*" In another one of his books, The Five Major Pieces to the Life Puzzle, he discusses reasons why certain people succeed and others don't, attributing this to five "*key components to success - philosophy, attitude, activity, results and lifestyle*".

One of my favorite quotes is by Tom Brady, arguably the Patriot's all-time most valuable quarterback, having earned seven Superbowl rings during his 22-season's career. He had once said during a press interview, "*To be successful at anything, you do not need to be special. You just need to be what most people aren't. Be consistent, determined and willing to work for it.*"

I believe all of these points are valid and yes, key components to achieving success. I would like to propose my top key fundamentals that have attributed to my personal development and success over the years, which are - **mindset**, **vision**, **knowledge**, **wisdom**, **consistency**, **determination**, and a willingness to **work hard** towards a specific goal.

1. Mindset. In my opinion, a person's mindset is the foundation for how information is **filtered**, **processed** and essentially **applied** towards any given situation or circumstance. Mindset can **accelerate**, **delay**, even **hinder** breakthroughs and ultimately determine the level of success in a person's life. A mindset is like a pair of glasses that are used to see a person's surroundings. Depending on the type of mindset, some objects and colors may appear to be distorted, fuzzy or unclear, while other things may appear to be hyper focused, brighter, or even larger than it really is. How does the expression go, "*Sometimes you are unable to see what is right in front of you? Or, unable to see the forest for the trees.*" This is because it is not just a matter of perspective, it is a matter of mindset. Depending on the mindset, a person can be blinded from seeing solutions and even opportunities that for other people may seem simple or obvious. It is all a matter of mindset. This is why a person's mindset forms the base level of the pyramid of my 7 key fundamentals for success.

2. Vision. A person's vision for the future will ultimately influence and help determine the direction that a person goes in life. Without vision, it is very difficult to design a **plan** or set specific **goals** that will lead towards a desired result. Without vision it is very difficult to develop or nurture inner desires, hope for the future, motivation and ambition.

"Where there is no vision, the people perish, but he that keep the law, happy is he." — Proverbs 29:18 (NKJV)

I think there is incredible wisdom that can be taken from this verse. Now, while a person's vision for their own future may change over time and as they mature in life, their vision is what gives them a focal point to head towards. It is that focal point that can be used in making important decisions in life, you can look at a situation and ask yourself, "*Will this decision take me closer to or farther away from the direction I know I want to head towards?*". Or, "*Does this decision add value or take away from what I already have?*". And ultimately, is that a positive or negative thing. Because sometimes, having something taken away from your life can be a positive thing. Essentially without vision, it is very difficult to develop a long-term plan and commit to the success of that plan. That is why people without vision tend to wander more and just go with the flow of where life takes them rather than continuing to make adjustment throughout their journey to ensure they end up in the right place.

Now don't misunderstand me, it can be great as a young adult to try a variety of things and go where opportunities take you, especially when you are using that as a journey of self-discovery to find out who you are, what your good at and even what you enjoy doing. I actually feel that my working career was exactly that, but no matter what new adventure I embarked on personally or professionally, I still maintained a sense of vision of where I wanted to go and what I wanted to achieve. There was always a sense of hope and forward-looking desire that I had in my life. If I was doing good, I wanted to then do better. If I was doing poorly, well then that was something I wanted to change as quickly as possible and be better.

I think some people that have lost their vision or ability to dream about the future tend to be drawn more into the now and present circumstances. This can diminish someone's hope that their current struggles and situation can change or improve over time. Which, if I am being honest, can be incredibly demotivating. It is this lack of hope that can affect a person's mental health, ambition or ability to self-motivate, which are all very important aspects of personal development.

In another translation of this is verse (NIV) it says, "*Where there is no revelation, people castoff restraint; but blessed is the one who heeds wisdom's instruction.*" Revelation is prophetic vision or vision that comes from God. The Hebrew word used to describe "*the people perish*" or "*people cast off restraint*" means to loosen, expose or uncover. This word has also been used inner changeable with ignoring, neglecting, or avoiding. Which what I have come to acknowledge in my own personal life, is that every time I have ignored wise instruction (whether from God or elsewhere), I have tended to neglect or even ignore the higher calling on my life. And I am of the personal belief that every person on this earth has a calling and purpose, it is up to us to discover what that purpose is and choose to do something about it.

3. & 4. Knowledge and Wisdom. Identifying the knowledge a person lacks requires study and research, while understanding the proper application of that knowledge involves the development of wisdom. To achieve success in any field, an individual must study and practice the application of what has been learned. It begins with mastering the fundamentals of the chosen area. For instance, someone aspiring to become a doctor would study medicine and anatomy. An individual aiming to be a business owner would focus on business principles, while an aspiring accountant would study finance, accounting, and tax law. Similarly, for someone seeking to build and grow wealth, the journey starts with studying successful individuals who have mastered wealth-building and learning how money works. This foundational step is essential for embarking on the path to financial freedom.

While people may become rich overnight by winning the lottery, or by coming into an inheritance, or success through their career, lasting wealth is not instantaneous, and it will take time to develop and grow. It will also take time to learn how to protect and manage that wealth so that it will last and not just be squandered in a short period of time or lost due to bad spending habits or in the next economic recession.

Statistical data shows that individuals who grow up without money and then quickly come into wealth—whether through fame, winning the lottery, or other sudden windfalls—often face significant challenges in maintaining their financial success. If they haven't taken the time to master the fundamentals of building and sustaining wealth or hired skilled financial professionals for guidance, many find themselves broke or back to their starting point within five years. This pattern raises an important question: why does this happen?

This often occurs due to a combination of factors, including **mindset** and a lack of **financial knowledge** and **wisdom**. Individuals who have never experienced significant wealth often focus on fulfilling long-held desires, purchasing items they have always dreamed of but may not necessarily need. For instance, they might buy their dream car, an expensive house, multiple vehicles or properties, or frequently travel to destinations they have always wanted to visit. This behavior often leads to a lifestyle that mirrors their newfound wealth. Unfortunately, without a sustained inflow of cash to support these expenses, they quickly find themselves in a position where their outgoing expenses match or exceed their income, leading to financial instability.

5. Consistency. Consistency in **behavior** and **actions** is essential for achieving a desired outcome or success. When a person identifies the need to change their mindset as part of their journey toward a goal, it is crucial to **stay the course** and remain **steadfast** in pursuing that transformation. If knowledge is the missing element, **dedicating regular time** to study and learning is vital. While setbacks and failures may occur along the way, the key is to consistently rise again, refocus on the ultimate goal, and persist. Taking accountability for failures involves identifying what went wrong, learning from the experience, and making adjustments to avoid repeating the same mistakes. Failure is a natural part of the learning process and does not determine success—what truly defines success is the commitment to never give up. Consistency is the foundation of achieving dreams and goals. Moreover, maintaining a positive outlook is important, as this journey often resembles a marathon rather than a sprint to the finish line.

I am reminded of an analogy I read or heard somewhere, comparing people to popcorn. When you cook popcorn, the kernels are all in the pan together, in the oil, at the same heat, and yet each individual popcorn kernel pops at different times but only when it's ready. Don't be discouraged when you do not "*pop*" as quickly as others but celebrate when you eventually do. Comparing yourself to others is futile, because we are all unique individuals, no one is the same and therefore our successes cannot be the same either.

"Comparison is the death of joy."
— Theodore Roosevelt, 1910

6. Determination. Ambition initiates the pursuit of a dream or goal, **motivation** provides the energy to sustain progress, and **determination** serves as the driving force that propels a person beyond their limits, no matter the obstacles encountered along the way. Determination embodies perseverance—the commitment to continue working toward success regardless of challenges or the time required to achieve it. This steadfast dedication to a course of action is essential for ultimate success. Together, determination, motivation, and ambition form a vital triad, each playing a critical role in ensuring progress and accomplishment. These components are fundamental to turning aspirations into reality.

It begins with ambition—a desire to accomplish, achieve, or become something different. Ambition can vary in intensity depending on the specific goal or area of focus. A person is either content with their current situation or has ambitions to pursue something new or reach a different destination. Motivation provides the initial fuel to propel someone forward and may help them start on the path toward their ambition. However, it is ultimately their level of determination to stay the course, despite challenges, that will enable them to cross the finish line and claim success.

All three components—ambition, motivation, and determination—require mindset development, as well as a strong belief in oneself and confidence in one's abilities. When a person lacks self-belief or doubts their ability to succeed, it often leads to disillusionment and eventually hopelessness. It is essential to recognize that self-doubt and hopelessness act like poison-tipped arrows to the mind. Without proper mental defense, much like a warrior protecting themselves with a shield, this poison can gradually erode ambition, motivation, and determination. The true battlefield is not external but within the mind, and it is the responsibility of each individual to safeguard and nurture it for success.

7. Hard work. Don't be fooled, anything worthwhile is going to involve hard work. If it was easy, everyone would do it. Hard work can take many forms, it can be **mental**, **emotional**, **physical**, or all of the above. One of the things that I contribute to the successes I had in my personal life and career has always involved my willingness to work hard, many times involving long hours, and sacrifice. A person's willingness and determination to work hard towards something will set them apart and naturally result in some level of success. However, the degree of success achieved will be up to them and involve many other factors.

A motto that has guided my life is, *"I don't chase **dreams**, I hunt **goals**."* For me, a dream represents something that exists solely in the imagination. While imagination and visualization are essential for shaping a person's reality and future, a dream remains intangible until it is spoken out loud, written down, and committed to as small, actionable goals. Without this transformation, a dream risks staying confined to the imagination, never fully realized. This is not to say that opportunities cannot arise to help someone achieve a dream but dreams alone require action and intention to yield results. Much like a tree, they must be nurtured, watered, and pruned to produce good fruit. This understanding is why I have developed habits that reflect the intentional pursuit of goals, treating them not as fleeting aspirations but as deliberate targets to be achieved.

A person might ask, "*Why hunting? How does hunting relate to achieving goals?*"

Again, this comes down to shifting the mindset. When I think about hunting, I don't think about it from a human's perspective, as a man might go into nature and hunt animals for sport or for food. I think of hunting from an animalistic perspective, like a predator would hunt their prey. One of my favorite memes is below, an image of a Lion running at full speed pursuing its prey.

Hunting is the practice of seeking, pursuing, capturing and ultimately killing prey. An animal, like this lion, is driven to hunt from hunger or a desire to provide for its family. That's it! A lion will be strategic and cunning about how it chooses to seek and pursue its prey because in the wild they are constantly on the verge of feast or famine. Life or death. Hunting is a matter of survival. If they fail, it is death, and therefore, failure is not an option. This is the mindset a person should adopt when approaching their goals. Imagine being the lion, with goals as the prey.

The key question becomes: how hungry is that person? This hunger serves as the driving force, pushing them beyond their limits to achieve their objectives. A strong sense of hunger compels a person to go the extra mile, wake up early, or stay up late, fueled by a deep commitment to success. It leads to prioritizing what truly matters, dismissing distractions such as binge-watching television, excessive socializing, or partying. Even habits that bring temporary joy or pleasure may lose their appeal as the focus shifts toward delayed gratification and the ultimate outcomes being pursued. This hunger sharpens a person's determination and aligns their actions with their long-term vision.

A cheetah may be the fastest land animal on earth, but it does not always catch the prey that it's chasing. When it fails, it must rest and then try again, if it is to survive. Therefore, as part of your mindset shift, a person must start visualizing their dreams and goals in this way. It must become a matter of survival where failure is not an option. "*You will catch your prey; you will succeed.*" It is only a matter of time and consistency.

When I started my personal development journey, my overall health was an immediate area of focus for me. So, for a short time, I hired a personal trainer to help teach me how to work out properly, how to build muscle and lose fat. One of the most valuable lessons this trainer taught me, was the concept of the "*point of failure*". Whenever I was doing exercise on a machine (or, free weights, like kettlebells, dumbbells, but always in a safe manner), he would essentially tell me to go to the point of failure. The goal in this exercise was to push my muscles until they couldn't go any further.

What I found most fascinating about this approach to exercise was realizing that my mind often imposed limits before my body actually reached its physical limit. For example, during leg extensions at a moderate weight, as my muscles began to burn and I struggled to fully extend my legs, my mind would signal that I couldn't go any further, prompting me to want to stop and rest. This is when my trainer would step in and say, "*No, you've got three more good reps in you.*"

And he was always right. More often than not, I had more than three reps left in me. He would push me to continue until I physically couldn't lift the weight anymore—"that was the true point of failure". Only then was the set complete. After a brief rest, I would repeat the exercise two more times to finish the full set before moving on to the next exercise, targeting a different muscle group (still focusing on legs during leg days). This process taught me that the mind often gives up before the body, and overcoming that mental barrier is essential to reaching one's full potential.

I followed a regimen with my trainer that focused on rotating muscle groups: one day for legs, one day for arms, and one day for back and core, then repeating the cycle. The rule was to never work the same muscle group two days in a row, as that increases the risk of injury. This schedule allowed each muscle group ample time to heal and recover before being targeted again. The results were impressive—after a year, I was physically the strongest I had ever been and had lost about 50 pounds overall. It was a powerful reminder that anything worthwhile requires time, dedication, and consistent hard work.

It is important to recognize that each of these key fundamentals develops gradually and does not come instantaneously. Growth occurs in stages, making it essential to set realistic expectations that can be achieved. A person should not become discouraged by failure or delays, as failure is an integral part of learning anything new. The key is to take time to rest, readjust, and remain consistent in the pursuit of progress.

CHAPTER 2

UNDERSTANDING MINDSETS: THE FOUNDATION OF TRANSFORMATION

The first step in understanding mindset is recognizing that humans are uniquely designed as a reflection of divine intention. According to Genesis, God created man in His image, making us distinct from any other creation in heaven or on earth. Like God, we are a trinity of body, soul, and spirit—a unique composition that mirrors our Creator. The body represents our physical form, the soul is our consciousness and sense of self, and the spirit connects us to God and higher purpose. It is crucial to focus on the soul and its relationship with the mind.

The soul is the essence of who we are, and it experiences, grows, and expresses itself through the mind, which acts as its command center. Think of the mind as a highly advanced **computer** and the body as its **biological network**. The body functions as an avatar, while the mind processes inputs, formulates decisions, and governs actions. The ***"operating system"*** of your mind—your mindset—is shaped by the **programs** running within it. These programs determine how you perceive, interpret, and respond to the world around you. Over time, they create a subconscious framework that defines your **behavior**, **decisions**, and **beliefs**.

The Origins of Your Programming

The programs that form your mindset are shaped by numerous factors, including your upbringing, cultural influences, educational experiences, and religious teachings. From childhood to the present, these inputs collectively create the foundation of how you think and act. However, the most empowering truth about mindset is this: **your programming can be changed**. If you are dissatisfied with your circumstances, your habits, or the person you have become, you have the ability to **rewrite** these internal codes.

Change begins with your willingness to take ownership of your mindset and invest the necessary effort to transform it. The extent of that change depends on your **determination**, **consistency**, and **commitment** to growth. Shifting your mindset requires a multifaceted approach, including meditation to quiet the mind, visualization to imagine your ideal self, belief in your ability to change, and deliberate physical actions to bring your vision to life. Transformation is not passive—it demands both introspection and action.

The Power of Choice and Control

"There are three things in life over which a person has complete control, and it all starts in the mind:
1. What they think and feel
2. What they say
3. What they do."
— Unknown Author

One of my favorite quotes, and a lesson I learned many years ago—perhaps from a preacher or motivational speaker, though the exact source escapes me—has left a lasting impact on my perspective. It conveys a profound truth: there are three key aspects of life over which a person has control—what they think and feel, what they say, and what they do. This simple yet powerful insight forms the cornerstone of personal transformation and mindset development, emphasizing that all change begins in the mind.

It is important to acknowledge that exceptions exist, particularly in cases of illness (including mental illness) and disability. There are people with mental illness that may cause them to struggle with having control over their thoughts, emotions and body. There are people born with genetic defects, disabilities or develop a disability later in life that effect these three areas we will be discussing, for example Multiple Sclerosis, Alzheimer's, and Tourette's.

While spiritual influences, such as demonic or unclean spirits, may contribute to illness within a person's body, and healing is possible through the blood of Jesus Christ, this discussion will focus on individuals who are not disabled or impaired by sickness. However, if you might have a disability or illness, don't give up hope. These principles can still be applied and used, but there may be a deep level of healing and prayer that should be incorporated in this process.

Mind. Your mindset is the **operating system** that governs your life, but you are the programmer. With intention and effort, you can rewrite limiting beliefs, overcome destructive habits, and align your **thoughts**, **emotions**, and **actions** with the person you aspire to be. Remember, transformation starts in the mind. By embracing the power of choice and taking control of your internal programming, you can create a life of purpose, fulfillment, and lasting change. Think of the mind as a central computer, serving as the processing hub for a vast network of biological machines interconnected through the central nervous system. These machines—organs, muscles, tendons, cells, and more—depend on the mind to function properly.

- **Processing information:** Like a computer, the mind processes vast amounts of information from the environment through our senses (sight, hearing, touch, taste, & spirit). The mind takes in data, analyzes it, stores it, and retrieves it when needed.

- **Memory:** Just as a computer has memory storage, the mind has the ability to store and retrieve information. This memory capacity allows us to learn from past experiences, make decisions, and solve problems.

- **Multitasking:** Computers can perform multiple tasks simultaneously, and our minds also have the capacity to multi-task. We can focus on different activities, thoughts, and emotions at the same time, similar to how a computer can run numerous programs concurrently. Your mind is also running underlying

- programing without you having to think about it, such as your heart pumping blood, your lungs breathing, your blood cells seeking out and metabolizing glycogen or fat for energy.

- **Programming:** The mind is influenced by our experiences, beliefs, and attitudes, which can be seen as the programming that shapes our thoughts and behaviors. We can learn and unlearn programming if we are open to that change. We can learn new ways of thinking and behaving, much like a computer can be programmed to perform new functions. This is how mindsets are formed.

- **Problem solving:** Both computers and the mind engage in problem-solving processes. Computers use algorithms and logical operations to solve problems, while our minds use creativity, critical thinking, and reasoning to address challenges we encounter.

- **Visualization:** While a computer has a screen that allows for images and information to be displayed visually, our minds are uniquely capable of creating mental images and scenes based on a combination of sensory inputs including memories and imagination. I would say one of the most underutilized and incredible supper powers a person possesses is their imagination. It is a muscle that needs to be developed, defined, and trained to be utilized effectively. This will involve learning and practicing meditation.

It is important for you to acknowledge that you are wonderfully and beautifully made by the creator, and that the human mind is far more complex and nuanced than any artificial intelligence system or technology that exists today. Our emotions, intuition, consciousness, spirit, and ability to form deep social connections which distinguish our minds from even the most advanced computer system. This leads to the first point, which can be divided into two parts. As a created human being, endowed with free will by the Creator, a person has control over two fundamental aspects: **(1) what they think** and **(2) what they feel**. But what does that really mean?

The human mind is uniquely designed with free will, granting a person the ability to determine both what and how they think. A person's mind, in essence, creates their reality. It processes data received from the surrounding environment, and the individual has the choice in how to interpret and respond to that data. The thoughts a person generates in response to external stimuli play a critical role in shaping their emotions, as it is their thoughts that give rise to feelings.

For instance, imagine a person listening to someone speak on a topic that holds personal significance. The speaker expresses an opinion that directly opposes the listener's beliefs. Furthermore, the speaker's tone, mannerisms, and words are hurtful and dismissive, targeting those who share the listener's perspective. These remarks might **trigger** memories of a painful or traumatic experience from the past. As a result, the listener finds themselves reliving those emotions as if the hurtful event is happening in the present moment. This is because the mind, through its thoughts, has connected the current experience to past memories, reigniting the associated feelings.

This example illustrates the power of the mind to shape emotional responses through thought. A person's ability to recognize and control this process is essential for emotional well-being and resilience. By choosing to reframe thoughts or consciously detach from **triggering interpretations**, an individual can take charge of their emotional state, breaking free from automatic reactions tied to past experiences. This awareness empowers a person to respond with clarity and intention, rather than being overwhelmed by emotions rooted in memory. Ultimately, a person's emotions will influence their decisions. This is why maintaining discipline is so important. The greater control an individual has over their thoughts and emotions, the better equipped they will be to make sound decisions, particularly in stressful or high-stakes situations.

This is why point #1 is so critical—if a person lacks control over their thoughts, it becomes nearly impossible to manage their emotional reactions to situations, often leading to poor decisions. Many can relate to moments when anger or frustration caused them to lash out, saying things they later regretted. In some cases, such moments of emotional impulsivity have cost individuals jobs, promotions, or even relationships.

At times, women, in particular, may be more passionate when discussing topics that matter deeply to them. However, this passion doesn't always translate well in professional settings. Speaking from personal experience, there have been instances where a boss has told me I was being emotional. It's a reminder that it's not always about what is said but how it is said. Emotions have a way of coming through in speech and being mindful of this can make a significant difference in how communication is received.

This leads to point #2: **individuals have control over what they say** and **don't say**. Words are incredibly powerful, much like a double-edged sword. They can bless or curse, uplift or harm, and every choice carries consequences. A person's words not only affect others but also themselves. It's possible to unintentionally curse oneself by speaking negative words or reinforcing limiting beliefs. Many people unknowingly speak negativity into their own lives and then wonder why they face repeated struggles. Being intentional and disciplined with words is vital to fostering positivity and avoiding self-inflicted obstacles.

"Death and life are in the power of the tongue: and they that love it shall eat the fruit thereof."
– Proverbs 18:21 (NKJV)

Remember, Jesus Christ is the Word of God, and the Holy Ghost dwells inside of you. A person's words have power and meaning and one day every person will have to give an account for every word they have spoken, the good and the bad. Those words that produced blessings or took them away, those words that have blocked the blessings from getting to themselves or others). Sometimes, through ignorance a person can become their own worst enemy if they do not have the knowledge and wisdom of how God's kingdom works.

This is why God instructs individuals to meditate on the scriptures—to think deeply about them, study their meaning, and speak the words out loud. The Word of God is alive and has the power to activate changes in the spiritual realm, influencing both a person and their circumstances. By speaking God's words over their life daily, a person can witness the transformative impact it brings. Reading and declaring the blessings that God has promised His children allows individuals to claim those promises for themselves and their loved ones, creating a powerful foundation of faith and hope.

"For the word of God is living and active, sharper than any two-edged sword, piercing to the division of soul and of spirit, of joints and of marrow, and discerning the thoughts and intentions of the heart."
– Hebrews 4:12 (NIV)

Point #3 emphasizes that **a person has control over their actions**, and what they choose to do will have consequences—either good or bad—depending on their decisions and responses. It is important to recognize that an individual is responsible for their own actions, not for the actions of others toward them. While a person cannot control what is done to them, they can control how they choose to respond. Even in situations where someone is coerced or deceived into acting against their best interests, the ultimate choice to act remains theirs. Additionally, it is essential to remember that inaction is also a form of action. Behaviors such as laziness, slothfulness, or procrastination can have consequences just as significant as direct actions.

"The first thing you do when you're in trouble is admit to yourself what you did to get there."
—Jessica Pearson, Suites

This quote resonates deeply, as it highlights the importance of self-reflection and accountability. When challenges or problems arise in a person's life, it is valuable to ask, "*What actions or decisions have led to this point?*" Often, the answers may not be immediately clear, as a person's mindset can obscure the truth. Sometimes, the same problems or patterns repeat multiple times before an individual recognizes the need to change unhealthy behaviors. Taking responsibility for one's current situation is crucial for growth. Without humility and a willingness to learn from mistakes, pride can take root, hindering personal development and progress.

"You can't control the wind, but you can adjust your sails."
— Unknown Author

Ultimately, everything outside of a person's **control**—such as **external circumstances** or the **actions of others**—does not fall under their responsibility. While these factors may influence outcomes in life, a person must remember the tools they do have: the **power** of their **thoughts**, **emotions**, **words**, and **actions**. It is not necessarily about what is happening to the person, but how they react. Additionally, the strength of their prayers and the words they speak are powerful weapons in navigating life's challenges. The true battlefield begins in the mind, and engaging in this internal warfare with intention and discipline is key to overcoming obstacles and moving forward.

"God, give us grace to accept with serenity the things that cannot be changed, courage to change the things which should be changed, and the wisdom to distinguish the one from the other."
— Serenity Prayer, attributed to theologian Reinhold Niebuhr (1892–1971)

Where should a person begin? It starts with asking what factors shape a mindset. For everyone, whether realized or not, a mindset is sculpted and programmed from childhood. Various influences, such as genetics, environment, experiences, and education, play a role in developing the mindset an individual has today. The first step in personal development is identifying and understanding one's current mindset.

1. Genetics: Genetics play a role in shaping a person's mindset, as traits like temperament and personality can be inherited from parents. However, beyond genetic traits, certain patterns can also be passed down through a person's bloodline. These are often referred to as generational curses, familiar spirits, or even demonic influences. Generational curses can manifest in various forms, such as inherited family sickness, infertility, broken relationships (whether familial or friendships), divorce, alcoholism, gambling, drug addiction, mental illness, rebelliousness, gluttony (obesity), or slothfulness (procrastination, unproductivity, laziness, and lack of motivation).

One of the most challenging generational curses to overcome is poverty. This is because poverty is a multi-dimensional curse, encompassing spiritual, physical, and soul components. The spiritual aspect may involve strongholds or beliefs passed down through family systems. The physical component includes real-world circumstances like lack of resources or opportunities, while the soul component ties to internalized feelings of lack, inadequacy, or despair. Addressing poverty as a generational curse requires a holistic approach to break its hold and create lasting change.

a. Body. The physical body enables a person to experience the world through the five senses: sight, sound, touch, taste, and smell. In the Bible, the body is often referred to as a tent, a temple, or a dwelling place for the spirit and the Holy Spirit, connecting it to the soul and physical existence. However, the body is inherently limited by these senses and cannot fully perceive the spiritual realm. For instance, human eyes can only see a limited distance and within a narrow range of the light spectrum. Technology has revealed that there are many other wavelengths in the light spectrum, some of which can be detected by cameras or other devices.

Similarly, human ears can only detect a specific range of sounds, whereas dogs have a heightened ability to hear frequencies beyond human capability. The same applies to the sense of smell; humans have a limited range compared to certain animals that can detect prey miles away or days after it has passed through an area. While it's a relief not to have such heightened senses in some situations, these limitations highlight that the physical senses offer only a partial perspective of reality. Unfortunately, many people rely solely on these physical senses to define truth and reality, overlooking the broader dimensions of existence beyond the tangible.

b. Spirit. The spirit is the life-giving force within a person's body, essential for sustaining both the body and the soul (mind). Without the spirit, neither the body nor the mind can survive. This is evident in the creation of Adam: God formed his body from the dust, but Adam only became a living being when God breathed His spirit into him. The significance of the spirit is also seen in cases where a person is on life support. While a machine can temporarily sustain a body by delivering oxygen, it cannot restore life if the spirit has departed. If the connection between body and spirit—sometimes referred to as the "*silver cord*"—is severed, the body will gradually cease to function once removed from artificial support. This process may take hours or days, but the body cannot sustain life without the spirit's energy.

The spirit can be compared to a renewable power source, much like the energy supply for a laptop. A laptop can operate briefly on battery power after being unplugged, but once the battery is depleted, the hardware shuts down without an external energy source. Similarly, the spirit is the renewable energy that sustains the body, providing it with life and vitality.

The spirit also equips a person with what is often referred to as the "*sixth sense*," which encompasses discernment and intuition. Unlike the body, the spirit never sleeps, tires, or ceases its activity. It constantly seeks connection and a relationship with its Creator. For many, this yearning is misunderstood and replaced with worldly pursuits, yet these efforts never fully satisfy. No level of achievement—be it success, wealth, power, influence, relationships, or prestige—can fill the void left by the absence of a deep connection with the Creator. The spirit longs for its original relationship and connection with God, which no earthly substitute can replace.

The spirit also experiences hunger, and it is nourished by what the Bible refers to as "*living water*," which comes only from God. Reading the Word of God allows this living water to flow, feeding and strengthening the spirit. This spiritual nourishment facilitates growth and renews the mind. The mind, closely connected to the body, requires constant renewal because the flesh is inherently weak and susceptible. All battles faced on earth are waged in the mind, which can be exhausting.

God's kingdom is abundant, overflowing with wealth and resources, and there is no lack in the Kingdom of Heaven. However, a generational curse of poverty can hinder a person's spirit from accessing the wealth and abundance that God has prepared for them in the spiritual realm. Such a curse, introduced through a person's bloodline, allows a spirit of poverty to act like a chain of bondage, holding the individual back and blocking their path to purpose. To break free from these chains and access the blessings God intends, the curse must first be broken.

c. Soul. The soul encompasses the mind, will, and emotions and serves as the battleground for both physical and spiritual struggles. It is within the soul that decisions are made, emotions are processed, and perspectives are shaped. The soul is vital because it acts as the interface connecting the body and the spirit, enabling them to communicate and influence each other. Through this connection, a person's physical actions can reflect their spiritual beliefs, while their spiritual state can affect their thoughts and emotions.

The relationship between the soul and the spirit is particularly significant, as the two are intricately linked. Many believe the Bible refers to this connection as the "*heart of man*," representing the inner core where thoughts, intentions, and spiritual truths converge. This connection is what allows a person to align their physical reality with their spiritual identity. For instance, when a person renews their mind with God's Word, it strengthens their spirit and empowers them to make better decisions, which are then carried out by the body.

However, because the soul is central to this relationship, it is also where battles often take place. Temptations, doubts, fears, and external pressures compete for control over a person's thoughts and will. The soul must navigate these challenges while maintaining harmony between the physical and spiritual realms. When the soul is aligned with God's truth, it acts as a bridge that allows the spirit to lead the body effectively. Conversely, when the soul is dominated by worldly influences, it can create disconnection, causing confusion, emotional turmoil, and poor decision-making.

Recognizing the soul's role as this vital connection highlights the importance of nurturing it through prayer, meditation, and reflection on God's Word. Strengthening the soul enables a person to better align their will with God's purpose, maintain emotional stability, and allow their spirit to guide their actions, fostering a balanced and fulfilling life.

2. **Environment:** The environment in which a child is raised—encompassing home life, school, and community—plays a crucial role in shaping their mindset. Positive and nurturing environments often foster a growth mindset, encouraging adaptability, resilience, and the pursuit of goals. Conversely, negative or stressful environments, such as those marked by poverty, can contribute to the development of a fixed mindset, limiting a person's ability to envision or strive for long-term success.

Poverty, as an example of a challenging environment, often instills a Now Mindset in children, where immediate needs and short-term thinking take precedence. Since topics like mindset development, financial literacy, and long-term planning are not typically taught in school, many individuals grow up unaware of how their environment has influenced their personal, professional, and financial outlook. This lack of awareness perpetuates cycles of struggle, as individuals may remain focused on the present without understanding the benefits of planning for the future.

On the other hand, environments characterized by wealth and abundance can offer a more nurturing and less restrictive atmosphere. Children raised in such settings often have greater opportunities to explore their creativity, dream bigger, and face fewer immediate limitations. However, it is important to note that not every child born into privilege achieves success. A variety of factors, including personal choices, external influences, and unforeseen challenges, can hinder development, even in families of moderate or significant means.

Typically, children raised in affluent environments are exposed early on to concepts like financial management, investing, recognizing good versus bad investments, networking, and influencing others. These formative years, enriched by learning, mentorship, and opportunities for growth, provide them with an earlier advantage in achieving success. This nurturing of a Future Mindset, rooted in long-term thinking and planning, is a key factor in their development. This book will explore how to cultivate and develop a Future Mindset, offering strategies for achieving lasting success and breaking free from limiting environments.

3. **Experiences:** A child's experiences play a pivotal role in shaping their beliefs about their abilities, intelligence, and potential. Positive experiences, such as encouragement, praise, and opportunities to grow,

can foster a growth mindset, building confidence and resilience. Conversely, repeated setbacks, criticism, or a lack of support may contribute to the development of a fixed mindset, where the child perceives their abilities as limited and unchangeable.

Consider how an individual's upbringing and early experiences might have shaped their current mindset. For instance, when trying something new—perhaps a sport or exploring a future career goal—how did the people around them respond? Were they encouraged to keep practicing after failures, celebrated for successes, or supported in dreaming big? Or were they met with criticism, indifference, or even mockery from parents, siblings, teachers, or peers? These early interactions can significantly influence the decisions a person makes as they transition into adolescence, young adulthood, and beyond.

Regardless of past experiences, it is never too late for a person to reevaluate and transform their mindset. Whether an individual is at the beginning of their career, middle-aged, or nearing retirement, they still have the opportunity to pursue goals and dreams for their future. A mindset is not fixed; it can evolve with effort, self-reflection, and a willingness to grow, allowing individuals to reshape their path and unlock new potential at any stage of life.

4. **Learning:** The way a child is taught to approach challenges, failures, and successes plays a critical role in shaping their mindset. Teaching resilience, perseverance, and the value of effort helps cultivate a growth mindset, enabling children to see challenges as opportunities rather than obstacles.

One of the remarkable aspects of the human mind is its capacity to learn, unlearn, and relearn behaviors, information, and the application of knowledge. Learning is an ongoing process, with individuals constantly acquiring new information while discarding what is deemed unnecessary or outdated. Often, the most lasting memories are formed during times of significant personal growth or through experiences that evoke strong emotions, particularly when lessons are tied to adversity or triumph.

A child's mindset is dynamic and continually evolving, influenced by countless factors from birth onward. Parents, caregivers, and educators play a vital role in fostering a positive and resilient mindset by providing encouragement, support, and opportunities for growth. While these formative years are crucial, it is never too late for an adult to unlearn negative patterns of thinking and develop a mindset focused on positivity, abundance, and success. With intention and effort, individuals can shift their perspectives and reshape their futures, regardless of their past experiences.

5. **Religion:** The foundation of beliefs, values, and moral guidelines instilled in a child or adult plays a significant role in shaping their mindset. The influence of religion or belief systems is profound, providing a framework for understanding the world and guiding behavior. While the topic of religion is vast enough to warrant its own book, its impact on mindset development is undeniable.

Some may argue that they have no religion, but this perspective can be challenged. Everyone operates from a set of beliefs, whether they acknowledge it as religion or not. For instance, beliefs such as denying the existence of God, rejecting the concept of moral absolutes, or embracing modern ideologies like an infinite number of genders are, in essence, value systems that influence behavior and perceptions. These frameworks, whether explicitly religious or secular, shape how individuals view themselves, others, and the world around them.

The key point is that religion itself does not necessarily determine a person's mindset. However, theologies, doctrines, and value systems derived from religious or philosophical beliefs significantly influence how a person thinks and approaches topics like success, wealth, and morality. These influences can shape a person's mindset development, either fostering growth or imposing limitations, depending on how they are understood and applied.

Understanding Scripture, Religion, and Theology: Clarifying Misinterpretations:

"For the love of money is a root of all kinds of evil, for which some have strayed from the faith in their greediness, and pierced themselves through with many sorrows."
— 1 Timothy 6:10 (NKJV)

An example of misunderstanding scripture can be found in 1 Timothy 6:10. Over the years, many people have used this verse to affirm their personal beliefs or justify why they have accepted lack or poverty in their lives. A common interpretation is that "*money is the root of all evil, therefore, it is better to be poor.*" However, this misses the key phrase: it is the love of money, not money itself, that is the root of all kinds of evil.

To understand this, consider the function of roots. Roots anchor plants, draw nutrients and water, and store reserves. Similarly, love is a powerful force that drives action, for better or worse. Love, both an emotion and a behavior, is characterized by intimacy, passion, and commitment. When Jesus was asked about the greatest commandment (Matthew 22:37-38), He replied: '*Love the Lord your God with all your heart, with all your soul, and with all your mind.*' This teaching directs individuals to evaluate their hearts and their motivations. If a person loves God above all else and sees money as a tool to serve Him, decisions are less likely to be influenced by greed or destructive desires. Love for God anchors decisions and ensures alignment with His purposes.

Is It Greedy to Desire Wealth?

Another common belief is that "*it is greedy to want to be rich; a person only needs enough to meet their basic needs.*" While happiness and service to God do not require wealth, it is essential to acknowledge two truths. First, God is not a God of lack—He is a God of multiplication. Throughout scripture, He blesses those who are faithful and obedient, such as Abraham, Jacob, Isaac, King David, Joseph, and Job. These men experienced trials but were also blessed abundantly and used mightily by God.

Let's examine the example of Job's life written of in the bible. Though he lost everything, including his family, his faithfulness resulted in blessings that exceeded what he had before. Similarly, Joseph endured betrayal, slavery, and imprisonment but ultimately rose to become second-in-command of Egypt, where his wealth and position allowed him to save his family and thousands of others during a great famine. These examples illustrate that wealth, when used for righteous purposes, can amplify a person's ability to fulfill God's will.

It is not greedy to desire wealth when the motivation is to serve others and glorify God. Wealth can enable acts of kindness and generosity, such as feeding the poor, funding missions, supporting businesses, or influencing positive change. Good works require time and resources, and it is challenging to help others if one struggles to meet their own basic needs.

A frequent concern for people in a religious mindset, is that "*money brings temptation, so it is better not to have it.*" While it is true that wealth can open doors to temptation, a person's moral character and relationship with God determine how they handle such challenges. This struggle is real, and individuals should guard themselves against the potential pitfalls of wealth. Strengthening moral discipline and remaining grounded in faith are key to resisting these temptations.

Does God Want His Children to Be Poor?

Some believe that "*The Lord wants me to be poor.*" This is a surprising and unfounded interpretation, as nowhere in scripture does God express a desire for His children to live in poverty. In Matthew 5:3, Jesus says: "*Blessed are the poor in spirit, for theirs is the kingdom of heaven.*" This refers to being spiritually humble and acknowledging dependence on God, not living in lack or material poverty.

Living in lack makes it difficult to be a blessing to others. A person who struggles to provide for their basic needs will find it challenging to contribute to others' lives and this includes their own. God's desire is for His children to thrive spiritually, emotionally, and materially so that they can serve as vessels of His love and blessings to the world.

CHAPTER 3

ACHIEVING SUCCESS THROUGH THE POWER OF A BALANCED MINDSET

One of the first things that I learned in my personal development journey is the importance of having a balanced mindset. It is essential as it empowers individuals to navigate life's challenges and opportunities with flexibility, strength, resilience and a clear sense of purpose. It involves integrating elements of different mindsets—such as focusing on the present while planning for the future, embracing growth while recognizing limits, and maintaining optimism while staying grounded in reality. A **balanced mindset** helps prevent extremes, such as being overly **risk-averse** or **recklessly impulsive**, and enables thoughtful **decision-making**. By fostering self-awareness and adaptability, a balanced mindset ensures that individuals can respond effectively to various situations, pursue their goals with clarity, and find fulfillment in both their journey and achievements.

Next, I began studying successful people to uncover the characteristics they shared. I noticed that successful individuals often exhibit similar traits and approaches, not just in their actions but also in their mindsets. They tend to **tackle challenges**, **solve problems**, and **seize opportunities** in comparable ways. What proved most valuable for me was learning to distinguish the mindsets that drive success from those that can hinder it. This understanding allowed me to recognize and adopt empowering mindsets while identifying and addressing the limiting ones.

Therefore, in order to identify a person's current mindset, it is important to understand that mindsets are not **rigid** or **mutually**

exclusive. In reality, elements of multiple mindsets often coexist and can shift depending on **context, circumstances**, and personal growth. A person's mindset is shaped by their **experiences**, **beliefs**, and **habits**, which means it can vary across different areas of life, such as relationships, career, health, and finances. Understanding this complexity allows for a more nuanced view of mindset development and self-awareness.

How Can Multiple Mindsets Coexist:

1. **Contextual Variation:** A person's mindset can vary depending on the context, showing a combination of growth and fixed mindsets in different areas of life. For instance, someone might have a **growth mindset** in their career, believing they can improve through effort and learning, yet exhibit a **fixed mindset** in relationships, thinking, "*I'm just not good at connecting with others.*" Similarly, a student might feel confident about improving their math skills, demonstrating a growth mindset, but believe they are inherently bad at sports and incapable of improving, reflecting a fixed mindset. This variation highlights how mindset is not universally applied but influenced by experiences, beliefs, and the specific situations an individual encounters.

I have personally experienced how my mindsets can vary depending on the context of my life. In my career and personal life, I have worked diligently over the last five years to cultivate growth, abundance, wealth, and positive mindsets. These efforts have led to significant personal and financial growth. However, when it comes to my physical health, I have struggled for over a decade to achieve my desired body type and maintain consistent weight loss.

In 2019, after graduating from California State University, Long Beach, I was fully committed to improving my physical health. I joined a gym and hired a personal trainer, one of the best decisions I've ever made. My trainer taught me how to work out effectively and designed a personalized workout regimen. For a year and a half, I exercised five days a week, spending 1.5 hours per session in the gym weigh training, and followed a strict diet. This included intermittent fasting and a balanced intake of lean proteins, healthy fats, and vegetables, while completely eliminating synthetic sugars, carbohydrates (including wheat and fruit), alcohol, juice, and fried foods.

This commitment paid off as I lost 50 pounds, significantly increased my strength, and improved my endurance through muscle-building. However, I hit a plateau at the 200-pound mark, where no matter how much effort I put in, I couldn't seem to break through. For over six months, I grappled with frustration, disappointment, and resentment. The constant physical pain from intense workouts and the challenge of maintaining a strict diet took its toll. At one point, I even considered liposuction to address the stubborn fat on my belly, arms, and thighs. Unfortunately, I was still too heavy to safely undergo the procedure. Eventually, I reached a breaking point, asking myself, "*Do I want to continue being miserable with intense workouts and strict diets, only to stay fat? Or should I let go, eat what I want, and still be fat?*" In my mind, both options would lead to the same result so I mine as well be happy right, instead of miserable and this is how I justified giving up on all the healthy behaviors I had implemented.

Looking back, I now realize that these feelings stemmed from a combination of a fixed mindset, scarcity mindset, and self-limiting beliefs. While I didn't fully believe that my body's ability to lose weight was predetermined, past experiences fed into my doubts and discouragement. Self-limiting beliefs, such as "*I'll never lose weight no matter what I do*," and comparing myself to others who seemed to achieve results more easily eroded my confidence and motivation. At the same time, I focused on what wasn't working instead of celebrating my progress, such as the 50 pounds I had already lost—classic symptoms of a scarcity mindset.

Moving forward, I am committed to addressing these mindsets and reframing my perspective. I plan to focus on what is within my control and celebrate healthy habits like exercising consistently and eating nutritious meals, regardless of immediate outcomes. My goal is to shift from a weight-loss-centered approach to prioritizing overall well-being, such as better sleep, increased strength, and reduced stress. I'll continue researching how factors like metabolism, hormones, and genetics influence weight loss and consider consulting with a dietitian, fitness coach, or therapist for tailored strategies and insights. By adopting a growth-oriented perspective and focusing on holistic health, I believe I can overcome these barriers and create a more sustainable path to achieving my goals.

2. **Overlapping Mindsets**: Certain mindsets can overlap and influence one another, creating a complex interplay of beliefs and behaviors. For example, a person with a **poverty mindset** might also exhibit a **scarcity mindset**, as both focus on perceived limitations. At the same time, they could demonstrate a growth mindset in personal development, actively working to overcome those limitations. A person struggling with saving money due to a poverty mindset might enroll in financial literacy courses, reflecting a **growth mindset** aimed at improving their situation. Additionally, this individual may have succeeded in obtaining a degree and is now striving to advance their career in that field. However, a person might still face financial struggles and debt, showing how overlapping mindsets can coexist, sometimes reinforcing challenges while also supporting efforts toward progress.

Without fully realizing it at the time, I was demonstrating how mindsets can coexist and overlap between the years of 2015 to 2020. It was the growth mindset that helped me to embrace challenges and prioritize earning a degree in order to achieve my goal of advancing my career. I continued to grapple with elements of a poverty and scarcity mindset after earning my degree, particularly when it came to financial struggles and managing debt during the COVID-19 pandemic and lockdowns. As I mentioned previously, these hardships and challenges were the catalyst that pushed me to seek out ways to improve my financial situation, leading me to explore investment opportunities. Ultimately, this journey sparked my interest in cryptocurrency, marking the beginning of a new chapter in my pursuit of financial growth and stability.

3. **Situational Triggers:** External factors can activate different mindsets, causing shifts in how individuals perceive and respond to situations. For instance, a person who generally operates with an **abundance mindset** might **temporarily** slip into a **scarcity mindset** during a financial crisis. Similarly, a typically optimistic entrepreneur might become risk-averse and overly cautious after experiencing a significant business loss. In such cases, their response may reflect a combination of **resilience** and **fear-based thinking**, showing how **situational triggers** can influence even well-established mindsets. These shifts highlight the dynamic nature of mindset and the impact of external circumstances on thought patterns and behaviors.

This reminds me of a pivotal conversation I had with my ex-husband during our marriage. At the time, he was a licensed Land Surveyor working for Los Angeles County, and occasionally, he took on side jobs for extra income on the weekend. Los Angeles Country had recently acquired robotic tripods that allowed a single surveyor to operate them, this new technology meant that rather than two people, only one was needed to record data points. The robotic tripod was able to operate and follow the person holding the data collector rod, and record points without having a person manual record points at the tripod. During our conversation, he mentioned how useful it would be to own one for his side jobs because this would mean he could take jobs and work on his own but dismissed the idea as unattainable because the equipment cost around $35,000 for a used and refurbished unit. His response reflected a scarcity mindset, focusing on the upfront cost and the perceived difficulty of affording such an investment. However, I viewed the situation differently, through a growth and abundance mindset. I saw the potential for this equipment to save him time and money while creating opportunities for greater independence and perhaps in the future the ability to work for himself full-time.

In my mind, I saw this equipment as the equivalent to hiring an employee, which was something we could not afford to do. So, I started by doing some calculations, an entry level land surveyor without a license earned approximately $70,000 annually. The way I saw it was if the equipment cost $35,000, then it was like we had hired an employee for six months, after which point we got to keep the employee but no longer had to pay for their services (it being a robot after all). When I explained this to him, he became excited and began researching financing options.

Within a week, we made the purchase, and he nicknamed his new "*employee*" Robi. This turned out to be the best decision for his career, because about a year later, Los Angeles County implemented new policies prohibiting licensed Land Surveyors from taking on side work, which had been a vital supplement to our income. Thanks to his investment in Robi, he was able to transition from working for the county to running his own business full-time. This experience highlights how shifting from a scarcity mindset to a growth and abundance mindset can open doors to opportunities that may initially seem out of reach, ultimately transforming challenges into steppingstones for success.

4. Transitioning Between Mindsets: People often transition between different mindsets as they grow or face new challenges. This dynamic nature allows for personal evolution and the gradual integration of more positive, growth-oriented perspectives over time. For example, someone who initially holds a negative mindset about their ability to succeed might, through intentional self-reflection and consistent effort, begin adopting a growth mindset. This shift highlights how mindsets are **not fixed** and can be **reshaped** to better support personal development and success.

At first, I had no idea how many different types of mindsets existed—now I see them everywhere, influencing every choice and challenge. This realization extends beyond my own life to the people around me as well. It's important to show yourself grace during the transition between mindsets, as growth is rarely a linear process. You may find yourself shifting between positive and negative mindsets as you navigate the challenges of personal development and adopt new behaviors that lead to success. This is a natural part of growth, and occasional setbacks or moments of doubt don't diminish your progress. Instead of being overly critical of yourself, recognize these transitions as opportunities to learn and strengthen your resilience. Celebrate your efforts and small victories along the way, understanding that developing a new mindset takes time, practice, and patience. Growth is a journey, not a destination, and every step—positive or challenging—brings you closer to becoming the best version of yourself.

Let's explore some examples of various mindsets and their key characteristics. You may find that you resonate with some of these, while others might be mindsets you'd like to cultivate further. Some may even evoke strong emotional reactions, and in those cases, it's helpful to note them in your journal to reflect on and revisit later.

Positive, Growth-Oriented, and Achievement-Oriented Mindsets

- **Growth Mindset** – Belief that abilities and intelligence can be developed through effort and learning.
- **Abundance Mindset** – Focus on opportunities, collaboration, and the belief that there is enough success for everyone.
- **Prosperity Mindset** – Emphasis on holistic well-being and creating abundance in all areas of life.
- **Gratitude Mindset** – A practice of focusing on what is good and

appreciated in life.

- **Optimistic Mindset** – Tendency to see the positive side of situations and believe in favorable outcomes.
- **Solution-Oriented Mindset** – Focus on finding answers and overcoming challenges rather than dwelling on problems.
- **Innovative Mindset** – A creative approach to thinking, constantly seeking new ideas and perspectives.
- **Open Mindset** – Willingness to consider new ideas and viewpoints without judgment.
- **Resilient Mindset** – Ability to bounce back and adapt to adversity or setbacks.
- **Wealth Mindset** – Emphasizes building financial stability and creating long-term financial success.
- **Prosperity Mindset** – Combines financial, emotional, and personal abundance for overall flourishing.
- **Rich Mindset** – Emphasis on creating and enjoying financial success while maintaining balance.
- **Ambitious Mindset** – Motivation to set and pursue bold goals with determination.

Present and Future-Focused Mindsets

- **Now Mindset** – Living fully in the present moment and taking immediate action.
- **Future Mindset** – Thinking long-term, setting goals, and planning for future success.
- **Proactive Mindset** – Taking initiative and control rather than reacting to situations passively.
- **Strategic Mindset** – Prioritizing actions based on long-term goals and systematic planning.

Negative and Limiting Mindsets

- **Fixed Mindset** – Belief that abilities and intelligence are static and cannot be changed.
- **Scarcity Mindset** – Focuses on lack, competition, and the idea that resources are limited.
- **Captivity Mindset** – Feeling trapped by circumstances, with little belief in the ability to change.
- **Negative Thinking** – Focusing on fears, doubts, and worst-case

scenarios.

- **Poverty Mindset** – A focus on financial struggle and a belief that wealth or success is unattainable, often leading to self-limiting behaviors.
- **Victim Mindset** – Attributes outcomes to external forces, avoiding responsibility or action.
- **Avoidance Mindset** – Avoids challenges or discomfort, often missing growth opportunities.
- **Perfectionist Mindset** – Sets unrealistically high standards, often leading to fear of failure.

Spiritual and Philosophical Mindsets

- **Purpose-Driven Mindset** – Aligns actions and decisions with a greater sense of meaning or mission.
- **Faith-Based Mindset** – Grounded in trust in a higher power or a guiding spiritual belief.
- **Holistic Mindset** – Focuses on integrating all aspects of life for balance and well-being.

While it's important to recognize these different types of mindsets, let's delve deeper into how multiple mindsets manifest in action.

1. Career: A person with a growth mindset might say, "*I can learn new skills to qualify for this promotion*," emphasizing their belief in growth and improvement. However, elements of a fear-based mindset can still influence their decision-making process, manifesting as negative thoughts like, "*But what if I fail and embarrass myself?*" This highlights the internal conflict between the desire to pursue opportunities and the fear of failure. Overcoming this conflict requires cultivating self-confidence, reframing failure as a learning opportunity, and taking small, intentional steps toward the goal. By focusing on the potential for growth and preparing for challenges with a proactive approach, individuals can gradually quiet their fears and move forward with determination and resilience.

2. Health: A person with a now mindset might say, "*I'll go for a run today to start building a habit*," emphasizing their belief in living fully in the present moment and taking immediate action. However, elements of a scarcity mindset could present themselves with thoughts like, "*I don't* *have the time or energy to commit to a full fitness routine.*" This highlights the internal conflict between taking proactive steps toward improvement and feeling constrained by perceived limitations. Balancing these mindsets requires shifting focus from what is lacking to what is possible, recognizing that small, consistent actions today can lead to meaningful progress over time.

3. **Finances:** A person with an abundance mindset might say, "*There are plenty of opportunities to grow my income,*" emphasizing their belief in focusing on possibilities and opportunity. However, elements of a poverty mindset could present themselves with thoughts like, "*I'll never get ahead because the system is stacked against me.*" This highlights the internal conflict between optimism about opportunities and deeply ingrained fears or doubts about external limitations. Navigating this conflict requires challenging limiting beliefs, reframing negative thoughts, and taking intentional steps to focus on what can be controlled. By reinforcing an abundance mindset, individuals can shift their perspective, recognizing that while systemic challenges may exist, there are still pathways to progress and success.

4. **Relationships:** A person with a collaborative mindset might say, "*Let's work together to solve this issue,*" emphasizing their focus on teamwork and achieving shared goals. However, elements of a fixed mindset could present themselves with thoughts like, "*They'll never change, so there's no point in trying.*" This highlights the internal conflict between a desire to foster cooperation and a deep-seated belief that change is impossible. Resolving this conflict requires recognizing that people and situations can evolve with effort and openness. By maintaining trust in the potential for growth, practicing patience, and focusing on building constructive communication, individuals can strengthen their collaborative mindset and create opportunities for meaningful progress and connection.

Recognizing multiple mindsets offers numerous benefits, as it allows for a deeper understanding of how different thought patterns influence behavior and decision-making. By identifying and understanding these mindsets, individuals can gain valuable insights into their strengths, challenges, and areas for growth. Here are a few key benefits:

1. **Enhanced Self-Awareness:** Recognizing multiple mindsets allows individuals to understand how their thinking adapts to different

situations, helping them identify strengths, areas for improvement, and patterns that either empower or limit them. For example, realizing you have a growth mindset in your career but a fixed mindset in personal relationships provides valuable insight, guiding you to focus on cultivating a more adaptable and positive approach in areas that need growth. This awareness is a critical step toward achieving balance and unlocking your full potential across all aspects of life.

2. **Improved Flexibility & Growth:** Awareness of various mindsets allows people to adjust their approach based on the context, leading to more effective problem-solving and decision-making, and allows them to shift from limiting beliefs to empowering ones. For example, transforming elements of a poverty mindset into an abundance mindset by focusing on gratitude and long-term planning. Or, for example, transforming elements of a fear or scarcity mindset into more empowering ones like growth or prosperity by focusing on opportunities, reframing challenges as learning experiences, and taking intentional steps toward abundance and self-improvement.

3. **Balanced Perspective:** Understanding that multiple mindsets coexist encourages a more nuanced view of personal and interpersonal dynamics, fostering empathy and collaboration. It can also help a person balance competing perspectives, for instance, a now mindset ensures immediate action, while a future mindset ensures strategic planning.

4. **Better Relationships:** Recognizing how different mindsets influence interactions can help improve communication and foster stronger connections with others, both professional and personal. For example, adopting a collaborative mindset in the workplace encourages open dialogue and teamwork, while being aware of a fixed mindset in a personal relationship might prompt you to work on patience and empathy. By understanding and addressing the impact of mindsets on interactions, individuals can build trust, resolve conflicts more effectively, and create more meaningful and productive relationships.

Balancing multiple mindsets requires actively managing and harmonizing them to create alignment and adaptability. This involves the following:

1. **Identify Dominant Patterns:** Reflect on your thoughts and behaviors in different areas of life. Identify where you exhibit empowering mindsets

and where limiting ones hold you back.

2. Reframe Limiting Mindsets: Challenge negative or fixed thoughts with evidence of your ability to grow and adapt. For example, if you have a scarcity mindset about time, practice prioritization and time management to feel more in control.

3. Leverage Positive Mindsets: Use areas where you have a strong mindset to inspire growth in weaker areas. For example, if you have a growth mindset in learning but a fixed mindset in relationships, apply the belief that effort leads to improvement to building stronger connections.

4. Stay Adaptable: Accept that mindsets can evolve and that experiencing setbacks in one area doesn't define your overall ability to grow. For example, if financial struggles trigger a poverty mindset, remind yourself of past successes where you overcame challenges through effort and creativity.

In conclusion, having elements of multiple mindsets is natural and reflects the complexity of human thought and behavior. By recognizing where different mindsets influence your decisions and actions, you can build self-awareness and work toward aligning your overall outlook with growth, abundance, and resilience. The goal isn't to eliminate every limiting mindset but to understand and transform them into opportunities for learning and development. Mindset development is a journey, and embracing this dynamic process is key to achieving balance and fulfillment. Success is not just about **actions**—it is about thinking **strategically**, staying **adaptable**, and aligning with a **balanced mindset**. By recognizing and shifting unhelpful thought patterns, you can achieve lasting personal and professional growth.

CHAPTER 4

UNLOCKING POTENTIAL: THE POWER OF MINDSET DEVELOPMENT AND SELF-AWARENESS

Your **mindset** is the lens through which you view the world, influencing how you think, feel, and act in every aspect of your life. It determines whether you see challenges as obstacles or opportunities, failures as setbacks or lessons, and your potential as fixed or limitless. Developing a positive, **growth-oriented mindset** is crucial for personal **growth**, **resilience**, and **achieving success**. This chapter explores the importance of mindset development and provides a practical guide for identifying your current mindset.

The Importance of Mindset Development

1. Mindset Shapes Your Reality: Your **mindset** profoundly affects how you perceive and respond to life's events. Two people can face the same challenge, yet their mindsets can lead to vastly different outcomes. A **positive, growth-oriented mindset** empowers you to see opportunities in adversity and take proactive steps toward improvement, while a **fixed** or **negative mindset** can lead to **fear**, **inaction**, and **stagnation**. For example, a **growth mindset** might encourage someone to view job rejection as constructive feedback and an opportunity to improve, while a fixed mindset might interpret it as proof of inadequacy, and a victim mindset might perceive it as discrimination.

2. Mindset Influences Your Actions: Your mindset determines your behaviors and habits, which directly affect your results. If you believe you can grow and improve, you're more likely to take risks, put in effort, and persevere. Conversely, if you believe success is beyond your reach, you're less likely to try in the first place. For example, someone with a proactive mindset might take daily steps toward their fitness goals, while someone with a defeatist mindset might not even start because they assume they'll fail.

3. Mindset Impacts Your Relationships: Your mindset also shapes how you interact with others. A collaborative mindset fosters teamwork and connection, while a scarcity mindset may lead to competition or mistrust. By developing an open and empathetic mindset, you can build stronger, more meaningful relationships. For example, an abundance mindset encourages celebrating others' successes, while a scarcity mindset might feel threatened by them.

4. Mindset Fuels Resilience: Life is unpredictable, and setbacks are inevitable. A resilient mindset equips you to face challenges with courage and adaptability, viewing failures as steppingstones rather than dead ends. For example, an entrepreneur with a resilient mindset might see a failed business venture as a learning experience, using it to refine their approach for the next opportunity.

5. Mindset Drives Long-Term Success: Success in any area—career, relationships, health, or personal growth—requires consistent effort and adaptability. Developing a mindset that embraces learning, persistence, and optimism is key to achieving and sustaining long-term success.

How to Identify Your Current Mindset

Understanding how to identify your current mindset is the first step toward developing a more empowering one. Here below is a structured approach to self-assessment:

1. Self-Reflection: Analyze Your Thoughts and Beliefs: Take time to reflect on your inner dialogue, especially when facing challenges or making decisions. You can start by asking yourself some of the below key questions:

- Do I believe my abilities are fixed, or do I think I can improve with effort? (Growth vs. Fixed Mindset)
- Do I focus more on possibilities or limitations? (Abundance vs.

Scarcity Mindset)
- How do I react to setbacks—do I see them as failures or opportunities to learn? (Resilient vs. Negative Mindset)
- Do I dwell on the past, focus on the present, or worry about the future? (Now vs. Future Mindset)

2. **Observe Your Reactions to Challenges:** Your immediate response to difficulties, obstacles and failures can reveal your mindset.

- **Growth-Oriented Response:** "*What can I learn from this? How can I improve?*"
- **Fixed Response:** "*I'm just not good at this; there's no point in trying.*"
- **Abundant Thinking:** "*There's enough success for everyone. How can I collaborate or find a solution?*"
- **Resilient Response:** "*This is hard, but I'll find a way through it.*"
- **Scarcity Thinking:** "*There's not enough to go around. I have to compete for every opportunity.*"
- **Defeatist Response:** "*This is too much; I can't handle it.*"

3. **Analyze Your Approach to Goals:** Your behavior toward goal-setting, including how you set and pursue goals often reflects your mindset.

- **Positive Indicators:** Setting ambitious goals and breaking them into actionable steps. Persisting through setbacks and seeking feedback.
- **Negative Indicators:** Avoiding goals for fear of failure or criticism. Giving up when progress is slow, or obstacles arise.

4. **Evaluate Your Interactions with Others:** Your mindset influences your relationships and interactions. Your feelings about others' achievements can also be an indication of mindset.

- **Collaborative Mindset:** "*How can we achieve this together?*"
- **Competitive or Scarcity Mindset:** "*Their success means less for me.*"
- **Abundance Mindset:** "*Their success inspires me. If they can do it, so can I.*"
- **Scarcity Mindset:** "*Their success takes away from my opportunities.*"

5. **Pay Attention to Your Language:** The words you use, both internally and externally, can reflect your mindset.

- **Positive Language** (Growth/Abundance Mindset): *"I can try something new," "This is challenging, but I can improve," "Let's find a way to make this work."*
- **Empowering Language:** *"I can improve," "This is an opportunity," "Let's find a solution."*
- **Limiting Language:** *"I'm not good at this," "It's impossible," "Why bother?"*
- **Negative Language** (Fixed/Scarcity Mindset): *"I'm not good at this," "I can't do it; it's too hard," "It's impossible to succeed."*

6. Evaluate Your Decision-Making Habits: Your decision-making process reveals whether you prioritize the present, future, or avoid action altogether.

- **Now Mindset:** *"What can I do right now to move forward?"*
- **Future Mindset:** *"How does this decision align with my long-term goals?"*
- **Captivity or Fear Mindset:** *"What if this doesn't work out? I'd better stay where I am."*

7. Examine Your Emotional Triggers: Notice how you feel when faced with failure, criticism, or someone else's success.

- **Positive Reactions:** Motivation to improve. Genuine joy for others' achievements.
- **Negative Reactions:** Self-doubt or resentment. Defensiveness or blame.

8. Seek Feedback from Others: Sometimes, those closest to you can provide valuable insights into your mindset. As part of this exercise, you might want to consider asking people trust the following questions:

- *"How do I usually respond to challenges or setbacks?"*
- *"Do I seem open to feedback and new ideas?"* or *"How would you describe my attitude toward setbacks and failures?"*
- *"Do you see me as someone who embraces challenges or avoids them?"*
- *"What areas do you think I could grow in?"*
- *"What do you think I focus on most when solving problems?"*

9. Track Your Patterns Over Time: Keep a journal to record your thoughts, decisions, and actions in different situations. Look for recurring themes in how you approach challenges, relationships, and opportunities.

- What challenges did I face today, and how did I respond?
- What's one thing I learned or accomplished today?
- How do I feel about the progress I'm making toward my goals?

10. Identify Patterns in Key Areas of Life: Break down your mindset in different contexts, such as work, relationships, health, and personal growth.

- **Work:** Do you seek out new challenges, or do you stick to what feels safe?
- Relationships: Are you open to connection and growth, or do you hold back due to fear or mistrust?
- **Health:** Do you believe you can improve your well-being, or do you feel stuck in your current habits?
- **Personal Growth:** Are you committed to learning and self-improvement, or do you avoid stepping outside your comfort zone?

11. Compare Mindsets to Common Frameworks: Use established frameworks, like Carol Dweck's Growth Mindset vs. Fixed Mindset, or Abundance Mindset vs. Scarcity Mindset, to pinpoint where your beliefs align.

- **Growth Mindset:** Focused on learning, effort, and improvement.
- **Fixed Mindset:** Belief that abilities are unchangeable.
- **Abundance Mindset:** Belief in limitless opportunities.
- **Scarcity Mindset:** Belief in limited resources and opportunities.

12. Test Yourself in New Situations: Challenge yourself with unfamiliar tasks or goals and observe how you respond.

- **Growth Response:** "*I'm not sure how to do this, but I'll figure it out.*"
- **Fixed Response:** "*This isn't something I'm good at, so I'll avoid it.*"

In summary, identifying your mindset is a process of self-awareness, honest reflection and personal growth. Once you've recognized your predominant mindset, you can take intentional steps to reinforce positive patterns and shift away from limiting beliefs. Your mindset reflects your attitudes, beliefs, and habitual ways of thinking that shape how you approach challenges, opportunities, and life in general. Mindsets are not fixed—they can evolve with effort and focus, enabling you to achieve greater personal and professional growth.

Common Mindset Types and Indicators

Successful people usually have several characteristics in common and so do their mindsets. They will usually approach challenges, problems, and opportunities in similar ways as well. Mindsets profoundly shape how we interpret and respond to the world. Below is an expanded exploration of common mindset types, their defining characteristics, indicators, and examples of how they manifest in everyday life. Understanding these mindsets can help identify areas for growth and guide the development of more empowering ways of thinking. It's worth mentioning that each of the mindsets discussed below could easily warrant an entire chapter, but for the sake of brevity, I will provide a concise overview of each.

Positive and Growth-Oriented Mindsets:

Growth Mindset. A Growth Mindset is defined by the belief that abilities, intelligence, and talents can be developed through effort, learning, and perseverance. It is characterized by a series of empowering behaviors and attitudes that drive personal and professional development. Individuals with this mindset embrace challenges as valuable opportunities to grow, seeing them as a chance to expand their skills and understanding. They actively seek feedback, using it as a tool for improvement rather than as a source of criticism. Failure is viewed not as a setback, but as a steppingstone to success, providing lessons that guide future efforts. A strong belief in the power of effort underpins their approach, as they recognize that consistent practice and dedication lead to improvement and mastery. Additionally, they find joy in the process of learning and personal development, appreciating the journey as much as the destination. This mindset fosters resilience, adaptability, and a lifelong commitment to growth.

As an example, a student struggling with math remains optimistic, thinking, "*If I keep practicing and seek help, I'll get better.*" This belief in the power of effort and learning drives them to persist despite difficulties. Similarly, a business owner whose first venture fails views the setback as a learning opportunity, asking, "*What lessons can I take from this to succeed next time?*" Both examples highlight how a growth mindset enables individuals to approach challenges with resilience and a focus on improvement, turning obstacles into stepping- stones for future success.

Abundance Mindset. An Abundance Mindset is defined by the belief that there are enough opportunities, resources, and success for everyone. It is characterized by positive attitudes and behaviors that foster collaboration, growth, and optimism. Individuals with this mindset celebrate others' achievements without jealousy, recognizing that someone else's success does not diminish their own potential. They willingly share resources and collaborate, understanding that working together creates greater value for everyone. Rather than dwelling on problems, they focus on finding solutions, approaching challenges with creativity and determination. Even in competitive environments, they maintain a sense of optimism, seeing opportunities where others might perceive threats or limitations. Additionally, they embrace change and challenges as avenues for growth, viewing them as chances to discover new possibilities and innovate. This mindset creates an environment of positivity and possibility, benefiting both the individual and those around them.

For instance, a colleague congratulates a team member on their promotion and offers support for their transition into leadership, demonstrating genuine encouragement and collaboration. Similarly, an entrepreneur openly shares business strategies with peers, believing that mutual success strengthens the industry as a whole. These actions reflect a belief in the power of shared growth and a focus on creating opportunities that benefit everyone involved.

Resilient Mindset. A Resilient Mindset is defined by the belief in the ability to recover and grow stronger after setbacks or adversity. It is marked by a set of empowering behaviors and attitudes that enable individuals to navigate adversity with strength and adaptability. Those with this mindset maintain a positive outlook during challenges, focusing on possibilities rather than being overwhelmed by difficulties. They actively seek solutions instead of dwelling on problems, channeling their energy toward progress. Failures are viewed as valuable learning experiences, prompting them to adapt their strategies and refine their approach. Resilient individuals also embrace change as a natural and inevitable part of life, seeing it as an opportunity for growth rather than a threat. Additionally, they build emotional strength through self-reflection and seeking support from others, fostering a sense of balance and confidence in the face of uncertainty. This mindset equips them to thrive even in the most challenging circumstances.

Such as, after losing a job, an individual quickly starts exploring new opportunities and acquiring new skills, demonstrating adaptability and a forward-thinking attitude. Similarly, when a team experiences a project failure, they come together to discuss what went wrong and collaboratively develop strategies to improve their approach for the future. Both examples highlight the ability to recover from setbacks with determination and a focus on growth, turning challenges into opportunities for progress.

Present and Future-Focused Mindsets:

Now Mindset. A Now Mindset is defined as focusing on the present moment, emphasizing immediate action and mindfulness. It is characterized by a focus on the present and a commitment to taking immediate, purposeful action. Individuals with this mindset seize current opportunities rather than procrastinating, ensuring that progress is made each day. They engage fully in tasks, minimizing distractions to maximize their productivity and presence. This mindset also involves appreciating and celebrating small, daily wins, recognizing the importance of incremental progress. To manage stress, they concentrate on what can be controlled in the moment, avoiding unnecessary worry about things beyond their reach. However, if not balanced, a now mindset may lead to neglecting long-term planning, which can impact future goals. Striking the right balance ensures that the benefits of this mindset are realized without sacrificing long-term aspirations.

In one case, a writer chooses to set aside an hour to draft a chapter, focusing on immediate progress rather than worrying about completing the entire book. In another case, a busy parent prioritizes being present by enjoying a family dinner without the distraction of work emails. Both examples illustrate the power of embracing the present moment to take meaningful actions and strengthen connections, fostering a sense of purpose and balance in daily life.

Future Mindset. A Future Mindset is defined as focusing on long-term goals, planning, and vision for the future. It is characterized by a focus on setting ambitious, strategic goals and working consistently toward achieving them. Individuals with this mindset prioritize investing time and effort into developing skills and acquiring knowledge that will yield long-term benefits. Their optimism about future opportunities keeps them motivated and forward-thinking, even when faced with challenges. They strive to balance current efforts with future rewards, ensuring that their actions today align with their long-term aspirations. However, if not well-balanced, a future mindset can sometimes lead to overlooking present opportunities, underscoring the importance of staying connected to both immediate and long-term priorities.

To illustrate, a recent graduate demonstrates forward-thinking by creating a five-year plan to advance their career while simultaneously pursuing further education to enhance their skills. Similarly, a family prioritizes saving for their child's college education over indulging in unnecessary luxuries, focusing on long-term benefits and financial stability. Both examples highlight the importance of planning and making sacrifices today to secure a brighter and more successful future.

Achievement-Oriented Mindsets:

Wealth Mindset. A wealth mindset is characterized by a focus on opportunities, abundance, and the belief in creating, managing, and growing resources responsibly. It emphasizes long-term planning, value creation, and the confidence to take calculated risks while maintaining a sense of gratitude and generosity. Individuals with this mindset embrace risk wisely, viewing calculated risks as valuable opportunities for growth and progress rather than something to fear or avoid. They focus on value creation, prioritizing the development of skills, assets, and networks that lead to sustainable success over time. Long-term planning is a key aspect of this mindset, as they look beyond immediate gratification and invest in future goals with patience and foresight. Acting with confidence, they trust in their ability to learn, adapt, and recover from setbacks, knowing that resilience is essential for achievement. Additionally, they understand the importance of generosity and collaboration, recognizing that sharing resources and working together contribute not only to their own success but also to the collective progress of their community. This mindset fosters growth, stability, and meaningful impact.

A business owner, for instance, invests time and resources into learning about emerging markets, recognizing it as an opportunity to expand and diversify income streams, even if it means stepping into unfamiliar territory. Similarly, an individual commits to saving and investing a portion of their income each month, understanding that small, consistent contributions can accumulate into significant wealth over time. In another example, a professional accepts a challenging leadership role, confident that it will not only enhance their skills but also open doors to greater opportunities in the future. These actions reflect the core principles of a wealth mindset: embracing growth, planning strategically, and making decisions with long-term benefits in mind.

Rich Mindset. A Rich Mindset is focused on enjoying financial success, cultivating wealth responsibly, and using resources to enhance quality of life. This mindset values not only accumulating wealth but also managing it wisely, sharing it generously, and maintaining balance between material achievements and personal fulfillment. It is marked by a thoughtful and balanced approach to wealth and financial success. Individuals with this mindset prioritize financial education, dedicating time to learning about saving, investing, and wealth-building strategies to make informed decisions. They actively seek opportunities to create multiple income streams, understanding the importance of diversifying earnings to establish long-term financial security.

This mindset also values balancing enjoyment with responsibility, recognizing that it is possible to enjoy wealth while maintaining financial discipline. Thinking long-term is a key principle, as they focus on achieving financial stability and building a legacy rather than indulging in short-term pleasures. Additionally, they practice gratitude and generosity, viewing wealth as a tool not only to enhance their own lives but also to uplift others and contribute to their communities. This approach fosters sustainable success, fulfillment, and a meaningful impact on the world.

To demonstrate, an entrepreneur reinvests profits into their business to fuel long-term growth while also allocating a portion for leisure and travel, demonstrating a balance between responsibility and enjoyment. Similarly, a professional works to diversify their income by starting a side hustle or investing in real estate, ensuring their financial security isn't reliant on a single source. In another example, a family prioritizes financial planning by creating a college fund for their children while still making time to enjoy vacations together. These examples highlight the rich mindset's focus on sustainable wealth-building, careful planning, and the ability to balance long-term goals with present enjoyment.

Success Mindset. A Success Mindset is characterized by a focus on achieving personal and professional goals through discipline, resilience, and intentional action. This mindset embraces growth, values perseverance, and maintains a clear vision of success while adapting to challenges and setbacks. It begins with goal-oriented thinking, where clear, actionable objectives are set and pursued with unwavering commitment. Resilience plays a central role, as obstacles are viewed not as setbacks but as opportunities to learn and grow. This mindset also prioritizes continuous improvement, with a constant focus on personal and professional development to enhance skills and capabilities. Confidence is another key characteristic, as individuals with a success mindset believe in their potential to succeed while valuing the effort and learning required to achieve their aspirations. Additionally, they take full responsibility for their actions and outcomes, avoiding blame or excuses, and instead focusing on solutions and accountability. Together, these traits create a foundation for sustained growth and achievement.

A professional demonstrates this mindset by developing a strategic plan to advance their career, such as earning certifications or building a strong network, and consistently taking steps to achieve their goals. Similarly, an athlete dedicates time to training and refining their skills, prioritizing progress over perfection, even in the face of a tough loss. Likewise, a student struggling with a challenging subject seeks tutoring, studies diligently, and views setbacks as temporary hurdles rather than defining failures. These examples highlight the focus, resilience, and proactive effort that characterize a success mindset.

Negative, Limiting and Fixed Mindsets:

Fixed Mindset. A Fixed Mindset is defined by the belief that abilities, intelligence, and talents are innate and unchangeable, like someone's DNA. It is characterized by behaviors and attitudes that limit personal growth and progress. Individuals with this mindset tend to avoid challenges out of fear of failure, preferring to stay within their comfort zone where success feels certain. They may feel threatened by the success others, interpreting it as a reflection of their own inadequacy rather than as inspiration or an opportunity to learn. Constructive criticism is often dismissed as a personal attack, making it difficult to use feedback for improvement. Additionally, they believe that effort is futile if talent doesn't come naturally, leading to a reluctance to try new things or persist through difficulties. This mindset reinforces a cycle of stagnation and missed opportunities for growth.

For instance, a musician avoids trying new techniques, thinking, "*I'm just not naturally gifted at this*," and therefore misses opportunities to improve their skills through practice. Similarly, a professional hesitates to apply for a promotion, believing, "*I don't have what it takes to succeed in that role*," allowing self-doubt to prevent them from pursuing growth and advancement. These examples highlight how a fixed mindset can lead to inaction and a reluctance to embrace challenges that foster development.

Scarcity Mindset. A Scarcity Mindset is defined by the belief that resources and opportunities are limited, creating fear of loss or competition. This focus on limitations can hinder personal and professional growth. Individuals with this mindset often view others' success as diminishing their own opportunities, fostering feelings of competition rather than collaboration. They may hoard resources or avoid sharing information, believing that doing so protects their position or advantage. This mindset prioritizes preserving what they have over seeking new opportunities for growth and advancement. A strong fear of taking risks further reinforces this behavior, as the potential for loss outweighs the possibility of gain. As a result, they often feel stuck in a cycle of lack or limitation, unable to break free from self-imposed barriers. This perspective not only restricts their progress but also limits their ability to embrace abundance and opportunity.

For instance, a manager withholds training opportunities from their team, fearing that empowering others might reduce their own value to the company. Similarly, an individual avoids networking, convinced that connections are a limited resource they cannot effectively compete for. These behaviors reflect a fear-based perspective that prioritizes self-preservation overgrowth and collaboration, ultimately hindering both personal success and the success of those around them.

Poverty Mindset. A Poverty Mindset is a mental attitude that prioritizes survival overgrowth, often characterized by fear, doubt, and a sense of helplessness. This mindset perpetuates cycles of limitation and inaction, preventing individuals from taking steps to improve their circumstances or pursue opportunities for success and fulfillment. More specifically this series of limiting beliefs and behaviors hinder financial and personal growth.

Individuals with this mindset often exhibit a reluctance to take risks or try new things, driven by a fear of failure or losing the little they have. They may view resources, success, or opportunities as finite, leading to feelings of competition or envy toward others. Immediate needs or gratification are frequently prioritized over long-term planning and investment, preventing the development of financial stability. This mindset is further reinforced by an internal dialogue that fosters feelings of unworthiness, inadequacy, or an inevitability of failure. Reluctance to engage in budgeting, saving, or financial management stems from fear or hopelessness, often resulting in over-reliance on external support, such as government programs or family assistance, rather than striving for independence. Extra income is often spent quickly, rather than being used to build financial security, reflecting a short-term focus. Opportunities for growth or success are unintentionally undermined due to fear or feelings of unworthiness, and failures are attributed solely to external factors rather than reflecting on personal responsibility or solutions. Additionally, this mindset is marked by a tendency to associate wealth with greed, immorality, or unfairness, leading to a rejection of the pursuit of financial success. These patterns perpetuate cycles of limitation and prevent individuals from achieving their full potential.

Here are some examples of how a poverty mindset reveals how fear, limiting beliefs, and systemic challenges can hinder progress and personal growth. For instance, an individual may refuse to invest in education or skill development due to fears of financial instability, missing opportunities for advancement. Similarly, someone might view a colleague's promotion as diminishing their own chances of success, fostering feelings of competition and inadequacy. Extra income, such as a tax refund, is often spent on non-essential items rather than being saved or used to pay off debt, reflecting a short-term focus. Internal dialogue might include thoughts like, "*I'll never be good at managing money*," or "*People like me can't succeed*," reinforcing a sense of hopelessness. Overwhelmed by the idea of creating a financial plan, some may ignore opportunities for budgeting or saving altogether.

Reliance on welfare benefits can also play a role, as individuals may avoid job opportunities or skill-building programs out of fear of losing essential support. This challenge is compounded by the fact that many welfare programs are not designed to bridge the gap between dependency and achieving a living wage, leaving individuals feeling trapped. Additionally, financial instability often leads to behaviors like using tax refunds for unnecessary purchases instead of building an emergency fund. Fear of rejection can cause individuals to miss deadlines or fail to prepare adequately for interviews, further limiting opportunities. Statements like, "*The system is rigged against me, so there's no point in trying*," or "*Rich people only care about themselves*," highlight a belief that external factors are insurmountable, rather than seeking to understand and emulate the habits that lead to success. These examples reflect how a poverty mindset creates barriers to growth and perpetuates cycles of limitation, often requiring a conscious effort and systemic change to overcome.

Negative Mindset. A Negative Mindset is defined by the tendency to focus on fears, doubts, and worst-case scenarios. It is characterized by a focus on obstacles and a tendency to see the worst in situations. Individuals with this mindset often dwell on problems rather than seeking proactive solutions, which can lead to a sense of stagnation. They frequently expect failure or disappointment, approaching challenges with pessimism rather than optimism. Setbacks are viewed as permanent and insurmountable, creating a belief that difficulties cannot be overcome. Gratitude and positivity are hard to find, as this mindset focuses on what is lacking or going wrong instead of recognizing opportunities or small victories. As a result, individuals may feel overwhelmed by challenges, further reinforcing their sense of defeat and limiting their ability to move forward.

For instance, after making a mistake at work, an employee might repeatedly think, "*I'll never be good enough for this job*," allowing one error to define their sense of worth and competence. Similarly, a student might avoid asking questions in class out of fear of embarrassment, assuming that seeking clarity would only highlight their shortcomings. These examples illustrate how a negative mindset can create barriers to learning, improvement, and self-assurance.

Fear-Based Mindset. A Fear-Based Mindset is dominated by fear of failure, rejection, or loss, leading to hesitation and inaction, often preventing individuals from pursuing growth or opportunities. People with this mindset tend to avoid taking risks, driven by a fear of negative outcomes that might result from stepping outside their comfort zone. They frequently overthink decisions, becoming stuck in analysis paralysis and unable to move forward. This mindset often leads to a constant need for approval or reassurance from others, reflecting a lack of confidence in their own judgment. Their thoughts are dominated by "*what could go wrong*" rather than exploring the possibilities of success or growth. Additionally, they struggle to embrace change, viewing it as a threat rather than an opportunity to adapt and improve. These patterns can significantly limit personal and professional development.

For instance, a talented professional may decline a leadership opportunity, worrying they won't succeed and allowing fear of failure to overshadow their capabilities. Similarly, an artist might hesitate to share their work publicly, fearing criticism and choosing to stay in their comfort zone rather than risk vulnerability. These examples demonstrate how fear can hold individuals back from pursuing growth, sharing their talents, and realizing their full potential.

Captive Mindset. A captive mindset is characterized by feelings of being trapped, powerless, or unable to change one's circumstances. It is rooted in limiting beliefs, external dependency, or past experiences, leading to inaction and a sense of helplessness. This mindset often prevents individuals from realizing their potential or pursuing opportunities for growth and freedom.

People with this mindset often believe that their circumstances are entirely shaped by external forces or other people, leaving them feeling powerless. They avoid taking risks or stepping outside their comfort zone, which leads to stagnation and missed opportunities for growth. This mindset is further reinforced by a dependency on external solutions, as they rely on others to solve problems rather than taking initiative. A lack of accountability is another key trait, with failures frequently attributed to external factors instead of reflecting on personal choices or actions. Additionally, there is a pervasive sense of hopelessness, as they feel that change is either impossible or futile, leading to resignation and a cycle of inaction. These patterns create significant barriers to personal growth and empowerment.

For instance, a person may remain in a toxic job, convinced they cannot find better opportunities elsewhere because they believe the "*job market is too competitive.*" Similarly, an individual might avoid pursuing a long-desired skill or goal, thinking, "*I'm too old to start now*" or "*People like me don't succeed,*" allowing limiting beliefs to stifle their growth. In another case, someone in an unhealthy relationship may feel trapped by financial dependency or fear of the unknown, avoiding the steps needed to seek freedom and improvement. These examples highlight how a captive mindset can create barriers to progress, often fueled by fear and self-doubt.

Victim Mindset. A victim mindset is characterized by a belief that external circumstances, other people, or uncontrollable events are entirely responsible for one's struggles or failures. This mindset often leads to feelings of helplessness, blame-shifting, and inaction, preventing individuals from taking ownership of their lives or making meaningful progress.

Those with this mindset consistently attribute failures or setbacks to external factors such as other people, systems, or bad luck, often feeling powerless to change their circumstances. This sense of powerlessness is compounded by an avoidance of responsibility, as accountability for problems is shifted to others rather than reflecting on personal actions or decisions. They tend to dwell on perceived injustices, focusing on unfairness and feeling targeted by life's difficulties. Instead of seeking solutions, they often prefer to complain about problems, resisting proactive efforts to resolve them. This mindset creates a cycle of stagnation, where individuals feel stuck and unable to move forward.

For instance, a student might attribute their poor grades to "*bad teachers*" rather than acknowledging their own lack of effort or preparation. Similarly, an employee who feels overlooked for promotions may blame favoritism, without considering how they could enhance their skills or contributions to increase their chances of advancement. In another case, a person facing financial struggles might repeatedly say, "*The system is rigged against me,*" using it as a justification for not improving their financial literacy or seeking new opportunities. These examples highlight how a victim mindset can perpetuate stagnation by focusing on external factors instead of fostering self-reflection and proactive solutions.

Avoidance Mindset. An avoidance mindset is characterized by a tendency to evade challenges, difficult situations, or uncomfortable emotions rather than confronting them directly. This mindset often stems from fear of failure, rejection, or discomfort and can lead to procrastination, missed opportunities, and stagnation.

Taking Action:

Once you've identified your current or most prominent mindset(s), you can begin to shift toward more empowering ones. Here's how:

1. **Acknowledge Limiting Beliefs:** Recognize thoughts that hold you back and challenge their validity.
2. **Focus on Growth:** Embrace challenges and view failures as opportunities to learn.
3. **Celebrate Progress:** Acknowledge small wins to build confidence and momentum.
4. **Surround Yourself with Positivity:** Seek supportive environments and role models who encourage growth and possibility.

In conclusion, your mindset is the foundation of your **actions**, **decisions**, and ultimately, your **success**. Developing a positive, growth-oriented mindset can transform how you approach life's challenges and opportunities. By identifying your current mindset and taking intentional steps to cultivate a more empowering one, you u**nlock your potential** to grow, thrive, and achieve your goals. Mindset development isn't just a one-time effort—it's a **lifelong journey** that shapes the **person you become** and the **impact you make** in the world.

CHAPTER 5

EXPLORING CAPTIVITY, POVERTY AND SCARCITY MINDSETS

Before we move on from the topic of mindsets, it's important to address some of the most limiting negative mindsets. Before we explore strategies for overcoming them, it is important to expand further on each of these mindsets and their characteristics.

The Captivity Mindset: A Barrier to Growth and Abundance

A **captivity mindset** refers to a psychological state where an individual feels **trapped** or **limited** by external **circumstances**, past **experiences**, or internal **beliefs**, preventing them from achieving their full potential. People with a captivity mindset often view themselves as **powerless**, **restricted**, or **stuck** in their current situation, even when opportunities for change or growth exist. This mindset may manifest in various areas of life, such as relationships, career, or personal development.

Common characteristics of a captivity mindset include:

1. Victim mentality:

Victim mentality is a psychological mindset where an individual consistently perceives themselves as the **victim** of circumstances, blaming **external factors** for their problems instead of **taking responsibility** for their actions or seeking **solutions**. This mentality can lead to feelings of helplessness, resentment, and a belief that success or happiness is unattainable because of forces beyond their control.

For example, someone with a victim mentality might blame their lack of career progress entirely on unfair management or workplace politics without reflecting on areas where personal improvement could help. Another example is a student who consistently attributes poor academic performance to bad teachers rather than poor study habits or lack of effort.

Another consideration is when someone attributes their lack of success or current position in society entirely to their DNA or the circumstances of their birth, believing they are inherently disadvantaged and powerless to change their future. For instance, a person might say, "*I'll never be successful because I wasn't born into a wealthy family*," or "*People like me can't achieve much because I didn't inherit the right genes or talents*." While it is true that circumstances of birth, such as socioeconomic background or genetic predispositions, can influence opportunities and challenges, adopting this mindset overlooks the potential for personal growth, hard work, and resourcefulness to create change. Instead of seeking ways to improve their situation, the individual remains stuck in a cycle of blame and resignation, limiting their capacity to take constructive action or develop the skills needed for success.

While real external challenges exist, a persistent victim mindset prevents **growth**, as it focuses on blame rather than constructive action. Shifting to a proactive approach, where individuals identify solutions and take responsibility, is essential for overcoming this limiting way of thinking.

2. Fear and doubt:

Fear and **doubt** are powerful emotions that can trap individuals in a **captivity mindset**, preventing them from pursuing their **goals** and reaching their full potential. Fear often manifests as an exaggerated anticipation of failure or negative outcomes, while doubt undermines self-confidence and the belief in one's abilities.

For example, someone with a fear of public speaking may avoid opportunities to present their ideas, even if it could advance their career, because they worry about judgment or making mistakes. Similarly, a person doubting their entrepreneurial abilities may never start a business despite having a solid plan, held back by "*what if*" scenarios of potential failure. This combination of fear and doubt creates mental barriers that reinforce inactivity and stagnation.

Feeling afraid of making decisions or trying new things due to fear of failure or uncertainty can lead to **paralysis by analysis**, where **overthinking prevents** action. This hesitation can cause missed opportunities, stagnation in personal and professional growth, and diminished self-confidence. When fear dominates decision-making, individuals may stick to familiar, safe routines even when change is necessary for progress.

For example, someone afraid to apply for a promotion might remain in an unfulfilling role, while another person hesitant to invest in learning new skills could fall behind in a competitive job market. Over time, this avoidance mindset can create regret and a sense of being "*stuck*," reinforcing feelings of inadequacy and further diminishing the willingness to take future risks. To **break this cycle**, it is essential to adopt a **growth mindset**, embrace mistakes as learning experiences, and focus on incremental progress rather than perfection.

Overcoming both emotions of fear and doubt requires cultivating courage, building confidence through small wins, and shifting focus from potential failure to possible success. By **challenging fear** and **doubt**, individuals can **break free** from a captivity mindset and move toward growth and achievement.

3. Low self-esteem:

Low self-esteem significantly contributes to a **captivity mindset**, where individuals feel trapped by their own perceived limitations and lack the confidence to pursue opportunities or personal growth. People with **low self-esteem** often believe they are **not good** enough, **smart** enough, or **deserving** of success, which leads to self-doubt, fear of failure, and reluctance to take risks.

For example, a talented artist might avoid showcasing their work because they feel it isn't "*worthy*" of public attention, missing out on potential recognition and growth. Similarly, someone with low self-esteem might settle for an unfulfilling job or unhealthy relationship, believing they lack the ability to achieve better outcomes. This mindset reinforces feelings of **helplessness** and prevents individuals from stepping out of their **comfort zones**.

Overcoming low self-esteem requires developing self-awareness, practicing positive self-talk, setting small, achievable goals, and celebrating progress, which can gradually build confidence and lead to a more liberated and proactive approach to life.

4. Fixed mindset:

A **fixed mindset**—the belief that **abilities**, **intelligence**, and **talents** are static and **unchangeable**—directly reinforces a captivity mindset, trapping individuals in self-imposed limitations and stifling growth. People with a fixed mindset often avoid challenges, fearing failure will expose their perceived inadequacies, and they resist feedback that contradicts their self-image.

For example, a student who believes they are *"bad at math"* may avoid studying or seeking help, assuming improvement is impossible, which ultimately limits their academic progress. Similarly, an employee who thinks leadership skills are innate rather than developed might never pursue promotion opportunities, believing they lack the natural talent required.

This perspective confines them to a cycle of inaction and missed potential. In contrast, adopting a growth mindset—recognizing that effort and learning lead to improvement—can break the captivity mindset by encouraging resilience, persistence, and a willingness to embrace challenges as opportunities for personal development.

5. Negative thinking:

Negative thinking is a pattern of thought that constantly focuses on **problems**, **obstacles**, and **limitations** rather than potential solutions or opportunities. People who engage in negative thinking regularly will focus on fears, doubts, and worst-case scenarios, often amplifying challenges and minimizing strengths or opportunities. This mindset frequently correlates with a captivity mindset, where individuals feel trapped by their circumstances, believing they lack the ability or resources to change their situation. Negative thinking reinforces this sense of entrapment, creating a cycle where perceived limitations hinder action and progress.

For example, someone stuck in a job they dislike might think, "*I'll never find another opportunity as good as this*," preventing them from exploring better career paths. Similarly, a person facing financial struggles might say, "*No matter what I do, I'll always be in debt*," which discourages them from budgeting or seeking new income sources. In relationships, negative thoughts like "*No one truly cares about me*" can isolate individuals further, reinforcing the captivity of loneliness.

Breaking free from a negative thinking mindset requires **shifting focus** from what is lacking to **what is possible**, enabling proactive steps toward change. In addition, breaking free from a captivity mindset involves shifting towards a growth mindset, where an individual recognizes their capacity for change, embraces challenges, and takes responsibility for their actions and choices. While for some this may seem incredibly difficult and perhaps even impossible to change how one thinks, but I assure you it is achievable.

Captivity Mindset of the Israelites Freed from Egypt:

The **captivity mindset** profoundly affected the Israelites after they were freed from slavery in **Egypt** and began their **40-year journey** in the wilderness. Despite their physical liberation, many of the Israelites struggled to free themselves from the mental and emotional chains of their former life in bondage. This mindset, characterized by fear, doubt, and a lack of trust in their ability to shape a better future, hindered their progress and prolonged their journey to the **Promised Land**.

1. Dependence and Fear of Change

After generations of slavery, the Israelites had become accustomed to relying on their Egyptian oppressors for **survival**, even under harsh conditions. When faced with the uncertainties of the wilderness, many longed to return to **Egypt**, despite the suffering they had endured there and despite that The Lord provided food and water (survival for all of their needs). This is evident in their frequent complaints, such as in Exodus 16:3, where they lamented, "*If only we had died by the Lord's hand in Egypt! There we sat around pots of meat and ate all the food we wanted,* *but you have brought us out into this desert to starve this entire assembly to death."* Their captivity mindset caused them to idealize the past and resist the challenges of change, even when freedom and abundance awaited them.

2. Lack of Faith and Trust

I believe strongly that faith needs action, and trust needs proof to be confirmed as true. And even though, God fulfilled his promises and provided proof to the Israelites that he would free them, provide for them and protect them; a person's mindset can cause a lack in faith and trust.

Which is precisely what happened with the Israelites, their captivity mindset made it difficult to fully trust God's promises and leadership through Moses. Despite witnessing miraculous events such as the parting of the Red Sea, the provision of manna, and water from a rock, they often doubted God's ability to provide for them. This lack of faith is highlighted in Numbers 14:3-4, when they questioned, "*Why is the Lord bringing us to this land only to let us fall by the sword? ... Wouldn't it be better for us to go back to Egypt?*" Their fear and lack of trust kept them spiritually bound, unable to embrace the freedom and blessings God had planned for them.

3. Complaints and Rebellion

The **captivity mindset** manifested in **persistent complaints** and **rebellion** against God and Moses. They grumbled about food, water, and the hardships of the journey, often expressing a desire to return to the familiarity of slavery in Egypt. This attitude not only revealed their ingratitude but also their difficulty in breaking free from the psychological patterns of submission and dependency ingrained during their time in bondage. Their rebellion culminated in significant consequences, such as when the Israelites refused to enter the Promised Land after hearing the spies' fearful report (Numbers 13–14). Their disobedience led God to decree that "*that generation*" would wander in the wilderness until they died, with only their children entering the Promised Land. He could not allow this mindset to continue on.

4. Resistance to Personal Responsibility

Freedom required the Israelites to take responsibility for their **faith**,

actions, and **relationship** with God. However, the captivity mindset often led them to blame Moses, God, or their circumstances for their struggles, rather than seeking solutions or growth. For example, when Moses was on Mount Sinai receiving the Ten Commandments, the people quickly reverted to old habits by building a golden calf and worshiping it, demonstrating their inability to take ownership of their covenant with God (Exodus 32).

5. Delayed Transformation

The Israelites had left Sinai (Numbers 10:11-36) on the 12th day of the second month of the second year after leaving Egypt. Shortly after, Moses then sent twelve spies to scout out the land of Cannan for 40 days, but when they returned ten out of the twelve spies gave a bad report. The 40 years in the wilderness was not only a punishment but also a necessary period for breaking the captivity mindset. During this time, God provided the Israelites with laws, guidance, and opportunities to develop faith, responsibility, and identity as a free people. The delay allowed a new generation—unshackled by the direct experiences of slavery—to rise with a mindset better suited to entering and conquering the Promised Land. This transformation underscores how deeply ingrained the captivity mindset was and how much effort was needed to replace it with a mindset of trust, faith, and freedom.

Lessons from the Captivity Mindset

- **Freedom Requires Inner Change:** Physical liberation is not enough; true freedom comes when individuals transform their thinking and embrace new responsibilities.
- **Faith is Essential for Progress:** A lack of trust in God's promises and leadership can keep people bound to old patterns, even when opportunities for growth and abundance are present.
- **Resisting the Past is Key to Moving Forward:** Idealizing past hardships or longing for "*the way things were*" prevents individuals from embracing the possibilities of the future.
- **Renewal Takes Time:** Breaking free from ingrained mentalities, habits, and fears is a process that requires patience, perseverance, and divine guidance.

The captivity mindset of the Israelites serves as a cautionary example of how deeply embedded mental and emotional chains can hinder progress, even in the face of miraculous opportunities. It reminds us of the importance of renewing our minds, trusting in God's plans, and embracing the challenges of growth as we journey toward our own "*Promised Lands.*"

America's history draws on parallels between the captivity mindset of the Israelites in the bible and the modern struggles of some Christian's in America, American slavery and woman's rights. The captivity mindset is a deeply ingrained way of thinking that persists even after physical liberation. It reflects the psychological, emotional, and cultural barriers that prevent individuals or groups from fully embracing freedom and their potential. This mindset has been evident throughout history—in the Israelites' journey from Egypt, in the aftermath of American slavery, and in the fight for women's rights. While physical emancipation represents a crucial first step, breaking free from the captivity mindset requires a transformation in beliefs, behaviors, and systems that perpetuate dependence, inequality, and self-limitation.

The Captivity Mindset in Modern America

Similar to the Israelites in Egypt, many people today may find themselves spiritually or mentally "***enslaved***" by dependence on worldly systems, policies, or cultural norms that conflict with their faith and divine calling. Here's how this dynamic is portrayed:

1. Dependence on the Government for Provision

Just as the Israelites looked back to Egypt for their physical sustenance, some people today might rely heavily on **government systems** or **policies** to meet their needs, even at the cost of spiritual principles or independence. Programs like welfare, healthcare, and other social safety nets, while often necessary and helpful, can sometimes foster a dependence that mirrors the Israelites' longing for the "*meat pots of Egypt.*" This reliance can create a captivity mindset where individuals feel unable to thrive outside of the government's control or intervention, rather than seeking God's provision and guidance.

Some individuals may prioritize government benefits over trusting God to provide through personal effort, community support, or creative solutions, unintentionally placing more faith in human systems than in divine provision or their own abilities. However, I believe we are approaching a time when many of these systems may fail, prompting a greater reliance on God's guidance. In such times, personal initiative, the strength of community, and innovative problem-solving will be essential to addressing challenges and building new systems that genuinely serve the well-being and best interests of the people.

2. Fear of Losing Comfort or Security

Many Christians, like the Israelites, may hesitate to step out in faith due to fear of uncertainty or the loss of comfort. In modern America, this often appears as an unwillingness to challenge cultural norms, policies, or systems that conflict with biblical principles. This captivity mindset prioritizes safety and stability over spiritual freedom, leading individuals to avoid taking bold steps for God. For example, some may refrain from speaking out against societal injustices, moral decay, or policies that contradict their beliefs, fearing the potential loss of jobs, social status, or personal comfort. This reluctance highlights the struggle between faith-driven action and the pull of worldly security.

3. Complaints and Grumbling

Just as the Israelites grumbled against Moses and God during their journey, many people today express dissatisfaction with their circumstances without taking action or trusting in God's plan. This mindset often focuses on problems rather than seeking divine solutions or actively working toward meaningful change. For instance, complaints about political corruption, moral decline, or societal challenges might dominate conversations among Christians, yet these grievances are often not paired with prayer, community engagement, or proactive efforts to create positive change. This approach highlights the need to shift from passive frustration to faith-driven action and collaboration.

4. Resistance to Responsibility and Faith

Freedom requires responsibility, faith, and trust in God's leadership. However, like the Israelites, some Christians today may resist taking personal responsibility for their spiritual growth or advancing God's kingdom, choosing instead to wait passively for church leaders, government officials, or community figures to act on their behalf. For example, a Christian might avoid evangelism, service, or activism, assuming these tasks are solely the roles of pastors, missionaries, or policymakers. This reflects a captivity mindset that underestimates the transformative power of individual obedience to God and the impact one person's actions can have on fulfilling His purposes.

5. Idolatry of Worldly Systems

When the Israelites built a golden calf during Moses' absence, it symbolized their return to familiar but false sources of security. Similarly, some Christians today place undue trust in political leaders, parties, or systems, treating them as ultimate sources of hope rather than relying on God and His guidance. For example, over-identifying with a political party or ideology and believing that the government alone can resolve spiritual or societal issues reflects a captivity mindset that prioritizes human systems over God's sovereignty. This misplaced trust can divert attention from God's instruction and His call to seek alternative, faith-driven solutions.

6. Fear of the Wilderness

Like the Israelites who feared the uncertainty of the wilderness, some Christians today resist stepping into spiritual or societal leadership because it demands courage, sacrifice, and trust in God. They may feel unprepared or unqualified, clinging to the predictability of the status quo, even if it limits their spiritual growth. For example, a Christian might hesitate to pursue a calling to ministry, missions, or social action due to concerns about financial instability, societal rejection, or the loss of worldly comforts. This reluctance underscores the challenge of trusting God's provision and embracing the unknown as a path to deeper faith and purpose.

The Captivity Mindset After American Slavery

The abolition of slavery in the United States was a monumental moment in history, yet it did not immediately free African Americans from the captivity mindset imposed by generations of systemic oppression. For centuries, enslaved people were taught to view themselves as inferior, dependent, and incapable of self-determination. These harmful beliefs were reinforced by laws, social structures, and cultural narratives that continued even after emancipation.

1. Psychological and Systemic Chains

Even after physical freedom, systemic racism, segregation, and economic inequality perpetuated the captivity mindset. Freed African Americans often faced limited access to education, employment, and land ownership, reinforcing feelings of inferiority and dependence on white systems of power. This mirrors the

Israelites' longing for Egypt, as many former slaves faced an uphill battle to assert their independence in a hostile society. For example, sharecropping systems and Jim Crow laws effectively re-enslaved African Americans economically and socially, making true freedom feel unattainable.

2. Breaking Free Through Empowerment

Despite these challenges, African Americans began to break free from this mindset through education, entrepreneurship, faith, and activism. Leaders like Frederick Douglass, Booker T. Washington, and Ida B. Wells inspired others to reject societal narratives of inferiority and claim their rightful place as equals. The Civil Rights Movement further dismantled systemic barriers, reflecting the Israelites' eventual journey into the Promised Land as a new generation emerged ready to fight for justice and equality.

Women's Rights and the Captivity Mindset

The struggle for women's rights similarly reveals the persistence of the captivity mindset. For centuries, women were confined to domestic roles, denied education, and excluded from political and economic power. These limitations fostered a mindset in many women—and in society at large—that their capabilities were inherently inferior to men's. This mindset was reinforced by cultural norms and institutions that perpetuated gender inequality.

Overcoming Societal Narratives

The captivity mindset among women was evident in beliefs that they were unfit for leadership, incapable of handling complex decisions, or destined solely for caregiving roles. These narratives were challenged by pioneers like Susan B. Anthony, Sojourner Truth, and Elizabeth Cady Stanton, who fought for suffrage, education, and labor rights. By breaking the societal chains, they inspired generations of women to reject the limitations imposed upon them. However, the fight for the right to vote wasn't just about political participation; it was about redefining women's place in society and their ability to contribute equally to the world.

The Ongoing Battle for Equality

Even today, remnants of the captivity mindset persist in wage gaps, unequal opportunities, and cultural biases. However, progress continues as more women step into leadership roles, advocate for equity, and challenge the systems that once held them back. This parallels the Israelites' journey, where full freedom required both systemic change and a renewal of individual and collective beliefs.

Woman Pastoring: A Modern Example of Breaking the Captivity Mindset

In many Christian traditions, the idea of women serving as pastors has been met with resistance, often stemming from longstanding cultural and theological interpretations that have limited women's roles in church leadership. However, as more Christians revisit scripture and consider the gifts and callings of women in ministry, many are recognizing that excluding women from pastoral roles reflects a captivity mindset—one rooted in tradition rather than the liberating principles of the gospel.

Breaking the Chains of Tradition

Consider the story of Pastor Sarah, a young woman who felt a strong calling to ministry from an early age. Despite her passion for serving God and her evident spiritual gifts, Sarah was discouraged by members of her community who believed women were not biblically authorized to lead a church. Comments like, "*You're better suited for children's ministry*," or "*Leadership is a man's responsibility*," reinforced a captivity mindset that confined women to certain roles, regardless of their abilities or callings.

However, Sarah found inspiration in examples from scripture, such as Deborah, who led Israel as a judge and prophet, and Priscilla, who taught and ministered alongside her husband, Aquila. With encouragement from mentors who recognized her calling, Sarah pursued theological education, honing her knowledge and leadership skills. Her faith and perseverance challenged the traditional narratives that had limited women's participation in ministry.

A Church Flourishing Under Her Leadership

When Sarah was finally invited to pastor a struggling church, her leadership breathed new life into the congregation. Her sermons, rooted in scripture and guided by the Holy Spirit, resonated deeply with the congregation. She initiated community outreach programs, created a mentorship network to support young leaders, and encouraged a culture of inclusion and collaboration. Under her guidance, the church grew spiritually and numerically, becoming a beacon of hope and service in the community.

Sarah's journey not only revitalized her church but also inspired other women to embrace their callings. Her success demonstrated that God equips both men and women for ministry, and that limiting leadership roles based on gender reflects human constructs rather than divine intent.

Sarah's story illustrates how the captivity mindset can hinder individuals and communities from fully experiencing God's plan. By breaking free from traditional restrictions and embracing God's liberating call, Sarah not only fulfilled her purpose but also helped her church and community flourish. Her example serves as a reminder that God's calling is not limited by gender, and that the church thrives when all members, regardless of their identity, are empowered to serve according to their gifts.

Breaking the Chains of Modern Oppression:

Today, many individuals unknowingly find themselves trapped within governmental and economic systems that can be oppressive, perpetuating cycles of dependency and limiting true freedom. These systems often create the illusion of choice and autonomy while subtly reinforcing structures that prioritize profit, control, and conformity over individual well-being. From mounting debt to stagnant wages, people are bound to frameworks that dictate the terms of their labor, consumption, and participation in society.

One of the clearest examples of modern economic oppression is the cycle of debt. Student loans, credit cards, and mortgages are marketed as pathways to success and stability, yet they often leave individuals saddled with financial burdens that take decades to escape. Governments and financial institutions design policies that favor corporations and lenders, leaving ordinary citizens with limited protections. In many cases, people work long hours not to build wealth or achieve their dreams but simply to service their debts, perpetuating a system where they are, in effect, laboring for entities that profit from their financial obligations.

The modern labor system itself can also feel like a form of enslavement. While employment is often necessary for survival, the structure of most jobs leaves little room for individual freedom. Many workers are expected to prioritize their roles over personal well-being, with long hours, limited benefits, and stagnant wages being the norm in many industries. Meanwhile, the wealth gap continues to widen, with economic gains disproportionately benefiting the elite. This disparity reflects a system where the efforts of the many support the luxuries of the few, creating an economic hierarchy that is difficult to escape.

Additionally, governmental systems play a significant role in reinforcing these dynamics. Policies that favor corporations, inadequate social safety nets, and taxation systems that disproportionately impact the middle and lower classes all contribute to the sense of systemic oppression. For example, large corporations often receive tax breaks and subsidies, while small businesses and individuals shoulder a heavier financial burden. This creates a framework where economic opportunities are skewed toward the already powerful, leaving little room for upward mobility.

The modern systems of economic and governmental oppression are deeply tied to the captivity mindset, where individuals feel trapped by circumstances they perceive as beyond their control. This mindset perpetuates feelings of helplessness, discouraging people from questioning the systems that confine them. For example, the belief that financial debt is an inevitable part of life or that working tirelessly for minimal advancement is simply "*how the world works*" reflects an acceptance of systemic constraints. This psychological captivity keeps individuals focused on survival rather than innovation, growth, or resistance to inequities. Much like the Israelites in the wilderness, who struggled to trust in their ability to thrive outside of Egyptian bondage, people today may hesitate to break free from systems that feel familiar, even if oppressive. Overcoming this captivity mindset requires not only recognizing the structural barriers in place but also cultivating a belief in one's ability to challenge and navigate these systems toward greater personal and collective freedom. By addressing both external oppression and the internalized beliefs that sustain it, individuals can begin to reclaim their agency and work toward a more equitable future.

Ultimately, the oppression of modern systems lies in their ability to obscure the reality of their control. Unlike historical forms of slavery or serfdom, where the chains were visible, today's systems operate through more subtle means: debt, labor exploitation, and policies that maintain inequality. To truly address this modern form of servitude, society must reimagine systems that prioritize human dignity, equitable opportunities, and freedom from oppressive economic and governmental constraints.

The Poverty Mindset: A Barrier to Growth and Abundance

A **poverty mindset** is a deeply ingrained belief system that perpetuates feelings of **scarcity**, **lack**, and **limitation**, regardless of one's actual financial or material circumstances. It goes beyond mere financial hardship to encompass a psychological state that affects how individuals perceive opportunities, resources, and their own potential for growth. This mindset often traps people in cycles of fear, self-doubt, and resistance to change, preventing them from pursuing a more abundant and fulfilling life.

Characteristics of a Poverty Mindset

1. Scarcity Mentality

A **scarcity mentality** is the belief that **resources**, **opportunities**, and **success** are **finite**. People with this mindset often feel that someone else's gain is their loss, leading to competition, envy, and an unwillingness to share or collaborate. For example, an employee might withhold knowledge from colleagues, fearing it will make them less valuable, or a person might resist investing in education or personal development, believing they cannot afford to take the risk. This perspective fosters a zero-sum approach to life, where perceived limitations overshadow potential opportunities. Shifting to an abundance mindset, where one recognizes that success and resources are often expandable, can help break this cycle. Collaboration, generosity, and a focus on creating value are key to overcoming the scarcity mentality.

2. Fear of Risk and Change

Fear is a dominant feature of the **poverty mindset**. Individuals may avoid taking risks, trying new things, or **pursuing growth** opportunities because they fear failure or loss. This fear often stems from past experiences of lack or failure, which reinforce the belief that the unknown is dangerous. For instance, someone might stay in a low-paying but stable job rather than seeking better opportunities because they fear rejection or instability. Similarly, a person may avoid investing in their future—such as starting a business or pursuing higher education—because of the perceived risk of financial loss. To counteract this fear, it is essential to reframe challenges as opportunities for growth and to view failure as a steppingstone to success. Building confidence through small, calculated risks can help individuals overcome their fear of change.

3. Entitlement and Dependence

A poverty mindset can sometimes manifest as a **sense of entitlement** or **overdependence** on **external support**. This occurs when individuals believe that others—whether family, government, or society—are responsible for improving their circumstances, rather than taking personal responsibility. For example, someone might rely entirely on social assistance without seeking ways to increase their income or skills. While external support can be necessary and beneficial, overdependence can lead to complacency and a lack of motivation to strive for self-sufficiency. Overcoming this aspect of the poverty mindset requires a shift toward personal responsibility and proactive problem-solving. Recognizing one's agency and potential to effect change is crucial for breaking free from dependence.

4. Negative Self-Image and Low Self-Worth

People with a poverty mindset often internalize feelings of unworthiness, believing they do not deserve success, happiness, or abundance. This **negative self-image** can lead to **self-sabotage**, where individuals unconsciously undermine their own efforts to improve their circumstances. For instance, a person might avoid applying for a promotion because they feel unqualified, even if they have the skills and experience required. Similarly, someone might spend impulsively rather than saving or investing because they believe they are not capable of managing money wisely. Breaking free from this aspect of the poverty mindset involves cultivating self-awareness, practicing self-compassion, and setting realistic goals that build confidence over time. Affirming one's value and potential is key to fostering a healthier self-image.

5. Resistance to Growth and Learning

A **fixed mindset**—the belief that abilities and intelligence are static—is a common feature of the poverty mindset. This perspective discourages effort, learning, and resilience, as individuals believe that success is determined by innate qualities rather than hard work and adaptability. For example, someone might say, "*I'm just not good with money*," and avoid learning about budgeting or investing. This resignation perpetuates cycles of financial mismanagement and missed opportunities. Adopting a growth mindset, where effort and learning are viewed as pathways to improvement, can help individuals overcome this limitation. Embracing challenges and seeking knowledge are essential steps toward personal and financial growth.

The Scarcity Mindset: A Barrier to Growth and Abundance

A **scarcity mindset** is a pervasive belief system rooted in the fear that **resources**, **opportunities**, and **success** are finite. This mindset traps individuals in a cycle of limitation and self-doubt, influencing how they perceive their potential and interact with the world. Regardless of actual circumstances, a scarcity mindset fosters feelings of lack and insecurity, creating psychological barriers that hinder growth and abundance. Overcoming this mindset is essential for unlocking creativity, collaboration, and the ability to thrive in both personal and professional life.

Characteristics of a Scarcity Mindset

1. Focus on Lack and Limitations:

A **scarcity mindset** directs attention to what is missing rather than what is possible. People with this mindset often dwell on their shortcomings, whether financial, emotional, or material, and believe they will never have enough. For instance, someone might constantly worry about their finances, even if they are financially stable, or feel they lack the skills needed to succeed despite having the resources to learn and improve. This focus on insufficiency creates a mental block, making it difficult to recognize or seize opportunities for growth. To counter this, shifting to an **abundance mindset**—where possibilities, resources, and opportunities are seen as plentiful—allows individuals to focus on solutions and potential rather than constraints.

2. Comparison and Envy:

A **scarcity mindset** often leads to constant comparison with others, creating feelings of **envy** and **inadequacy**. Instead of being inspired by others' successes, individuals with this mindset view someone else's achievement as a threat to their own. For example, a colleague receiving a promotion might lead to thoughts like, "*They got the opportunity I'll never have*," rather than recognizing the promotion as proof that success is attainable. This competitive outlook can damage relationships and **stifle collaboration**, reinforcing the belief that success is limited to a select few. Overcoming this requires embracing the idea that success is not a zero-sum game. Celebrating others' achievements and seeking opportunities to collaborate can shift the focus from competition to collective growth.

3. Fear of Taking Risks:

The scarcity mindset breeds **fear of failure** and **loss**, discouraging individuals from stepping out of their **comfort zones**. This fear often stems from a belief that failure will deplete already limited resources, making risks seem insurmountable. For instance, someone might hesitate to invest in a new business venture or professional development course because of the upfront cost, even if the potential returns far outweigh the risks. This avoidance of risk keeps individuals stuck in the status quo, unable to grow or capitalize on opportunities. Reframing failure as a learning experience and taking small, calculated risks can help break this cycle. Building confidence through incremental successes reinforces the belief that taking chances leads to growth.

4. Over-Hoarding and Resource Mismanagement:

A scarcity mindset often leads to **hoarding resources**, whether **time**, **money**, or **possessions**, out of **fear** that they **will run out**. Paradoxically, this behavior can lead to resource mismanagement, as individuals fail to invest their resources wisely. For example, someone might save money excessively but avoid investing it in ways that could generate long-term wealth, or they may stockpile items they don't need while neglecting essential expenditures. This hoarding behavior stems from a fear of scarcity rather than a strategy for growth.

Learning to use resources intentionally—such as budgeting, investing, and prioritizing experiences over possessions—can help shift the focus from scarcity to abundance.

5. Fixed Mindset and Resistance to Growth:

The **scarcity mindset** is often **tied** to a **fixed mindset**, where individuals believe that their **abilities**, **intelligence**, and **circumstances** are **static**. This belief discourages effort and learning, as individuals assume they cannot change their situation. For instance, someone might avoid pursuing a higher-paying job because they believe they lack the skills, or they might dismiss opportunities for personal growth with statements like, "*I'm not the kind of person who can succeed in that field.*" Adopting a growth mindset—where effort and learning are seen as keys to improvement—empowers individuals to overcome these self-imposed limitations. Viewing challenges as opportunities to develop new skills fosters **resilience** and opens the door to greater possibilities.

Overcoming a **captivity**, **poverty**, and **scarcity mindset** is essential for unlocking the full potential of a growth and abundance mindset. These limiting mindsets keep individuals trapped in cycles of fear, doubt, and inaction, preventing them from pursuing opportunities, taking risks, and realizing their dreams. Embracing a growth and abundance mindset, however, shifts the focus to possibilities, **resilience**, and the belief that success and resources are plentiful and achievable. It empowers individuals to break free from the mental and emotional barriers that hold them back, fostering confidence, creativity, and collaboration. By challenging **limiting beliefs** and adopting behaviors rooted in **gratitude**, self-awareness, and **perseverance**, individuals can transform their outlook and create a life of purpose, fulfillment, and limitless potential. The journey to this transformation begins with a decision to let go of the past and step boldly into a future of growth and **abundance**.

CHAPTER 6

UNDERSTANDING THE SIMILARITIES AND DIFFERENCES OF THE RICH AND WEALTHY

Rich and wealthy individuals are often grouped together, as both possess significant financial resources, but their approaches to money, success, and lifestyle diverge in critical ways. While they share similarities in their pursuit of financial success, their mindsets, priorities, and habits often reflect contrasting philosophies. Understanding these similarities and differences can help clarify the distinctions between being rich and being truly wealthy, offering a roadmap for those aspiring to achieve financial freedom and abundance.

The way we approach time and priorities has a profound impact on our decisions and outcomes. A ***"Now Mindset"*** focuses on immediate gratification, short-term rewards, and present-day concerns, often at the expense of future growth and opportunities. Conversely, a ***"Future Mindset"*** emphasizes long-term goals, delayed gratification, and strategic planning to create sustainable success. Understanding the differences between these mindsets is crucial for achieving balance, making meaningful progress, and building a fulfilling life.

Similarities Between Rich and Wealthy Individuals

1. Desire for Financial Prosperity:

Both **rich** and **wealthy** individuals prioritize **financial success** as a key goal. They understand the importance of money in achieving personal and professional aspirations, and they actively work toward building financial resources. Whether through careers, businesses, or investments, both groups recognize that financial stability opens doors to opportunities and security.

2. Work Ethic and Ambition:

Rich and wealthy individuals often share a strong work ethic and a drive to succeed. They are typically ambitious, resourceful, and willing to put in the effort needed to achieve their goals. This shared trait is a cornerstone of their financial achievements.

3. Value of Opportunities:

Both groups seize opportunities to grow their wealth. Whether it's through career advancement, entrepreneurial ventures, or strategic investments, rich and wealthy individuals understand the value of identifying and capitalizing on opportunities that align with their financial goals. Despite these similarities, the ways in which rich and wealthy individuals approach money, lifestyle, and long-term planning reveal significant differences.

Differences Between Rich and Wealthy Individuals

Focus on Income vs. Net Worth:

Rich Individuals often define their financial success by their ability to earn a **high income**, focusing on **active income streams** such as salaries, bonuses, or business profits. Their wealth is heavily dependent on continuous work or the ongoing performance of their ventures to sustain their lifestyle. This reliance on **active income** creates a vulnerability: if the income stream stops—due to job loss, market changes, or personal circumstances—their lifestyle may quickly become unsustainable. Rich individuals frequently equate financial success with their capacity to earn and spend, often prioritizing immediate gratification and outward displays of affluence over long-term security.

This mindset can lead to living paycheck to paycheck, even at high income levels, as spending often rises to match or exceed earnings. For example, they may invest in luxury homes, cars, and vacations without allocating sufficient resources to savings or investments that grow over time. While this approach can create the appearance of wealth, it lacks the stability and resilience associated with true **financial freedom**.

Rich individuals may also miss opportunities to build passive income streams or assets that generate value independently of their efforts. By focusing solely on earning and spending, they often overlook the importance of financial planning, diversification, and creating a sustainable foundation for the future. This short-term focus highlights a critical distinction between being rich and being wealthy: the former depends on active income, while the latter builds security through assets and strategic long-term planning.

There are many examples of this among celebrities, athletes, and musicians who experienced financial struggles due to a reliance on active income and a "*rich mindset*," illustrating how living beyond their means or failing to plan for the future can lead to financial instability.

Mike Tyson earned over $400 million during his boxing career, making him one of the highest-paid athletes of his time. However, his lavish spending on mansions, exotic pets, cars, and jewelry, combined with legal issues and mismanagement of funds, left him bankrupt by 2003. His wealth was tied directly to his earnings in the ring, and once his boxing career slowed, his income couldn't sustain his extravagant lifestyle. Tyson's story highlights the dangers of equating financial success with high earnings and spending without investing in long-term assets.

MC Hammer achieved massive success in the late 1980s and early 1990s with hits like "*U Can't Touch This*." At the peak of his career, he reportedly earned $30 million annually. However, his lavish spending on a massive mansion, luxury cars, and supporting an entourage of over 200 people quickly drained his wealth. By 1996, he filed for bankruptcy with over $13 million in debt. Hammer's case illustrates how an overreliance on active income and excessive spending can lead to financial collapse when the income stream diminishes.

Allen Iverson, a former NBA superstar, earned an estimated $200 million during his career from salaries and endorsements. However, his extravagant spending on jewelry, cars, and a large entourage left him in financial distress. Iverson reportedly struggled to pay bills and maintain his lifestyle after retiring from the NBA. His example underscores the risks of failing to save and invest, as his active income ended when his basketball career did, leaving him without sustainable wealth.

Nicolas Cage earned significant wealth through his acting career, with some reports estimating he made over $150 million between 1996 and 2011. However, Cage spent excessively on luxury items, including multiple mansions, exotic cars, rare artifacts, and even a dinosaur skull. His spending outpaced his income, and he faced financial troubles and unpaid taxes, forcing him to sell off many of his assets. Cage's story demonstrates how focusing on spending and material possessions without adequate financial planning can lead to instability.

Toni Braxton, a Grammy-winning singer, filed for bankruptcy twice despite earning millions from her successful music career. She cited poor financial management, excessive spending, and unfavorable contracts as key factors in her financial difficulties. Her case highlights how living beyond one's means and failing to secure financial independence can leave even high earners in financial distress.

Johnny Depp, one of Hollywood's most recognizable actors, reportedly earned over $650 million throughout his career. However, his extravagant spending on luxury properties, fine art, yachts, and a $30,000-per-month wine habit left him in financial turmoil. Depp's financial woes illustrate the risks of failing to manage wealth responsibly and relying too heavily on continuous high earnings to sustain an unsustainable lifestyle.

Many high earners face financial struggles due to an overreliance on active income, excessive spending on lavish lifestyles, and a lack of financial planning. Without creating passive income streams or investing in appreciating assets, their resources are often depleted faster than they can be replenished. Poor money management and inadequate preparation for the end of their high-earning careers leave them financially vulnerable. These examples underscore the importance of adopting a ***"wealth mindset,"*** which prioritizes long-term security through investments, diversification, and living within or below one's means. By shifting from a rich mindset to a wealth mindset, individuals can build lasting prosperity and avoid common financial pitfalls.

Wealthy individuals prioritize building **net worth** over merely earning a high income, focusing on creating sustainable financial independence (i.e., "*Future Mindset*"). They understand that true wealth comes from acquiring and growing assets—such as **investments**, **businesses**, and **real estate**—that appreciate in value over time and provide **consistent passive income**. For the wealthy, financial success is not defined by how much they earn but by how well their assets work for them, even when they are not actively engaged in generating income.

To achieve this, they cultivate multiple streams of passive income, including rental properties, dividends from stocks, royalties from intellectual property, or income from businesses that require minimal day-to-day involvement. These diversified income streams ensure that their wealth continues to grow and sustain their lifestyle, regardless of external economic fluctuations or personal circumstances.

In addition to creating **passive income**, wealthy individuals often reinvest a portion of their earnings into new opportunities, further compounding their wealth. This long-term approach to financial management provides a level of freedom that allows them to focus on personal passions, family, and legacy-building rather than being tied to continuous work. By emphasizing sustainability, diversification, and smart investments, wealthy individuals create a financial foundation that supports both present enjoyment and future **security**.

Now it is still unclear what the legacy of some of these individuals below might be, as several have had past association, friendships or other linkages to individuals like Jeffery Epstein and Sean Combs (P. Diddy), and continued investigations are underway. The purpose here below is to illustrate examples of celebrities, athletes, musicians, tech moguls, and entrepreneurs who exemplify the principles of building wealth through net worth, passive income, and long-term investment strategies.

LeBron James (Athlete) is not only one of the highest-earning athletes in the world but also a prime example of someone who focuses on building net worth. Beyond his NBA salary, LeBron has diversified his income through investments in companies like Blaze Pizza, where he owns a significant stake, and Fenway Sports Group, giving him partial ownership in sports teams like the Boston Red Sox. He also co-founded SpringHill Company, a production company, creating another revenue stream. These ventures generate passive income and build wealth that extends far beyond his basketball career.

Rihanna (Musician and Entrepreneur) transitioned from a successful music career to becoming a billionaire by building her net worth through her business ventures. Her cosmetics brand, Fenty Beauty, and her lingerie line, Savage X Fenty, are major contributors to her wealth. By owning a significant portion of these companies, she earns passive income from their ongoing success. Her focus on creating scalable businesses ensures financial sustainability that is not dependent on album sales or performances.

Oprah Winfrey (Media Mogul) is a quintessential example of a wealthy individual who has built long-term wealth through strategic investments and multiple revenue streams. After creating and growing her media empire, she invested in diverse ventures, including a significant stake in Weight Watchers (now WW International). She also owns her production company, Harpo Studios, which continues to generate income. Her focus on asset ownership has turned her media success into a lasting legacy.

Ashton Kutcher leveraged his acting income to invest in tech startups, creating significant wealth through passive income and equity stakes. He co-founded A-Grade Investments and has invested in companies like Uber, Airbnb, and Spotify, all of which grew exponentially in value. By focusing on acquiring assets that generate long-term returns, Kutcher has built a financial portfolio that far exceeds his acting earnings.

As the founder of Amazon, **Jeff Bezos** (Tech Mogul and Entrepreneur) exemplifies the concept of building wealth through equity and asset growth. While Amazon initially struggled to turn a profit, Bezos's focus on reinvesting earnings into the company paid off as its value skyrocketed. Even after stepping down as CEO, Bezos's net worth continues to grow through his equity in Amazon and investments in ventures like Blue Origin and The Washington Post. This approach ensures his wealth is not tied solely to his active role in the company.

The founder of Spanx, **Sara Blakely**, (Entrepreneur) built her wealth by owning and scaling her company. Instead of focusing on high income, she reinvested in her business, growing its value exponentially. When she sold a majority stake in Spanx to Blackstone, she retained equity in the company, ensuring she continues to benefit from its success while also creating significant passive income.

George Clooney transitioned from acting to wealth-building through his investment in Casamigos Tequila. He co-founded the brand with friends and later sold it to Diageo for up to $1 billion. By maintaining ownership stakes during the brand's growth, Clooney demonstrated how focusing on asset creation can yield massive financial rewards.

Elon Musk's wealth is primarily tied to his ownership stakes in Tesla, SpaceX, and other ventures. Rather than focusing on earning a salary, Musk reinvests in his companies, which continue to grow in value. His focus on building assets that appreciate over time makes him one of the wealthiest individuals in the world, showcasing the power of long-term thinking and passive wealth creation.

Reese Witherspoon turned her acting career into a wealth-building enterprise by founding Hello Sunshine, a media production company focused on female-driven stories. She recently sold a majority stake in the company to Blackstone but retained equity, ensuring continued passive income. This move exemplifies leveraging initial success to create lasting wealth.

Wealth-minded individuals prioritize diversification, building multiple income streams through businesses, investments, and assets that provide financial stability and growth. They adopt a long-term focus, investing in ventures that appreciate over time rather than relying solely on active income, which requires continuous effort. A key element of their strategy is **ownership**, as they acquire **equity** in **businesses** and **assets** that generate value and sustain their financial independence even after their primary careers wind down. By emphasizing **net worth**, **sustainability**, and **passive income**, these individuals demonstrate how a wealth mindset can lead to lasting financial success and true independence.

Spending vs. Investing:

Rich and wealthy individuals share the common goal of pursuing a fulfilling life, but their approaches to achieving this differ significantly. While both groups enjoy the advantages of their financial resources, their mindsets shape how they use them. One of the most significant differences between the now mindset and the future mindset is how resources—such as time, money, and energy—are allocated.

A **Now Mindset** often focuses on spending resources for immediate gratification, such as entertainment, convenience, or fleeting pleasures. This can lead to exhaustion, financial strain, or burnout. This mindset values spontaneity and emotional connection, which can make life feel vibrant and meaningful in the moment. **Rich individuals** often prioritize immediate satisfaction, focusing on pleasures, accomplishments, and material gains that bring joy or status in the present. They value spontaneity, indulgence, and emotional connection, which can make life feel vibrant and rewarding in the short term. For instance, a rich individual might splurge on luxury experiences, high-end cars, designer clothing, or lavish vacations, viewing these as markers of personal success and fulfillment. These outward displays of wealth often serve to reinforce their status and enjoyment in the moment. However, their spending habits are typically centered on showcasing or experiencing their wealth rather than investing in strategies to grow or sustain it over time.

A **Future Mindset**, however, prioritizes investing resources in ways that yield lasting benefits and focuses on building a foundation for sustained fulfillment. This includes investing in education, skills, relationships, and health. People with a future mindset see resources as tools for creating long-term value, understanding that small, consistent investments compound over time. **Wealthy Individuals** take a future-focused approach to fulfillment, prioritizing sustainability and long-term well-being over immediate gratification. They emphasize strategies such as financial planning, skill development, and personal growth to build a foundation for lasting prosperity.

For the wealthy, fulfillment is not solely about enjoying the present but about creating stability, freedom, and opportunities for the future. This often involves investing in appreciating assets like stocks, businesses, or real estate, ensuring their wealth continues to grow and provide value over time. They view money as a tool to generate opportunities and achieve meaningful goals, rather than simply a means to indulge in material consumption. Wealthy individuals also focus on nurturing relationships and contributing to causes that align with their values, reflecting a broader and more enduring vision of success. By balancing present enjoyment with future security, they cultivate deeper and more sustainable fulfillment, ensuring that their actions today contribute to a prosperous and purposeful life in the long run.

While their approaches differ, both mindsets ultimately strive to enrich life—either in the present or down the road. Both the **Now and Future Mindsets** focus on gratification but in different time frames. The now mindset seeks instant rewards, prioritizing enjoyment and satisfaction in the present moment. This mindset can be valuable for celebrating achievements, forming relationships, and taking a well-deserved break from long-term goals. On the other hand, the future mindset delays gratification, recognizing that sacrifices today can lead to greater rewards tomorrow. It involves putting off short-term pleasures to invest in actions that yield long-term benefits, such as career advancement, financial independence, or personal development. The key difference lies in the scope of their vision: the now mindset operates within a short horizon, while the future mindset looks beyond immediate gains to focus on sustainable outcomes.

Short-Term vs. Long-Term Thinking: Limited Perspective vs. Big-Picture Thinking

Rich Individuals often times use the **Now Mindset**, prioritizing instant results and immediate gratification, often disregarding the long-term consequences of decisions. Individuals with this mindset tend to focus on short-term rewards, whether it's impulsive spending, neglecting savings, or avoiding tasks that lack immediate payoffs. While this approach may offer temporary satisfaction, it often leads to stagnation and missed opportunities over time. This is evident in the behavior of some rich individuals, who prioritize enjoying their wealth in the present through lucrative jobs, high-return investments, or luxury lifestyles. While these decisions can yield quick success, they often lack sustainability due to their focus on the here and now.

In contrast, Wealthy Individuals with a Future Mindset adopts a broader perspective, recognizing the value of patience, discipline, and consistent effort in achieving long-term success. Individuals with this mindset are willing to make sacrifices today for greater rewards tomorrow. They invest in personal growth, plan strategically, and align their actions with their long-term vision. Wealthy individuals embody this future-focused approach by prioritizing financial freedom through strategic planning, long-term investments, and delayed gratification. Rather than seeking immediate returns, they focus on opportunities that compound over time, understanding that true success often requires years—or even decades—

to materialize.

Moreover, wealthy individuals value intelligence and acknowledge the importance of leveraging the expertise of others. They hire advisors or specialists with the skills and wisdom to help them navigate challenges and achieve their goals. This willingness to collaborate and adapt reflects a commitment to building sustainable success rather than chasing fleeting gains.

The difference between these mindsets also extends to perspective. A now mindset often operates with a **limited view**, focusing on immediate circumstances and assuming they will remain constant. This narrow perspective can lead to fear, hesitation, and missed opportunities for growth, as individuals fail to anticipate or adapt to change. For example, someone with a now mindset might avoid pursuing additional training, believing their current skills are sufficient indefinitely.

By contrast, a future mindset embraces big-picture thinking, acknowledging that circumstances evolve and requiring adaptability to navigate change. This mindset encourages dreaming big, planning strategically, and maintaining optimism about what lies ahead. For instance, someone with a future mindset might proactively invest in education or skill development to prepare for career changes, recognizing the importance of continuous growth in an ever-changing world.

Ultimately, the future mindset's emphasis on long-term thinking and adaptability allows individuals to build resilience and take advantage of evolving opportunities, while the now mindset's focus on immediate gratification often limits their potential for sustained success. By combining big-picture thinking with a willingness to make thoughtful sacrifices, the future mindset paves the way for enduring fulfillment and achievement.

Emotional Reactions vs. Logical Decisions:

The decision-making processes of the Now and Future Mindsets differ fundamentally in their focus and approach. The **now mindset** is often driven by **emotional reactions** and a desire for comfort, relief, or **immediate pleasure**. While this can lead to **impulsive decisions**, such as overspending or indulging in unhealthy habits that feel gratifying in the moment, these choices may create challenges and setbacks over time. This mindset tends to prioritize **short-term satisfaction**, often at the expense of **long-term stability**.

In contrast, the future mindset emphasizes logical, deliberate choices aligned with long-term objectives. It encourages individuals to carefully weigh the pros and cons, anticipate consequences, and make decisions that support their broader values and goals. For example, someone with a future mindset might invest in further education or save for retirement, even if it requires sacrificing leisure or disposable income in the present. This approach focuses on building a foundation for sustainable success and fulfillment.

Despite their differences, both mindsets share a common need for self-awareness. Understanding your emotions, values, and priorities is crucial to making choices that truly reflect what matters most to you—whether in the moment or for the future. Without this clarity, even well-intentioned decisions can miss the mark.

The now mindset often leads to reactive thinking, where individuals respond to immediate needs or crises without considering how their actions fit into a larger plan. This reactive approach can create cycles of urgency and stress, as short-term fixes rarely address deeper or underlying issues. On the other hand, a future mindset fosters proactive planning. Those with a future-oriented perspective anticipate potential challenges and prepare for them in advance. This foresight allows for clearer, more confident decision-making, reducing the likelihood of being overwhelmed or derailed by unexpected events. By integrating the strengths of both mindsets with self-awareness, individuals can balance present enjoyment with future security.

Scarcity vs. Abundance Mindset: A Key Difference Between Rich and Wealthy Individuals

A fundamental distinction between rich and wealthy individuals lies in how they perceive opportunities and resources—through the lens of a scarcity mindset or an abundance mindset. This perspective not only shapes their financial behaviors but also reveals how they approach the present and future, intertwining with the now and future mindsets.

Rich Individuals: Scarcity Mindset and the Now Focus

Rich individuals often operate with a scarcity mindset, rooted in the belief that resources, wealth, and opportunities are finite. This perspective can lead to fear-driven behaviors, such as hoarding wealth, avoiding collaboration, or competing aggressively to maintain their financial status. They may feel that any loss or missed opportunity is irreversible, causing anxiety and an overwhelming need to focus on short-term gains.

This scarcity-driven approach aligns closely with a now mindset, as it prioritizes immediate results and protection of current assets over long-term growth and sustainability. For example, a person with this mindset might decline to share business strategies or network connections, fearing it will diminish their own success. Similarly, they might overextend themselves financially to maintain a high-status lifestyle, believing they must "*prove*" their wealth in the present to secure their social standing.

The downside of this perspective is that it limits creativity and growth. By focusing solely on protecting what they have in the moment, rich individuals may miss opportunities to invest in their future or build relationships that could lead to greater prosperity.

Wealthy Individuals: Abundance Mindset and the Future Focus

Wealthy individuals, in contrast, embrace an **abundance mindset**, viewing resources and opportunities as plentiful and often expandable. This perspective fosters a sense of optimism and confidence, enabling them to focus on **long-term growth** rather than **short-term competition**. Instead of fearing loss, they see challenges and risks as opportunities to learn, innovate, and create even more wealth.

This **abundance mindset** aligns with a **future-focused approach**. Wealthy individuals are more likely to collaborate with others, share resources, and invest in ventures that may not yield immediate returns but promise significant benefits over time. For example, someone with this mindset might mentor others, invest in community projects, or share knowledge freely, understanding that lifting others up creates a ripple effect of success that benefits everyone, including themselves.

Wealthy individuals recognize that success is not a zero-sum game; someone else's achievements do not detract from their own. This outlook not only reduces stress and competition but also cultivates strong networks and partnerships that can amplify their financial and personal success over the long term.

Scarcity vs. Abundance: Impact on Decision-Making:

The **scarcity mindset** drives reactive, **fear-based decisions**, such as clinging to existing resources or avoiding calculated risks. This often results in short-term gains but limits potential for sustainable growth. For example, a rich individual might focus on saving money in a low-interest account to avoid perceived risks, missing out on the benefits of higher-yield investments.

The **abundance mindset**, however, encourages proactive, growth-oriented decision-making. Wealthy individuals are willing to take risks and delay gratification because they trust in their ability to recover and adapt. For instance, they might invest in real estate or start a business, knowing that these ventures could yield exponential returns in the future.

The Takeaway: Choosing an Abundance Mindset

Transitioning from a scarcity mindset to an **abundance mindset** involves shifting focus from short-term protection to long-term growth, aligning your now and future mindsets. Recognize that opportunities and resources are not fixed; they can expand with creativity, collaboration, and persistence. Instead of asking, "*How can I keep what I have?*" adopt a future-focused question like, "*How can I use what I have now to create more in the future?*" By embracing this abundance-driven perspective, you not only unlock your potential for financial success but also cultivate a mindset of resilience, generosity, and optimism that leads to a truly fulfilling life.

The now and future mindsets, though distinct, can work together to create a more balanced and fulfilling life. The now mindset brings spontaneity, emotional connection, and the ability to savor the present moment. It reminds us to celebrate small victories, nurture relationships, and take breaks from the demands of long-term pursuits. Meanwhile, the future mindset provides structure, direction, and a sense of purpose. It ensures that your actions today align with your larger goals, paving the way for sustained success and security. By integrating these perspectives, you can embrace the best of both worlds—fully enjoying the present while steadily working toward the life you envision for the future.

While the future mindset is essential for achieving long-term success, it's crucial to strike a balance between preparing for tomorrow and appreciating today. A rigid focus on the future can lead to burnout, stress, and the feeling of missing out on life's simple pleasures. Conversely, living entirely in the moment can result in unfulfilled potential and regrets over missed opportunities. The key is to blend these mindsets effectively—enjoy the present without losing sight of your long-term goals. Celebrate small achievements, prioritize rest and relaxation, but ensure that your daily actions contribute to your bigger vision. A balanced approach allows you to live fully in the moment while building a sustainable and prosperous future.

Ultimately, the now and future mindsets represent two distinct approaches to time, priorities, and decision-making. While the now mindset offers immediate comfort and gratification, the future mindset focuses on building lasting success and fulfillment. Cultivating a **future-oriented perspective** and aligning your actions with **long-term goals** empowers you to break free from **reactive patterns** and create a life of purpose, abundance, and achievement. Remember, the choices you make today shape the future you will experience tomorrow, making it essential to balance spontaneity with strategy for a meaningful and well-rounded life.

The now mindset and the future mindset each have their strengths and weaknesses, but they share a **common goal**: to create a life of meaning and fulfillment. Recognizing their differences and similarities allows you to harness the power of both perspectives. Embrace the present with gratitude and intention while keeping your eyes on the horizon, ensuring that your daily actions contribute to your long-term vision. By balancing spontaneity with strategy, you can build a life that is both joyful in the moment and secure for the future.

CHAPTER 7

ROADBLOCKS TO VICTORY & THE BLUEPRINT FOR SUCCESS

Now that you have a clearer understanding of common mindsets, let's explore the obstacles that can hinder success and positive growth. Not long ago, I watched a video of someone who claimed to ask ChatGPT a question, "*If you were the Devil, if you were Satan, how would you stop someone from being successful?*"

The response he received was very profound and compelling, and I have to admit, at first, I thought it was just click bate. So, I decided to investigate this for myself, in order to verify ChatGPT's response. The results may surprise you.

ChatGPT's 12 Responses:

'If I were the devil and my goal was to stop someone from being successful, I would employ subtle and insidious tactics designed to undermine their confidence, sow doubt, and create distractions. Success often depends on clarity, perseverance, and a strong mindset, so targeting these areas would be the most effective strategy. Here's how that could look:

1. Plant Self-Doubt and Fear

The enemy often whispers thoughts of inadequacy, **fear of failure**, and **self-doubt** into our minds, convincing us that we're not smart, talented, or worthy enough to succeed. These lies cause hesitation, discouraging us from taking risks or pursuing opportunities, and may lead to giving up at the first sign of difficulty. Thoughts like,

"*You're not good enough to achieve this. Don't even try—you'll only embarrass yourself*," can paralyze progress and keep us from realizing our true potential. Recognizing and rejecting these lies is crucial for overcoming such negative influences.

2. Distract Them with Immediate Gratification

The enemy often shifts focus from long-term goals to fleeting pleasures and distractions, encouraging **procrastination** and indulgence in **time-wasting activities**. This tactic derails progress, causing a loss of focus and momentum, and often leads to delaying or abandoning meaningful pursuits. Thoughts like, "*Why work on that project now? You deserve to relax and binge-watch another episode*," can seem harmless but gradually undermine discipline and dedication, keeping individuals from achieving their full potential. Recognizing these diversions is key to staying on track.

3. Foster a Scarcity and Poverty Mindset

The enemy often sows a **scarcity mindset**, convincing individuals that opportunities and resources are **limited**. This creates envy, competition, and a fear of taking risks, leading them to hoard resources, avoid collaboration, and shy away from challenges out of fear of losing what little they have. Thoughts like, "*There's not enough to go around. If someone else succeeds, it means you'll fail*," fuel this mindset, trapping them in a cycle of insecurity and stagnation. Overcoming this lie requires embracing an abundance mindset and trusting in the availability of opportunities for all.

4. Surround Them with Negative Influences

The enemy often places **toxic**, **discouraging**, or **complacent individuals** in our lives who **criticize**, **belittle**, or **distract** us from **pursuing our goals**. This negativity can create an environment that stifles motivation and reinforces limiting beliefs. For example, a friend might dismiss someone's dreams by saying, "*Why aim so high? Be realistic and settle for what you already have*." Such influences can derail progress and diminish confidence, making it essential to recognize and distance ourselves from harmful relationships while seeking uplifting and supportive connections.

5. Encourage Comparison and Envy

The enemy often shifts focus to others' achievements, creating feelings of inadequacy and convincing individuals that they'll never measure up. This **comparison** traps them in a **cycle of wasted energy**, as they dwell on perceived shortcomings rather than concentrating on their own unique journey and progress. Thoughts like, "*Look at how far ahead they are—you'll never catch up*," can discourage action and hinder growth. Breaking free from this mindset requires redirecting attention to personal goals and celebrating individual progress.

6. Promote Procrastination and Perfectionism

The enemy often tricks individuals into believing they need to wait for the ***"perfect time"*** or ***"perfect conditions"*** before taking action. This mindset leads to endless planning, researching, and second-guessing, ultimately preventing them from starting at all. Thoughts like, "*You're not ready yet—wait until everything is perfect before moving forward*," create a cycle of procrastination and missed opportunities. True progress begins when action is taken, even in imperfect circumstances.

7. Emphasize Failure Over Growth

The enemy often twists setbacks into evidence of incompetence, discouraging individuals from seeing mistakes as opportunities to learn and grow. This fear of failure prevents them from taking risks or trying again, keeping them stuck in a cycle of doubt. Thoughts like, "*You failed once, so why bother trying again? You're clearly not cut out for this*," undermine confidence and halt progress. Overcoming this mindset requires reframing failure as a steppingstone toward growth and resilience.

8. Sow Discontent and Unfulfillment

The enemy often convinces individuals that no matter how much progress they make, it will never be enough to bring true happiness or success. This leads to a constant cycle of dissatisfaction, where they endlessly chase new goals without pausing to appreciate their achievements. Thoughts like, "*You'll only be happy once you achieve X—but even that might not be enough*," fuel this mindset, robbing them of contentment and joy. Breaking free requires practicing gratitude and finding fulfillment in the present while pursuing future goals.

9. Overwhelm Them with Busyness

The enemy often fills life with **endless tasks** and **obligations**, creating the illusion of productivity while leaving little time for meaningful progress or reflection. This tactic keeps individuals so preoccupied with **busyness** that they lose focus on their true goals. Thoughts like, "*You don't have time to work on your dreams—you're already too busy managing everything else*," reinforce this **cycle of distraction**. To overcome it, one must prioritize what truly matters and make intentional space for pursuing personal growth and purpose.

10. Undermine Their Faith or Belief System

The enemy often sows doubt in an individual's purpose, worth, or connection to a higher power, causing them to question whether their efforts have any significance. Without a strong sense of purpose or spiritual grounding, they lose motivation and direction, feeling aimless and discouraged. Thoughts like, "*What's the point of working so hard? None of it will matter in the end*," can lead to despair and stagnation. Overcoming this requires reconnecting with one's faith, values, and sense of meaning to restore clarity and drive.

11. Erode Their Discipline and Consistency

The enemy often promotes laziness, inconsistency, and a reliance on fleeting motivation rather than cultivating disciplined habits. This approach leads to a strong start but a lack of follow-through, ultimately sabotaging progress. Thoughts like, "*You don't have to work on it today—there's always tomorrow*," foster procrastination and delay meaningful action. Breaking this cycle requires building consistent habits and prioritizing discipline over momentary feelings to ensure sustained growth and success.

12. Exploit Their Weaknesses

The enemy often targets insecurities, bad habits, or vices, amplifying them to derail focus and success. These weaknesses become distractions, pulling individuals away from their goals and trapping them in destructive cycles of behavior. Thoughts like, "*You'll never overcome this habit—it's just who you are,*" reinforce a sense of hopelessness and prevent growth. Overcoming this requires recognizing these lies, seeking strength through self-discipline and faith, and taking deliberate steps to break free from limiting patterns.

The enemy's greatest weapon is subtlety, using small, seemingly harmless distractions and doubts to derail a person's path to success. By cultivating awareness, discipline, and a positive mindset, individuals can resist these tactics and thrive, no matter the challenges they face.'

Roadmap to Shifting Your Mindset:

To achieve success, a person must intentionally cultivate habits, attitudes, and strategies that align with their goals and values. Success isn't just about achieving external milestones; it's about developing resilience, self-awareness, and a sense of purpose. Additionally, implementing key strategies is essential to effectively overcome the enemy's obstacles and safeguard your progress toward personal and spiritual growth. Here's a guide to what a person can do to set themselves up for success.

Steps for Creating and Developing Positive Routines:

1. Align Your Actions with Your Purpose:

Aligning your actions with your **purpose** is essential for creating a fulfilling and meaningful life. Start by defining your "*why*"—the deeper reason behind your goals—and ensuring that your aspirations align with your values and passions. When your actions are **rooted in purpose**, they fuel **motivation** and provide a **sense of direction**, making success not only achievable but also deeply rewarding. Reflecting on questions like, "*Why am I pursuing this goal, and how does it align with my purpose?*" helps maintain focus and ensures that your efforts contribute to a life of authenticity and significance. It is important to stay connected to your faith or guiding principles to maintain clarity and motivation.

Developing who you want to be begins with defining the character and values you aspire to embody. This process requires self-reflection to identify the traits and principles that align with your vision for a meaningful life, such as integrity, kindness, perseverance, or humility. Cultivating these qualities involves intentional daily actions, making choices that reflect your desired character even in small moments. Surround yourself with role models who inspire growth and encourage accountability, while seeking to learn from mistakes and challenges along the way. Grounding your values in timeless principles, such as those found in Scripture—"*Whatever is true, whatever is noble, whatever is right, whatever is pure, whatever is lovely, whatever is admirable—if anything is excellent or praiseworthy—think about such things*" (Philippians 4:8)—ensures that your development is rooted in authenticity and purpose. Over time, consistent effort in shaping your character will align your actions with your values, transforming you into the person you aspire to be.

Understanding your "*why*" begins with uncovering the core motivations that drive your goals and decisions. Ask yourself, "*What truly inspires me?*" and "*What is the deeper reason behind what I'm pursuing?*" Identifying your "*why*" helps you connect your actions to your values and passions, giving your life a sense of purpose and direction. Once you gain clarity about what motivates you—whether it's personal growth, making a positive impact, or providing for loved ones—it's time to move from reflection to action. Break your goals into small, actionable steps that align with your purpose, and start building momentum. Taking intentional action bridges the gap between aspiration and reality, turning your "*why*" into tangible progress and fulfillment.

2. Journaling and Goal Setting

Journaling, **goal setting**, and **tracking progress** are essential practices for personal growth and success. Journaling provides a space for self-reflection, helping you clarify thoughts, identify patterns, and express gratitude, which fosters mental clarity and emotional well-being. Goal setting creates a roadmap for your aspirations, giving direction and purpose to your efforts, while breaking down big dreams into manageable steps. Tracking progress ensures accountability, allowing you to celebrate milestones, learn from setbacks, and make adjustments as needed. Together, these practices create a cycle of intentionality and improvement, empowering you to stay focused, motivated, and aligned with your long-term vision.

To achieve your goals, start by setting a clear long-term vision and breaking it down into actionable steps you can accomplish each day. Prioritize progress over perfection, as small, consistent efforts build momentum and lead to significant results over time. This approach keeps you motivated by demonstrating how your daily actions contribute to your larger aspirations. Adopting a mindset like, "*What can I do today to move closer to my goal?*" helps maintain focus and ensures steady progress toward your vision.

3. Take Consistent and Disciplined Action

Developing **habits** and **routines** that align with your goals is essential for **long-term success**. Rather than relying on fleeting motivation, focus on building **consistency** through disciplined, small actions that compound over time to create significant results. Each day presents an opportunity to make progress, no matter how small. Adopting a mindset of asking yourself, "*What small step can I take today to stay on track?*" helps maintain focus and ensures steady advancement toward your objectives.

Remember, developing a positive routine is a powerful step toward living a purposeful and fulfilling life. By understanding your priorities, setting clear goals, and building habits rooted in faith and discipline, you can create a routine that supports your personal growth and aligns with God's plan for you. Remember, routines aren't about perfection but about consistency and intentionality. Take small, steady steps, and trust the process as you move closer to becoming the best version of yourself.

4. Manage/Remove Distractions and Stay Focused:

To manage **distractions** and stay focused, it's essential to **prioritize** your time and energy by **eliminating activities** that divert you from your goals. For many, this involves stepping away from social media and limiting time spent scrolling through unproductive content. Others may need to reduce the hours spent watching TV, playing video games, or engaging in similar distractions. By consciously removing these interruptions, you create space for steady progress without being sidetracked by unimportant tasks or negative influences. To reinforce this focus, shift your mindset by regularly asking yourself, "*What is the most important task I can focus on today?*" This simple question can help redirect your thoughts and actions toward meaningful priorities, enabling you to achieve your goals more effectively.

5. Overcoming Vices and Replacing with Virtues:

A natural progression from managing distractions is dropping **vices**. To overcome vices, one must practice a combination of self-awareness, intentional effort, self-discipline, and seek guidance through prayer, scripture, and support from others. It may also be helpful to study spiritual and practical tools for transformation. The first step is recognizing the vice and its impact on your life—acknowledging how it hinders your growth, relationships, or spiritual walk. Replace the harmful habit with a positive one; for example, swap idle scrolling on social media with reading, prayer, or exercise. **Replacing vices** with **virtues**—such as replacing dishonesty with truthfulness or laziness with diligence—leads to personal transformation and spiritual growth. Set clear goals and boundaries, such as limiting exposure to environments or triggers that encourage the vice. Surround yourself with supportive people who encourage accountability and celebrate progress. Consistently pray for strength, guidance, and forgiveness, as God provides the power to overcome (Philippians 4:13). Finally, practice patience with yourself—breaking free from vices is a process, and small, consistent changes lead to lasting transformation. Ultimately, vices are obstacles to living a fulfilling, virtuous, and God-centered life, and recognizing and addressing them is essential for holistic well-being.

6. Meditation and Reflection:

Meditation is a powerful practice that promotes **mental clarity**, **emotional** balance, and spiritual well-being. By taking time to quiet the mind and focus inward, meditation helps reduce stress, improve concentration, and foster a sense of peace. It allows you to step back from the noise of daily life, gaining perspective and cultivating mindfulness, which enhances your ability to respond to challenges with calm and intention. Spiritually, meditation provides an opportunity to connect with God, reflect on His Word, and seek guidance, as encouraged in Scripture: "Be still, and know that I am God" (Psalm 46:10). Regular meditation nurtures self-awareness, strengthens resilience, and creates space for personal growth, making it an essential tool for holistic well-being.

7. Develop a Positive Self-Talk Habit

Cultivate self-awareness by recognizing negative thoughts and patterns, then challenging them with truth and positivity. Replace **self-criticism** with empowering **affirmations** and **constructive** feedback, avoiding harsh judgments of yourself or others. Stop comparing yourself to others and celebrate your unique progress. Positive self-talk strengthens confidence and reinforces your belief in your ability to succeed. Embrace thoughts like, "*I have the strength and skills to overcome any obstacle*," to foster resilience and a growth-oriented mindset.

Positive self-talk is a transformative habit that reshapes how you perceive challenges and opportunities. By consciously choosing empowering language, you can reframe setbacks as learning experiences and obstacles as steppingstones to growth. This habit not only improves your mental well-being but also enhances your ability to take decisive action, even in difficult situations. Additionally, speaking kindly to yourself fosters self-compassion, helping you to recover more quickly from mistakes and build emotional resilience. When you stop using words poorly against yourself and others, you create a mental environment where positivity and self-belief thrive. Over time, consistent **positive self-talk** shifts your mindset, allowing you to approach life with **confidence**, clarity, and a stronger **sense of purpose**.

Implement Key Strategies for Success:

Implementing key strategies for success is essential to turning aspirations into reality. Success doesn't happen by chance; it requires intentional planning, discipline, and consistent effort. By adopting practical approaches, such as setting clear goals, cultivating productive habits, and maintaining a growth mindset, you can overcome obstacles and stay focused on your vision. These strategies not only guide you toward achieving your objectives but also empower you to navigate challenges with resilience and confidence. With the right tools and mindset, success becomes a deliberate and achievable journey.

1. Cultivate Confidence and Belief in Yourself:

Replace **self-doubt** with **self-affirmation** and confidence in your abilities, understanding that growth is achieved through effort, not just innate talent. This mindset allows you to take bold steps toward your goals, even when faced with uncertainty. Embrace thoughts like, "*I am* *capable of learning, growing, and succeeding. Each challenge is an opportunity to improve,"* to build resilience and stay motivated on your journey.

2. Adopt Multiple Positive and Growth-Oriented Mindsets:

Success and fulfillment are rooted in the way you think. By adopting multiple positive mindsets—such as a growth mindset, abundance mindset, future-focused mindset, and wealth mindset—you can transform challenges into opportunities and chart a path toward lasting progress. These mindsets work together to shape how you view yourself, your goals, and the world around you, empowering you to take consistent action toward success.

By adopting an abundance mindset this allows you to shift towards the belief that opportunities and resources are plentiful, and success is not a limited commodity. Instead of competing with others, focus on collaboration and celebrating their achievements. This perspective shifts your energy from envy or fear to gratitude and optimism, making you more open to discovering unexpected possibilities. For instance, when someone else succeeds, remind yourself, "*There's more than enough success to go around, and I'm ready to create my own.*" Adopting this mindset not only fosters positivity but also enhances your willingness to share knowledge, ideas, and resources, creating a ripple effect of growth for yourself and others.

Adopting a **growth mindset** means emphasizing the belief that abilities, intelligence, and talents are not fixed but can be developed through effort, learning, and perseverance. With this mindset, challenges become opportunities to grow, and failures are seen as stepping- stones to success. When faced with obstacles, ask yourself, "*What can I learn from this experience?*" By focusing on continuous improvement, you embrace the journey of growth, cultivating resilience and a strong belief in your potential. This mindset is essential for overcoming self-doubt and staying motivated, even when progress feels slow.

Adopting a **future-focused mindset** encourages you to look beyond your current circumstances and envision the possibilities that lie ahead. By aligning your actions with your long-term goals, you stay motivated and maintain a sense of purpose. Instead of dwelling on past mistakes or current limitations, concentrate on what you can achieve with consistent effort and strategic planning. Visualizing your desired future, combined with actionable steps to get there, empowers you to make decisions today that align with your vision of tomorrow.

Adopting a **wealth mindset** involves viewing money and resources as tools for growth, impact, and creating value—not as ends in themselves. This mindset encourages you to focus on financial literacy, smart investments, and developing skills that generate long-term benefits. Rather than seeing wealth as something only a select few can achieve, recognize that financial success comes from intentional planning, disciplined habits, and a belief in your ability to create opportunities. A wealth mindset helps you approach money with responsibility, generosity, and confidence, knowing that prosperity is achievable and sustainable.

By integrating an **abundance mindset**, **growth mindset**, **future-focused mindset**, and **wealth mindset**, you can develop a holistic approach to personal and professional growth. These mindsets complement each other, enabling you to face challenges with confidence, celebrate progress, and remain focused on your unique journey. Together, they transform your perspective from one of limitations to one of boundless possibilities, empowering you to approach life with optimism, resilience, and a clear sense of purpose. When these mindsets form the foundation of your actions, success becomes not only attainable but also deeply rewarding and meaningful.

3. Prioritize Mental and Physical Health

Health, both mental and physical, is foundational to achieving success and maintaining a **positive mindset**. Your body and mind are interconnected, and neglecting either can hinder your ability to focus, stay motivated, and handle challenges effectively. Physical health—through proper nutrition, exercise, and rest—fuels your energy levels and resilience, while mental health—through mindfulness, stress management, and emotional awareness—keeps you balanced and capable of clear, constructive thinking. A healthy body supports a healthy mind, and together, they create the conditions for a growth-oriented mindset. When you prioritize your well-being, you're better equipped to face obstacles with **confidence**, sustain long-term progress, and embrace opportunities for personal and professional growth. Developing habits that nurture your health reinforces the belief that you are capable of and deserving of success, creating a positive cycle of mindset and self-care.

Expanding on the connection between health and mindset, maintaining mental and physical well-being also enhances your ability to cultivate resilience and adapt to life's challenges. A strong, healthy body enables you to manage stress more effectively and increases stamina, allowing you to remain productive and engaged in your goals. Similarly, prioritizing mental health by practicing gratitude, seeking therapy when needed, or engaging in mindfulness activities reduces anxiety and fosters a calm, focused mind. Together, these practices create a fertile environment for a growth mindset, where you view challenges as opportunities rather than setbacks. Poor health, on the other hand, can lead to fatigue, negative thinking, and diminished motivation, which undermine your ability to stay consistent and focused. By committing to holistic health, you empower yourself to pursue success with clarity, strength, and a mindset that embraces positivity and progress.

4. Surround Yourself with Positive Influences:

Building a network of supportive, growth-minded individuals is essential for personal development, as these connections inspire and challenge you to be your best. Surround yourself with people who encourage your goals, provide motivation, and offer valuable perspectives. Seek out encouraging, like-minded people who uplift and inspire you. Pair this with a daily habit of reading and reflecting on positive content, such as a chapter from Psalms each morning, to cultivate a mindset of gratitude and growth. A positive environment reinforces your aspirations, strengthens your resolve during challenges, and equips you with insights to navigate your journey. Start each day by asking yourself, "*Who can I learn from or connect with today to help me grow?*" to stay focused on fostering meaningful relationships and personal progress.

The influence of those we surround ourselves with cannot be underestimated, as bad company has the power to corrupt even the strongest morals. Scripture warns us in 1 Corinthians 15:33 (NIV): "*Do not be misled: 'Bad company corrupts good character.*" When we consistently engage with individuals who disregard values of integrity, kindness, or truth, their attitudes and behaviors can subtly infiltrate our own, leading us to compromise on principles we once held firmly. Negative influences can normalize gossip, dishonesty, or indulgence in harmful habits, eroding the foundation of good morals over time. Just as iron sharpens iron (Proverbs 27:17), the wrong relationships can dull our spiritual and ethical edge, making it critical to seek friendships that inspire us to grow closer to God and uphold righteousness. By choosing our companions wisely, we protect our character and remain aligned with God's will for our lives.

To cultivate a **positive environment**, it's equally important to identify and remove **toxic**, **manipulative**, or **negative** influences from your **circle of influence**. Start by reflecting on your interactions and assessing how certain individuals make you feel after spending time with them—do they uplift and inspire you, or leave you drained and discouraged? Pay attention to patterns of manipulation, constant criticism, or behaviors that undermine your confidence and goals. Once identified, establish healthy boundaries by limiting contact with these individuals or disengaging from conversations that foster negativity. Be assertive but kind when communicating your need for distance, focusing on your commitment to personal growth. Seek to replace these interactions with those who share your values and vision, creating a circle of influence that supports and strengthens you. By taking proactive steps to surround yourself with positivity, you create the space needed to thrive emotionally, mentally, and spiritually.

Setting healthy boundaries is crucial for limiting the impact of negative behaviors from friends, family, or colleagues on your success. Begin by clearly defining your personal **limits** and **identifying behaviors** that **hinder** your **progress**, such as constant criticism, unrealistic demands, or persistent negativity. Communicate these boundaries assertively but respectfully. For example, with a friend who frequently dismisses your goals, you might say, "*I value our friendship, but I'd prefer not to discuss my plans if the conversation isn't supportive.*" With family members who pressure you into commitments that disrupt your focus, try stating, "*I can't take on that responsibility right now, but I appreciate your understanding.*" In a workplace setting, address a colleague's unproductive behavior by expressing your needs: "*I need to stay focused on this project, so I'd appreciate keeping our discussions work-related.*"

Reinforce these boundaries by consistently upholding them, even when it feels uncomfortable. By doing so, you protect your time, energy, and mental well-being, ensuring that external negativity does not derail your success.

5. Practice Gratitude and Contentment:

Regularly reflecting on your achievements and expressing gratitude, even during challenging times, can foster a positive mindset and keep you motivated. Start by writing down 5-10 things you're grateful for and reading this list daily, adding to it as time progresses. Gratitude helps you focus on what's going well, reduces stress, and reinforces positivity. Remind yourself with thoughts like, "*I am grateful for the progress I've made and the lessons I've learned,*" to stay encouraged and grounded in your journey.

Gratitude is a **powerful tool** for transforming your **mindset** and sustaining **motivation**. When you actively acknowledge the good in your life, you shift your focus away from what's lacking and toward the blessings, progress, and opportunities you've experienced. This practice rewires your brain to notice positivity and reduces the tendency to dwell on setbacks or stressors. By making gratitude a daily habit—such as journaling about moments of joy, personal growth, or even the challenges that taught you valuable lessons—you cultivate resilience and emotional well-being. Over time, your gratitude practice becomes a source of encouragement, reminding you of your strength and the many reasons to remain hopeful. It not only enhances your current outlook but also equips you to approach future challenges with confidence and optimism.

6. Embrace Failure as a Learning Opportunity:

View setbacks and failures as opportunities for valuable feedback rather than final outcomes. Take time to analyze mistakes, uncover lessons, and adjust your approach accordingly. Embracing failure as a natural part of growth allows you to keep moving forward, building resilience with each challenge. Remind yourself, "*This didn't work as planned, but I can learn from it and try again,*" to maintain focus and grow stronger after every obstacle.

Embracing failure as a **learning opportunity** is essential for personal and professional **growth**. Each setback provides insights into what works and what doesn't, helping you refine your strategies and build better solutions. Rather than seeing failure as a reflection of your abilities, view it as a steppingstone toward success. Cultivating this perspective fosters resilience, teaching you to persevere and adapt in the face of adversity. Additionally, normalizing failure as part of the journey removes the fear of making mistakes, encouraging you to take calculated risks and explore new opportunities. Remember, some of the greatest innovations and achievements were born from repeated failures that paved the way to breakthroughs. When you shift your mindset to value the lessons failure brings, you unlock your potential to grow, improve, and ultimately succeed.

7. Practice Financial and Resource Management:

Developing **financial discipline** begins with creating a budget, saving for the future, and investing in opportunities that align with your goals. By prioritizing **financial literacy**, you can make informed decisions that build stability and freedom, reducing unnecessary financial stress. This stability allows you to focus on personal and professional growth with greater confidence. Reflecting on questions like, "*How can I use my resources wisely today to secure my future?*" helps you stay intentional and proactive in managing your finances.

Building a solid financial foundation is about more than just managing money—it's about creating a life of stability, opportunity, and purpose. Budgeting ensures you have a clear understanding of where your money is going, allowing you to prioritize essential expenses, eliminate unnecessary spending, and allocate resources toward your goals. Saving provides a safety net for unexpected challenges and opens doors to future opportunities, while investing helps your money grow and work for you over time. Developing financial literacy empowers you to make strategic decisions, such as diversifying income streams or identifying worthwhile investments, that align with your long-term vision. Beyond reducing financial stress, responsible money management fosters a sense of control and peace of mind, enabling you to focus on personal growth and meaningful pursuits. With discipline and a future-focused mindset, financial freedom becomes a tool for unlocking opportunities and achieving your dreams.

8. Prioritize Personal Growth and Lifelong Learning:

Commit to continuous learning by engaging with books, courses, mentorship, and personal reflection. Cultivating a mindset of curiosity and openness to new knowledge helps you stay adaptable and better equipped to navigate challenges. This dedication to growth ensures that you're always improving, expanding your skills, and gaining fresh perspectives. Regularly asking yourself, "*What can I learn today that will help me grow?*" keeps you focused on development and fuels your journey toward success.

Continuous learning is a lifelong investment in yourself that enhances not only your skills but also your mindset and resilience. By seeking knowledge from diverse sources, such as books, podcasts, or interactions with mentors, you gain a broader perspective and stay ahead in an ever-changing world. Learning also fuels innovation, as new ideas and insights spark creativity and problem-solving abilities. Beyond formal education, personal reflection is a key component of growth, allowing you to assess experiences, identify lessons, and refine your approach. In a fast-paced environment, adaptability becomes a vital skill, and a commitment to learning ensures you remain flexible and prepared for unforeseen challenges. Embracing this mindset creates a ripple effect, enhancing confidence, expanding opportunities, and positioning you as a lifelong learner capable of thriving in any circumstance.

9. Practice Mindfulness and Balance:

Staying present and mindful in your daily activities is key to maintaining a healthy work-life balance. By focusing on the present moment, you can reduce stress, enhance focus, and approach tasks with clarity and purpose. Balancing work with rest and personal time prevents burnout, ensuring you remain energized and motivated as you pursue your goals. Regularly reflecting on questions like, "*Am I taking care of my mind, body, and spirit while working toward my goals?*" helps you stay aligned with both your personal well-being and professional aspirations.

Expanding on this, **mindfulness** allows you to fully engage with each task, strengthening your ability to prioritize and manage responsibilities effectively. Balance, on the other hand, creates space for self-care and relationships, which are vital for long-term success and fulfillment.

Incorporating activities like meditation, exercise, or time with loved ones can recharge your energy and foster creativity. A mindful and balanced approach not only enhances productivity but also cultivates a sense of joy and purpose, making your journey toward success sustainable and enriching.

10. Identify a Coach, Mentor or Accountability Partner:

Having a **personal coach**, **mentor**, or **accountability partner** can significantly enhance your journey toward success by providing **guidance**, **motivation**, and **support**. A coach or mentor brings valuable experience and insights, helping you identify blind spots, set realistic goals, and develop effective strategies for achieving them. They offer constructive feedback and encouragement, keeping you on track and challenging you to grow beyond your comfort zone. An accountability partner ensures you stay committed to your plans by regularly checking in on your progress and holding you responsible for the promises you make to yourself. Their presence fosters consistency, builds discipline, and keeps you motivated during difficult times. Moreover, having someone invested in your success can provide a sense of partnership and reassurance, making your goals feel more attainable and your journey more fulfilling.

Beyond guidance and accountability, a coach, mentor, or accountability partner also provides an invaluable external perspective that can help you navigate challenges and opportunities more effectively. They can identify patterns you may overlook, offer creative solutions to problems, and share lessons from their own experiences. This relationship also fosters personal and professional growth by encouraging continuous learning, whether through exposure to new ideas, resources, or networks. Additionally, a mentor or coach can serve as a source of inspiration, modeling behaviors and attitudes that align with your aspirations. The encouragement and validation they offer during setbacks can boost your confidence and resilience, helping you maintain focus even when progress feels slow. With their consistent support, you're not only more likely to achieve your goals but also to develop the habits and mindset necessary for sustained success.

Incorporating prayer into the process of working with a coach, mentor, or accountability partner adds a profound spiritual dimension to your growth journey. Prayer helps you seek God's wisdom and guidance as you set goals, make decisions, and navigate challenges, ensuring that your efforts align with His purpose for your life. It fosters a sense of humility and reliance on God's strength, reminding you that success is not achieved solely through your own efforts but through His provision and grace. Regular prayer also brings clarity and peace, helping you stay grounded in your values and maintain perspective during times of uncertainty or difficulty. By inviting God into this process, you create a foundation of faith that not only supports your ambitions but also deepens your relationship with Him, making your journey more meaningful and spiritually enriching.

10. Take Calculated Risks:

Stepping outside your **comfort zone** is essential for growth and innovation. By embracing new opportunities and carefully evaluating risks, you open yourself to experiences that challenge your limits and expand your potential. Taking bold steps, even when uncertain, builds confidence and resilience, helping you overcome fear and hesitation. Reflecting on questions like, "*What's one bold step I can take today toward my dreams?*" encourages action and keeps you focused on progress, even in the face of challenges.

Stepping out of your comfort zone also fosters creativity and adaptability, as it pushes you to think differently and approach problems with fresh perspectives. When you take calculated risks, you're not only increasing your chances of success but also building the mental and emotional fortitude to handle setbacks. Each step outside your comfort zone teaches you something valuable, whether it's a new skill, insight, or understanding of yourself. Over time, these small acts of courage compound, transforming fear into confidence and dreams into reality.

11. Celebrate Successes—Big and Small:

Acknowledging your **achievements**, no matter how small, is a powerful way to **build momentum** and **confidence**. By celebrating progress, you reinforce positive habits and maintain motivation for the journey ahead. Each success, whether a completed task or a step closer to your goal, serves as a reminder of your capabilities and fuels your desire to keep moving forward. Reflecting on thoughts like, "*What win can I celebrate* *today, and how can I build on it?*" keeps your focus on growth and progress rather than perfection.

Expanding further, celebrating achievements cultivates a mindset of gratitude and positivity, which boosts resilience and helps you stay inspired during challenges. Recognizing even minor wins shifts your perspective from what is still left to accomplish to how far you've already come. This habit fosters a **cycle of confidence** and **action**, as each celebration encourages you to tackle the next goal with enthusiasm. Over time, acknowledging progress transforms your journey into a series of meaningful milestones, keeping you energized and aligned with your long-term vision.

In conclusion, success is a result of intentional habits, a strong mindset, and consistent effort. By cultivating confidence, focusing on long-term vision, surrounding yourself with positivity, and embracing challenges as opportunities for growth, you can create a foundation for sustained success. Every step, no matter how small, brings you closer to your goals when aligned with purpose, discipline, and belief in your potential. The journey to success is as much about **personal transformation** as it is about achieving **external milestones**. Start today, and let every action build toward the future you envision.

CHAPTER 8

STRENGTHENING YOUR MIND AND BOUNDARIES THROUGH BIBLICAL PRINCIPLES

Training your mind to be stronger than your feelings and establishing firm boundaries requires a deliberate effort to align your thoughts, emotions, and actions with God's truth. While emotions like empathy, anger, and passion are natural, allowing them to dictate your decisions can lead to sin, imbalance, or relational harm. Scripture provides guidance on how to master these aspects of our lives with wisdom, discipline, and faith.

1. Train Your Mind to Be Stronger Than Your Feelings

Emotions are a **divine** gift, meant to **enrich** our **experiences** and deepen our **connections** with others and with God. They allow us to feel joy, love, compassion, and conviction, but when left unchecked, they can also lead us into fear, anger, doubt, and impulsiveness. Feelings, while powerful, are not always reliable guides for decision-making, as they can be influenced by circumstances, past experiences, and fleeting desires. To walk in alignment with God's will, we must train our minds to be stronger than our emotions, ensuring that our choices are rooted in wisdom, faith, and self-control rather than momentary impulses.

Scripture reminds us that the **heart** can be **deceitful**, leading us astray if we rely solely on **feelings** rather than on **God's truth**:

"The heart is deceitful above all things and beyond cure. Who can'

understand it?" — Jeremiah 17:9, (NKJV)

Instead of conforming to worldly influences or emotional whims, believers are called to renew their minds through Scripture, prayer, and spiritual discipline. By doing so, we gain clarity and discernment, allowing us to make decisions that align with God's good, pleasing, and perfect will:

"Do not conform to the pattern of this world, but be transformed by the renewing of your mind. Then you will be able to test and approve what God's will is—his good, pleasing and perfect will."
— Romans 12:2, (NIV)

Applying This Principle in Daily Life:

- **Pause and Seek Wisdom:** Before making decisions based on emotions, **take time** to **pray**, **reflect**, and **seek biblical wisdom** to ensure alignment with God's will.
- **Develop Spiritual Discipline:** Consistently reading Scripture, engaging in prayer, and surrounding yourself with Godly counsel strengthens your ability to remain steadfast in faith rather than being swayed by emotions.
- **Practice Self-Control:** Learning to control reactions, remain patient in challenges, and trust in God's timing helps build emotional resilience and spiritual maturity.

By training our minds to be stronger than our feelings, we cultivate a spirit of discernment, stability, and faith, allowing us to walk confidently in God's purpose rather than being led by temporary emotions.

2. Set Boundaries Stronger Than Your Empathy

Empathy is a Christlike virtue, allowing us to share in others' burdens, extend compassion, and reflect God's love. It enables us to offer support, encouragement, and understanding to those who are struggling. However, without healthy boundaries, empathy can become misguided, leading to emotional exhaustion, enabling harmful behaviors, or even compromising personal values. While we are called to love and serve others, we must also ensure that our help is rooted in wisdom rather than obligation or guilt.

Scripture provides guidance on balancing compassion with discernment:

- "*Above all else, **guard** your heart, for everything you do flows from it.*" (Proverbs 4:23, NIV) – **Setting boundaries** is **not selfish**; it is an act of stewardship over your heart, mind, and **well-being**. Without proper boundaries, constant emotional giving can lead to spiritual depletion, making it difficult to serve effectively.

- "*Carry each other's burdens, and in this way you will fulfill the law of Christ. If anyone thinks they are something when they are not, they deceive themselves.*" (Galatians 6:2-3, NIV) – We are called to help bear one another's burdens, but this does not mean taking on responsibilities that others must learn to handle themselves. There is a distinction between supporting someone and taking on their full weight.

Application: Practicing Healthy Boundaries in Compassion

- **Establish Clear Boundaries:** Loving others does not mean neglecting personal responsibilities, emotional well-being, or spiritual health. Even Jesus, after ministering to large crowds, took time to withdraw, rest, and pray:
  – "*But Jesus often withdrew to **lonely** places and prayed.*" (Luke 5:16, NIV)
  – Prioritizing time for renewal allows for continued service without burnout.

- **Discern Between Helping and Enabling: True empathy** should **empower** others, not foster **dependence** or reinforce **destructive behaviors**. There is a difference between offering a hand to lift

- someone up and carrying them indefinitely. Pray for wisdom and discernment to know when to step in, when to set limits, and when to say no. Boundaries are an act of love, as they encourage personal responsibility and growth.

By setting boundaries stronger than your empathy, you honor God's call to serve while preserving your own well-being and values. Healthy boundaries enable sustainable compassion, ensuring that you can continue to reflect God's love without compromising your own spiritual and emotional health.

3. Do Not Let Passion or Revenge Lead You to Sin

Passion is a **powerful** and **God-given force**, capable of driving individuals to achieve great things, defend justice, and stand boldly for truth. When guided by the Holy Spirit, passion fuels righteousness, perseverance, and godly action. However, **unchecked passion**—whether in the form of anger, ambition, or desire for justice—can lead to sinful behaviors such as **vengeance**, **pride**, **impulsivity**, and **bitterness**. Without self-control and spiritual discernment, passion can shift from righteous motivation to **destructive force**, pulling individuals away from God's will.

Scripture warns against allowing anger or personal vengeance to dictate our actions:

- "*In your* ***anger*** *do not sin: Do not let the sun go down while you are still angry, and do not give the devil a foothold.*" (Ephesians 4:26-27, NIV) – Anger itself is not sinful, but when left unchecked, it becomes a gateway to sin, leading to resentment, unforgiveness, and even reckless actions. The enemy exploits unchecked anger to create division, hatred, and destruction in relationships.

- "*Do not take revenge, my dear friends, but leave room for God's wrath, for it is written: 'It is mine to avenge; I will repay,' says the Lord.*" (Romans 12:19, NIV) – Taking justice into our own hands removes trust in God's sovereignty. **Vengeance** belongs to **the Lord**, and attempting to repay evil with evil only leads to further pain and separation from His will.

Application: Keeping Passion Aligned with God's Will

- **Surrender Vengeance to God:** When wronged, it is natural to feel hurt, angry, or betrayed, but acting out of bitterness or retaliation does not lead to healing. Instead of seeking revenge, trust in God's justice. He sees every injustice and promises to handle all things in His perfect timing. Choosing forgiveness over resentment frees the heart from the burden of bitterness and allows God's peace to take root.

- **Channel Passion into God's Work:** Passion, when directed toward righteous pursuits, is an incredible force for spiritual growth, kingdom impact, and personal transformation. Rather than allowing anger or revenge to consume your energy, redirect that intensity into prayer, ministry, serving others, or growing in faith. Passion can be used for mentoring, advocacy, creative expression, or leadership within the church—all of which honor God and fulfill His purpose.

By allowing the Holy Spirit to govern emotions and desires, passion can be used as a tool for God's glory rather than a weapon for destruction. The key to avoiding sin is to remain rooted in faith, trust in God's justice, and direct passion toward fulfilling His will. When passion is aligned with God's purpose, it becomes a force of transformation, healing, and divine impact rather than a source of sin.

4. Do Not Let Anger Control You

Anger is a natural and God-given emotion, designed to alert us to injustice, wrongdoing, or personal boundaries being crossed. However, while anger itself is not inherently sinful, allowing it to **control** us can lead to destructive behaviors, broken relationships, and spiritual disconnection. When anger lingers unchecked, it can evolve into **bitterness**, **resentment**, or even **revenge**, which are barriers to peace, healing, and righteousness. God calls us to **manage anger** with **wisdom**, **patience**, and **self-control**, ensuring that our emotions serve His purpose rather than leading us into sin.

Scripture offers guidance on how to handle anger in a way that honors God:

"My dear brothers and sisters, take note of this: Everyone should be quick to ***listen****, slow to* ***speak*** *and slow to become* ***angry****, because human anger*

- *does not produce the righteousness that God desires.*" (James 1:19-20, NIV) – This passage reminds us that anger, when acted upon impulsively, often leads to unrighteous behavior. Instead of reacting in the heat of the moment, God calls us to pause, listen, and respond with wisdom.

- "*A fool gives full* ***vent*** *to his spirit, but a wise man* ***quietly*** *holds it back.*" (Proverbs 29:11, ESV) – Unrestrained anger is a sign of foolishness, not strength. A wise person exercises self-control and discretion, ensuring that emotions do not lead to harmful words or actions.

Application: Managing Anger in a Godly Way

- **Practice Self-Control:** Before reacting in anger, pause, pray, and seek God's guidance. Taking time to calm down and reflect can prevent harsh words, rash decisions, or irreversible damage to relationships. Anger should be processed through wisdom, not unleashed in frustration.

- **Choose Reconciliation Over Resentment:** Jesus calls His followers to seek peace, even when wronged:
  – "*Blessed are the peacemakers, for they will be called* ***children*** *of God.*" (Matthew 5:9, NIV)

Instead of allowing anger to fester into bitterness, believers are called to pursue reconciliation, extend grace, and let go of **resentment**. **Forgiveness** does not mean excusing wrongdoing, but it does mean entrusting justice to God and refusing to be enslaved by anger.

When anger is surrendered to God and managed with wisdom, it can be transformed into a force for positive change rather than destruction. Controlled, righteous anger can be used to stand for justice, defend the oppressed, and inspire action for God's kingdom, but uncontrolled anger leads only to division and sin. By practicing patience, self-control, and reconciliation, believers can ensure that their emotions serve God's purpose rather than lead them away from His will.

Practical Steps for Mastering Emotions and Boundaries

1. Stay Rooted in Scripture:

- Read daily passages that address emotions and self-control. Meditate on verses like Galatians 5:22-23, which lists self-control as a fruit of the Spirit.
- Memorize verses that counteract specific struggles, such as Philippians 4:6-7 for anxiety or Proverbs 15:1 for anger.

2. Pray for Strength and Discernment:

- Ask God to guide your emotions and help you recognize when feelings are clouding your judgment.
- Pray for wisdom in setting and maintaining healthy boundaries.

3. Surround Yourself with Accountability:

- Seek trusted friends, mentors, or spiritual leaders who can help you stay aligned with God's will.
- Share your struggles and victories with those who will encourage you to grow.

4. Model Christlike Behavior:

- Follow Jesus example of balancing compassion with conviction. He showed empathy while maintaining firm boundaries, as seen when He cleansed the temple (John 2:13-17) and addressed the Pharisees with truth (Matthew 23).

5. Regularly Examine Your Heart:

- Reflect on your motivations and feelings to ensure they align with God's purposes.
- Confess and repent when emotions or actions have led you astray and seek God's grace to do better.

Emotions are not inherently bad, but they are unreliable guides. By training your mind with God's Word and strengthening your boundaries with wisdom, you can master your feelings rather than being mastered by them. As Paul writes in 2 Timothy 1:7 (NIV): "*For the Spirit God gave us does not make us timid, but gives us power, love, and self-discipline.*" Embrace this truth and let God's Spirit lead you into a life of strength, peace, and purpose.

CHAPTER 9

FINANCIAL EVOLUTION AND THE GREAT WEALTH TRANSFER

Throughout the modern era in Western culture, numerous technological revolutions have transformed industries and societies. While this book does not delve into the specifics of each historical revolution, it is crucial to understand a common thread among them: each was driven by **three primary engines** for growth—**new cheap inputs**, **innovative products**, and advanced processes. In every era, individuals who recognized these opportunities, invested in emerging technologies, and adapted to the changes reaped significant benefits, often building substantial wealth.

Today, two concurrent industrial revolutions are reshaping the global landscape, offering similar opportunities for those who are prepared. To take advantage of this transformative period, a person must focus on three critical actions: paying close attention to developments, identifying and understanding trends, and taking decisive action. This book will provide insights, perspectives, and strategies to help navigate these steps and position oneself for success in the evolving economy.

Since 1975, the **Third Industrial Revolution** has significantly transformed information and telecommunications, ushering in a digital era that continues to shape economic, social, and technological landscapes. In 2000, the Fourth Industrial Revolution began, advancing financial and scientific technologies by integrating hardware, software, and biology into cyber-physical systems. This era emphasizes breakthroughs in connectivity and communication through the internet, with experts predicting transformative innovations in robotics, artificial intelligence, nanotechnology, quantum computing, biotechnology, the Internet of Things (IoT), the Industrial Internet of Things (IIoT), decentralized consensus, fifth-generation wireless technologies (5G), 3D printing, renewable energy, and fully autonomous vehicles.

A pivotal moment within this revolution occurred in 2008 with the introduction of **Bitcoin**, which fundamentally altered the banking and financial system. Bitcoin, the first cryptocurrency and digital asset financial system, was introduced by an unknown entity or group under the pseudonym Satoshi Nakamoto. On October 31, 2008, Nakamoto's white paper was published on Bitcoin.org, laying out a decentralized digital currency concept. Bitcoin was officially launched in January 2009. To this day, the true identity of Satoshi Nakamoto remains unknown, sparking speculation about whether it could be an individual, a government entity, or an organization. Regardless of its origins, Bitcoin has given rise to a groundbreaking financial ecosystem.

Since Bitcoin's inception, thousands of additional cryptocurrencies and tokens have emerged, each with its own networks, utilities, and technological purposes. By 2023, it was estimated that 5% to 7% of the world's money was involved in cryptocurrency, amounting to approximately $1 to $2.48 trillion. While these figures reflect a growing sector, they represent a small percentage of the global financial landscape, indicating significant room for expansion. Cryptocurrencies, no longer in their infancy, are entering a phase of rapid development, marked by substantial growth and growing pains. Regulatory clarity, widespread adoption, and further technological advancements will likely define the next stage of evolution for this emerging market.

Unlike most technologies, which typically launch at high prices and become more affordable over time, cryptocurrencies tend to begin at **low** prices, **increasing** in **value** as their market capitalization grows. For example, in 1971, the first personal computer cost around $750 (equivalent to approximately $4,500 today), while today, personal computers can be purchased for as little as $200. Conversely, cryptocurrencies often start at minimal values and appreciate as more global financial resources are directed into the market. This dynamic offers a unique investment opportunity, as early adopters can benefit from significant price appreciation over time.

FINANCIAL EVOLUTION AND THE GREAT WEALTH TRANSFER

Throughout history, financial systems have evolved alongside advancements in technology, shaping the way societies operate and how value is exchanged. From bartering goods to the use of gold and silver coins, to paper money and modern banking, each step forward has transformed economies and lives. Today, the world stands on the precipice of another **revolutionary shift**: the transition from **fiat-based financial** systems to **blockchain-based** decentralized assets.

The Evolution from Fiat to Blockchain

Cryptocurrency and **Blockchain** technology remains a topic of significant contention, with many skeptics questioning its permanence, legitimacy as money, susceptibility to manipulation, and potential for misuse in tracking and controlling consumer behavior. Admittedly, when Bitcoin first emerged, I shared many of these concerns, which initially deterred me from exploring or investing in cryptocurrency. At the time, I even believed that this technology might become part of the so-called **"*Beast*" system**—a centralized global financial system tied to end-times prophecy. As a result, I wanted nothing to do with it.

However, after extensive research and reflection, I have developed a more nuanced understanding of cryptocurrency and its potential role in shaping the future. While some of my initial concerns and assumptions may hold partial truth and could be used to fulfill prophecy, I now recognize how this technology could be used in meaningful and transformative ways, even within the framework of God's broader plan. One key realization was that the evolution of how civilizations exchange currency is a constant process. Change is inevitable, and individuals must either adapt and participate in the transition or risk being left behind, ultimately forced into the new system during its mass adoption phase.

The evolution of currency and payment systems has been an ongoing process throughout history, driven by the needs of societies and the technological advancements of the times. Each era has introduced new methods of exchange, reflecting changes in economies, cultures, and innovations. Below is an expanded overview of the progression of currency and payment methods over the last several hundred years:

1. **Commodities as Currency:** Historically, civilizations relied on **tangible commodities** such as **gold**, **silver**, **precious metals**, jewels, grain, and

agricultural products for bartering and trade. These items held intrinsic value and were exchanged for goods and services. While such commodities are still viewed as a store of value today and remain integral to investment portfolios, they are no longer practical for everyday transactions due to their bulk, variability in quality, and difficulty in transporting.

2. **The Introduction of Coins:** Around 600 BCE, the invention of standardized coins made from pure gold and silver revolutionized trade. These coins established a uniform system for determining value based on size and weight, making transactions more efficient. Coins remained the dominant form of currency for centuries, fostering economic stability and enabling the growth of trade networks across regions.

3. **The Invention of Paper Money:** In the 7th century A.D., the Tang dynasty in China introduced paper money to simplify larger monetary transactions. Unlike coins, paper money was lightweight and easier to carry in bulk. This concept spread to Europe in the 1600s, with paper currency being adopted as a means to fund military expeditions and other large-scale expenditures. By 1690, the U.S. began issuing **paper money**, setting the stage for the **modern banking system**.

4. **The Birth of Checks:** In 1762, British banker Lawrence Childs created the **first checks**, offering a new way to transfer funds without the need to physically exchange cash. Checks gained popularity as a secure and convenient method of payment, especially for businesses purposes. Many banks now facilitate digital check payments, allowing customers to schedule bill payments electronically while the bank handles the printing and mailing of checks.

5. **The U.S. Federal Reserve and Paper Currency:** In 1914, the establishment of the U.S. Federal Reserve brought about the issuance of the first federal notes. Initially valued at $10, these notes quickly became a widely accepted form of currency, eventually expanding to include various denominations ranging from $1 to $100. This marked a significant step toward a unified monetary system in the United States.

6. **The Emergence of Credit Cards:** The first credit card, known as the Diners Club Card, was introduced in 1950. Initially accepted by 28 restaurants and two hotels, it required users to pay off balances in full

each month. Over time, credit cards evolved into a widely accepted payment method, offering revolving credit with interest, rewards programs, and enhanced security through chip technology. Today, credit cards are a cornerstone of global commerce.

7. **The Rise of Debit Cards:** By the 1970s, banks began piloting debit cards linked to personal bank accounts. With the proliferation of ATMs in the 1980s and 1990s, debit cards became a popular alternative to cash and checks. Today, they are one of the most frequently used payment methods, offering convenience and security for everyday transactions.

8. **The Shift to Fiat Currency:** In 1971, President Nixon **removed** the U.S. dollar from the **gold standard**, transitioning the country to a **fiat currency system**. Under this system, the value of money is not backed by a physical commodity like gold but by the trust and authority of the issuing government. While the decision to shift to a fiat currency provided flexibility for economic policies, it also enabled the unchecked printing of money, ultimately leading to inflation and currency devaluation. The lack of transparency has ultimately eroded public trust and strained economies worldwide. Fiat currency, backed by governments rather than physical commodities, has been the cornerstone of the global financial system for over a century. However, it is not without significant flaws and appears to be approaching the limits of its sustainability. Much like a house built on shifting sand, such a system cannot stand indefinitely.

9. **Digital and Mobile Payments:** Since the late 1990s, digital and mobile payment technologies have transformed how financial transactions are conducted. Applications such as Apple Pay, Venmo, Google Pay, PayPal, and Zelle offer speed, convenience, and widespread acceptance, making them popular across all age groups. For younger generations, like Gen Z, digital wallets have become the norm. Many view physical cards and cash as outdated, signaling the shift toward a cashless society. It is also worth noting that during the 2008 financial crisis, in particular, it revealed vulnerabilities in the centralized banking system, leaving many searching for alternatives to the current fiat currency system.

10. **The Birth of Bitcoin and Digital Currencies:** Enter **blockchain technology**. Introduced through Bitcoin in 2009 by the enigmatic Satoshi Nakamoto, blockchain offered a **decentralized**, **transparent**, and **secure**

way to record and verify transactions. This technology laid the groundwork for a New Financial System—one that removes the need for intermediaries, empowers individuals, and opens the door to innovation on an unprecedented scale. Since Bitcoin's inception, thousands of digital assets have been created, each with unique utilities and purposes. Cryptocurrencies, decentralized finance (DeFi), and tokenized assets have expanded the possibilities for how wealth can be stored, transferred, and grown. Blockchain is not merely a tool for financial transactions; it represents a new era of financial inclusion and opportunity.

The progression of currency and payment methods reflects humanity's ingenuity in addressing the evolving needs of trade, security, and convenience. From bartering goods to digital wallets, each stage of this journey has brought about transformative changes. The advent of blockchain and cryptocurrencies represents the next significant leap, offering unprecedented opportunities for transparency, decentralization, and innovation in the global financial system. This ongoing evolution challenges individuals and institutions alike to adapt and prepare for the future.

Defining The Great Wealth Transfer

The "***Great Wealth Transfer***" refers to the massive shift of financial assets and economic power from traditional systems to **digital, blockchain-based systems**. Unlike generational wealth transfers of the past, where assets moved within **families** or between **demographics**, this transfer is **global in scale** and technological in nature.

This transformation is creating a once-in-a-lifetime opportunity for individuals, businesses, and nations. As trillions of dollars shift from fiat to digital assets, those who understand and prepare for this transition stand to benefit immensely. It is not just about financial gains—it is about reimagining how value is created, exchanged, and preserved in the 21st century.

The **Great Wealth Transfer** is also leveling the playing field. In the past, access to wealth creation **opportunities** was often **limited to the elite** or well-connected. Blockchain democratizes access, allowing anyone with an internet connection to participate in the global financial ecosystem. From investing in cryptocurrencies to engaging with decentralized applications (dApps), the opportunities are vast and accessible.

Why Understanding This Transition is Critical

This financial evolution is not a distant possibility; it is happening now. The shift to digital assets is already disrupting industries, redefining economies, and challenging traditional systems of power. For individuals, businesses, and governments, understanding this transition is not optional—it is essential.

1. **For Individuals:** This transition offers unprecedented opportunities to build wealth, achieve financial independence, and break free from the limitations of traditional banking. **Blockchain technology** enables **individuals** to become their **own bank** by providing tools for securely managing and transacting value without the need for traditional financial intermediaries. Through decentralized systems, individuals can create and control their own digital wallets, which serve as private vaults for cryptocurrencies and other digital assets. These wallets are protected by cryptographic keys, giving the owner full authority over their funds and transactions.

Unlike traditional banks, blockchain-based financial systems operate 24/7 and allow for peer-to-peer transactions that are fast, **transparent**, and often more cost-effective. Additionally, **decentralized finance (DeFi)** platforms enable individuals to **lend**, **borrow**, and earn interest on their assets directly, replicating banking functions without the **middleman**. This self-sovereign approach to finance empowers individuals with greater control, security, and financial freedom, eliminating the reliance on traditional banking systems. However, it also presents risks, including volatility, scams, and the need for financial literacy. Education and preparation are key to navigating this landscape.

2. **For Businesses:** Blockchain technology is fundamentally transforming the way businesses operate across industries by introducing greater **transparency**, efficiency, and trust into operations. In supply chain management, for instance, blockchain provides an immutable ledger that allows companies to track the origin, movement, and authenticity of goods in real-time. This capability enhances **accountability**, **reduces fraud**, and **fosters trust** among stakeholders, including consumers who demand more visibility into how products are sourced and manufactured.

In the realm of finance and payments, blockchain is revolutionizing **cross-border transactions** by enabling faster, cheaper, and more secure payments. Traditional international payment systems often involve multiple intermediaries, resulting in delays and high fees. Blockchain eliminates these inefficiencies, allowing businesses to transact directly with their partners globally, often settling payments within minutes instead of days. This is particularly advantageous for small and medium-sized enterprises (SMEs) that rely on cost-effective and timely payments to remain competitive.

Moreover, **smart contracts**—self-executing contracts with terms directly written into code—are **automating business** processes like invoicing, royalty distribution, and legal agreements. This automation reduces administrative overhead and minimizes the risk of human error or fraud, allowing businesses to operate more efficiently.

Businesses that proactively adopt and integrate blockchain technology not only improve operational efficiency but also position themselves as leaders in innovation. They gain a competitive edge by offering more transparent, secure, and cost-effective solutions to customers. Conversely, businesses that resist or delay embracing these advancements risk becoming obsolete in a rapidly evolving digital landscape. As blockchain adoption grows, companies across sectors will find that staying relevant and competitive requires understanding and leveraging this transformative technology.

3. For Governments: The rise of **decentralized finance (DeFi)** presents a significant shift in the global financial landscape, challenging the traditional control that central banks and governments have wielded over monetary systems. DeFi, with its decentralized networks and permissionless protocols, enables individuals to conduct financial transactions—such as lending, borrowing, and trading—without relying on traditional banking institutions. This newfound autonomy undermines the centralized power structures that have historically regulated the flow of money, posing both opportunities and challenges for governments.

For policymakers, this shift necessitates a delicate balancing act. On one hand, the innovative potential of DeFi and blockchain technology can drive economic growth, enhance financial inclusion, and reduce inefficiencies in traditional systems. By fostering a supportive regulatory environment, governments can encourage innovation, attract investment, and position themselves as leaders in the global digital economy. Forward-thinking policies can also enable the development of central bank digital currencies (CBDCs), allowing governments to retain some level of monetary control while embracing the benefits of blockchain technology.

On the other hand, the decentralized nature of DeFi creates regulatory challenges. The absence of centralized intermediaries makes it harder to enforce anti-money laundering (AML) and combat the financing of terrorism (CFT) regulations. Tax compliance becomes more complex, as governments struggle to track and monitor transactions occurring on decentralized networks. Additionally, the volatility and speculative nature of many digital assets raise concerns about financial stability and consumer protection.

To address these challenges, governments must craft frameworks that strike a balance between promoting innovation and ensuring stability. This includes implementing clear regulatory guidelines for cryptocurrency exchanges, DeFi platforms, and blockchain developers. Collaboration with international organizations and other governments will also be critical, as the decentralized and borderless nature of blockchain technology requires a coordinated global approach to regulation.

Moreover, public education and transparency about the benefits and risks of DeFi are essential. By engaging with stakeholders, including the private sector and blockchain communities, policymakers can create a more inclusive regulatory environment that fosters trust and collaboration. Governments that successfully navigate this transition will not only mitigate potential risks but also unlock the immense economic potential of decentralized finance, ensuring their relevance in an increasingly digitized world.

The Great Wealth Transfer is not just about money—it is about the future of how societies function and preparing for the Great Harvest. Those who take the time to understand this shift, invest in the right opportunities, and adapt to new technologies will not only thrive but also contribute to shaping the next era of financial and societal evolution.

Global Financial System Reforms and Initiatives

The transition to a new financial system aligned with the **United Nations' Agenda 2030** and other global initiatives involves a series of strategic milestones aimed at fostering sustainable development, financial inclusion, and environmental responsibility. While this book will not delve directly into these specific topics, it is important to acknowledge the ongoing initiatives and provide an estimated timeline of the remaining key phases and actions anticipated in the coming years. These developments are closely tied to and will directly drive the adoption of the new financial system and blockchain technology.

2015-2019: Foundations Laid for Sustainable Finance

- **2015**: Adoption of the 2030 Agenda for Sustainable Development and the Paris Agreement, establishing global commitments to sustainable development and climate action.
- **2017**: Formation of the G20 Sustainable Finance Study Group, later renamed the Sustainable Finance Working Group (SFWG), to enhance the mobilization of sustainable finance.
- **2018**: Launch of the UN Secretary-General's Strategy for Financing the 2030 Agenda, focusing on aligning global financial systems with sustainable development goals.

2020-2023: Strategic Planning and Initial Implementation

- **2020**: Development of the G20 Sustainable Finance Roadmap to guide international efforts in scaling up sustainable finance.
- **2021**: Introduction of the Financial Stability Board's (FSB) framework for the regulation and supervision of crypto-asset activities, addressing the rise of digital assets.
- **2022**: UNEP Finance Initiative marks 30 years, highlighting the evolution and integration of sustainable finance practices within the industry.
- **2023**: Global leaders advocate for reforms in the international financial architecture to better support sustainable development and climate resilience.

2024-2026: Accelerated Implementation and Policy Integration

- **2024**: The FSB advances the implementation of its regulatory framework for crypto-assets and monitors the financial stability implications of digital innovations, including tokenization and artificial intelligence.
- **2025**: The UK and EU plan to transition to T+1 settlement cycles in financial markets, enhancing efficiency and reducing systemic risk.
- **2026**: Ongoing reforms in global financial institutions aim to increase support for sustainable investments, particularly in developing economies.

2027-2030: Full Integration and Global Adoption

- **2027**: The EU targets the implementation of shorter trade settlement times, aligning with global standards to improve market liquidity and stability.
- **2028**: International financial institutions are expected to have fully integrated climate considerations into their funding and operational frameworks, supporting a resilient net-zero transition.
- **2029**: Global financial systems anticipate widespread adoption of interoperable digital currencies and assets, enhancing cross-border transactions and financial inclusion.
- **2030**: Achievement of the **Sustainable Development Goals (SDGs)**, with financial systems fully aligned to support sustainable development, eradicate poverty, and address climate change.

his timeline represents an estimated roadmap based on current global initiatives and policy directions. Actual progress will depend on various factors, including political will, technological advancements, and collaborative efforts among nations and institutions.

As the world transitions from the old to the new, this book will serve as a guide to understanding the mechanics of the Great Wealth Transfer, the opportunities it presents, and the steps needed to participate. The journey ahead is transformative, and those who prepare will be well-positioned to navigate and benefit from the financial revolution that is reshaping the world.

CHAPTER 10

THE END OF AN ERA

Throughout history, humanity has relied on various financial systems to facilitate trade, store value, and manage economies. Each iteration has reflected the needs and limitations of its time. The current financial system, built on fiat currency and central banking, has dominated the global economy for over a century. While it brought innovation and growth, this system is showing signs of strain, revealing key limitations that make a transition inevitable.

Origins of Fiat Currency and Central Banking Systems

The concept of **fiat currency**—a type of money that has value because governments declare it legal tender—dates back centuries. Unlike money backed by tangible assets such as gold or silver, fiat currency derives its worth from trust in the issuing government and its ability to maintain economic stability.

The modern fiat system began to take shape in the 20th century, particularly after the **Bretton Woods Agreement** in 1944. This agreement established the **U.S. dollar** as the world's reserve currency, backed by **gold**. Other nations pegged their currencies to the dollar, creating a system of relative stability. Under this system, the dollar was pegged to gold at a fixed rate of $35 per ounce, while other countries agreed to maintain fixed exchange rates relative to the dollar.

The Bretton Woods Agreement also led to the creation of two major institutions: the International Monetary Fund (IMF) and the World Bank. However, in 1971, President Richard Nixon **ended** the U.S. dollar's direct **convertibility to gold**, eliminating the gold standard and making it a **purely fiat currency**, citing concerns that the nation's gold reserves were insufficient to back the growing number of dollars in circulation.

By 1973, the **Bretton Woods system** had fully **collapsed**, allowing countries to adopt flexible exchange rate systems where currencies were no longer tied to the price of gold. This shift allowed governments to print money without being constrained by gold reserves, fundamentally altering global economics.

During the 1970s, the US dollar's position as the global reserve currency was strengthened with the introduction of the petrodollar system. After the **1973 oil crisis**, the United States negotiated an agreement with Saudi Arabia and other major oil-producing nations to price oil **exclusively in US dollars**. This arrangement required countries to hold US dollars to buy oil, significantly boosting the currency's demand.

Consequently, the US dollar became the dominant currency for international trade, leading many countries to maintain dollar reserves. This arrangement enabled the United States to fund its trade deficit by printing more dollars, as these were needed worldwide for purchasing oil and other essential commodities. The US dollar's status as the world's reserve currency stems from a combination of factors, notably the **Bretton Woods Agreement** and the **petrodollar** system. The dollar's central role in global trade has had profound effects on the world economy and remains a subject of ongoing debate among economists and policymakers.

Additionally, central banking has become a cornerstone of this system. Institutions like the Federal Reserve in the United States were established to control monetary policy, stabilize economies, and manage inflation. Central banks wielded immense power, determining interest rates, printing money, and acting as lenders of last resort during financial crises. While fiat currency and central banking systems brought flexibility and growth, they also introduced vulnerabilities. Trust in the system is paramount, but as history has shown, that trust is not guaranteed.

Sam's Endless Party: A Tale of Debt, Dollars, and Denial

Imagine if someone named "*Sam*" decided that every time they faced a small inconvenience, they threw a huge party to cheer themselves up. Got a flat tire? Party! Forgot their anniversary? Bigger party! The problem is, Sam doesn't have enough money for these parties, so he decides to max out every credit card he has. When the cards are full, he starts borrowing from neighbors, distant cousins, and even the mailman.

Now, decades later, Sam has gotten older but unfortunately not wiser. Sam's parties have become legendary, but he is living in a mansion built entirely on IOUs. His fridge is full of expired leftovers, and the gardens surrounding the house have wilted because the electricity to run the sprinkler system is unpaid.

What does Sam plan to do about this you might ask? His answer, throw another party to brainstorm solutions.

This is kind of where the U.S. government is with its national debt. It keeps hosting grand spending initiatives and borrowing to cover costs, thinking that future "*Sam*" will figure out how to pay for it all.

The twist? The entire neighborhood—representing the American population—is being billed for Sam's reckless spending. They're stuck paying for the balloons, the DJ, and even the interest on the caterer's unpaid invoices. Every time someone questions this setup, Sam shrugs and says, "*We're all in this together!*"

Meanwhile, the neighbors are left wondering if Sam will ever figure out how to budget or if they're doomed to a lifetime of footing the party bill.

The moral of this story is that reckless and unsustainable spending, whether by an individual or a government, eventually catches up and creates consequences for everyone involved. Just as Sam's actions burden his neighbors with his debts, poor financial management by a government can lead to economic instability, increased taxes, inflation, and a loss of trust from its citizens. It highlights the importance of accountability, responsibility, and planning for the future rather than relying on short-term fixes and deferring problems indefinitely.

Key Limitations of the Current System

1. Inflation and Devaluation of Fiat Currencies:

One of the **most significant weaknesses** of **fiat currencies** is their susceptibility to **inflation**. When governments print money to address economic challenges, it increases the money supply, reducing the purchasing power of each unit of currency. This can lead to rising prices and economic instability.

Hyperinflation is an extreme example, where a currency **loses its value** at an alarming rate. Historical instances, such as in Weimar Germany in the 1920s or Zimbabwe in the 2000s, demonstrate the devastating effects of uncontrolled inflation. Even in stable economies, gradual inflation erodes savings and diminishes wealth over time, disproportionately affecting those with limited financial means.

2. Lack of Transparency in Traditional Banking:

Traditional banking systems often operate behind closed doors, leaving consumers with little understanding of how their money is managed. Central banks make critical decisions about monetary policy with minimal public input, and commercial banks engage in opaque practices, such as **fractional reserve banking**, where they **lend out more** money than they **hold in deposits**.

This lack of transparency can lead to **mismanagement** and **corruption**. For example, the **2008 financial crisis** exposed the fragility of the banking system and the consequences of **unchecked risk-taking**. Many people lost their homes, jobs, and savings due to decisions made by financial institutions that prioritized profit over stability.

3. Global Debt and Its Unsustainable Trajectory:

Global debt has reached staggering levels, surpassing **$300 trillion** in 2023. Governments, corporations, and individuals rely heavily on borrowing to sustain operations and lifestyles. While debt can stimulate growth, the current trajectory is unsustainable. Countries often resort to borrowing to fund social programs, infrastructure, and defense. However, servicing this debt requires increasing amounts of revenue, leading to higher taxes or cuts in essential services. Developing nations are particularly vulnerable, as they struggle to repay loans from international institutions, perpetuating cycles of poverty and dependence. The reliance on debt also creates systemic risks. If one major economy defaults, it can trigger a domino effect, destabilizing global markets and economies.

As of December 2024, the U.S. national debt has surged to approximately $36.09 trillion, a staggering increase from just $371 billion in 1970. This represents a more than 97-fold growth over five decades, fueled by policy choices, economic crises, and escalating federal spending on areas like healthcare, defense, foreign aid and social programs.

This relentless growth has significantly affected the debt-to-GDP ratio—a critical measure of a country's financial health. In 1970, the debt-to-GDP ratio was around 36%, meaning the debt was relatively modest compared to the overall economic output. However, by 2023, it had soared to over 122%, signaling that the national debt is growing at a much faster rate than the economy itself.

This alarming trend underscores another dimension of the unsustainability of continued borrowing and unchecked spending. As debt outpaces economic growth, it raises concerns about the nation's ability to manage its obligations in the long term, potentially burdening future generations with even greater economic challenges.

Historical Context: The Expiration of the Petrodollar Agreement

In June 2024, the longstanding **petrodollar agreement** between Saudi Arabia and the United States has **officially expired**, marking a pivotal shift in global economic dynamics. Saudi Arabia has since ceased exclusively selling oil in U.S. dollars and now accepts **multiple currencies**, including the **Chinese yuan**, **euros**, and **yen**. This decision reflects a broader move to diversify away from reliance on the dollar, significantly altering the landscape of international trade. Additionally, Saudi Arabia has embraced digital currencies as part of its economic diversification strategy, including exploring the use of Bitcoin and potentially **Central Bank Digital Currencies (CBDCs)**. Notably, Saudi Arabia is participating in projects like mBridge, a multi-CBDC platform, which further reduces its dependency on the dollar for transactions.

This transition has raised serious concerns about its potential impact on the U.S. economy. The reduced global demand for the dollar could result in increased inflation, higher interest rates, and disruptions in bond markets. While the exact consequences remain uncertain, this shift diminishes the dollar's role as the dominant global reserve currency. It also signals a broader trend among nations seeking alternatives to the dollar for trade and financial transactions. Such changes suggest the beginning of a geopolitical and economic realignment that may have profound implications for the global financial system.

Although detailed statistics on the proportion of Saudi oil currently sold in non-dollar currencies remain undisclosed, the significance of this move cannot be overstated. This development is a major step toward diversifying international trade away from dollar dominance, potentially setting the stage for a financial reset. Should this trend continue, it may contribute to the eventual decline of the U.S. dollar's world reserve status and the end of the fiat currency era.

The death of the old financial system appears inevitable, ushering in a new one that will reshape the global economic order. Unfortunately, this monumental shift has received little attention from mainstream media, leaving the American public largely unaware of the approaching storm until it may be too late.

As Dr. Pippa Malmgren, an economist and former advisor to President George W. Bush, stated at the World Government Summit in March 2022: ***"We are about to abandon the traditional system of money and accounting and introduce a new one."*** Dr. Malmgren, a respected authority in economics and international relations, has highlighted this transition as part of a broader global strategy to redefine how economies function. With her extensive background in economic policy and technology entrepreneurship, her warning underscores the urgency of preparing for these changes.

The shift away from the petrodollar and the exploration of new financial systems reflect a critical juncture in global economics. Nations are actively recalibrating their trade practices, embracing technological advancements, and reducing reliance on legacy systems. For individuals, businesses, and governments, understanding and adapting to these developments will be essential to navigating this transformative era.

The flaws in our current financial system are not new. Throughout history, economic models have risen and fallen, often replaced by systems better suited to the times. Historical patterns suggest that when financial systems fail to adapt, they collapse, often leading to significant social and economic upheaval. The weaknesses of the fiat and central banking system mirror those of past systems on the brink of obsolescence.

The Collapse of the Old and Need for a New Financial System

The limitations of the current financial system—persistent inflation, lack of transparency, and unsustainable debt—highlight the need for change. Blockchain technology and decentralized finance (DeFi) offer a promising alternative, addressing many of these issues by creating a transparent, secure, and efficient system.

As this book will explore, the world is on the verge of a major transformation. Understanding the flaws of the old financial system is the first step in preparing for the opportunities and challenges of the new era. By learning from the past, an individual can position themselves to thrive in the age of decentralized finance and blockchain technology.

It is important to be aware of how the collapse of the old financial system and the crash of fiat currencies could manifest, understanding that it will likely happen in a series of interconnected events accompanied by consequences that will ripple across global economies.

1. Hyperinflation and Currency Devaluation:

As fiat currencies lose their purchasing power, the threat of hyperinflation becomes a stark reality. **Hyperinflation**, characterized by a **rapid** and **uncontrollable rise in prices**, could render basic goods and services unaffordable for the average citizen. Everyday items like food, fuel, and medicine could see exponential price increases, leading to economic instability and widespread hardship. Currency devaluation, a key driver of such crises, typically occurs when confidence in a **nation's economy** or **monetary policies erodes**. This can happen for several reasons, including **excessive money printing** to cover ballooning government debts, a diminished foreign demand for the currency (as illustrated by the recent decline of the petrodollar system), and a general loss of faith in central banking policies.

The warning signs of such a collapse are often evident long before the full impact is felt. Rapidly rising prices of essential goods and services signal the diminishing value of the currency. Black market currency exchanges may emerge, offering better rates than official ones as citizens and businesses seek alternatives to preserve their wealth. In such environments, people increasingly turn to more stable foreign currencies, tangible assets like gold, or digital assets such as cryptocurrencies as safer stores of value.

The implications of this shift extend beyond personal finances, as businesses struggle to maintain operations, supply chains become disrupted, and social unrest brews. Recognizing these signs early and taking steps to diversify wealth into stable or appreciating assets becomes critical for individuals and nations seeking to mitigate the fallout from a collapsing fiat currency system.

2. Revaluation of Undervalued Foreign Currencies:

Undervalued foreign currencies, such as the **Iraqi dinar**, **Vietnamese dong**, **Ugandan shilling**, and **Indian rupee**, have long been seen as potential candidates for revaluation due to their perceived disparity between their nominal exchange rates and the true value of their economies. Revaluation occurs when a country's currency is adjusted upward in value relative to other currencies, often reflecting stronger economic fundamentals or **improved monetary policy**. For countries with undervalued currencies, revaluation could be driven by factors such as the discovery or increased exploitation of natural resources, economic reforms, trade surpluses, or a shift in geopolitical significance.

For example, Iraq, with its vast oil reserves, has the potential for its dinar to be revalued if political stability and infrastructural development continue to improve, attracting foreign investment. Similarly, Vietnam, known for its manufacturing and export growth, could see its dong rise in value as the country strengthens its trade position and integrates more deeply into global markets. In Uganda, investments in oil exploration and infrastructure development could enhance the value of the shilling. Meanwhile, India's rupee, backed by a growing economy, expanding technology sector, and increasing international trade, could also gain strength with the right policy measures.

Revaluation of these currencies could bring significant opportunities for foreign investors holding large amounts of undervalued notes, but it could also present challenges. Governments must carefully manage such shifts to avoid destabilizing inflation, trade imbalances, or capital flight. Moreover, geopolitical dynamics, debt obligations, and reliance on external markets can influence whether revaluation occurs and how it impacts a country's economy.

For individuals and businesses, tracking economic indicators like GDP growth, trade balances, foreign reserve levels, and government policy in these regions can offer clues about potential currency revaluations. While the prospect of investing in undervalued currencies carries potential rewards, it also requires caution, as political instability or economic mismanagement could hinder or delay revaluation efforts.

2. Banking and Liquidity Crises:

Traditional banks could find themselves under severe strain during a financial crisis as individuals and businesses begin to lose trust in the system. This erosion of confidence could **trigger widespread panic**, prompting depositors to rush to withdraw their funds in what is commonly known as a **bank run**. As more people attempt to liquidate their savings, banks—bound by fractional reserve practices where only a small percentage of deposits are kept in reserve—may quickly run out of liquidity. The inability to meet **withdrawal demands** can cripple financial institutions and cause widespread economic disruption.

In an attempt to stabilize the situation, central banks might intervene with capital injections or emergency funding. While these measures could temporarily ease the immediate liquidity crisis, they often come at a cost.

Injecting large sums of money into the economy, particularly in the form of **newly printed currency**, could **exacerbate inflation** and further undermine public trust in the banking system. This creates a vicious cycle where efforts to prevent collapse only deepen the financial instability.

The signs of such a crisis would likely be visible to those paying attention. Long lines at banks and ATMs, as people scramble to access their funds, could become a common sight. In more extreme cases, governments and financial institutions might impose restricted withdrawal limits or enforce "*bank holidays*," temporarily shutting down banking operations to prevent further depletion of reserves. Smaller financial institutions, unable to withstand the mounting pressures, may face insolvency and collapse, triggering further panic and consolidating power among larger banking entities.

This chain reaction could ripple through the broader economy, disrupting supply chains, reducing credit availability, and creating widespread uncertainty. For individuals and businesses, diversifying assets—such as holding funds in decentralized digital currencies or tangible assets like gold—can provide a level of security in these unpredictable scenarios. For policymakers, addressing the root causes of mistrust and improving systemic transparency will be essential to avoiding or mitigating such crises in the future.

3. Debt Defaults and Sovereign Crises:

Countries burdened by **unsustainable levels of debt** face the growing risk of defaulting on their loans, a scenario that could ripple through global markets and trigger widespread economic instability. **Sovereign debt crises** often occur when nations cannot meet their debt obligations due to high interest payments, declining revenues, or eroding investor confidence. When a country defaults, it undermines the trust of international lenders and foreign investors, potentially leading to capital flight and a sharp contraction in the domestic economy. The ripple effects of such crises can be profound, especially for countries reliant on international lending or dependent on the confidence of foreign investors to stabilize their economies.

Key signs of an impending sovereign debt crisis include governments delaying or defaulting on bond payments, which signals a lack of liquidity or fiscal mismanagement. Credit rating agencies may downgrade a country's rating, further deterring investors and increasing borrowing costs. In such scenarios, countries often turn to international organizations like the International Monetary Fund (IMF) for bailouts or restructuring agreements, which may come with stringent austerity measures that can lead to social and political unrest.

The domino effect of a sovereign debt crisis can destabilize other nations, particularly those with interconnected financial systems or trade dependencies. For example, if a major economy defaults, it could result in reduced trade flows, lower commodity prices, and heightened risk aversion in global markets, making it more difficult for other countries to secure financing. Financial institutions holding significant amounts of sovereign bonds from defaulting nations could also face losses, further spreading the crisis.

To mitigate such risks, nations need to prioritize sound fiscal policies, maintain healthy foreign reserves, and diversify their economies to reduce reliance on volatile external funding. International cooperation and innovative financial solutions, such as debt restructuring or new financial instruments, may also be critical in addressing the underlying vulnerabilities of heavily indebted nations. For investors and businesses, understanding the dynamics of sovereign debt and monitoring early warning signs can help navigate potential risks and opportunities in a fragile global economic environment.

4. Disruption in Global Trade:

As fiat currencies lose stability, the global trade system could face significant disruptions. The U.S. dollar has long served as the dominant reserve currency, facilitating the majority of international trade agreements. However, if its value erodes or nations lose confidence in its reliability, countries may struggle to settle trade transactions efficiently. This instability could lead to the emergence of alternative systems, such as **bartering**, bilateral agreements, and the adoption of alternative currencies like cryptocurrencies or central bank digital currencies (CBDCs). These alternatives would aim to provide stability and flexibility in trade but may take time to gain widespread acceptance and efficiency.

The destabilization of fiat currencies could result in sharp declines in imports and exports as nations face difficulties securing agreements under fluctuating exchange rates. Supply chain disruptions could compound these challenges, leading to shortages of essential goods like food, medicine, and energy. Countries reliant on imports for critical resources might be forced to seek alternative suppliers or prioritize self-sufficiency in certain industries, further straining global trade relationships.

In response, many nations could accelerate the use of digital currencies or local currencies in trade settlements. **Cryptocurrencies** and **CBDCs**, with their potential for **instant**, **transparent**, and **decentralized transactions**, could provide a viable alternative for cross-border payments. For example, regional trade agreements might adopt a shared digital currency to bypass reliance on fiat reserves. Bartering systems and bilateral agreements between nations could also reemerge, enabling trade without the need for a stable global currency.

This transition period may be marked by economic uncertainty and geopolitical tensions as nations vie for influence in shaping the new trade landscape. Businesses and governments will need to adapt by diversifying supply chains, exploring new markets, and embracing innovative technologies that facilitate efficient and secure trade practices. Understanding these evolving dynamics will be crucial for navigating a potential reconfiguration of the global economic order.

5. Surge in Alternative Assets:

As **fiat currencies weaken** and public **trust** in traditional financial systems erodes, individuals and institutions are likely to seek refuge in **"*safe haven*" assets** such as **gold**, **silver**, and **cryptocurrencies**. These alternatives are often viewed as more stable stores of value during times of economic uncertainty. Historically, precious metals like gold and silver have been favored during financial crises due to their intrinsic value, scarcity, and long-standing role as a medium of exchange. With increased demand, the prices of these metals could soar to unprecedented levels, further solidifying their status as reliable hedges against inflation and currency devaluation.

In addition to traditional safe havens, digital assets like cryptocurrencies may see explosive growth in adoption and value. Cryptocurrencies offer unique advantages, including portability, transparency, and independence from centralized financial institutions, making them attractive alternatives for both individuals and businesses. As trust in fiat currencies falters, digital assets like Bitcoin, Ethereum, and stablecoins could become increasingly mainstream for everyday transactions. For instance, retailers and service providers may begin accepting cryptocurrencies as payment to cater to a growing base of crypto-savvy consumers.

Beyond serving as a means of exchange, blockchain technology enables the tokenization of traditional assets, such as real estate, art, and commodities. Tokenized assets offer fractional ownership, liquidity, and ease of transfer, making previously illiquid investments accessible to a broader audience. This innovation could further drive the shift away from fiat-dominated systems and reshape how assets are traded and valued globally.

These shifts signal a profound transformation in the global financial landscape. Rising gold and silver prices, widespread cryptocurrency adoption, and the tokenization of traditional assets all point to a future where decentralized and alternative assets play a central role in preserving wealth and facilitating trade. For individuals and organizations, understanding and adapting to these emerging trends will be critical to safeguarding financial stability and taking advantage of new opportunities in the evolving economic landscape.

6. Rise of Central Bank Digital Currencies (CBDCs):

In response to the growing instability of fiat currencies, governments worldwide may turn to **Central Bank Digital Currencies (CBDCs)** as a modern solution to bolster financial systems and maintain control over monetary policy. Unlike decentralized cryptocurrencies, CBDCs operate on centralized blockchains, giving central banks unparalleled oversight and control over the currency's distribution and usage. By leveraging blockchain technology, CBDCs could enable real-time transactions, reduce the cost of cash handling, and improve the efficiency of monetary policy implementation. However, while this innovation offers promising benefits, it also raises significant concerns about privacy, autonomy, and the potential for overreach in surveillance.

The introduction of CBDCs could be accompanied by strategic measures to encourage adoption. Governments might phase out physical cash, positioning digital currency as a more secure and convenient alternative. To further incentivize adoption, they could offer benefits such as tax rebates, subsidies, or seamless integration with social welfare programs, making CBDCs appealing to both businesses and individuals. However, the shift to a fully digital currency system would likely mean increased monitoring of financial transactions, potentially eroding the privacy traditionally associated with cash-based systems. For example, **governments** could **track spending habits**, **freeze accounts**, or impose negative interest rates directly through CBDC platforms, raising questions about the **balance between security** and **personal freedom**.

Signs of this transition may include governments gradually reducing cash circulation, introducing legislation to enable CBDC infrastructure, and piloting these currencies in controlled environments. Countries like China have already made significant strides with their digital yuan, while other nations, including the European Union and the United States, are actively exploring CBDC frameworks.

While CBDCs could address many challenges posed by failing fiat systems, their centralized nature presents a double-edged sword. They offer unprecedented efficiency and control but at the potential cost of financial privacy and individual autonomy. As governments push forward with these systems, it will be crucial for policymakers to establish ethical and transparent frameworks to ensure that CBDCs serve the broader public interest without compromising fundamental freedoms. For individuals, understanding the implications of CBDCs and preparing for a cashless society will be key to navigating this transformative shift in global finance.

7. Social and Political Unrest:

The **collapse of fiat currencies** could trigger widespread economic instability, leading to significant **societal dissatisfaction** and **unrest**. As the value of money erodes, savings diminish, and purchasing power declines, the resulting hardships may exacerbate inequality and unemployment. People facing financial insecurity, coupled with frustration over government mismanagement, could be driven to protest, strike, or demand sweeping changes. Such conditions can ignite political upheavals, as citizens rally against perceived injustices and call for **radical monetary reforms**.

This unrest might manifest in several ways. **Protests** and **demonstrations** could become a common occurrence, with people expressing **outrage over inflation**, **job losses**, and the erosion of their savings. Strikes, particularly in essential industries, could disrupt the already strained supply chains, further deepening economic woes. Political polarization could intensify as opposing factions blame different ideologies or policies for the crisis, leading to heightened tensions within societies. Grassroots movements advocating for alternative monetary systems—such as cryptocurrencies or community-based economies—might gain traction, challenging traditional power structures and financial institutions.

Historical examples, such as the hyperinflation crisis in 1920s Germany or the 2001 Argentine economic collapse, illustrate how such turmoil can destabilize nations. In Germany, economic despair contributed to the rise of extremist ideologies, while in Argentina, massive protests and social unrest forced political leaders to resign. Similarly, today's interconnected world could see these crises ripple across borders, amplifying global instability.

Governments and institutions must anticipate and address these potential flashpoints by implementing strategies to mitigate economic pain. Policies such as universal basic income, targeted financial aid, or job creation programs could help stabilize societies during periods of transition. Furthermore, fostering open dialogue and transparency about monetary **reforms** could reduce public distrust and pave the way for smoother adaptation to new financial systems. For individuals, understanding these dynamics and preparing for potential disruptions—such as by diversifying income streams or investing in resilient assets—will be critical to weathering such turbulent times.

8. Wealth Redistribution and Financial Reset:

In the aftermath of a **fiat currency collapse**, a coordinated ***"financial reset"*** may emerge as a global strategy to stabilize economies and address widespread financial disarray. This reset could involve measures such as large-scale debt forgiveness, revaluation of currencies, or the implementation of entirely new monetary systems designed to rebuild trust in the financial landscape. While these actions might aim to restore stability and alleviate economic strain, they could also result in profound shifts in wealth distribution, fundamentally altering financial hierarchies and societal structures.

Key aspects of this reset might include the introduction of global digital currencies backed by tangible assets like gold, silver, or commodities. Such currencies could provide a stable and universally accepted medium of exchange, replacing volatile and unreliable fiat systems. Governments might also debate implementing policies such as universal basic income (UBI) to ensure a baseline standard of living, or wealth taxes to redistribute resources more equitably. These approaches would likely aim to prioritize financial inclusion, ensuring that underbanked and marginalized populations have access to resources and opportunities in the new system.

The implications of a financial reset would be far-reaching. While some individuals and institutions could benefit from debt relief or currency revaluation, others might experience significant losses, particularly if wealth is heavily concentrated in outdated or devalued assets. Social tensions could arise as debates over fairness, taxation, and redistribution intensify. Policymakers would face the delicate task of balancing economic recovery with equity, ensuring that the reset fosters long-term stability rather than exacerbating divisions.

Historically, resets have occurred after periods of extreme financial distress, such as the **Bretton Woods Agreement** after World War II, which established the U.S. dollar as the global reserve currency. In a similar vein, a modern reset could redefine the global financial order, potentially shifting power from traditional economic hubs to emerging markets or nations that embrace innovative technologies like blockchain and digital assets. For individuals, staying informed about potential resets and diversifying wealth into resilient, tangible, or digital assets could be critical strategies for navigating and thriving in this transformative period.

In conclusion, the **collapse** of the **old financial system** and **fiat currencies** would likely unfold in phases, with significant economic, social, and political consequences. While the transition could be tumultuous, it also presents opportunities for those prepared to adapt. Understanding these signs and proactively diversifying into stable assets like gold, real estate, or decentralized technologies can mitigate risks and position individuals to thrive in the new financial era.

CHAPTER 11

THE EMERGENCE OF BLOCKCHAIN TECHNOLOGY

The digital age has revolutionized nearly every aspect of modern life, from communication and commerce to education and entertainment. Amid this wave of innovation, one technology has emerged with the potential to fundamentally reshape the global financial system: blockchain. Originally developed as the foundation for Bitcoin, blockchain technology has since grown into a powerful tool with applications far beyond cryptocurrency. Its decentralized, transparent, and secure nature makes it a groundbreaking alternative to traditional systems.

The Birth of Blockchain: What It Is and How It Works

As previously mentioned, blockchain was introduced to the world in 2008 through a whitepaper titled **Bitcoin: A Peer-to-Peer Electronic Cash System**, authored by an individual or group under the pseudonym Satoshi Nakamoto. The whitepaper proposed a revolutionary way to conduct financial transactions without the need for a central authority, such as a bank or government.

At its core, a **blockchain** is a **digital ledger** that records transactions across a network of computers. Unlike **traditional ledgers** maintained by a single authority, blockchain operates on a **decentralized network**, meaning no single entity has control over the entire system. Each transaction is grouped into a "***block***," which is then added to a "***chain***" of previous transactions, creating an unalterable history.

Blockchain's decentralized structure is maintained by a network of participants, often referred to as nodes. These **nodes** validate transactions through a **consensus mechanism**, such as **Proof of Work (PoW)**, utilized by Bitcoin or **Proof of Stake (PoS)** adopted by Ethereum. Once a block is validated, it is added to the chain, ensuring that every participant in the network has an identical copy of the ledger. This innovation addressed long-standing challenges in digital transactions, such as double spending, by providing a transparent and tamper-proof way to verify and record data.

Key Characteristics of Blockchain

Blockchain technology is far more than just the foundation for cryptocurrency; it serves as a transformative tool for enhancing **transparency**, security, and efficiency across diverse industries such as healthcare, supply chain management, legal services, and finance. It owes its transformative power to several key characteristics that set it apart from traditional systems.

1. Decentralization:

Traditional financial systems are built on centralized infrastructures, where trusted **intermediaries** such as banks, payment processors, and clearinghouses play vital roles in managing transactions, maintaining records, and ensuring the flow of funds. These centralized authorities act as gatekeepers, overseeing the transfer of money, verifying identities, and safeguarding sensitive data. While effective for centuries, this model comes with inherent inefficiencies, high costs, and vulnerabilities. Centralized systems are prone to delays, single points of failure, and the potential for abuse of power or manipulation by those in control.

Decentralization, a core principle of blockchain technology, addresses these limitations by enhancing resilience and accessibility. Unlike centralized systems that rely on a single server or authority, decentralized networks operate through a distributed system of nodes. This structure ensures that even if some nodes go offline due to technical issues, cyberattacks, or natural disasters, the network remains operational, safeguarding data integrity and transaction processing. Every participant in the network has access to the same data, preventing any single entity from exercising undue control or influence.

By removing intermediaries, blockchain reduces transaction costs, accelerates processes, and strengthens security. It facilitates direct peer-to-peer transactions, eliminating the need for central authorities to validate or oversee them. This distributed approach enhances the robustness of the system, as there is no single point of failure—if one node is compromised, the rest of the network continues to function seamlessly.

Beyond operational efficiencies, decentralization marks a profound shift in power dynamics within financial systems. Individuals regain control over their financial activities, and the system becomes inherently transparent, reducing opportunities for corruption, fraud, and censorship. Blockchain technology decentralizes trust, creating a more equitable financial ecosystem that benefits participants across borders, particularly those excluded from traditional banking systems. This transformation holds the potential to redefine how value is exchanged, stored, and managed globally.

Decentralization also plays a crucial role in democratizing access to financial services. Traditional banking systems often exclude individuals in underbanked or unbanked regions due to infrastructure gaps, lack of documentation, or economic barriers. Decentralized networks bypass these limitations by enabling secure, direct transactions without the need for intermediaries. With just an internet connection and a digital wallet, individuals can participate in the global economy—sending, receiving, and storing value with ease.

Moreover, decentralization reduces the risk of censorship or manipulation by centralized authorities, fostering greater financial autonomy. It drives innovation in areas such as microfinance, remittances, and decentralized finance (DeFi) platforms, building a more inclusive financial ecosystem. By empowering individuals and communities traditionally left out of global financial systems, decentralization transforms not only technological infrastructure but also the lives and opportunities of countless people around the world. This paradigm shift underscores blockchain's capacity to create a financial system that is fairer, more resilient, and globally inclusive.

2. Transparency:

Blockchain's **transparency** is among its most transformative and appealing features, offering an unprecedented level of openness in the management and tracking of data. Every transaction within a blockchain network is recorded on a distributed ledger that is visible to all participants. While the personal details of users remain **encrypted** and **secure**, the **transaction data** itself is **openly accessible** and **immutable**. This combination of privacy and openness fosters trust and accountability across various applications, from financial systems to supply chains.

Transparency in blockchain technology provides a powerful tool for combating fraud, corruption, and mismanagement. In traditional systems, opaque processes often leave room for unethical practices, errors, or inefficiencies to go unnoticed. Blockchain eliminates this opacity by creating a shared, tamper-proof record of all transactions. Each entry on the ledger is time-stamped and cryptographically secured, making it virtually impossible to alter or delete data without the consensus of the network. This ensures that all parties involved can independently verify the integrity of the information.

One compelling application of blockchain's transparency is in supply chain management. By recording every step of a product's journey from origin to destination, blockchain can provide verifiable proof of authenticity, ethical sourcing, and compliance with regulatory standards. For instance, in industries like agriculture or pharmaceuticals, blockchain can be used to confirm that goods have been sustainably sourced or stored under appropriate conditions, offering peace of mind to consumers and stakeholders. Companies adopting this technology can build greater trust with their customers by demonstrating accountability and ethical practices.

Beyond supply chains, blockchain's transparency has far-reaching implications in industries such as finance, healthcare, and governance. In financial systems, it can reduce fraud by providing a clear, auditable trail of all transactions, helping regulators and institutions monitor for irregularities. In healthcare, blockchain can be used to maintain accurate patient records while ensuring privacy and security. Governments, too, can leverage blockchain to enhance transparency in public spending, elections, and aid distribution, reducing opportunities for corruption and inefficiency.

The global potential of blockchain's transparency becomes even more evident when addressing cross-border transactions and international aid. In cross-border payments, blockchain provides real-time visibility into the movement of funds, reducing delays and increasing trust between parties. In humanitarian efforts, it ensures that financial aid and resources reach their intended recipients without mismanagement or diversion.

Ultimately, blockchain's transparency creates a more equitable and trustworthy ecosystem by empowering individuals and organizations to operate with greater integrity. By providing an open and verifiable record of transactions, it enables collaboration, accountability, and innovation across industries, fostering a new era of trust in the digital age. As more sectors embrace this technology, the potential to build systems that are not only efficient but also ethically sound becomes a reality.

3. Security

Blockchain technology offers an unparalleled level of security, making it a trusted solution for safeguarding data and transactions across various industries. At the core of this security are advanced cryptographic techniques that encrypt transactions and link them together in an immutable chain of data blocks. Each block contains a **cryptographic hash** of the previous **block**, creating an interconnected system that is **virtually tamper-proof**. Altering any block would require recalculating and modifying all subsequent blocks in the chain, an endeavor that is computationally infeasible, especially in a decentralized network.

A key component of blockchain's security lies in its decentralized nature. Unlike traditional systems that rely on a central authority or server, blockchain operates across a distributed **network of nodes**. Each node has a copy of the entire ledger, ensuring that no single point of failure exists. This redundancy makes blockchain networks resilient to cyberattacks, as compromising one node does not affect the integrity of the entire system. In fact, to successfully manipulate a blockchain, an attacker would need to control the majority of nodes—an extraordinarily difficult feat in large, decentralized networks.

Blockchain networks also employ robust consensus mechanisms, such as Proof of Work (PoW) or Proof of Stake (PoS), to verify and validate transactions before they are recorded on the ledger. These mechanisms require network participants to reach agreement on the validity of a transaction, ensuring that fraudulent or invalid entries are rejected. This collective validation process adds another layer of security, making it extremely difficult for malicious actors to manipulate the system.

For example, in a PoW system like Bitcoin, participants (miners) must solve complex mathematical puzzles to add a new block to the chain. This process requires significant computational resources, discouraging potential attackers by making fraudulent activities economically unviable. In PoS systems, participants must stake their own assets as collateral to validate transactions, aligning their financial interests with the security of the network.

Beyond transaction security, blockchain's architecture protects against data breaches and unauthorized access. Data stored on the blockchain is encrypted and accessible only to those with the appropriate keys, ensuring privacy while maintaining transparency. This makes blockchain an ideal solution for industries such as finance, healthcare, and supply chain management, where data integrity and confidentiality are critical.

Additionally, the immutability of blockchain records enhances its reliability. Once a transaction is added to the blockchain, it cannot be altered or deleted, providing a permanent and verifiable audit trail. This feature is particularly valuable in sectors where trust and accountability are paramount, such as legal contracts, government records, and financial reporting.

In an era of increasing cyber threats, blockchain's multi-faceted security measures offer a powerful defense against hacking, fraud, and data manipulation. By combining cryptographic protections, decentralized architecture, and consensus-driven validation, blockchain provides a secure foundation for digital transactions and data management. As industries continue to adopt this technology, blockchain's robust security will play a crucial role in fostering trust and resilience in the digital economy.

4. Immutability:

Once a transaction is recorded on a blockchain, it becomes virtually unchangeable. This characteristic, known as immutability, ensures that every piece of data entered into the ledger is permanently preserved, creating a reliable and unalterable historical record. **Immutability** is achieved through **cryptographic hashing** and the decentralized nature of blockchain networks. To alter a transaction, one would need to manipulate the data across all copies of the ledger stored on numerous nodes, which is computationally infeasible for established and widely distributed blockchains.

This feature enhances accountability, as users cannot retroactively modify or delete data to hide errors, fraudulent activity, or unethical practices. It creates a tamper-proof system where the integrity of information is safeguarded, fostering trust among participants. Blockchain immutability ensures that once data is written, it remains secure and auditable, making it a valuable tool in addressing concerns related to fraud and data manipulation.

Applications of Immutability Across Industries: Immutability is particularly advantageous in sectors where trust, transparency, and data accuracy are critical. Below are some examples of how this feature is being utilized:

Healthcare: Blockchain technology offers transformative solutions across multiple sectors by leveraging its immutable nature. In healthcare, blockchain provides a secure platform for storing medical records. Once a record is entered into the blockchain, it becomes unalterable, ensuring that a patient's medical history remains accurate and free from tampering. This reliability is particularly critical in areas such as treatment history, insurance claims, and research data integrity. Additionally, blockchain addresses the global issue of counterfeit medications by creating a transparent and tamper-proof record of transactions throughout the drug supply chain. By tracking every stage, from manufacturing to distribution, blockchain ensures that only authentic products reach consumers, fostering trust and safety in the pharmaceutical industry.

In the realm of legal services, blockchain's immutability underpins innovations like smart contracts and evidence storage. Smart contracts are digital agreements that execute automatically once predefined conditions are met, offering fairness, transparency, and efficiency in contractual arrangements. Furthermore, blockchain can securely store legal evidence, ensuring that it remains unaltered from submission to adjudication. This enhances the integrity of legal proceedings and builds confidence in the judicial process by safeguarding critical data against tampering or manipulation. Through these applications, blockchain demonstrates its potential to enhance accuracy, trust, and accountability across critical sectors.

Finance: Blockchain technology offers significant advantages to financial institutions by maintaining an immutable ledger of transactions. This ensures accuracy and transparency, minimizing disputes and helping institutions comply with regulatory standards. Additionally, blockchain creates reliable audit trails that auditors can utilize to access transparent, tamper-proof records of financial activities. This not only simplifies the auditing process but also reduces the potential for fraud, enhancing trust in financial operations.

Supply Chain Management: Blockchain technology enables comprehensive tracking of goods throughout every stage of production and distribution, creating an unalterable record of a product's journey. This ensures greater accountability by allowing stakeholders to verify the origins and movement of goods, reducing the risk of fraud and counterfeiting. Furthermore, blockchain enhances transparency for consumers who prioritize ethically sourced products, offering them verifiable proof of authenticity and adherence to ethical standards in production and supply chains.

Government and Public Sector: Blockchain technology has transformative applications in areas such as land registry and voting systems. By creating a permanent and tamper-proof record of land ownership, blockchain reduces disputes and curtails corruption in property transactions, providing a transparent and secure system for managing real estate ownership. Similarly, blockchain-based voting systems offer a reliable solution for ensuring the integrity of electoral processes. Once a vote is cast, it becomes immutable, preventing any alterations or deletions and fostering greater transparency and trust in democratic systems. This innovative approach enhances accountability and reduces the potential for fraud in these critical societal functions.

While immutability offers numerous benefits, it is not without challenges. The inability to alter data means errors must be corrected through additional transactions rather than direct modifications. For example, if a mistake is made in recording a medical record or financial transaction, a new entry must be added to the blockchain to rectify it, potentially complicating data management.

Additionally, the immutable nature of blockchain raises concerns about privacy, particularly in cases where sensitive personal data is involved. Innovations such as zero-knowledge proofs and encrypted blockchain solutions are being explored to address these concerns while maintaining the integrity of immutable records.

As blockchain technology continues to evolve, its immutability will remain a cornerstone feature, driving trust and reliability across diverse applications. From preventing fraud to ensuring data accuracy and transparency, immutability is set to transform industries and redefine how information is managed and trusted in the digital age. By providing a secure, tamper-proof framework, blockchain enables a new era of accountability and trust in systems that previously relied on fallible intermediaries.

Introduction to Bitcoin: The Pioneer of Decentralized Finance

Bitcoin, launched in January 2009, was the first real-world application of blockchain technology. Often referred to as ***"digital gold,"*** **Bitcoin** was designed as a decentralized form of currency that could operate independently of governments and traditional financial institutions.

Bitcoin introduced the concept of peer-to-peer transactions, allowing individuals to send and receive money directly without intermediaries. Transactions are verified by network participants through the Proof of Work consensus mechanism, which involves solving complex mathematical puzzles to validate blocks.

One of Bitcoin's most revolutionary aspects is its **fixed supply**. Unlike fiat currencies, which can be printed at will, Bitcoin has a cap of **21 million coins**, making it **deflationary in nature**. This scarcity has contributed to its appeal as a store of value, similar to precious metals.

Bitcoin's success paved the way for a broader movement known as

decentralized finance (DeFi). Today, thousands of cryptocurrencies and blockchain-based projects have built upon Bitcoin's foundation, exploring use cases in areas such as smart contracts, **decentralized applications (dApps)**, and tokenized assets.

A Catalyst for Change

The emergence of blockchain technology marks a turning point in the evolution of financial systems. Its ability to decentralize power, enhance transparency, and secure data positions it as a viable alternative to traditional systems plagued by inefficiencies and inequalities. As blockchain continues to evolve, its applications are expanding into industries ranging from healthcare and supply chain management to voting and identity verification. However, it was Bitcoin's pioneering use of this technology that demonstrated its potential to disrupt and transform the global economy. The journey from the old financial system to one powered by blockchain and decentralized assets has only just begun. Understanding the fundamentals of blockchain is essential for anyone seeking to navigate and capitalize on the opportunities presented by this new era of innovation.

The Rise of Digital Assets

The emergence of blockchain technology laid the foundation for the rise of digital assets, transforming the way people think about value, ownership, and financial systems. While Bitcoin is the pioneering cryptocurrency, it has paved the way for a diverse ecosystem of digital assets that go far beyond its initial scope. Ethereum, altcoins, stablecoins, Non-Fungible Tokens (NFTs), and Decentralized Finance (DeFi) platforms have expanded the possibilities of blockchain technology, introducing new utilities and applications. This chapter explores the evolution of digital assets, their key categories, and their transformative potential.

Beyond Bitcoin: Ethereum and the Growth of Altcoins

Bitcoin was the first cryptocurrency to introduce the concept of decentralized digital money, but its design primarily focuses on serving as a store of value and a medium of exchange. **Ethereum, launched in 2015** by Vitalik Buterin, expanded the potential of blockchain by introducing the concept of **smart contracts**. These self-executing contracts allow developers to build **decentralized applications (dApps)** on the Ethereum network, opening the door to countless new use cases.

Ethereum's programmability and **flexibility** have inspired the creation of thousands of alternative cryptocurrencies, often referred to as "***altcoins***." These altcoins serve various purposes, ranging from enhancing transaction speeds and privacy to enabling specific industry applications. Popular altcoins like Binance Coin (BNB), Cardano (ADA), and Solana (SOL) have gained traction as they cater to unique niches within the blockchain ecosystem. This diversification has turned the digital asset space into a vibrant and competitive marketplace, driving innovation and adoption across sectors.

Key Asset Categories

The digital asset ecosystem comprises several distinct categories, each with its unique characteristics and applications:

1. Cryptocurrencies:

Cryptocurrencies are the backbone of the digital asset world. They function as digital currencies that use cryptography for secure transactions and operate on decentralized networks. Bitcoin remains the most well-known cryptocurrency, but many others, like Ethereum, Litecoin, and Ripple XRP, serve additional purposes beyond monetary transactions.

Cryptocurrencies have gained recognition as a legitimate asset class, with applications ranging from remittances and microtransactions to investments and cross-border payments. They provide an alternative to traditional fiat currencies, particularly in regions with unstable economies or limited access to banking services.

2. Stablecoins:

Stablecoins address one of the main challenges of cryptocurrencies: volatility. These digital assets are **pegged** to a stable value, such as a **fiat currency** (e.g., USD) or a commodity (e.g., gold), making them more suitable for everyday transactions and savings.

Examples include Tether (USDT), USD Coin (USDC), Dai (DAI) and Ripple (RLUSD). Stablecoins bridge the gap between traditional finance and the digital asset world by enabling seamless transactions, reducing risk, and providing a reliable medium of exchange.

3. NFTs (Non-Fungible Tokens):

Non-Fungible Tokens (NFTs) represent unique **digital assets** that **cannot** be exchanged on a **one-to-one basis** like cryptocurrencies. They are often used to tokenize ownership of art, music, videos, virtual real estate, and other digital or physical items.

NFTs gained significant attention in 2021 when **digital artwork** and **collectibles** sold for millions of dollars. However, their utility extends beyond art; NFTs can represent proof of ownership, intellectual property rights, or even event tickets, creating new possibilities for industries like gaming, entertainment, and real estate.

4. Decentralized Finance (DeFi) Platforms:

Decentralized Finance (DeFi) platforms leverage blockchain technology to recreate traditional financial services like lending, borrowing, and trading without intermediaries. Using smart contracts, DeFi platforms enable users to access financial services in a permissionless and transparent manner.

Popular DeFi platforms like Uniswap, Aave, and Compound have revolutionized the financial sector by providing alternatives to traditional banking systems. DeFi's rapid growth underscores its potential to democratize finance and empower individuals with greater control over their assets.

The Utility of Digital Assets

Digital assets are not just speculative investments; they serve practical and transformative purposes across various industries. Here are some of the key utilities:

1. Payment Systems:

THE EMERGENCE OF BLOCKCHAIN TECHNOLOGY

Cryptocurrencies such as Bitcoin and stablecoins like USDC are revolutionizing the way payments are made, offering fast, secure, and low-cost solutions that traditional financial systems struggle to match. Unlike traditional banking systems, which often require several business days to process international transfers, blockchain-based payment systems enable transactions to be completed in seconds or minutes, regardless of the distance between sender and recipient. This speed is a game-changer for cross-border payments, eliminating the delays and inefficiencies caused by intermediaries like correspondent banks.

The cost advantage is equally significant. Traditional systems often impose high fees for international transactions due to exchange rates, intermediary charges, and service fees. Cryptocurrencies, on the other hand, operate on decentralized networks that significantly reduce overhead costs. For instance, a transaction involving millions of dollars can be processed on the blockchain for a few dollars or less, making it an attractive option for both individuals and businesses. This low-cost model is particularly beneficial for remittances, where high fees have historically eroded the value of money sent by expatriates to their families in developing countries.

Another transformative feature of blockchain-based payment systems is their accessibility. Unlike traditional banks, which operate on fixed schedules and close on weekends and holidays, cryptocurrency networks run 24/7, ensuring that transactions can be initiated and completed at any time. This always-on nature is especially valuable for emergencies or time-sensitive payments, providing a level of flexibility and reliability that traditional systems cannot offer.

Blockchain technology also enhances financial inclusion by providing banking services to unbanked and underbanked populations. With just a smartphone and internet access, individuals who lack access to traditional financial institutions can use cryptocurrencies and stablecoins to send, receive, and store money securely. This is particularly impactful in regions where banking infrastructure is limited or unreliable.

Furthermore, cryptocurrencies can facilitate micropayments, which are often impractical with traditional payment systems due to high fees. These tiny transactions are critical for enabling new business models, such as pay-per-use services, content monetization, and decentralized applications (dApps).

The combination of speed, cost efficiency, accessibility, and inclusivity positions blockchain-based payment systems as a powerful tool for reshaping global finance. As adoption grows and technology evolves, these systems are poised to play a pivotal role in creating a more connected and equitable financial ecosystem.

2. Smart Contracts

Smart contracts, first introduced by Ethereum, are transforming industries by automating complex processes and executing agreements without the need for intermediaries. These self-executing contracts run on blockchain technology, ensuring that predefined conditions are met before actions are triggered. By removing the need for manual intervention, smart contracts enhance efficiency, transparency, and security while significantly reducing costs and the potential for human error or fraud.

One of the most prominent applications of smart contracts is in Decentralized Finance (DeFi). Platforms like Uniswap and Aave leverage smart contracts to enable services such as automated lending, borrowing, and trading. For instance, a user can lend cryptocurrency to a liquidity pool and earn interest, with the entire process managed by a smart contract. The terms of the loan, including interest rates and collateral requirements, are encoded into the contract, ensuring fairness and transparency for all parties involved. They are widely used in DeFi, supply chain management, insurance, and legal services, ensuring transparency and reducing the risk of fraud.

3. Tokenized Real-World Assets

Blockchain technology has introduced the concept of **tokenization**, which involves converting **real-world assets** like **real estate**, **stocks**, **commodities**, or **art** into digital tokens on a blockchain. These tokens represent ownership or rights to the underlying asset, enabling a secure, transparent, and efficient way to buy, sell, and trade assets. Tokenization has the potential to revolutionize traditional financial markets by increasing accessibility, enhancing liquidity, and democratizing investment opportunities.

One of the most transformative aspects of tokenization is the ability to enable fractional ownership. Traditionally, high-value assets such as luxury real estate or rare artwork were accessible only to wealthy investors or institutions. With tokenization, these assets can be divided into smaller, more affordable shares, represented by tokens. For instance, a $5 million luxury property could be tokenized into 5,000 tokens, each worth $1,000. This allows a broader range of investors to participate in asset ownership and benefit from its appreciation or income, such as rental yields.

Tokenization also addresses one of the biggest challenges in certain asset classes: liquidity. Markets for assets like real estate, private equity, or fine art are often illiquid, meaning it can take months or even years to sell or exchange them. With tokenized assets, secondary markets can be created, where investors can trade tokens representing their ownership. For example, platforms like RealT already allow investors to buy and trade tokens representing ownership stakes in U.S. rental properties, providing liquidity that would otherwise be unavailable in traditional real estate markets.

Beyond real estate, tokenization is making waves in other sectors. In the stock market, tokenized securities allow for 24/7 trading, breaking free from the constraints of traditional trading hours. Commodities like gold and oil can also be tokenized, enabling investors to own fractions of these assets without the need for physical storage or handling. Companies like Tether Gold are already offering tokens backed by physical gold, making it easier for individuals to invest in and trade this historically stable asset.

Art and collectibles are another area seeing the benefits of tokenization. High-value art pieces, such as a Picasso painting, can be tokenized so that multiple people can co-own a fraction of the piece. Platforms like Maecenas are pioneering this space, allowing investors to diversify their portfolios with exposure to fine art without requiring millions of dollars upfront. The tokenization of real-world assets also enhances global accessibility and inclusivity. Investors from anywhere in the world can participate in markets that were previously limited by geography or financial barriers. Blockchain's transparency ensures that all participants have access to the same information, reducing fraud and increasing trust in these transactions.

Furthermore, smart contracts—automated programs that execute agreements based on predefined conditions—can be integrated with tokenized assets to streamline operations such as dividend payouts, rent distributions, or profit sharing. This automation reduces administrative costs and ensures that investors receive their returns efficiently and transparently. Tokenization represents a significant leap forward in financial innovation, transforming how assets are bought, sold, and managed. By breaking down barriers to entry, enhancing liquidity, and leveraging blockchain's security and transparency, tokenization opens up a world of possibilities for investors and asset owners alike. As adoption grows, it is expected to reshape traditional markets and create new opportunities in the global economy.

A New Frontier in Finance

The rise of digital assets signals a paradigm shift in how value is created, stored, and exchanged. From cryptocurrencies and stablecoins to NFTs and DeFi platforms, digital assets are redefining industries and creating new opportunities for individuals, businesses, and governments. As this ecosystem continues to evolve, understanding the nuances of digital assets and their applications is critical for navigating the transition from traditional systems to a decentralized future. The journey is just beginning, and those who adapt early will be well-positioned to thrive in this new era of innovation and opportunity.

CHAPTER 12

OPPORTUNITIES WITHIN THE GREAT WEALTH TRANSFER

The global financial landscape is undergoing a monumental transformation as economies move from traditional fiat systems toward digital and blockchain-based financial frameworks. This shift is driven by advancements in technology, changing consumer behaviors, and the need for more efficient and transparent financial systems. This chapter explores the ongoing transition, the factors driving the move towards a cashless society, the emergence of Central Bank Digital Currencies (CBDCs), the roles of governments and private companies, and the phases of adoption that are paving the way for a fully digital economy.

The Push Towards a Cashless Society

In recent years, the idea of a **cashless society** has gained significant momentum. The rise of **digital payment platforms** like Apple Pay, PayPal, Venmo, and mobile banking applications has transformed the way people transact. Increasingly, physical cash is being replaced by digital alternatives, particularly in urban and technologically advanced regions.

The Benefits of a Cashless Society are Clear:

- **Convenience:** Digital transactions are faster, more efficient, and reduce the need for **physical currency handling**.
- **Transparency:** Digital payments leave an **electronic trail**, reducing the risk of **corruption** and tax evasion.

- **Security:** Advanced encryption and authentication methods make digital payments safer than carrying physical cash.

The **COVID-19 pandemic** further **accelerated** this trend, as people sought **contactless payment methods** to minimize physical contact. Retailers and businesses adopted digital payment solutions at unprecedented rates, propelling the transition to a cashless economy. While the convenience of these systems is undeniable, the implications for privacy, accessibility, and financial equity are topics of ongoing debate.

Central Bank Digital Currencies (CBDCs): Bridging Traditional Finance with Blockchain

Central Bank Digital Currencies (CBDCs) represent a pivotal step in the transition from **fiat** to **digital**. Unlike decentralized cryptocurrencies such as Bitcoin, CBDCs are digital forms of a nation's fiat currency, issued and regulated by central **banks**. CBDCs aim to combine the efficiency and transparency of blockchain technology with the stability and oversight of traditional financial institutions.

Key Features of CBDCs:

- **Centralized Oversight:** Unlike cryptocurrencies, which operate on decentralized networks, CBDCs are controlled by central banks, allowing for regulatory compliance and monetary policy enforcement.
- **Increased Efficiency: CBDCs** reduce transaction **times** and **costs**, particularly for **cross-border payments.**
- **Financial Inclusion:** CBDCs can provide unbanked populations with access to **digital financial services** through mobile devices.

Countries like China, Sweden, and Nigeria are leading the charge with pilot programs and national rollouts of their CBDCs. The Chinese Digital Yuan, for example, has already seen widespread use in domestic trials, demonstrating the potential for CBDCs to reshape global financial systems.

While **CBDCs** offer numerous benefits, they also raise concerns about **privacy** and **centralized control**. Governments will need to strike a delicate balance between leveraging the advantages of digital currencies and addressing these challenges.

As of January 2025, several countries have fully launched Central Bank Digital Currencies (CBDCs), with their respective central banks spearheading these initiatives:

- **The Bahamas:** The Central Bank of The Bahamas introduced the Sand Dollar in October 2020, becoming the first country to officially launch a CBDC.
- **Nigeria:** The Central Bank of Nigeria launched the e-Naira in October 2021, aiming to enhance financial inclusion and facilitate easier remittances.
- **Jamaica:** The Bank of Jamaica rolled out its CBDC, JamDex, to promote digital payments and improve access to financial services.
- **Eastern Caribbean Currency Union (ECCU):** The Eastern Caribbean Central Bank introduced DCash, a digital version of the Eastern Caribbean dollar, to modernize payment systems across member countries.
- **China:** The People's Bank of China has been piloting the digital renminbi (e-CNY) in various cities, with plans for a broader rollout.
- **India:** The Reserve Bank of India launched the Digital Rupee pilot, aiming to explore the feasibility of a digital currency in enhancing the country's payment systems.
- **Russia:** The Bank of Russia has been developing the Digital Ruble, with pilot programs initiated to assess its integration into the financial system.

These developments reflect a growing global interest in CBDCs as nations seek to modernize their financial infrastructures, enhance payment efficiencies, and promote **financial inclusion**.

The Role of Private Companies and Governments in Driving Adoption

The transition from fiat to digital is not solely the result of government initiatives; private companies are playing a critical role in driving adoption and innovation.
Private Companies:

- Technology firms like **PayPal**, **Square**, and **Coinbase** have developed platforms that make digital currencies **accessible** to the masses.

- Blockchain-focused startups and developers are creating decentralized financial (DeFi) applications, tokenized assets, and smart contracts, which are expanding the use cases of digital currencies.

Governments:

- **Governments** are increasingly recognizing the potential of blockchain technology to improve financial systems and reduce inefficiencies.
- **Regulatory frameworks** are being developed to address the challenges posed by digital currencies, including consumer protection, anti-money laundering (AML), and know-your-customer (KYC) requirements.

The collaboration between governments and private companies is critical to building a robust and inclusive digital financial ecosystem. Governments provide the **regulatory clarity** needed for **stability**, while private companies innovate and expand the boundaries of what is possible in the digital economy.

Several financial institutions have developed or are in the process of developing their own stablecoins, aiming to enhance transaction efficiency, reduce costs, and integrate blockchain technology into their services. Notable examples include:

- **JPMorgan Chase:** Introduced JPM Coin, a U.S. dollar-pegged stablecoin designed to facilitate instantaneous **cross-border payments** and streamline transactions between institutional clients.
- **Societe Generale – Forge (SG-Forge):** Launched the EUR CoinVertible, a Euro-backed stablecoin available to retail investors, aiming to modernize payment systems and enhance transaction efficiency within the European financial market.
- **Mitsubishi UFJ Financial Group (MUFG):** Developed the MUFG Coin, a Japanese yen-pegged stablecoin intended to facilitate secure and efficient digital transactions within Japan's financial ecosystem.
- **USDF Consortium:** A collective of U.S. banks collaborating to issue a bank-minted stablecoin known as USDF, aiming to provide a secure and regulated digital currency for various payment applications.
- **Visa:** While not a bank, Visa has launched a tokenization network to enable banks to issue their own stablecoins, facilitating the

- integration of digital currencies into traditional financial systems.
- **Deutsche Bank:** Through its asset management arm, DWS, Deutsche Bank plans to launch a stablecoin by 2025, aiming to integrate digital currencies into traditional banking services.
- **BBVA:** The Spanish banking group BBVA is collaborating with Visa on a pilot project to develop a stablecoin, reflecting a growing interest among European banks in digital currencies.
- **Standard Chartered:** Leading a consortium, Standard Chartered is testing a stablecoin pegged to the Hong Kong dollar, indicating a strategic move to enhance digital payment solutions in the Asian market.

These initiatives reflect a growing trend among traditional financial institutions to adopt blockchain technology and develop proprietary stablecoins, seeking to improve transaction processes and remain competitive in the evolving digital economy.

Phases of Adoption: From Early Adopters to Mainstream Integration

The transition from fiat to digital is unfolding in distinct phases, reflecting the natural progression of technological adoption.

1. **Early Adopters:** Early adopters of **digital currencies** primarily consisted of cryptocurrency enthusiasts and tech-savvy individuals who were quick to **recognize** the **potential of blockchain technology**. These pioneers embraced digital assets like Bitcoin and Ethereum, helping to establish their utility and legitimacy in the financial and technological landscapes. By using, promoting, and investing in these emerging currencies, **early adopters** laid the groundwork for broader adoption, showcasing how blockchain technology could revolutionize areas such as payments, transparency, and decentralized systems. Their efforts created the foundation for the cryptocurrency ecosystem that continues to expand today.

2. **Institutional Adoption:** In recent years, the adoption of digital assets has moved beyond early enthusiasts to include **major financial institutions**, hedge funds, and corporations. These entities have recognized the transformative potential of cryptocurrencies and blockchain technology, leading to significant investments in the sector. Companies such as Tesla, MicroStrategy, and Square have made headlines

by **incorporating cryptocurrencies** like Bitcoin into their balance sheets. These strategic moves not only reflect confidence in the long-term value of digital currencies but also signal a broader acceptance of blockchain as a cornerstone of the future financial ecosystem. Institutional involvement has further legitimized cryptocurrencies, encouraging more businesses and investors to explore opportunities in the digital asset space.

3. **Regulatory and Governmental Integration: Governments** around the world are actively working to integrate digital currencies into their economies by developing **Central Bank Digital Currencies (CBDCs)** and establishing regulatory frameworks for the broader cryptocurrency market. These efforts aim to modernize financial systems, enhance transparency, and provide secure digital payment options. **Central banks** are exploring ways to **issue CBDCs** that can coexist with traditional fiat currencies, offering a state-backed alternative to private cryptocurrencies.

This phase of integration also involves collaborations between governments and private companies. Such partnerships are facilitating the transition to digital financial systems by leveraging the technological expertise of the **private sector** and the **regulatory authority of governments**. These joint efforts are designed to ensure that digital currencies are implemented **efficiently** and **securely**, while addressing concerns about privacy, cybersecurity, and market stability. This cooperation marks a critical step toward widespread adoption and a more seamless transition into a digital-first financial future.

4. **Mainstream Adoption:** Mainstream adoption of digital currencies represents a pivotal phase in the evolution of the global financial system, where digital assets become an integral part of everyday transactions. Activities such as buying groceries, paying rent, or even tipping service workers could seamlessly involve cryptocurrencies or Central Bank Digital Currencies (CBDCs). As businesses and payment platforms integrate digital currency options, their use is expected to become as common as credit cards or cash.

A **key factor** in this transition will be **widespread financial education** and the development of accessible technologies. Ensuring that individuals from all demographics—regardless of age, income, or technological proficiency—can participate in the digital economy is essential for equity and inclusivity. Initiatives to simplify digital wallets, increase public understanding of blockchain technology, and enhance digital infrastructure will help bridge the gap between early adopters and the general population, fostering a more inclusive financial ecosystem.

In summary, the transition from fiat to digital is not just an evolution of currency; it is a reimagining of the global financial system. The push toward a cashless society, the development of CBDCs, and the collaborative efforts of governments and private companies are shaping a new era of economic activity. By understanding the phases of adoption and the challenges and opportunities they present, individuals and businesses can position themselves to thrive in the digital financial landscape.

This shift is not just about technological innovation—it is about creating a financial ecosystem that is more inclusive, efficient, and adaptable to the needs of a rapidly changing world. As this transition continues to unfold, those who are informed and prepared will be best equipped to navigate and benefit from the new digital economy.

Identifying Areas of Growth During the Transition

The transition from traditional financial systems to blockchain-based digital ecosystems represents a generational opportunity for individuals and businesses to build and preserve wealth. This ***"Great Wealth Transfer"*** is creating new pathways for financial growth, especially for those who are informed and proactive. By identifying key areas of opportunity, developing strategic approaches to wealth creation, and understanding how to manage risk in a volatile market, individuals can position themselves to thrive in this evolving financial landscape.

Investing in Cryptocurrencies and Blockchain Technology

The cryptocurrency market, with its rapidly expanding ecosystem, is at the forefront of the wealth transfer. Bitcoin, Ethereum, and a myriad of altcoins have demonstrated their potential as both stores of value and innovative financial tools. Beyond individual cryptocurrencies, investing in blockchain technology companies offers exposure to the infrastructure supporting decentralized finance (DeFi), smart contracts, and tokenized assets.

Key Points:

- **Early Adoption Advantage:** Many cryptocurrencies are still in their growth phase, offering significant **upside** potential for **early investors**.
- **Institutional Involvement:** Major corporations and financial institutions are adopting blockchain, further legitimizing the space and driving demand.
- **Broader Applications:** Blockchain's potential extends beyond currency, revolutionizing industries such as healthcare, supply chain, and energy.

Opportunities in DeFi and Staking

Decentralized finance (DeFi) is reshaping traditional financial services by offering decentralized platforms for lending, borrowing, trading, and earning interest without intermediaries. Staking, where investors lock up their cryptocurrency to support network operations and earn rewards, is another lucrative opportunity within the blockchain ecosystem.

Key Points:

- **High Yields:** DeFi platforms often provide higher interest rates compared to traditional savings accounts or investments.
- **Accessibility:** DeFi and staking platforms are open to anyone with internet access, promoting financial inclusion.
- **Evolving Ecosystem:** As DeFi continues to mature, new tools and platforms are emerging, creating additional opportunities for early participants.

Tokenization of Real Estate and Other Traditional Assets

Tokenization allows real-world assets, such as real estate, art, or commodities, to be represented as digital tokens on a blockchain. This innovation makes traditionally illiquid assets more accessible and divisible, democratizing investment opportunities.

Key Points:

- **Fractional Ownership:** Investors can **own a fraction** of **high-value assets**, lowering barriers to entry.

- **Global Accessibility:** Tokenized assets can be bought and sold globally, increasing liquidity and market participation.
- **Transparency:** Blockchain technology provides an immutable record of ownership, enhancing trust and reducing fraud.

Strategies for Wealth Creation:

Dollar-Cost Averaging in Cryptocurrency

Dollar-cost averaging (DCA) is a strategy where an investor consistently purchases a **fixed dollar amount** of a particular asset at **regular intervals**, regardless of **market conditions**. This method reduces the impact of volatility and avoids the pitfalls of trying to time the market.

Benefits of DCA:

- Reduces **emotional decision-making** during market fluctuations.
- Provides a **disciplined approach** to building a cryptocurrency portfolio.
- Allows investors to **accumulate more assets** when prices are low.

Maximizing Market Opportunities with Limit Orders

Profiting from market spikes, dips and even crashes can be strategically achieved by using buy and sell limit orders, which allow investors to automate their trades at predetermined price levels. This approach is particularly useful in volatile markets, as it allows individuals to capitalize on price fluctuations while mitigating the emotional decision-making that often accompanies rapid market movements.

- A **buy limit order** enables a person to purchase an asset at or below a specified price, capitalizing on sudden dips in the market. For example, if a cryptocurrency typically trades at $50 but experiences volatility, setting a buy limit order at $45 ensures the purchase only occurs if the price drops to that level, maximizing potential gains.

- A **sell limit order** helps lock in profits by automatically selling an asset when it reaches a target price. If the same cryptocurrency spikes to $60, a sell limit order ensures the asset is sold, capturing profits without requiring constant monitoring of the market.

Portfolio Diversification in Digital Assets

Diversification is a fundamental principle of **risk management**. Within the **digital asset** space, diversification involves spreading investments across various asset classes, including cryptocurrencies, stablecoins, NFTs, and tokenized real-world assets.

Key Considerations:

- **Asset Allocation:** Balance high-risk, high-reward assets (e.g., altcoins) with more stable options (e.g., Bitcoin or stablecoins).
- **Sector Exposure:** Invest in different sectors within the blockchain space, such as DeFi, gaming, or enterprise blockchain solutions.
- **Geographic Diversity:** Explore projects from different regions to reduce exposure to regulatory risks in a single country.

Understanding and Managing Risk in a Volatile Market

The cryptocurrency market is known for its high volatility, which can lead to significant gains or losses. Successful investors understand the importance of managing risk and adopting strategies to protect their investments.

Risk Management Strategies:

- **Set Stop-Loss Orders:** Automatically sell assets if their price falls below a predetermined level to **limit losses**.
- **Invest Only What Can Be Afforded to Lose:** Allocate a portion of funds that will not jeopardize financial stability if lost.
- **Stay Informed:** Regularly research and monitor market trends, regulatory developments, and project updates to make informed decisions.
- **Use Secure Wallets:** Protect digital assets by using **hardware wallets** or other secure storage solutions to prevent hacking and theft.

In conclusion, the wealth transfer driven by blockchain technology and digital assets offers unprecedented opportunities for financial growth. By identifying areas of innovation, such as cryptocurrencies, DeFi, and tokenized assets, and adopting strategies like dollar-cost averaging and portfolio diversification, individuals can harness the potential of this evolving financial landscape. However, the key to success lies in understanding and managing risk, ensuring that investments are both informed and sustainable.

This transition marks a new era of financial possibilities, and those who embrace it with preparation and strategy will be well-positioned to thrive in the digital economy. The journey requires not only foresight but also resilience and adaptability—traits that will define the new generation of wealth builders.

CHAPTER 13

THE GOLDEN TRINITY OF WEALTH BUILDING

Let's explore what I call ***"The Golden Trinity"*** of building wealth: **Knowledge**, **Wisdom**, and **Discernment**. These three foundational principles are essential for positioning an individual in the right place, at the right time, and making the right decisions. Learning how to acquire and apply these principles will be the key to long-term financial success. Throughout this book, the importance of practicing the ability to learn, unlearn, and relearn information has been emphasized—a critical skill in an ever-evolving financial landscape. This requires recognizing that there is knowledge an individual may lack and must acquire to adapt and grow.

If an individual was educated in the public school system, they were likely taught how to become a successful employee or laborer. Schools focus on developing specific skill sets designed for the workforce—how to trade time for money—but they rarely teach how money works, how to grow it into wealth, or how to make it work for them. If a person's goal is to break free from the cycle of working 40-50 hours per week, living paycheck to paycheck, and building someone else's wealth, a mindset shift is necessary. Understanding the principles of investing and financial management is crucial.

For those aspiring to become their own boss, learning how to create a successful business—one that provides value through a service, product, or both—is essential. For individuals aiming to become investors, developing the ability to research and identify assets with potential for future growth is critical. They must also learn how to acquire these assets

Choosing a Vehicle:
*Financial knowledge is very important in determining **what** investments, assets, and strategies are right for you.*

Knowing the Season:
*Discernment is necessary to receive confirmation on **when** to take position. Timing is key for any fruitful investment, and God speaks to his children through discernment.*

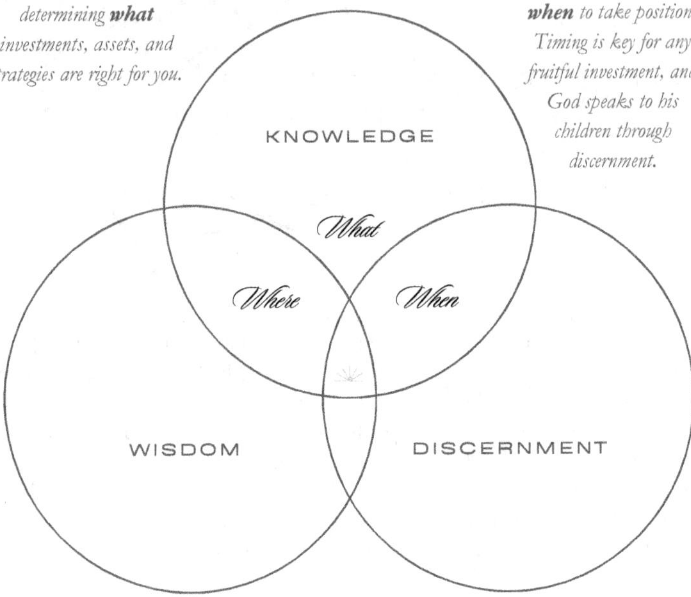

Taking Position:
*Wisdom is utilizing both knowledge and discernment to know what to invest in, when to invest, and **where** to be positioned. Your position involves knowing the location **where** your money should be invested, the type/form of asset, where to safely store your assets and at time the geographical location as well.*

The Golden Trinity:
This is where you want to be, 'The Golden Trinity' of building wealth. To be in the right place, at the right time, and doing the right thing.

and safely store them to protect their financial future.

Step One: Acquiring Knowledge

Knowledge is the accumulation of **information**, **facts**, and **skills** acquired through **education**, **experience**, and **learning**. It represents understanding and awareness of specific subjects or fields, often gained through study, training, research, and hands-on experience.

For example, an individual well-versed in finance understands investment principles, market trends, and financial analysis. This knowledge may come from formal education, independent study, or practical experience. To build wealth, a person must learn the financial principles that the wealthy utilize—what money is, how it works, how to build and grow it, and how to protect it. The financial system today is vastly different from past decades and will continue to evolve, especially as society transitions into new financial technologies and systems.

A lack of knowledge is a significant disadvantage. Without **financial literacy**, individuals may make poor investment choices, fail to protect assets, or miss lucrative opportunities. Knowledge enables a person to choose the right investment vehicles and develop the confidence to navigate financial markets wisely.

Consider driving a car: before taking a driving test, a person undergoes education and practice. On test day, an individual would naturally choose a car they are familiar with, rather than a vehicle with an unfamiliar manual transmission. Investing works the same way. A person must understand the financial vehicles they use—their risks, benefits, and potential for growth.

Money serves as the vehicle that has the potential to transport an individual toward financial goals. It is up to the person to choose the right investment vehicle, understand its features and future potential, and position it for safety and security while earning passive income. Unlike traditional vehicles that depreciate, the assets discussed in this book have significant upside growth potential.

Step Two: Applying Wisdom

Wisdom is the ability to **apply knowledge** effectively. It involves sound judgment, critical thinking, and practical insight. Wisdom allows an individual to make well-reasoned decisions based on logic rather than emotion.

King Solomon, when given the opportunity to ask God for anything, chose wisdom above wealth, power, or long life. This pleased the Lord, and because of his wise request, Solomon was also granted wealth and honor beyond any king before or after him (2 Chronicles 1:7-12). Similarly, an individual should seek wisdom first to guide financial decisions.

Financial wisdom means knowing when to **invest**, when to **hold**, and when to **sell**. It also means **avoiding financial traps**, such as investing in dying industries or volatile markets without proper research. As the world moves into an era of digital assets, blockchain technology, and evolving financial systems, wisdom is more critical than ever.

Step Three: Developing Discernment

Discernment is the ability to make sound decisions by perceiving beyond the surface. It allows an individual to recognize the **right opportunities** at the **right time** and determine whether an **investment**, business move, or financial decision is aligned with long-term goals. Timing is everything in investing. **Knowing when** to **buy**, when to **sell**, and when to **hold** requires more than financial knowledge—it requires discernment. Discernment acts as a compass, guiding individuals through uncertain markets and helping them make spiritually and financially sound choices.

For many, **discernment** comes through **intuition**, spiritual insight, or practical experience. Some individuals experience gut feelings, while others receive **divine guidance** through **prayer**, **dreams**, or **visions**. The key is spending time with God to sharpen the ability to hear from Him. Just as **relationships** require **time**, **trust**, and **communication**, so does developing spiritual discernment.

Applying Knowledge, Wisdom, and Discernment in Wealth Building

To build and sustain wealth, an individual must apply all three elements:

- **Knowledge** helps in understanding financial principles and investment opportunities.
- **Wisdom** enables the application of knowledge effectively, managing risk and making sound financial decisions.
- **Discernment** ensures that a person is positioned correctly in the right investment, at the right time, in the right place.

A failure to properly integrate these three principles can lead to significant financial risk. Consider the following scenarios:

- **Right Place & Right Time, but Wrong Investment:** An individual exchanges foreign currency and becomes a millionaire but fails to move their money into safe assets before the US dollar crash.
- **Right Investment & Right Location, but Wrong Timing:** A person invests in Bitcoin at an all-time high, only for the market to crash before securing profits.
- **Right Investment & Right Timing, but Wrong Location:** An individual stores gold in a bank safety deposit box, only for the bank to fail and seize assets.

Building wealth is not just about **making money**—it's about making the **right choices** at the **right time**. The financial world is changing rapidly, and new opportunities are emerging. By seeking knowledge, applying wisdom, and developing discernment, an individual will be positioned to not only build wealth but also **protect** and **sustain** it.

Whether an individual is investing in precious metals, cryptocurrency, real estate, or stocks, the key question should always be: Am I in the right investment, at the right time, in the right place? Understanding and mastering The Golden Trinity will empower an individual to take control of their financial future and build lasting wealth that aligns with God's purpose for their life.

How God Speaks Through Dreams, Visions, and Prophetic Words

Throughout history, God has spoken to His children in various ways, including **dreams**, **visions**, and **prophetic words**. These divine messages serve as **guidance**, warnings, and revelations to help believers navigate the complexities of life. The Bible is filled with examples of God revealing His plans through supernatural encounters. In Joel 2:28, God declares,

"And it shall come to pass afterward, that I will pour out my Spirit on all flesh; your sons and your daughters ***shall prophesy****, your old men shall* ***dream dreams****, and your young men shall* ***see visions****."* This prophecy is reiterated in the New Testament in Acts 2:17, emphasizing that in the last days, divine communication will become more prominent.

As we move into 2025 and beyond, it will become increasingly important for believers to seek the Lord's instruction in all aspects of life, including financial decisions. Markets are unpredictable, and economic systems are evolving rapidly. However, God is not limited by human knowledge—He knows the beginning from the end and desires to guide His children in making wise choices. Through dreams, visions, and prophetic words, He provides insights on when to enter and exit markets, which assets to invest in, how much to allocate, and the timing of critical events. By actively seeking His voice, believers can position themselves for financial security and divine provision in uncertain times.

Dreams have historically been a means by which God reveals future events and hidden wisdom. In the book of Genesis, Joseph was given prophetic dreams that ultimately led him to prepare for a famine, ensuring not only his survival but also the survival of Egypt and his family. Similarly, God can reveal financial shifts, economic downturns, and strategic investment opportunities to those who are listening. Visions, which are supernatural insights given while awake, allow believers to receive clear direction and understanding regarding what steps to take in their financial and spiritual lives.

Prophetic words—whether received personally or through trusted prophetic voices—can confirm what God is speaking. The Bible instructs believers to test every prophecy (1 Thessalonians 5:20-21) and align it with Scripture to ensure its authenticity. When an individual receives a prophetic word about financial decisions, it should be weighed against biblical principles, prayer, and discernment. Seeking wise counsel from spiritually mature believers is also crucial in understanding the application of these divine messages.

As the world enters a time of financial shifts, geopolitical changes, and technological advancements, God will continue to speak to His people, providing wisdom, strategy, and supernatural insight. Those who remain attuned to His voice, obedient to His leading, and diligent in their financial stewardship will be positioned to thrive rather than merely survive. The key is to cultivate a lifestyle of prayer, fasting, and spiritual sensitivity, allowing the Holy Spirit to illuminate the path forward in both personal and financial matters.

The Importance of Like-Minded Friendships in Spiritual Growth

Having a friend who is **like-minded** and shares similar spiritual giftings is invaluable in the journey of faith. Such friendships create a **strong spiritual support** system, fostering mutual encouragement, accountability, and **confirmation** of **God's direction**. These relationships are more than just companionship; they are a God-ordained partnership that helps individuals navigate life's challenges with faith and discernment.

When two individuals are aligned in their faith and sensitivity to the Holy Spirit, they can discern, interpret, and validate divine messages together, ensuring clarity and wisdom in decision-making. This alignment strengthens their ability to hear from God accurately, offering reassurance in moments of doubt and uncertainty.

The Lord often uses others to confirm His instructions, whether through dreams, visions, or direct prophetic words. For example, a believer may receive a prophetic word about a major life decision but remain unsure of how to proceed. A spiritually like-minded friend might receive a similar revelation through a dream or word from God, providing much-needed confirmation and peace. This has been evident in my own life, where God has used my close friend, Heather, to reinforce the revelations and instructions He has given me directly. At times, I have received dreams or visions about significant financial decisions, and without me mentioning them, Heather has later shared a similar message from the Lord, confirming the steps I needed to take.

Having a trusted friend who understands the spiritual realm and operates in similar giftings allows for deeper discussions, strengthened faith, and a heightened awareness of God's voice. These relationships foster an environment where believers can share insights, pray together, and encourage one another in their walk with God. In seasons of uncertainty, such a friendship serves as a beacon of wisdom and reassurance, reminding believers that they are not alone in their spiritual journey.

These friendships can also serve as **spiritual iron sharpening iron** (Proverbs 27:17). For example, if one friend begins to drift away from spiritual disciplines, the other can provide loving accountability, encouraging them to stay in prayer, study the Word, and seek God's guidance. Additionally, when facing spiritual attacks, like-minded friends can stand in agreement, intercede, and offer scriptural encouragement, reinforcing faith and perseverance.

In the Bible, we see many examples of divinely orchestrated friendships that contributed to fulfilling God's purposes. **Jonathan** and **David** had a **friendship** built on **spiritual alignment** and **loyalty**, providing David with much-needed encouragement during times of trial (1 Samuel 18:1-4). Similarly, Moses had Aaron and Hur to support him in battle by holding up his arms when he grew weary, leading to victory for Israel (Exodus 17:12).

As we approach 2025 and beyond, the importance of these friendships will only grow. The spiritual and financial landscape is rapidly evolving, and having spiritually aligned friends who can discern the times and provide wise counsel will be crucial. Whether navigating economic shifts, prophetic insights, or personal growth, these friendships will serve as a divine anchor, keeping believers firmly rooted in their faith and aligned with God's plan.

For instance, the Lord has used my friendship with Heather North to affirm the messages and guidance provided to me by the Lord and some of which is shared below. Many of these words, dreams, and visions were detailed on my YouTube channel, Digital Dollars Now, before events in the cryptocurrency market unfolded. To see all posts on my prophetic dreams please visit this channel. Here below are just some of the key highlights to a few prophetic words and dreams:

Heather received a word from The Lord saying, "*April 15th*", (which is also Tax Day), "*something is going to happen that will impact taxes*". (It is unclear if it will happen in 2025 or further in the future)

I personally received a dream on 11/18/2024 about taxes, and in that dream, I was telling a work colleague, "*You should invest in Crypto, now is the time!"* The conversation shifted to taxes, and I said, "*Trump is going to abolish income tax & set a straight sales tax policy but before he does, he will abolish tax on crypto gains.*"

On January 19th, 2025, during a joint prayer session with Heather, we received the following: Heather heard, "*Sell now, opportunities to buy later.*" Before hearing this, she saw the Shiba dog (which we understood as a reference to sell our holdings for Shiba Inu). Then the Lord reminded Heather about her earlier vision, that everything (Cryptocurrency) dropped, and everything fell, like it flatlined. And that The Lord told her while she was taking a shower "*to take her gains now, opportunity to buy later.*" Then The Lord said, "*volatile times ahead not only in the markets (both stocks and crypto), but with the national security of the USA.*"

Heather had a vision that showed a lot of unexpected destruction that impacted the whole USA. The Lord specifically showed her the Washington Monument, and that something would happen to it. During that same vision The Lord showed her Wallstreet going down and how people on Wallstreet were freaking out because it was an unexpected thing.

The Lord spoke to Heather saying, "*you will not miss this! This is Divine! Step where I am calling you to step and do not do it out of fear - know that I am with you. And if you make a mistake and if you make a wrong decision... I will help you correct it. You will not miss it.*"

We both continued to pray, asking for confirmation that we should sell both our XRP and Shiba Inu holdings. It was at this point that The Lord said to Heather, "*I tell you when there is a bull run about to happen, and you prepare for it. But when I tell you there is about to be a crash happening, then you're hesitant.*" He wanted us to see that multiplication is easier to receive than loss—after this prayer session both Heather and I sold all of our holdings in both XRP and Shiba Inu, setting buy limit orders for ranges we had felt lead to.

Side Note: The below is a timeline of price points that preceded this prayer session and that took place exactly 2 weeks after this word was given. The Lord had us pull out of the market right before the dump of these two cryptocurrencies.

- Jan 15, 2025 – XRP hits $3.40
- Jan 17, 2025 – Shiba Inu hits $0.000025
- Feb 2, 2025 – XRP crashes to $1.78 and Shiba crashes to $0.000012

The Lord reminded Heather of a Poem she had received years earlier, and said hold onto this knowledge:

April showers brings **May** Flowers,
June sight brings **July's** fright,
August storm brings full form,
September's plunder will bless **October's** number's

On 1/31/2025, the Lord told Heather, "*I did not call everyone out of the market, but I want you all-in for the crash and you need liquidity. That is your position.*" He also said, "*I am about to level the playing field.*" He also referenced 7 mountains and spoke: "*cryptocurrency, stocks, corporations, debt, politics, and Hollywood.*" (Each of which connects back to the 7 Mountains)

He showed Heather the exposure of corruption would lead into the economic collapse, saying "*The money they used to buy assets is corrupt money, dirty deals.*" The Lord continued and said, "*Corrupt money will not stand in the economy He is establishing.*" He then said, "*Remember your dream, 2025 is the year of the wealth transfer, IT IS THE YEAR TO INVEST.*" The Lord said, "*In your dream that was My Angel Proclaiming it to the political arena. That is what will happen. They will level the playing field.*"

The Lord spoke to Heather saying, "*There will be executions. The severity of the crimes will call for execution. The truth behind the darkness is so vile, and that 'Heather' only knows the surface.*" She felt like she had a good idea of how bad things are, but it doesn't sound like it. He added, "*Infiltration of every arena. I gave them a chance to turn (to Jesus), and they refused... There is going to be many suicides once the dominos start falling. This will be unprecedented, like nothing seen before. This is My time to clean house. Just like the time of Noah, Sodom, and Gomorrah. Remember the word about Noah and the door shutting (given last fall)? I gave sufficient grace.*"

On 11/26/2024 during a prayer session with The Lord, He given me a word that aligns with Heathers above. He said, *"Time of my anointed."* I saw a desert beetle, like a scarab that was scurrying in the dark between a rock and sand. It was trying to hide underground because it was being hunted. I heard, *"Exposure! It is found."* Then I saw a long wooden scepter squishing the beetle. *"They can't hide much longer from their wicked deeds. Their time is almost finished. The door is closing."* Then I saw a golden door in heaven and the Lord was shutting it. There were all kinds of insects scurrying across the floor and flying through the air trying to get through the door before it closed, and it was too late. *"The Doors I shut no man can open. The Doors I open no man can shut. Exposure!"*

Then I saw the late Queen Elizabeth and *'The Biden'*. Then I saw a plastic face mask hanging in someone's hand, they are holding it out as if to say, *"see ... look at this"*. Then I saw Scooby doo (the cartoon) unmasking the villain. Then the Lord spoke, *"Nothing is as it appears. The veil of deception is being lifted. This will be really hard for many. Even you will be shocked by some of what you will see. Prepare to be amazed. Technology is more advanced than you think. People will have to shut down, because they cannot take it."* I understood this as cognitive dissonance. That they will know the truth but continue to believe the lie. Then I saw in the spirit a noose hanging and several others being hung for executions. Then I saw people being lined up and taken up on a gallows platform in pairs of six to be hung. The line from the gallows was very long, and the criminals had their hands tied behind their back. The gallows were out in the open, somewhere in an open plain, kind of a flat area (and it reminded me of Texas).

A ways off from the gallows was a pile of bodies of those who had been executed already. I was then showed an image of hands, and there was blood on the hands. I knew in the spirit that this was the innocent blood that these criminals had shed (and that they were now being judged for their crimes). The Lord then showed me the image of children and I saw tears streaming down their faces. It was at this point that I felt the weight of this word being really heavy on my spirit, and I felt really sad. I also felt sick like I wanted to throw up.

Then I heard, *"More must be done. The enemy will not escape the wrath of God. They will call out wanting the rocks to fall on them. They are hiding underground. They are everywhere, like vermin. They will not escape. I need my people, my children, to step up. They will be needed during this hour."*

The Lord spoke to Heather about the stone that President Trump has (a metaphor for the stone that King David used to kill Goliath), "*Trump does not yet realize the full magnitude of this* **stone**. *But he will receive tangible proof very soon and he will put the agencies in order. There are enemies in his camp, and he is aware of it. Putin will partner with Trump, there will be a world stage set that will take out every leader and player that is a part of these heinous crimes. That will be* **GESARA**. *There will be a sifting of documents. This is not just the U.S.; this will have a global impact. They will PACT together to restore humanity. That is why it is vital the U.S. pulls out of NATO, WHO, Green Pact deal, and all of the others because they are all guilty of crimes against humanity. You can see there is a much bigger picture. When you think about crypto, they will still have their shares and the opportunity to buy more. Some I have called out of the market to maximize their holdings. Remember the East to the West. This is not just a flash crash this is an economic reset globally. All debt will be cancelled. Personally, and globally. Then it will be time to rebuild the world.*" Then The Lord showed her that the amount of money held by the people that are going to be exposed for dirty money will be enough to collapse the markets.

On 12/09/2024, I had an XRP dream where I saw a trading graph for XRP, the image was black, and the trading looked to be volatile. I could sense that XPR wanted to climb upwards, but it was hitting resistance. Then all of a sudden, the right half of the chart went white (completely blank) and I heard the following words, "*It is coming! The Reset is coming soon! Financial Reset!*"

In 2022, I had a dream that XRP had a run from around $10 to $15 and then crashed below $10. It happened so quickly that there was not time to react, move my XRP onto the exchange or sell it. At that time, I did not have my XRP on the exchange or sell limit orders set.

On 12/13/2024, I had a dream of a gold coin, I knew it was Shiba Inu, and it had a Shiba dog on the face of the coin. Then the dog began to howl really loud, and I heard the Lord say, *"Bull. Spike. Crash."* This was repeated three times.

It is worth noting that Heather has seen visions of two spikes for Shiba Inu, the first to $1 and a second to around $13.

During a combined prayer session on 2/14/2025, the Lord gave the below words. I am adding this information here not to instill fear but to be prayed on and prepared for.

"Many deaths coming, people getting boils on their skin." (perhaps due to nuclear radiation poisoning) "Invisible missiles, Kim Jong Un, North Korea." Saw something exploding in the air over the middle of the United States, likely what North Korea will set off (possible EMP & or nuclear bomb). Heard, *"Heart Attacks."* (People dropping dead because their heart stops, this could be because of EMF exposure or the EMP bomb) The Lord said, *"Detox now, detox from heavy metals and the vaccines. Watch the skies. Watch the waters. Enemy close!"* He also told me in a separate dream to stop drinking coke (soda). This was important.

"The Harlot (spoken of in Revelation) = Free-Masons. Under the Harlot is many churches, many denominations that all feed into this Beast System. What is under these churches? A place of worship and sacrifice (not of Me). The Harlot will burn. The Vatican will burn. The 4 winds of change will align with the 7 mountains, much to be unpacked in this hour. Wars and rumors of war. All 7 mountains will fall, they will be laid bare for all eyes to see. There is no more time left, the door is closed! The wicked will be taken out, many arrested, many captured, (there may be casualties and deaths). The masks will be taken off. Some people are not who they pretend to be (Actors/people playing a part)."

Then I heard in the spirit, *"Off with their heads!"* This is from Alice in Wonderland, the Queen of Hearts said this. Then I heard, *"Mad Hatter."* Note, the Mad Hatter was beheaded by the Queen of Hearts. *"Many stories convey truth, you will see, it will shock many. Be mindful of your surroundings."*

On 2/16/2025 I had a dream and then when I woke up The Lord continued to provide more information:

In my dream I was watching a news broadcast on a mounted TV on the wall, I knew that I was in a foreign country, because the news was in another language, I recognized this as Dutch. I heard *"Copenhagen"*, which is in Denmark. Then I heard, *"Klaus Schwab"*, he is German, I knew that's important but not sure why. There were two women with me that I did not know. They were flipping through a notebook and discussing what index funds they wanted to invest in, the notebook had drawings that one of the women drew from the day before. Then on the TV, it was discussing index funds and stocks, it showed the names of many index funds, but I only recognized that they were also talking about Klaus Schwab. Then the TV screen changed to show the trading for the past day, I saw the date August 2nd. It was written as 8/2. No year, but I felt like it was this year 2025. On 8/2 all of the index funds on the screen took a dive, the markets were crashing fast in the red and there was shock and chaos going on. Klaus Schwab was among them, I saw his name written, like it was an Index fund. I was trying to take a picture of the screen but when I did the camera on my phone turned the TV screen orange and red, distorting the image so that it was unclear. I was unable to take the picture on my phone.

The two women that were with me in the room, were sitting at a desk in front of an old PC computer, and one of the women said, "*Don't worry, I can print the graph for you.*" She knew I wanted to capture what was happening. Then I asked, "*Didn't we talk yesterday about the markets crashing?*" I started to look back through my journal, and the ladies start looking through theirs. But their notebook did not have words in it, they had drawings. The lady's notebook of drawings was in colored pencil. There was a woman drawn side facing, she was young, beautiful and brunette. (I think the drawing of the woman was the wife of the President of Ukraine, Zelenskyy) Then there was a drawing of 5 men standing in a V-shape alignment, the man in front looked like the President of Ukraine, Zelenskyy. Then there was a drawing of the names of all the index funds and stocks that were on the tv screen, but it did not show the chart crashing downward or the date like the TV. So, I asked her to go ahead and print from the computer what I was seeing on the tv, so that I could share this with people. The drawings were professional and beautiful.

After I woke up from this dream I heard, "*Don't buy the index funds, buy the stocks when they crash. Many retirement accounts are going to be affected when the markets crash because they invest in indexes and not the direct stocks. It's going to make you dizzy, the storm that's coming.*" Then I saw myself sitting in a chair being spun around really fast. The scene shifted and was sitting in front of the old computer in my dream, and on the screen is a graph (I knew it was crypto, possibly bitcoin) and it was crashing sharply downward, and I heard, "*Plunder! Stocks will crash first followed by the crypto market. Get your baskets ready.*" Then I saw, large loafs of bread falling from the sky, and I was trying to catch the bread in a wooden basket as it fell. These were really big loaves of bread, like one loaf of bread filled the entire basket. Then I heard *"Manna" and "He's providing provision."*

I then heard, *"Klaus Schwab is going down. He will be made low. His sins laid bare for all to see."* I saw the late Queen Elizabeth, I have seen her before in previous words. I sensed there is something hidden in the British Monarchy. I saw King Charles III. He's going to pass away. Prince William will become king (I heard '*this year*'). I had to look this up because honestly thought Prince William was already king, but I guess he's next in line.

I heard, *"Hollywood will be judged this year."* I saw the P. Diddy trial and heard *"All roads lead to Rome"*, then I saw the Vatican. I saw Robin Williams as Peter PAN (in the movie '*Hook*'). Not sure what this means but I heard *"Kids being stolen in the night. Wickedness in plain sight, Hollywood mocks the wicked deeds that they do and puts them in movies. Be ready, it comes quickly.*" I saw a waterfall of rushing water over Rocky cliffs. It looks like Niagara Falls. "*There is no holding back these waters. It will wash away everything in its path.*"

In our spiritual journey, like-minded friendships play a crucial role in fostering growth, encouragement, and accountability. Surrounding ourselves with those who share our faith and values strengthens our walk with God, providing wisdom, support, and confirmation of His guidance in our lives. These relationships help us stay grounded in truth, uplift us during challenges, and inspire us to pursue our divine purpose. As iron sharpens iron, so do these friendships refine and strengthen our faith, reminding us that we are never alone in our pursuit of spiritual growth.

CHAPTER 14

2025 IS THE YEAR OF THE WEALTH TRANSFER—IT IS THE YEAR TO INVEST

The Lord recently reminded my friend Heather North of a poem that He had given her several years ago. I believe this poem is relevant to this year and goes along with the other word she was given where He told her, "***2025 is the year of The Wealth Transfer—It is the Year to Invest.***"

April showers bring **May** flowers,
June sight brings **July** fright,
August storm brings full form,
September's plunder will bless **October's** numbers

I received a word from the Lord on 2/10/2025 confirming this, it is listed here below:

"Be diligent. Follow my instructions. Don't be discouraged, all things work together for good for those who love me. Be consciously aware of your actions and how this effects your surroundings.

Change is coming swiftly, and many will be caught unprepared because they are focusing on the world stage of distractions, rather than what I am doing in this hour. I have called many too fast and pray, and to listen for my divine instructions but they are unable to hear me because their ears are blocked, and heart are not in the right place.

They are foolish and they will be a part of those that mourn when the blessings come. I have called you to sell in this hour for a reason, to position you so you can buy when the crash happens. Have faith in the instructions that have been given to you.

You have seen the flood waters come and washing over these crypto assets eroding their profit. You are now in the lull, but more water is coming. (Reminded me of my flood dream) *These waters will be more violent and massive, washing over the market with violent purpose and washing it clean. A cleansing is coming, a financial reset.*

Stay in position to fill your baskets. More instructions are coming when it is time. Be calm, and do not fear what you are about to see.

The stage is set, the dominoes are lined up, what is about to happen will cause panic in the markets. The wicked will flee, they will pull what liquidity they can to protect themselves. This is being guided by my divine hand. This will be the ***first plunge****, the first opportunity for my children to plunder.*

But a second is coming, much greater than the first. You must be vigilant and listen for my instructions. The ***second plunge*** *will also be caused by* ***panic*** *from* ***world events*** *but also by economic failures.*

Do not fear this fall in the fall, it is necessary to build something new. It is part of the financial reset. The financial reset is not just one event, it is a ***cascade progression*** *of* ***events*** *over the next* ***ten months****.*

It is all happening in 2025, the year of The Great Wealth Transfer, this is the year to plunder the land, the year to invest and take profits. Multiplying what I have given you. ***Do not bury your talents in the ground*** *during this season, be diligent and active, follow my instructions and you will be blessed.*

Be happy and joyful for you are mine, and I am yours. The best is yet to come. Your sorrows will be turned to joy. My blessings are for those who love me, who listen to my words and act accordingly.

Keep your eyes and heart fixed on me, my daughter. You are precious in my sight."

A Prophetic Perspective on The Timeline of The Great Wealth Transfer:

I initially believed that the wealth transfer would begin in 2025, marked by significant price surges in prophetic coins like Shiba Inu and XRP. These gains, I anticipated, would generate substantial profits, serving as seed money for further market events throughout the year. While we did witness a notable increase in XRP, which reached a new all-time high of $3.40 on January 15th, Shiba Inu also experienced a run-up in November and December of 2024, peaking at $0.000033. Admittedly, I had hoped Shiba Inu's surge would reach somewhere between $0.10 and $1.00. However, on January 19th, the Lord provided clear instructions to exit the market, warning of an impending downturn and signaling that there would be opportunities to buy back into the market at a later date.

Stage 1: First Plunge

It has become increasingly clear, through both prophetic words from the Lord and vivid dreams, that a significant financial reset is on the horizon. This reset is expected to bring a sharp downturn in the cryptocurrency market, and potentially even the stock market, leading to a steep decline in the prices of key assets. However, for those who have heeded God's guidance, this downturn will not be a cause for fear, but rather an opportunity—an appointed time to multiply their crypto holdings by buying in at deeply discounted prices. This event will serve as both a test of faith and a moment of divine positioning for those who have been listening to His instructions.

One particular dream I received painted a striking picture of what is to come. In this dream, a flood engulfed the top of a mountain, unfolding in two distinct stages. The **first wave** of flooding surged through a church, causing extensive damage and sweeping away many people who had been positioned inside. I believe the mountain symbolized the cryptocurrency market, while the church represented specific key assets that both myself and others have been led to invest in. The destruction within the church suggests that many will be unprepared for the volatility, and as a result, they may suffer great financial losses or be forced out of the market entirely.

The second wave, however, was even more devastating. This massive surge completely obliterated the church, washing everything away in what appeared to be a cleansing process. This could signify a deeper purging within the financial system—a dismantling of corrupt structures, a reset of market dynamics, or even the removal of those who have built their financial foundations on unstable ground. It also serves as a spiritual metaphor, reinforcing the idea that only those who are firmly anchored in God's direction will withstand the coming storm and be positioned for restoration and increase when the floodwaters recede.

It is not yet clear if this first plunge will involve a staged downturn over time, a flash crash or a combination of both. Therefore, I would suggest being prepared with buy limit orders set on the exchange(s). As this financial shift approaches, it is crucial to remain vigilant, seeking wisdom and discernment from the Lord. Those who are faithful stewards of the resources entrusted to them will find themselves strategically placed for multiplication and influence in the new financial era that follows.

Key Assets to consider acquiring during this first plunge:

- Shiba Inu (SHIB)
- Ripple (XRP)
- Bitcoin (BTC)
- Ethereum (ETH)
- Stellar Lumens (XLM)
- Wrapped Ether (WETH)
- Pepe (PEPE)
- Solana (SOL)
- Cardano (ADA)
- Flare (FLR)
- XDC Network (XDC)
- Electroneum (ETN)
- Terra Luna Classic (LUNC - Now LUNA)
- Hedera Hashgraph (HBAR)

It is possible that this plunge could occur at any point leading up to April. The poem above specially refers to April showers which could symbolize cleansing, and it is well known that often times floods occur during rain showers. And The Lord has called out the date of April 15th, as a date of importance. Therefore, time will tell how these events will unfold.

Stage 2: First Bull & Spike

The first line of the above poem and well-known saying, "***April's** showers* *brings **May's** flowers*", carries deep symbolic meaning, representing growth, renewal, and the fulfillment of what has been sown. Just as the first blossoms on a fruit tree signal the beginning of the process that ultimately leads to a bountiful harvest, so too does this imagery reflect the financial and spiritual cycles we are about to witness. The flowers must first bloom and be pollinated before they can bear fruit, much like the market's initial surges that will later lead to the harvesting of profits. Those who have positioned themselves wisely and followed divine instruction will be able to reap the rewards of this season of financial transformation.

The Lord has also impressed upon me the importance of reviewing the market trends of Bitcoin in 2021, as they hold prophetic insight into what we may witness in 2025. Looking back, Bitcoin experienced a powerful bull run that began in December 2020, reaching its first peak on April 13, 2021, at an all-time high of approximately $64,000. This was followed by a sharp decline before another surge occurred between October 19 and November 28, 2021, when Bitcoin again reached around $64,000, only to be followed by another significant downturn leading into a prolonged bear market.

Now, in December 2024, we have observed Bitcoin following a similar pattern, trending upward and recently reaching a new all-time high of $109,000. While it remains uncertain whether this is the peak of Bitcoin's first major rally, the historical pattern suggests the strong possibility of two distinct bull run spikes occurring in 2025—just as in 2021. This insight serves as a guide for those navigating the markets, allowing them to anticipate key turning points and make strategic financial decisions in alignment with God's timing. By paying attention to these patterns and seeking wisdom, those who are led by the Lord can be prepared to maximize the opportunities that arise during this unfolding financial cycle.

Consider Utilizing Profits to Invest in Other Key Assets:

- Gold and Silver (and other precious metals such as Copper)
- Foreign Currencies (Iraqi Dinar, Vietnamese Dong, Uganda Shilling)
- Land (farmland)
- Real Estate and Development projects

In conclusion, while recognizing patterns and market trends provides valuable insight, the true key to success lies in exercising wisdom, discernment, and obedience to the Lord's instructions. As the **second-stage bull** run unfolds, it will be crucial to take profits at the right time, ensuring that the resources gained can be effectively stewarded for future opportunities and Kingdom purposes. Timing will be everything, and those who remain attuned to God's guidance will be best positioned to navigate this season with clarity and confidence. By trusting in His direction rather than solely relying on market analysis, investors can move with divine precision, securing both financial increase and spiritual alignment in this unfolding wealth transfer.

Stage 3: Volatility—June & July

June Sight—The Coming Exposure and Market Shifts:

This period is likely to be marked by extreme volatility in the financial markets, presenting both challenges and opportunities. For those with knowledge of trading and the discernment to navigate these fluctuations, it may serve as a pivotal moment to multiply assets. However, wisdom and divine guidance will be essential, as sudden shifts could redefine entire economic sectors overnight.

The Lord has spoken of leveling the playing field across the Seven Mountains—Cryptocurrency, Fiat Currencies, Stocks, Corporations, Debt, Politics, and Hollywood—and June Sight appears to be the moment when exposure begins to unravel the hidden corruption within these spheres. It is my belief that June will act as a trigger month, where key dominoes begin to fall, setting off a chain reaction that will impact all seven mountains. Hidden financial manipulation, unethical corporate dealings, political deception, and the deep entanglement of corrupt money across these sectors will begin to come to light.

As exposure intensifies, the old financial system—built on deception and greed—will begin to crumble, making way for the new economy the Lord is establishing. "*Corrupt money will not stand in the economy The Lord is establishing.*" The shifts we see in June will not be minor; they will be groundbreaking, revealing how deeply intertwined these mountains have been in the preservation of power and control.

Those who are prepared will not only witness history unfold but will also be positioned to take part in the righteous restructuring that follows.

Crimes Against Humanity—A Global Reckoning:

President Donald Trump has recently been given critical documents—files that hold far greater significance than he may yet realize. These documents, referred to in a prophetic word given to Heather by the Lord as "*the **Stone***"—symbolic of the very stone David used to defeat Goliath—carry the potential to expose unprecedented levels of corruption and crimes against humanity.

In this revelation, the Lord also stated, "*President Trump will receive tangible proof very soon, and he will put the agencies in order. There will be a sifting of documents. This is not just the U.S.; this is a global impact. They will PACT together to restore humanity. That is why it is vital the U.S. pulls out of NATO, WHO, Green Pact deals, and all of the others because they are all guilty of crimes against humanity.*"

The magnitude of this coming exposure will be staggering, affecting not only the United States but the entire world. What has been concealed within global institutions—hidden under the guise of political alliances, humanitarian efforts, and environmental initiatives—will be laid bare. Corruption, deception, and unspeakable crimes that have been perpetrated under the cover of these powerful organizations will be exposed, leading to a reckoning unlike anything seen before.

The Lord has personally revealed to me that even I will be shocked by the depth of this depravity. The unveiling of these crimes will be so disturbing that many will struggle to accept the truth. Those who have orchestrated and enabled these atrocities will not escape justice. Arrests will be made, and judgments will be carried out. However, tragically, some of those implicated will choose to take their own lives rather than face the consequences of their actions. The scale of this unfolding event will be unprecedented—a moment in history that will reshape the world's understanding of power, corruption, and divine justice.

This is a pivotal time, one that will demand strength, discernment, and unwavering faith. As these revelations come to light, the nations will be forced to choose between truth and deception, justice and complicity. The Lord is bringing forth a season of cleansing, and those who stand for righteousness will witness the greatest exposure of evil in modern history.

Additionally, the trial of Sean Combs (P. Diddy) is scheduled to begin in May 2025, and while it is highly likely that the proceedings will take place behind closed doors—much like the Jeffrey Epstein case—the magnitude of the allegations suggests that complete secrecy may not be possible. Given the nature of the crimes reportedly linked to these events, the truth may eventually surface despite efforts to suppress it.

This case is not just about one individual but potentially exposes a vast network involving high-profile figures, including celebrities, business moguls, and influential politicians on a global scale. The connections and implications run deep, touching multiple industries and power structures. While mainstream narratives may attempt to downplay or control the public perception of this trial, the sheer weight of the evidence and the involvement of multiple key players may make it impossible to fully conceal. The world has witnessed similar scandals in the past, where hidden truths were eventually brought to light despite efforts to suppress them. This trial could serve as a pivotal moment, revealing the extent of corruption and exploitation within elite circles. The question remains: how much will be revealed to the public, and how will society respond when confronted with these disturbing realities?

Brad Garlinghouse and Gary Gensler—"*Black Ties*":

In the coming months, we may witness revelations that link Brad Garlinghouse, CEO of Ripple, and Gary Gensler, Chair of the SEC, in a potential collusion—what some might call a "*Black Ties*" connection. While this is not a "*Thus says the Lord*" prophecy, but rather my personal opinion based on an informed observation. There are however, strong indications that the long-standing SEC lawsuit against XRP has strategically suppressed its price under the guise of regulatory uncertainty. This legal battle has lingered for years, effectively stalling retail and institutional confidence in XRP's market potential.

Yet, despite this suppression, Ripple's XRP network has continued to experience massive growth, making significant strides in global financial adoption. The recent launch of their stablecoin, RLUSD, is just one example of their ongoing expansion. XRP has now been integrated into financial systems across all seven continents, solidifying its global presence. Japan, in particular, stands out as a key adopter, with projections suggesting that by 2025, nearly 80% of its banks will utilize XRP for cross-border transactions. Beyond Japan, financial institutions in major economies—including the United States, Canada, India, Brazil, China, the United Arab Emirates, the United Kingdom, Australia, Sweden, and Thailand—have also partnered with Ripple, recognizing the efficiency and scalability of its blockchain network.

With such widespread institutional adoption and a growing ecosystem of financial integrations, the question remains: why has XRP's price remained artificially low, failing to break the $5 threshold? Given its utility, adoption rate, and potential to revolutionize global financial transactions, one would expect its value to be far higher. This ongoing price suppression raises serious questions about the true motives behind the SEC's actions and whether certain high-profile figures, including Gensler, have played a role in delaying XRP's full market potential. If these connections are indeed exposed, it could mark a turning point—not only for XRP but for the entire cryptocurrency industry—revealing deeper layers of manipulation within regulatory agencies and financial markets.

Elon Musk's Forensic Team—Unmasking Corruption and Government Waste:

Elon Musk and his forensic investigative team have uncovered shocking levels of financial misconduct within the federal system, revealing a staggering accumulation of wealth among government workers earning moderate salaries. The findings suggest that individuals in bureaucratic positions—who should have limited earning potential—have somehow amassed millions of dollars, raising serious questions about bribery, money laundering, and embezzlement within government agencies. Even more astonishing is the discovery that Social Security payments are still being issued to recipients who, on paper, are over 150 years old—an undeniable indication of widespread fraud and systemic exploitation of taxpayer funds.

These revelations expose not only financial mismanagement but also the deeply rooted corruption that has allowed government officials and fraudulent entities to siphon vast amounts of money unchecked. Musk's team has further identified a massive amount of wasteful spending across multiple government sectors, where funds meant for public welfare and infrastructure have been funneled into unaccountable programs, shell companies, and questionable foreign transactions. This level of exposure could serve as a catalyst for long-overdue financial accountability, potentially leading to mass investigations, policy reforms, and the restructuring of agencies that have long operated without true oversight. However, with such high stakes, the resistance to these revelations will likely be fierce, as those benefiting from this corruption will seek to silence and discredit those bringing the truth to light. What unfolds next may be pivotal in determining whether the public finally demands full transparency and whether justice will be served for the years of financial deception that have burdened the economy and working-class citizens.

July's Fright—A Dark Plot Unfolding:

The term "***July's Fright***" likely foreshadows a period of terror and unrest, potentially brought on by coordinated attacks from sleeper cells that have been infiltrating America's borders unchecked over the past four years. The Lord has revealed that one of the targets may be the Washington Monument, where a significant attack could result in substantial damage—an act designed not only to create chaos but to strike at the heart of the nation's identity and history. If this revelation is accurate, it is imperative that we cover this in fervent prayer, asking for divine intervention to thwart these plots before they come to fruition.

Beyond this specific attack, there are likely other violent operations being planned, intended to serve as distractions—diverting attention away from the broader exposure of corruption and financial reckoning that is unfolding. These events will be orchestrated to instill panic, weaken national morale, and justify further governmental overreach. However, as believers, we must stand in faith, praying for protection, wisdom, and the exposure of these plots before they can be carried out. While July's Fright may represent a period of shaking, it is also an opportunity for intercession, where the power of prayer can dismantle the plans of the enemy and bring divine protection over the land. Now more than ever, vigilance and spiritual discernment will be critical as we navigate these turbulent times.

Stage 4: Second Plunge

August Storm—The Coming Justice:

The term "***August Storm***" carries a prophetic weight, likely symbolizing the coming wave of **mass arrests** and judgment for the **crimes** that have been committed in secret for far too long. Much like a powerful storm that arrives suddenly, cleansing the land and washing away **corruption**, this event will serve as a divine reckoning—a moment where long-hidden injustices are brought to light and the guilty are held accountable. The intensity of this storm suggests that the exposure and subsequent arrests will not be isolated incidents but a widespread, coordinated effort to dismantle deeply embedded systems of evil. As with any great upheaval, there will be resistance, chaos, and uncertainty, but ultimately, this storm will be one of justice and restoration. For those who have been awaiting this moment, August Storm is not a sign of fear, but of long-overdue vindication—a turning point where the scales of justice begin to tip in favor of truth and justice. The world will not emerge unchanged; this storm will alter the course of history, shaking corrupt institutions and paving the way for a new era of righteousness, accountability, and divine order.

Dirty Money—The Collapse Trigger:

In a prophetic word given to Heather by the Lord, He revealed, "*The amount of money held by the people that are going to be exposed for **dirty money** (and **crimes against humanity**) will be enough to **collapse the markets**.*" This statement carries profound implications—not just for financial markets, but for the global power structure as we know it.

It is highly likely that when arrests begin and **large-scale asset seizures** take place, the **liquidation** of these ill-gotten funds will **trigger an economic collapse**. Many of the individuals and organizations implicated in these crimes have amassed vast fortunes—wealth accumulated through corruption, exploitation, and manipulation. Once these assets are confiscated and removed from circulation, the ripple effect on financial institutions, hedge funds, and corporate empires could be catastrophic. Even before these major events occur, we could see people liquidating assets in an attempt to run and hide from persecution.

What remains uncertain is how long this liquidation process will take. Will it unfold rapidly, creating an immediate market shock, or will it be a slow and systematic unraveling that leads to a prolonged downturn? Regardless of the timeline, I strongly believe that this financial reset and the resulting market collapse will coincide with the **second purge**, which is discussed further below.

This event will mark a turning point in the global financial system—an unavoidable reckoning where the structures built on deception and greed will come crashing down. While the immediate effects will be unsettling, this reset will also pave the way for a new, more transparent financial order. Those who are prepared, both spiritually and strategically, will have the opportunity to navigate this transition and be positioned for the rebuilding that follows. This will not just be an **economic collapse**; it will be the beginning of a divinely orchestrated **transfer of wealth**—one that shifts financial power away from the corrupt and into the hands of those who are aligned with **God's purposes**.

September's Plunder—The Transfer of Wealth:

The term "***September's Plunder***" likely signifies the aftermath of a financial collapse—a time when the markets, having crashed under the weight of **judgment** and **exposure**, will present unprecedented opportunities for God's people to acquire assets at drastically reduced prices. This will not be an ordinary **economic downturn**, but a divinely orchestrated transfer of wealth, where those who have followed God's wisdom and prepared in advance will be positioned to reclaim what was once held by corrupt institutions and individuals.

The collapse of cryptocurrency markets, stock markets, and other key sectors will shake the foundations of global finance, yet for those who have been listening and waiting, this will be a season of divine restoration. Just as the Israelites plundered Egypt after generations of oppression (Exodus 12:35-36), September's Plunder will be a time when the righteous step into ownership, acquiring land, businesses, technologies, and financial assets that were once monopolized by the elite. This will not be a moment of greed, but of stewardship—where God's people will be entrusted with resources to establish His **Kingdom economy**, ensuring that wealth is used for righteous purposes, to uplift communities, and to fund the next great move of God. Those who recognize this moment will step into the greatest financial repositioning of our time, fulfilling biblical prophecy that "*the wealth of the wicked is stored up for the righteous*" (Proverbs 13:22).

Key Assets to consider acquiring during the second plunge:

All **ISO 20022 compliant tokens** - ISO 20022 is a global standard for financial messaging that aims to harmonize data exchange between financial institutions, enhancing **interoperability** and **efficiency**. Several cryptocurrencies have aligned themselves with this standard to facilitate better integration with traditional financial systems.

Notable ISO 20022 compliant cryptocurrencies include:

- **XRP (Ripple):** Designed for fast and cost-effective cross-border payments, XRP is a prominent example of a cryptocurrency adhering to the ISO 20022 standard.
- **Stellar Lumens (XLM):** Stellar focuses on facilitating cross-border transactions and has adopted ISO 20022 to enhance its interoperability with existing financial infrastructures.
- **Cardano (ADA):** Known for its research-driven approach, Cardano has embraced ISO 20022 to ensure seamless communication with traditional financial systems.
- **IOTA (MIOTA):** Tailored for the Internet of Things (IoT), IOTA utilizes ISO 20022 to standardize data exchange between IoT devices and financial institutions.
- **Quant (QNT):** By leveraging the Overledger protocol, Quant enables interoperability between various blockchain networks and aligns with ISO 20022 to facilitate integration with traditional finance.
- **Algorand (ALGO):** Algorand's blockchain platform supports both financial and non-financial applications and has adopted ISO 20022 to enhance its compatibility with existing financial systems.
- **Hedera Hashgraph (HBAR)**: Utilizing a unique consensus algorithm, Hedera Hashgraph has aligned with ISO 20022 to improve its interoperability with traditional financial infrastructures.
- **XDC Network (XDC)**: Focused on enterprise use cases, the XDC Network has adopted ISO 20022 to facilitate seamless integration with global financial systems.

By aligning with ISO 20022, these cryptocurrencies aim to bridge the gap between digital assets and traditional finance, promoting broader adoption and more efficient financial transactions.

Other cryptocurrencies to consider acquiring include:

- Shiba Inu (SHIB)
- Bitcoin (BTC)
- Ethereum (ETH)
- Wrapped Ether (WETH)
- Pepe (PEPE)
- Solana (SOL)
- Cardano (ADA)
- Flare (FLR)

Again, it is worth repeating, consider utilizing profits to invest in **other key assets**:

- Gold and Silver (and other precious metals such as Copper)
- Foreign Currencies (Iraqi Dinar, Vietnamese Dong, Uganda Shilling)
- Land (good farmland that can be used for agricultural farming or livestock)
- Real Estate (both residential and commercial)
- Development properties and projects
- Fortune 500 stocks and lesser-known stocks (Such as Zion Oil)

Stage 4: Second Bull Run & Spike

September's Plunder Will Bless October's Numbers:

The financial shift set to take place in "***September's Plunder***" will lay the foundation for a powerful economic surge in "***October's Numbers***". As wealth is repositioned and assets are acquired at a fraction of their true value, the influx of money re-entering the markets is likely to **trigger** a significant **bull run** in cryptocurrency. Investors who strategically plundered undervalued assets during the **September collapse** will see their holdings multiply in **October** as confidence and liquidity return to the financial landscape. Additionally, October may be the month when undervalued foreign currencies undergo long-awaited revaluation, including the **Iraqi Dinar**, **Vietnamese Dong**, and the **Uganda Shilling**. If these currencies rise to their true market value, it could mark a monumental shift in global wealth distribution, blessing those who have positioned themselves accordingly. Regardless of how these events unfold, October is shaping up to be a time of divine restoration, where the resources transferred in September begin to flourish and grow, marking a season of financial blessing and opportunity.

Christmas in November—A Season of Financial Blessings:

The prophetic word ***"Christmas in November"*** suggests that an unexpected wave of financial blessings will arrive ahead of the traditional holiday season, bringing a time of supernatural provision and breakthrough for God's people. This could be the moment when the long-awaited wealth transfer manifests to new heights and in tangible ways, possibly through a **second bull run** in cryptocurrency, the release of withheld financial resources, or the fulfillment of major economic shifts such as currency revaluations and debt cancellations. What would normally be expected in December—**gifts**, **abundance**, and **celebrations**—will come early, marking November as a month of divine acceleration and provision.

This event will not only be about personal financial gain but also about positioning God's people to sow into **Kingdom initiatives**, fund ministries, and uplift communities. The wealth that was once controlled by corrupt hands will begin to flow into the hands of the righteous, enabling them to build, restore, and establish God's purposes on Earth. Just as Christmas represents joy, giving, and the arrival of something miraculous, ***"Christmas in November"*** will be a prophetic fulfillment of financial blessings and answered prayers at a scale that will shock the world.

Debt Cancellation and a New Economic Era:

The Lord has said, *"**All debt will be cancelled, both personally and globally**. Then it will be **time to rebuild the world**."* Therefore, be encouraged because this global debt cancellation is another critical aspect of the unfolding financial transition into the new economic system being established. The Lord spoke about a stone—a significant, game-changing event—that involves **President Trump** partnering with **Vladimir Putin** to expose and dismantle **corrupt global leadership**. This divine orchestration will set the stage for the removal of leaders and institutions involved in **crimes against humanity**, making way for a restructured financial and political system. The result of this exposure and removal may lead to the implementation of **GESARA** (**Global Economic Security and Reform Act**)—a worldwide financial reset designed to eliminate illegitimate debt, restore economic fairness, and redistribute wealth more equitably. If this unfolds as expected, it will mark one of the greatest financial liberations in modern history, freeing nations and individuals from oppressive debt structures that have enslaved economies for decades. This shift will not only impact personal finances but also restore sovereignty to nations, releasing them from financial control mechanisms imposed by corrupt institutions. The world is on the brink of a radical economic transformation, and those who are prepared will witness the dawn of a new financial system built on transparency, accountability, and divine justice.

A Critical Warning—Protect Your Wealth Before the Collapse:

I want to issue a strong warning: "*Keep your **gold, silver**, and **cash out of the banks!***" What exactly do I mean by this? The banking system is part of the old financial system and as part of the transition to the new system, first the old system must be taken down. The Federal Deposit Insurance Corporation (FDIC) only insures bank deposits up to $250,000 per banking category—a limit that provides little security in the event of a major financial collapse. Given the growing instability within the banking sector, I strongly advise against keeping more than this insured amount in any single bank or category.

When the long-foretold banking failures and the collapse of the old financial system finally unfold, I do not believe we will see the same government bailouts that rescued banks in previous crises. Unlike in 2008, where trillions were printed to prop up failing institutions, the coming transition into a new financial system will likely mark the final death of the current fiat-based economy. The government will no longer have the ability to print money indefinitely to patch financial holes, and the U.S. dollar's role as the world's reserve currency will face unprecedented threats. As fiat currency loses its purchasing power, those who remain dependent on the traditional banking system could see their savings wiped out overnight.

This is why diversification into real, tangible assets is critical at this stage of the wealth transfer. The time to secure your wealth is now—before **systemic failures** take hold. This means moving away from **fiat currency dependence** and placing your resources into hard assets such as **gold**, **silver**, **cryptocurrencies**, and other stores of value that cannot be manipulated by central banks or government entities. **Precious metals** have historically held their worth through financial collapses, serving as a hedge against inflation and monetary instability. Meanwhile, blockchain-based assets and **decentralized financial systems** provide an alternative pathway for those looking to preserve and grow their wealth outside of traditional institutions.

The collapse of the old system is not a question of if, but when. Those who take proactive steps to exit the fiat system and position themselves in alternative assets will be far better prepared to navigate the transition into the new economy. Do not wait until it is too late—take action now to secure your financial future.

The Inevitable Sequence: Currency Revaluation, Fiat Collapse, and Banking System Failure

It is highly likely that these three major financial events will occur in sequential order, leading to a complete restructuring of the global economic system. First, the revaluation of foreign currencies—such as the Iraqi Dinar, Vietnamese Dong, and Uganda Shilling—will serve as the initial trigger. This revaluation will expose the true suppressed value of these assets, flooding markets with new liquidity while simultaneously devaluing artificially inflated fiat currencies like the US Dollar and Euro. Second, the collapse of the fiat-based dollar system will follow, as the revaluation event undermines the dominance of the US and European financial order.

With fiat money losing credibility and purchasing power, the ability to print endless amounts of currency to sustain economic stability will rapidly diminish. Third, the banking collapse will be the inevitable consequence, as financial institutions reliant on the old fiat system will fail to absorb the shock, leading to bank runs, liquidity shortages, and widespread panic. Without government bailouts—since fiat money will no longer hold its former strength—many major banks will shut down or restructure, marking the death of the old financial system. This sequence of events will pave the way for a new financial paradigm, where wealth is redistributed, decentralized systems rise, and assets like gold, silver, and digital currencies take center stage. Those who have prepared ahead of time will be in the best position to navigate this shift and step into the new economic reality with wisdom and financial security.

In conclusion, the months ahead will usher in a profound shift in the global financial and economic landscape, marked by exposure of corruption, divine judgment, wealth transfer, and a complete restructuring of economic systems. These events will not be minor adjustments but seismic shifts that will reshape markets, governments, and financial institutions as we know them. The most important thing is not to fear what is coming, but to prepare wisely—physically, mentally, and spiritually. Physically, this means securing tangible assets such as gold, silver, and cryptocurrencies, diversifying wealth, and staying informed on economic trends.

Mentally, it requires a mindset of discernment, the ability to adapt to rapid changes, and the wisdom to navigate uncertainty. Spiritually, preparation means drawing closer to God, seeking His guidance and divine wisdom, and standing firm in faith, knowing that these changes are part of His greater plan. Those who position themselves with foresight and obedience will not only endure this transition but will be strategically placed to thrive, bless others, and steward the resources that will be transferred into the hands of the righteous. This is not just a season of financial change—it is a **Kingdom shift**, and those who are prepared will step into unprecedented opportunities for influence, provision, and purpose.

CHAPTER 15

TOOLS AND STRATEGIES FOR BUILDING WEALTH

The emergence of blockchain technology and digital assets has revolutionized how individuals approach wealth-building. With a growing array of tools and strategies, it is now possible to invest, earn passive income, and diversify portfolios in ways previously unimaginable. This chapter explores practical methods for buying, selling, and safely storing digital assets, the role of wallets and exchanges, the importance of diversification, and opportunities for generating passive income.

Buying and Selling Digital Assets:

For anyone entering the world of digital assets, understanding the process of purchasing, selling, and securely storing cryptocurrencies is critical. It is essential to not only understand these activities but also to become confident in performing them to avoid costly mistakes that could lead to financial losses.

1. **Choose a Reputable Exchange:** Platforms like **Coinbase**, **Binance**, and **Kraken** are popular options for beginners geographically located in the United States. These exchanges offer user-friendly interfaces and support for a variety of cryptocurrencies. For individuals located outside the United States, region-specific platforms are often available, tailored to meet the needs and regulations of their respective geographical areas.

Exchange Types:

- **Centralized Exchanges (CEXs):** Platforms like Coinbase and Binance are user-friendly but require trust in the exchange's security measures.
- **Decentralized Exchanges (DEXs):** DEXs like Uniswap and PancakeSwap allow peer-to-peer trading without intermediaries, offering greater privacy but requiring more technical knowledge.

When choosing a cryptocurrency platform, several factors should be carefully considered to ensure a secure and seamless experience. Reputation is key—researching reviews and ratings can provide insights into the platform's reliability and user satisfaction. Security measures are equally important; look for platforms that offer strong encryption, utilize cold storage for funds, and provide insurance policies to protect against potential breaches. Additionally, the platform's supported assets should align with the cryptocurrencies a person intends to trade or invest in. Finally, it's crucial to evaluate **fees**, including **transaction**, **withdrawal**, and deposit charges, as these can significantly impact overall returns, especially for frequent traders. Taking these factors into account can help individuals select a platform that best suits their needs and priorities. The choice of wallets and exchanges can significantly impact the security and ease of managing digital assets.

2. Set Up an Account: This typically involves providing identification and completing a **Know Your Customer (KYC)** verification process. KYC is a process used by financial institutions and businesses to verify the identity of their customers. It involves collecting personal information such as government-issued identification, proof of address, and sometimes financial details. The primary goals of KYC are to prevent fraud, money laundering, and illegal activities by ensuring that customers are legitimate and compliant with regulatory standards.

3. Deposit Funds: Depositing funds into a cryptocurrency exchange account is a straightforward process designed to accommodate users of all experience levels. Most platforms offer multiple funding options, including transferring money from a linked bank account or using a credit or debit card. Bank transfers are typically the most economical choice, often coming with minimal fees and higher transaction limits, making them ideal for larger deposits. Credit and debit cards provide the convenience of instant funding, though they may incur slightly higher fees. Exchanges guide users step-by-step through the process, from linking accounts to confirming deposits, ensuring a smooth experience. The flexibility and ease of these funding options allow users to start trading or investing in cryptocurrencies quickly and without unnecessary complications.

4. **Place an Order:** Once funds are deposited into a cryptocurrency exchange account, an individual can start purchasing cryptocurrencies by placing orders tailored to their trading preferences. A "***market order***" allows for the immediate purchase of a cryptocurrency at the current market price, making it an ideal choice for beginners or those who want quick execution. On the other hand, a "***limit order***" gives users more control, allowing them to set a specific price at which they are willing to buy a cryptocurrency. This option is useful for those aiming to capitalize on price fluctuations or adhere to a strict budget. Most exchanges

- **Security best practices:** Adopting robust security practices is essential for safeguarding cryptocurrency investments. Enabling **two-factor authentication (2FA)** on accounts adds an extra layer of protection by requiring a secondary verification method, such as a code from a mobile app. Using strong, unique passwords for wallets and exchange accounts further minimizes the risk of unauthorized access. Additionally, it is crucial to regularly back up wallet keys and store these backups in secure and multiple locations, such as encrypted drives or physical safes, to protect against data loss or theft. By implementing these practices, individuals can significantly enhance the security of their digital assets.

The Importance of Diversification:

Diversification is a cornerstone of effective **wealth-building**, particularly in the volatile landscape of digital assets, stocks, commodities, currencies, and other investment vehicles. By spreading investments across various asset classes, individuals can mitigate risk, balance potential losses in one area with gains in another and create a more resilient financial portfolio capable of withstanding market fluctuations. Combining traditional investments with digital assets creates a balanced portfolio that mitigates risk while maximizing growth potential.

Digital Asset Diversification

1. **Cryptocurrencies:** Diversification in cryptocurrency is a key strategy to mitigate risk while capitalizing on the potential growth of various digital assets. By investing in a blend of **well-established coins** and promising **altcoins**, investors can protect themselves from market volatility and increase the chances of benefiting from different trends within the crypto space. For instance, **XRP (Ripple)** stands out for its focus on facilitating cross-border payments with a strong use case in the banking sector, providing stability and adoption. **XLM (Stellar)**, similar to XRP, aims to improve financial infrastructure by connecting traditional financial institutions to blockchain technology, offering potential in global remittances. XDC (XDC Network) focuses on enterprise blockchain solutions, enhancing supply chain and trade finance, positioning it well for institutional adoption. **HBAR (Hedera Hashgraph)** is notable for its high-speed consensus mechanism, offering a scalable and energy-efficient platform for decentralized applications, which could be crucial in the future of decentralized finance.

On the more speculative side, **SHIB (Shiba Inu)** has gained significant attention as a meme coin but has since expanded its ecosystem with projects like ShibaSwap and the Shiba Inu Metaverse, drawing in a large and dedicated community. Many in the prophetic community have shared dreams and words from God suggesting that SHIB will soon experience a surge in value, with many seeing its potential rise as a divine signal of prosperity for those who hold it. Similarly, **LUNC (Terra Luna Classic)**, though rooted in controversy after the collapse of the original Terra ecosystem, has been revitalized by its community. Prophetic voices have indicated that LUNC will also experience a significant uptick in value, with several visions showing a pattern of coins rising shortly after one another, giving hope to those invested in its revival. These insights from the prophetic community suggest a period of notable growth for these altcoins, offering believers in these visions a sense of confidence that their investments could pay off in the near future. I have personally received prophetic dreams about Ripple XRP reaching $15 and Shiba Inu "*Howling*", and which I have shared in more detail on my YouTube channel '*Digital Dollars Now*'.

IOTA stands out by using its Tangle technology rather than traditional blockchain, enabling feeless and scalable transactions, particularly beneficial for the Internet of Things (IoT). ALGO (Algorand) is a promising project focused on creating a decentralized, scalable blockchain with low transaction costs and a strong emphasis on sustainability, positioning it as a potential key player in DeFi and enterprise applications. **Cosmos (ATOM)** aims to solve blockchain interoperability by allowing different networks to communicate and share information seamlessly, potentially transforming the way blockchains collaborate. On the more speculative side, PEPE has emerged as a meme coin with a dedicated community, tapping into the popularity of internet culture and meme-driven markets. **VOLT (Volt Inu)**, another meme coin, is attempting to integrate staking and passive income opportunities for holders, with aspirations to leverage decentralized finance tools for its ecosystem, though it remains highly volatile. **FLR (Flare token)** adds another intriguing layer to the mix, offering interoperability between different blockchains, with a particular focus on bringing smart contract functionality to assets like XRP, **Litecoin**, and others that don't have native smart contract capabilities, making it an important player in expanding blockchain utility. By incorporating a variety of coins like these into a portfolio, investors can balance risk and reward while staying ahead of shifting market trends.

The diversification of cryptocurrency investments opens the door to innovative and speculative assets, offering both high-risk and high-reward potential. Such as **WKC (Wiki Cat)**, a lesser-known altcoin, is a more risky yet potential high-reward investment, often seen as an **emerging meme coin** with a vibrant following. Additional coins like **BNB Tiger**, **BNB Lion**, and **Tigermoon** reflect the growing trend of meme and community-driven tokens, which, while speculative and volatile, can experience rapid growth due to social media hype, large communities, and ambitious projects or tokenomics. Although these tokens can yield substantial rewards for early investors, they also carry significant risks, and investors should approach them cautiously, balancing the potential for high returns with the inherent volatility of these assets.

2. Stablecoins: Stablecoins are digital assets designed to provide stability by pegging their value to a fiat currency, commodity, or basket of assets. Popular examples include Tether (USDT), USD Coin (USDC), and Binance USD (BUSD), which are often linked to the US dollar. These coins serve as a "*safe haven*" during market downturns, offering a store of value and mitigating the volatility typically associated with cryptocurrencies like Bitcoin or Ethereum. While stablecoins provide certain benefits, such as a stable value and use in cross-border transactions or as a medium for trading other cryptocurrencies, they come with inherent limitations and risks. For instance, their use in transactions can sometimes be more expensive than transferring cryptocurrencies like **XRP or XLM**, which are designed for fast and low-cost payments. Additionally, stablecoins lack the potential for significant price appreciation, as their value is intentionally fixed to their underlying asset. This means they function more as a financial tool for stability rather than an investment opportunity.

However, there are risks to consider with stablecoins, especially in times of economic uncertainty. If the currency to which a stablecoin is pegged, such as the US dollar, experiences significant devaluation or collapse, the stablecoin's value would also be at risk. For example, Tether (USDT), which is linked to the US dollar, could lose its stability if the dollar weakens dramatically due to inflation, economic instability, or shifts in global reserve currency dynamics. Additionally, questions about transparency, reserve audits, and regulatory scrutiny add to the uncertainty surrounding some stablecoins.

With the looming economic challenges and the potential for significant shifts in the financial landscape, relying solely on stablecoins for stability may pose a higher risk than anticipated. While they can play a role in portfolio management or as a temporary store of value, they should be approached cautiously. Diversifying into other asset classes, such as cryptocurrencies with utility (like XRP and XLM), precious metals, or real-world assets, could provide a more balanced strategy to weather future financial uncertainties.

3. NFTs: Non-fungible tokens (NFTs) have emerged as a groundbreaking asset class, offering exposure to digital art, collectibles, and virtual real estate. Unlike traditional cryptocurrencies, which are interchangeable, NFTs represent unique assets verified on a blockchain. This distinctiveness opens opportunities for investors to diversify their portfolios by venturing into sectors that merge technology, creativity, and ownership.

Digital art has become one of the most prominent use cases for NFTs, allowing artists to tokenize their work and sell it directly to collectors. High-profile sales, like Beeple's "*Everyday's: The First 5,000 Days*," which sold for $69 million, have demonstrated the potential value of this market. Collectibles, such as virtual trading cards and branded merchandise, are another lucrative sector, offering fans a way to own rare and exclusive digital items.

Virtual real estate is also revolutionizing the concept of property ownership. Platforms like Decentraland and The Sandbox enable investors to buy, sell, and develop parcels of land in digital metaverses. These virtual properties can generate income through leasing, hosting events, or advertising, creating a new revenue stream in an increasingly digital world.

NFTs provide a means of diversifying investments by tapping into emerging digital economies. However, as with any asset class, there are risks, including market volatility, speculative pricing, and the evolving regulatory landscape. Conducting thorough research, understanding the underlying value of NFTs, and ensuring alignment with long-term financial goals can help investors navigate this innovative space.

4. **DeFi Projects: Decentralized Finance (DeFi) projects** are transforming the traditional financial ecosystem by offering innovative, permissionless, and transparent financial services through blockchain technology. Unlike traditional financial institutions, which rely on intermediaries like banks or brokers, DeFi platforms operate through smart contracts—self-executing code on decentralized networks like Ethereum. These platforms enable users to access services such as lending, borrowing, staking, yield farming, and trading without the need for intermediaries, often resulting in reduced fees and increased accessibility.

One of the most popular applications of DeFi is decentralized lending and borrowing. Platforms like Aave and Compound allow users to lend their cryptocurrencies to earn interest or borrow against their holdings as collateral. This model creates a peer-to-peer system that eliminates the need for traditional credit checks and bureaucracy, making financial services available to a broader audience, including those in underbanked regions.

Another innovative DeFi concept is yield farming, where users earn rewards by providing liquidity to decentralized exchanges or other protocols. Platforms like Uniswap and SushiSwap enable liquidity providers to earn transaction fees and governance tokens, creating opportunities for passive income. DeFi projects also introduce synthetic assets—blockchain-based representations of real-world assets like stocks or commodities—allowing users to gain exposure to traditional markets without needing a centralized intermediary.

However, DeFi is not without risks. Smart contract vulnerabilities, market volatility, and regulatory uncertainty pose challenges for participants. As the sector evolves, thorough research and risk management are critical for investors. Despite these risks, DeFi represents a paradigm shift in how financial services are delivered, democratizing access, fostering innovation, and paving the way for a more inclusive financial future. For investors, exploring DeFi projects offers not only diversification but also an early foothold in a rapidly expanding ecosystem.

Traditional Investments:

1. Stocks, bonds, and mutual funds: Investing in stocks, bonds, and mutual funds has long been a cornerstone of wealth-building strategies, offering opportunities for growth, income, and portfolio diversification. Stocks represent ownership in companies and provide the potential for significant returns through price appreciation and dividends. Bonds, on the other hand, has historically offered more stable income by paying interest over a fixed term, making them a safer option during periods of economic uncertainty. Mutual funds allow investors to pool resources and diversify across a range of assets, reducing individual stock risk while benefiting from professional management.

However, these investments are not without risk, especially in the context of an anticipated stock market crash. With global economic instability, inflation concerns, and geopolitical tensions, the stock market could face significant volatility in the near future. A major market downturn could wipe out substantial wealth for those who are overly exposed to equities or heavily leveraged in their investments. Bond markets, particularly those tied to government debt, may also face challenges, such as rising interest rates, which can devalue existing bonds.

Despite the risks, market downturns often present unparalleled opportunities for savvy investors. As the saying goes, "***Buy when there's blood in the streets.***" During a stock market crash, many high-quality stocks will be available at deeply discounted prices. This can be an opportune time for long-term investors to enter the market or increase their holdings, especially in companies with strong fundamentals, growth potential, or reliable dividends.

To navigate these turbulent times, investors should maintain a well-diversified portfolio and have cash reserves ready to deploy during a downturn. Conducting thorough research and focusing on long-term investment horizons can help mitigate risks and capitalize on opportunities. While market crashes can be intimidating, they often serve as a reset, paving the way for future growth and prosperity for those prepared to act.

The anticipated wealth transfer presents a unique opportunity for a new wave of **companies** to **emerge**, particularly those founded by **Christians** and rooted in **kingdom-based principles**. These businesses, driven by morals, ethics, and a commitment to serving others, could redefine the corporate landscape. With a focus on integrity, transparency, and community impact, these enterprises aim to prioritize purpose over profit while still delivering exceptional value. For investors, these startups and companies represent an ideal opportunity to align financial growth with personal values. Investing in such businesses not only offers the potential for substantial returns as they tap into unmet market needs but also supports a larger mission of creating a positive societal impact. These ventures and Initial Public Offing (IPOs) could emerge in a variety of sectors, including education, renewable energy, healthcare, and technology, bringing innovation alongside ethical practices. As these kingdom-based businesses grow, they may become some of the most sought-after investment opportunities in the new financial era.

2. Real Estate: Investing in real estate, particularly through rental properties and other avenues like commercial spaces, vacation homes, and real estate investment trusts (REITs), can be an excellent way to build wealth and generate passive income. Owning rental properties allows investors to earn consistent cash flow through tenant payments, while also benefiting from potential property appreciation over time. Vacation rentals, supported by platforms like Airbnb and VRBO, can be especially lucrative in high-demand tourist destinations, often providing higher returns than long-term leases. Moreover, REITs offer a way to invest in real estate without directly owning property, providing dividends and liquidity while diversifying investment portfolios.

However, timing is critical when investing in real estate. Currently, many markets are at their peak, with property values driven to record highs by low interest rates and high demand over recent years. Investing at such levels carries the risk of purchasing overvalued assets, which may depreciate in a market correction or downturn. Furthermore, the potential for a financial crisis, such as the anticipated fiat currency collapse, introduces additional risks. Economic instability could lead to widespread layoffs, hyperinflation, and an increase in non-payment of rents as tenants struggle to meet their financial obligations. In such scenarios, landlords with mortgaged properties could face significant financial strain, potentially jeopardizing their ability to meet monthly mortgage payments.

For investors considering mortgaging real estate, caution is paramount. The 2008 mortgage crisis serves as a stark reminder of how quickly over-leveraging can lead to financial ruin. During that period, property values plummeted, and many property owners were unable to keep up with their mortgage payments due to job losses and a collapse in rental income. I personally foresee a similar scenario unfolding in the near future if current economic trends continue. Over-leveraging, particularly in a market that may be approaching a peak, could result in foreclosures and significant losses if tenants' default on rent payments.

To mitigate these risks, potential investors should carefully assess market conditions, prioritize properties in stable or growing rental markets, and maintain a strong cash reserve to cover unexpected expenses or vacancies. Additionally, avoiding over-leveraging and ensuring that rental income significantly exceeds mortgage obligations can provide a safety buffer. While real estate remains a powerful tool for wealth creation, a prudent and well-researched approach is essential to weather potential market downturns and economic uncertainties.

3. **Land and Agriculture:** The future potential of increased value in land and agriculture is a compelling opportunity for forward-thinking

investors. As global dynamics shift and concerns about food security grow, investing in fertile farmland in strategic areas could become one of the most lucrative and impactful ventures. Land dedicated to sustainable farming practices and organic production is likely to see increased demand, especially in a future where environmental challenges, climate irregularities, and food shortages loom.

One critical driver for this value lies in the potential for future famines or disruptions in global food supply chains. Factors such as chemical trials, harmful substances released into the atmosphere, and weather manipulation experiments could significantly affect crop yields and farming conditions in certain regions. Investing in agricultural land positioned in climates less vulnerable to these risks—or equipped with advanced, sustainable farming infrastructure—could provide a reliable source of food production and ensure the long-term viability of these assets.

Additionally, the increasing awareness and demand for non-genetically modified (non-GMO) food and ethically raised livestock are reshaping consumer preferences. Landowners who focus on growing organic crops and raising animals without antibiotics or harmful chemical exposure, adhering to grass-fed and pasture-raised principles, stand to benefit from the premium prices associated with these high-quality products. This shift away from industrialized farming practices reflects a growing consumer desire for healthier, more sustainable food options.

Beyond financial rewards, investing in agriculture carries significant societal benefits. Landowners in this sector could play a pivotal role in addressing future food shortages by contributing to local and global food security. As traditional supply chains become less reliable due to environmental or economic pressures, independent agricultural operations could fill critical gaps, providing communities with access to fresh, nutritious food.

In summary, land and agriculture represent a unique investment opportunity that combines economic potential with ethical and societal impact. For those who see the value in cultivating farmland strategically, embracing sustainable and chemical-free practices, and raising livestock responsibly, the future holds not only the promise of financial rewards but also the fulfillment of contributing to a healthier, more resilient world.

4. **Commodities:** Commodities like gold, silver, copper and various other precious metals have long been regarded as safe-haven assets, particularly during times of economic uncertainty or financial instability. Their intrinsic value, scarcity, and universal acceptance make them a reliable store of wealth, especially when confidence in fiat currencies wanes. In the event of a financial reset or a fiat currency collapse, gold and silver could play a critical role as alternative mediums of exchange and as assets that retain value. Historically, during periods of hyperinflation, currency devaluation, or geopolitical unrest, these precious metals have experienced significant appreciation in value. As central banks around the world continue to stockpile gold and silver as a hedge against currency risks, individuals may also benefit from including these tangible assets in their portfolios. With the potential for increased demand in a post-reset economy, commodities like gold and silver could become even more valuable, serving as essential tools for wealth preservation and financial security.

Beyond their role as safe-haven assets, gold and silver have critical applications in technology and industry, making them even more valuable in a modern economy. Silver, known for its exceptional conductivity, is a key component in the production of electronics, including computers, circuits, and solar panels. Its role as a conductor in electrical systems ensures that it remains indispensable in emerging technologies such as renewable energy and electric vehicles. Similarly, gold's unique properties, such as resistance to corrosion and superior conductivity, make it essential in high-tech applications like semiconductors, aerospace equipment, and medical devices. Both metals are vital to technological advancement, further solidifying their importance as both investment vehicles and industrial necessities.

Looking to the future, the increasing demand for these metals in technology, combined with the potential collapse of fiat currencies, could significantly drive up their value. Personally, I foresee gold reaching a price of around $10,000 per ounce within the next decade, as it retains its status as a **global store of value** and sees expanded use in technology. **Silver**, often referred to as "***poor man's gold***," is poised to follow closely behind, with a predicted valuation of approximately $4,000 per ounce.

As industrial demand rises and the global financial system undergoes potential restructuring, both metals are set to play critical roles, making them indispensable assets for both investors and industries alike.

Benefits of Diversification

Diversifying your assets across various investment classes, including cryptocurrency, precious metals, foreign currency, land, and real estate, can be a powerful strategy for navigating the unpredictable financial landscape of the coming years. Each of these assets offers unique benefits —cryptocurrencies provide the potential for high returns, precious metals serve as a hedge against inflation, foreign currency can protect against economic instability, and land and real estate often offer long-term growth and stability. However, the key to successful diversification lies in timing these investments to buy into them at the right season. With market conditions constantly shifting, it's essential to remain sensitive to the signs and guidance that may come, especially in times of volatility. Listening to God's instruction and seeking His wisdom will be crucial as we approach uncertain times, ensuring that our decisions are not only financially sound but also aligned with His greater plan. Trusting in divine timing will help navigate these investment opportunities with confidence and discernment, positioning us for future prosperity.

"Invest in seven ventures, yes, in eight; you do not know what disaster may come upon the land."
— Ecclesiastes 11:2 (NIV)

This verse emphasizes the importance of diversification, a principle often applied in financial planning. The wisdom here suggests spreading investments across multiple opportunities to mitigate risks, as no one can predict future challenges or **economic downturns** (except The Lord of course). This timeless advice aligns with sound financial strategies for building resilience and long-term wealth.

Diversification is a **fundamental strategy** in investment planning, designed to reduce overall risk by spreading investments across multiple asset classes. By allocating funds into a mix of assets—such as stocks, bonds, real estate, commodities, and digital assets—investors can mitigate the impact of poor performance in any single investment. This approach ensures that losses in one area can be offset by gains in another, creating a more balanced and resilient portfolio.

Generating Passive Income: Staking, Lending, and Yield Farming

One of the most exciting aspects of the digital financial system is the ability to generate passive income. Unlike traditional investments, digital assets offer innovative methods for earning returns.

Staking: Staking is the process of **locking up** a certain amount of cryptocurrency in a blockchain network to support its operations, such as transaction validation. In return for their participation, **users earn rewards**, which are often distributed in the form of additional cryptocurrency. Notable examples of blockchain networks that utilize staking include Ethereum 2.0, Cardano, and Polkadot.

Staking is a fundamental process in many blockchain networks that operate on a Proof of Stake (PoS) or related consensus mechanisms. It involves participants committing a certain amount of cryptocurrency to the network, effectively "*staking*" their assets. This stake acts as a form of collateral that helps secure and maintain the integrity of the blockchain. By doing so, participants play a crucial role in ensuring the network's operations, such as **validating transactions**, producing new blocks, and maintaining overall security.

Unlike mining in Proof of Work (PoW) systems, which relies on computational power, staking depends on the quantity of cryptocurrency held and locked by the participant. The more cryptocurrency staked, the higher the chances of being selected to validate transactions or create new blocks. This makes staking more energy-efficient compared to mining, as it does not require significant computational resources.

In return for their contribution, stakers earn rewards, typically in the form of additional cryptocurrency. These rewards serve as an incentive for users to participate in the network and can vary depending on factors such as the network's rules, the total amount staked, and the participant's share of the stake.

Staking also has other benefits beyond rewards. It often grants participants governance rights, allowing them to vote on key proposals and decisions regarding the network's future development. This gives stakeholders a voice in shaping the ecosystem they are invested in.

Popular blockchain networks that use staking include Ethereum 2.0, which transitioned from Proof of Work to Proof of Stake to improve scalability and energy efficiency; Cardano, which employs a unique PoS protocol called Ouroboros; and Polkadot, which uses staking as part of its Nominated Proof of Stake (NPoS) model to secure its multichain ecosystem.

Overall, staking is not only a way to earn passive income but also a mechanism to contribute to the stability and growth of blockchain networks. It has become a cornerstone of modern blockchain technology, fostering a decentralized, sustainable, and participatory financial ecosystem.

Lending: Platforms such as Aave and Compound have revolutionized the financial landscape by enabling individuals to lend their digital assets to others in exchange for interest payments. These decentralized finance (DeFi) platforms operate on blockchain technology, creating a secure and transparent environment for peer-to-peer lending without the need for traditional intermediaries, such as banks. This system allows asset holders to put their idle cryptocurrency to work, earning passive income while retaining ownership of their assets.

The lending process is straightforward: users deposit their digital assets into a liquidity pool on the platform. Borrowers can then access these funds, often by providing collateral in the form of other cryptocurrencies to minimize the risk of default. Lenders earn interest, which is dynamically adjusted based on supply and demand for the assets within the pool. For instance, if a particular cryptocurrency is in high demand for borrowing, the interest rate for lending that asset increases, providing higher returns for lenders.

One of the significant advantages of lending through platforms like **Aave** and Compound is the flexibility they offer. Lenders can withdraw their funds at any time, subject to the availability of liquidity, making it a convenient option for those looking to earn income without locking their assets for extended periods. Additionally, many platforms support a wide range of digital assets, from stablecoins like USDC and DAI to more volatile cryptocurrencies, allowing users to choose their preferred risk-reward profile.

Beyond earning interest, lending in the DeFi ecosystem contributes to the overall growth and functionality of decentralized finance. By providing liquidity, lenders enable borrowers to access capital for various purposes, such as trading, leveraging, or participating in other DeFi protocols. This interconnected system fosters a vibrant and dynamic financial ecosystem that operates independently of traditional financial institutions.

However, it's essential to consider the risks associated with crypto lending. Factors such as market volatility, smart contract vulnerabilities, and liquidation risks for borrowers can impact the security of funds. As a result, users should conduct thorough research and exercise caution when participating in DeFi lending.

Overall, lending on platforms like Aave and Compound offers a compelling opportunity to generate passive income while supporting the decentralized economy. As the DeFi sector continues to grow, these platforms are likely to play an increasingly vital role in reshaping how individuals interact with and benefit from financial services.

Yield Farming: Yield farming, also known as **liquidity mining**, is a strategy in the decentralized finance (DeFi) ecosystem where individuals provide liquidity to decentralized exchanges (DEXs) or lending platforms in exchange for rewards. These rewards are typically distributed in the form of tokens, which may include the platform's native governance tokens or other cryptocurrencies. By participating in yield farming, users can generate returns on their idle cryptocurrency holdings, often earning significantly higher yields than traditional financial instruments offer.

The process of yield farming involves depositing assets into liquidity pools—smart contracts that facilitate trading or lending on DeFi platforms. For example, on decentralized exchanges like Uniswap or SushiSwap, users provide equal values of two cryptocurrencies to a trading pair's liquidity pool, enabling smooth trading operations. In return, they receive a share of the trading fees generated by the pool and may also earn additional rewards, such as governance tokens. Similarly, on lending platforms like Aave or Compound, users can lend their assets to borrowers and earn interest while potentially receiving bonus tokens.

While yield farming has the potential to be highly lucrative, it is considerably more complex and risky than other DeFi strategies. The rewards often depend on factors like the demand for the liquidity pool, the value of the reward tokens, and the platform's fee structure. However, these high yields come with significant risks:

- **Market Volatility:** Cryptocurrencies are inherently volatile, and the value of assets deposited in liquidity pools can fluctuate dramatically. This exposes yield farmers to impermanent loss—a phenomenon where the value of deposited assets decreases compared to simply holding them.
- **Smart Contract Vulnerabilities:** Yield farming relies on smart contracts, which are susceptible to bugs or exploits. A single vulnerability in a platform's code can lead to significant losses if malicious actors exploit it.
- **Regulatory Risks:** As DeFi operates in a relatively unregulated space, changing regulations or crackdowns could impact the operations of yield farming platforms or the value of their tokens.
- **Complexity:** Yield farming often requires a deep understanding of how DeFi platforms work, including liquidity pool dynamics, staking mechanisms, and the associated risks. Mistakes in navigating these processes, such as selecting an unreliable platform or mismanaging funds, can result in losses.

Despite these risks, yield farming remains a popular strategy for those seeking high returns in the DeFi ecosystem. To mitigate potential downsides, participants are encouraged to diversify their investments, research the platforms they use, and monitor their positions closely. Additionally, tools and analytics platforms are available to help users evaluate opportunities and manage their yield farming strategies more effectively. In summary, yield farming is a sophisticated and high-risk approach to earning rewards in the DeFi space. While it offers substantial earning potential, it requires careful planning, continuous monitoring, and a willingness to navigate the inherent complexities and risks of decentralized finance.

Building wealth in the digital age requires an understanding of the tools and strategies available for managing digital assets effectively. By mastering the basics of buying, selling, and storing cryptocurrencies, choosing the right platforms, diversifying investments, and leveraging opportunities for passive income, individuals can position themselves for long-term financial success. As this new financial landscape evolves, staying informed and adaptable will be the keys to unlocking its full potential.

CHAPTER 16

THE LONG-TERM OPPORTUNITY OF INVESTING IN ISO 20022-COMPLIANT CRYPTOCURRENCIES

Investing in cryptocurrencies that are ISO 20022 compatible or compliant presents a promising long-term opportunity for those looking to align their portfolios with the future of global financial systems. ISO 20022 is an international messaging standard designed to streamline communication between financial institutions, particularly for cross-border payments, settlements, and data transfers. **Cryptocurrencies** compliant with **ISO 20022** are well-positioned to **integrate** seamlessly with this evolving global standard, potentially making them key players in the future of financial **interoperability**.

Why ISO 20022 Compliance Matters

- **Alignment with Global Financial Systems:** ISO 20022 is being adopted by major financial institutions, including central banks and global payment networks like **SWIFT**. Cryptocurrencies compliant with this standard are more likely to be integrated into these systems, offering a bridge between traditional finance and blockchain technology.
- **Adoption by Institutions:** ISO 20022-compliant cryptocurrencies are primed for institutional use, making them attractive investments as banks, corporations, and governments increasingly adopt blockchain for faster and more secure transactions.
- **Future-Proof Investments:** As ISO 20022 becomes the global standard for financial messaging, compliant cryptocurrencies are more likely to remain relevant, offering stability and long-term growth potential in a

volatile market.

- **Interoperability:** Compliance ensures these cryptocurrencies can communicate seamlessly with existing financial networks, making them more versatile and likely to gain mainstream adoption.

Cryptocurrencies That Are ISO 20022 Compliant

Several cryptocurrencies are already ISO 20022 compliant or compatible, making them strong contenders for **long-term investment**:

- **XRP (Ripple):** Known for its focus on **cross-border payments**, XRP is designed to facilitate **fast**, **low-cost transactions**, making it a natural fit for ISO 20022 standards.
- **XLM (Stellar):** Stellar focuses on financial inclusion and cross-border payments, particularly for **underbanked populations**, and aligns with ISO 20022 requirements.
- **XDC (XDC Network):** A hybrid blockchain platform optimized for **international trade** and **finance**, XDC's adherence to ISO 20022 standards ensures compatibility with global financial messaging systems. XDC Network is designed for enterprise and trade finance applications, emphasizing compliance and interoperability.
- **HBAR (Hedera Hashgraph):** Hedera offers enterprise-grade blockchain solutions with a focus on **speed**, **security**, and **energy efficiency**, aligning with ISO standards.
- **IOTA (MIOTA):** Designed for the Internet of Things (IoT), IOTA's architecture enables secure data and value transfer, with ISO 20022 compliance enhancing its applicability in standardized financial messaging. IOTA's use cases extend beyond finance, but its compliance makes it suitable for data and payment interoperability.
- **Algorand (ALGO):** Known for its high-performance blockchain, Algorand is positioned for financial and decentralized application (dApp) use cases.
- **Quant (QNT):** Quant's Overledger technology enables **interoperability across blockchains**, making it a key player in connecting **various financial systems**.
- **Cardano (ADA):** A decentralized Proof-of-Stake blockchain platform emphasizing security and scalability, Cardano's compliance with ISO 20022 facilitates interoperability with existing financial infrastructures.

These cryptocurrencies' compliance with ISO 20022 positions them favorably for integration into the evolving landscape of global finance, promoting interoperability, efficiency, and broader adoption.

The Long-Term Investment Case

1. **Institutional Adoption and Use Cases:** Cryptocurrencies that align with ISO 20022 are poised to be integrated into real-world applications, including cross-border payments, supply chain finance, and central bank digital currencies (CBDCs). This makes them attractive to **institutional** investors looking for compliant and scalable solutions.

2. **Enhanced Regulatory Clarity:** ISO 20022 compliance may signal greater regulatory approval, as these cryptocurrencies are built to operate within established financial frameworks, reducing the risks associated with non-compliance.

3. **Potential for Mass Adoption:** As **governments** and **central banks** implement ISO 20022 for financial communication, compliant cryptocurrencies could become integral to new payment systems, driving demand and value.

Navigating Market Volatility and the Future of Cryptocurrency Regulation

Due to the anticipated volatility in the markets, it is highly likely that governments and financial institutions will introduce new **regulatory frameworks** to bring greater oversight, security, and compliance to the cryptocurrency space. While **regulation** can provide legitimacy and stability to digital assets, it will also eliminate or marginalize many cryptocurrencies that fail to meet compliance standards or lack **real-world utility** within the evolving financial landscape. The enforcement of stricter guidelines will expose projects with poor **governance**, inadequate **security** measures, or speculative foundations, leading to their decline or complete removal from major exchanges.

To mitigate risk and ensure long-term viability, investors should consider focusing on cryptocurrencies that are ISO 20022 compliant, as these assets are designed to align with future financial infrastructure.

ISO 20022 is a global messaging standard that enables efficient, secure, and structured communication between financial institutions, banks, and payment networks. It is particularly crucial for cross-border transactions, remittances, settlements, and regulatory reporting, making it a cornerstone of the next-generation financial ecosystem. Cryptocurrencies that meet these standards will likely be preferred by banks, governments, and corporations, ensuring their adoption, stability, and long-term growth potential.

By investing in ISO 20022-compatible cryptocurrencies, individuals and institutions position themselves for success in an increasingly regulated and interoperable financial system. These assets are not only **compliant** with emerging financial protocols but are also poised to play a vital role in global trade, institutional finance, and digital asset settlements. As **regulations** tighten and the industry matures, investors who strategically align with **standardized**, **secure**, and **compliant** digital assets will be well-prepared to navigate future market shifts while capitalizing on the long-term growth of the **crypto-driven** financial revolution.

CHAPTER 17

CHALLENGES AND RISKS IN THE DIGITAL ERA

The shift from traditional financial systems to a blockchain-based digital economy brings immense opportunities for innovation and growth. However, it also introduces a host of challenges and risks that must be addressed. Navigating these issues is critical for individuals, businesses, and governments aiming to participate in this new era responsibly and successfully. This chapter explores the key risks and challenges in the digital asset landscape, including regulatory uncertainty, security concerns, market volatility, and environmental impacts.

Regulatory Uncertainty and Evolving Laws:

One of the most significant challenges facing the digital asset space is the **lack of consistent** and clear **regulatory frameworks**. As cryptocurrencies and blockchain technologies continue to disrupt traditional financial systems, governments worldwide are struggling to establish rules that balance innovation, consumer protection, and financial stability. This regulatory uncertainty creates risks for investors and developers alike, as unclear guidelines can lead to sudden crackdowns, market instability, or outright bans in certain jurisdictions. For instance, ambiguous tax policies, inconsistent treatment of digital assets as securities or commodities, and differing compliance requirements make it challenging for businesses and individuals to navigate the market confidently.

However, as the cryptocurrency market matures, the push for regulatory clarity is gaining momentum. While this shift will bring greater legitimacy and trust to the industry, it will also have significant consequences for the ecosystem. Many existing projects and tokens that fail to comply with emerging regulatory standards are likely to disappear, posing substantial risks for investors involved in these assets. Projects lacking transparency, utility, or robust compliance frameworks may not **survive** the increased scrutiny, leading to a consolidation of the market around more compliant and fundamentally sound cryptocurrencies.

In this regulatory **shakeout**, coins and projects aligned with international standards, such as those adhering to the ISO 20022 messaging standard for financial transactions, are well-positioned to thrive. Coins like XRP, XLM, and other ISO 20022-compliant assets are designed to integrate seamlessly with traditional financial institutions, offering enhanced interoperability, efficiency, and compliance. These features make them attractive options as global regulators seek to modernize payment systems and encourage blockchain adoption within regulated frameworks.

As regulatory clarity emerges, the stage will be set for the mass adoption of blockchain technology. This period of adoption will likely drive significant growth for compliant cryptocurrencies, particularly those that meet institutional and regulatory requirements. Financial institutions, governments, and enterprises are expected to adopt these blockchain-based solutions at scale, creating new demand and driving value for tokens that facilitate secure and efficient cross-border payments, data exchange, and financial inclusion.

In conclusion, while the path to regulatory clarity introduces risks—such as the disappearance of non-compliant projects—it also presents opportunities for well-positioned assets to rise to prominence. Investors who understand this dynamic and focus on projects with strong fundamentals, regulatory readiness, and real-world utility stand to benefit significantly as the industry transitions into its next phase of growth and adoption.

Global Inconsistencies: Global adoption of digital assets is marked by stark inconsistencies, with countries taking vastly different approaches to cryptocurrencies, ranging from outright bans to full integration into their financial systems. For instance, **China** has implemented a sweeping **ban**

on cryptocurrency **trading** and **mining**, citing concerns over financial stability and energy consumption. In contrast, **El Salvador** made history in **2021** by becoming the first country to adopt **Bitcoin** as **legal tender**. This bold move aimed to promote financial inclusion, reduce remittance costs, and attract foreign investment, with mixed results that have sparked debates worldwide.

Beyond El Salvador, other countries have also begun to embrace Bitcoin and other digital assets as forms of payment. The Central African Republic (CAR) followed El Salvador's lead in 2022, adopting Bitcoin as legal tender to stimulate its economy and integrate into the global financial ecosystem. In nations like **Switzerland**, Bitcoin is recognized as a means of payment in several regions, such as the canton of Zug, often referred to as "***Crypto Valley***," where local taxes can even be paid in cryptocurrency. Similarly, Japan, one of the earliest adopters, has classified Bitcoin and certain other digital assets as legal property, enabling their use in payments and transactions under regulatory oversight.

Other digital assets, such as XRP, have also found acceptance in certain countries and industries as a form of payment. XRP, known for its speed and low transaction costs, has been integrated into financial systems for cross-border payments and remittances. In regions like Southeast Asia, particularly in the Philippines, XRP is used by payment providers and financial institutions to facilitate remittances efficiently. **Japan** has also shown interest in **XRP**, with collaborations between Ripple and Japanese financial giants to streamline domestic and international transactions. Countries that emphasize blockchain innovation and financial technology, such as Singapore, have further explored the utility of XRP and similar assets within their payment ecosystems.

As the global landscape evolves, some countries remain in a gray area, developing regulations that cautiously encourage adoption while addressing risks. The **European Union**, through initiatives like the **MiCA (Markets in Crypto-Assets)** Regulation, is working toward harmonized standards for digital assets, potentially paving the way for broader adoption of cryptocurrencies, including Bitcoin and XRP, as forms of payment.

In summary, the global stance on digital assets varies widely, with some nations embracing cryptocurrencies like Bitcoin and XRP as payment solutions, while others remain cautious or outright prohibitive. These inconsistencies highlight the importance of understanding local regulations and trends, as they significantly impact the adoption and utility of digital assets on a global scale. As more countries explore the benefits of blockchain technology, the gap between restrictive and progressive approaches may narrow, fostering a more unified and inclusive global financial system.

Tax Implications: The taxation of cryptocurrencies remains a significant challenge due to unclear and inconsistent regulations across jurisdictions. In the United States and many other countries, cryptocurrencies are typically classified as **assets**, which means that gains from trading, selling, or exchanging digital currencies are subject to **capital gains taxes**. However, other jurisdictions treat cryptocurrencies as currencies or commodities, leading to a fragmented and often confusing tax landscape. This lack of consistency creates compliance challenges for both individuals and businesses, making it difficult to navigate reporting obligations, deductions, and exemptions.

In the U.S., cryptocurrency tax compliance can be particularly burdensome. Every transaction, including using cryptocurrency to purchase goods and services or exchanging one digital asset for another, may trigger a taxable event. This complexity has led to calls for reform, with advocates urging the government to establish clearer and more uniform tax policies for digital assets. In response, some policymakers have proposed measures to simplify the tax treatment of cryptocurrencies.

One notable proposal came from **President Donald Trump**, who suggested **eliminating taxes** on **U.S.-based** cryptocurrencies to foster innovation and maintain the country's leadership in blockchain technology. This plan aimed to remove capital gains taxes on transactions involving U.S.-origin digital assets, making it easier for businesses and individuals to use cryptocurrencies in everyday commerce and encouraging broader adoption. If implemented, this policy could significantly reduce the administrative burden on taxpayers and stimulate growth within the domestic crypto industry.

Several U.S.-based cryptocurrencies could potentially benefit from such a policy, including:

- **XRP:** Developed by Ripple Labs, XRP is designed for fast, low-cost cross-border payments and is widely used in the financial sector.
- **XLM (Stellar Lumens):** Created by the Stellar Development Foundation, XLM facilitates cross-border transactions and financial inclusion, especially in underserved regions.
- **Algorand (ALGO):** Known for its scalability and energy efficiency, Algorand supports a wide range of blockchain applications and is based on a U.S.-origin protocol.
- **Hedera (HBAR):** A decentralized public network offering high-speed transactions and governance by major corporations, Hedera is gaining traction in various industries.
- **Orchid network (OXT):** The project aligns with a focus on privacy, decentralized technology, and open-source principles, aiming to address global concerns about internet freedom and online privacy.
- **Cardano (ADA):** Although its development is global, much of its foundational research and partnerships are tied to U.S.-based academic and tech institutions.
- **Tezos (XTZ):** A blockchain platform known for its self-amending protocols and strong presence in the U.S. developer community.

A tax policy that exempts these U.S.-based cryptocurrencies from capital gains taxes could accelerate their adoption by reducing the financial and administrative barriers for users and businesses. Moreover, it would position the United States as a more crypto-friendly environment, attracting investment, talent, and innovation in blockchain technology.

Globally, other countries have taken steps to clarify or simplify cryptocurrency taxation. For example, Germany exempts cryptocurrency gains if the assets are held for more than a year, encouraging long-term investment. Similarly, **Portugal** has a crypto-friendly **tax regime** with **no capital gains tax** on **individual** cryptocurrency **transactions**. These examples highlight the potential benefits of clear and supportive tax policies in fostering innovation and adoption.

In conclusion, while the current patchwork of cryptocurrency tax rules creates significant challenges, proposals like President Trump's plan to eliminate taxes on U.S.-based cryptocurrencies could mark a pivotal step toward clarity and growth. By aligning tax policies with the unique characteristics of digital assets, governments can encourage adoption, reduce compliance burdens, and position themselves at the forefront of the global blockchain revolution.

Anti-Money Laundering (AML) and Know Your Customer (KYC): These regulations are critical tools used by regulators worldwide to combat illicit activities such as **money laundering**, **terrorist** financing, and **fraud** in the financial system. These measures require businesses, particularly financial institutions and cryptocurrency platforms, to **verify** the **identity** of their users, monitor transactions, and report suspicious activities. While AML and KYC frameworks are essential for maintaining security and ensuring compliance with legal standards, they pose unique challenges in the context of decentralized platforms that prioritize user privacy and anonymity.

In the cryptocurrency space, the implementation of AML and KYC measures often creates a tension between regulatory compliance and the core principles of decentralization. Many decentralized platforms, such as DeFi protocols and decentralized exchanges (DEXs), operate without a central authority, making it difficult to enforce KYC and AML requirements. These platforms are built on the ethos of anonymity and permissionless access, allowing users to interact directly without revealing their identities. Introducing KYC requirements to such platforms can undermine their decentralized nature, potentially deterring users who value privacy.

Furthermore, AML and KYC measures can create significant hurdles for decentralized platforms. Verifying user identities requires substantial resources, infrastructure, and ongoing monitoring, which can increase operational costs for smaller platforms. These compliance requirements may also slow down the onboarding process for users, reducing the platform's appeal compared to traditional financial systems or fully anonymous alternatives.

However, there is growing pressure from regulators to address these challenges as the cryptocurrency industry matures. High-profile cases of money laundering and illicit activity in the crypto space have led to calls for stricter oversight, with regulators emphasizing the importance of

AML and KYC compliance even for decentralized entities. Some platforms are exploring innovative solutions, such as implementing **decentralized identity (DID)** systems or **zero-knowledge proof (ZKP)** technologies, which allow users to verify their identities or meet compliance standards without revealing sensitive personal information. These approaches aim to strike a balance between regulatory compliance and the preservation of user privacy.

Additionally, platforms that fail to comply with **AML** and **KYC regulations** risk losing access to critical infrastructure, such as fiat-to-crypto on-ramps or partnerships with traditional financial institutions. Non-compliance can also lead to legal penalties, reputational damage, and exclusion from certain markets.

In conclusion, while AML and KYC measures are necessary for combating illicit activities and ensuring the integrity of financial systems, they present significant challenges for decentralized platforms that value user privacy and anonymity. As regulators continue to focus on integrating these measures into the cryptocurrency space, the industry will need to adopt innovative solutions to balance compliance with decentralization. This ongoing tension highlights the importance of fostering dialogue between regulators, platforms, and users to develop frameworks that support both security and privacy in the evolving financial landscape.

Impact on Innovation: Over-regulation or unclear regulatory frameworks can significantly hinder the growth and development of blockchain technology by creating an environment of uncertainty and barriers to entry. Blockchain is a rapidly evolving technology with the potential to transform industries such as finance, supply chain, healthcare, and more. However, regulatory hurdles can stifle innovation by discouraging startups, developers, and investors from fully exploring blockchain's potential.

Blockchain technology has the potential to revolutionize industries and redefine economic systems, but over-regulation risks stifling this transformative potential. By fostering an environment that encourages innovation while addressing risks through smart, adaptable policies, regulators can enable startups and developers to explore blockchain's full potential. Collaboration between governments, the private sector, and the blockchain community will be crucial to creating a balanced framework that supports growth, innovation, and security.

Understanding and staying updated on regulatory developments is crucial for navigating this uncertain landscape. Working with legal experts and adhering to best practices in compliance can mitigate potential risks.

Security Concerns: Scams, Hacks, and Safeguarding Digital Assets:

Security is a critical concern in the digital era. While blockchain technology is inherently secure due to its decentralized nature, the broader ecosystem of wallets, exchanges, and DeFi platforms is vulnerable to various threats.

Scams and Fraud: Scams and fraud are prevalent in the cryptocurrency space, with malicious actors frequently exploiting the lack of regulation and the inexperience of new investors. Common schemes include **rug pulls**, where developers create fraudulent projects or tokens, artificially inflate their value, and then abruptly withdraw all funds, leaving investors with worthless assets. **Phishing attacks**, which trick users into revealing sensitive information like **private keys** or **wallet credentials**, are another widespread tactic. A notable example of such fraudulent activity occurred in 2021 with the Squid Game token scam. This fake cryptocurrency was launched under the guise of being inspired by the popular TV series. The token's value skyrocketed due to widespread hype, but its creators disappeared with millions of dollars in investor funds, leaving participants with significant losses. Such incidents highlight the importance of due diligence and caution in the volatile world of cryptocurrencies.

Exchange Hacks: Centralized cryptocurrency exchanges, which serve as custodians for users' funds by holding them in wallets, are frequent targets for hackers. These platforms often store large amounts of digital assets in centralized systems, making them attractive to cybercriminals. Exchange hacks can lead to substantial financial losses for both the platform and its users, undermining trust in the broader cryptocurrency ecosystem.

A prominent example of this is the **2014 Mt. Gox hack**, where one of the largest cryptocurrency exchanges at the time suffered a catastrophic breach. Hackers stole approximately 850,000 Bitcoin, worth hundreds of millions of dollars at the time and billions by today's standards. This incident resulted in the exchange's bankruptcy and left thousands of users unable to recover their funds. It also served as a wake-up call for the industry, emphasizing the need for robust security measures.

While security practices have improved since the Mt. Gox era, exchange hacks remain a significant risk. Some more recent incidents include the 2019 hack of Binance, one of the largest and most reputable exchanges, where attackers stole over $40 million worth of Bitcoin. These breaches demonstrate that even leading platforms are not immune to sophisticated attacks.

To mitigate the risks associated with exchange hacks, users are encouraged to take proactive measures. One of the most effective strategies is to minimize reliance on centralized exchanges for long-term storage of funds. Instead, users can transfer their assets to personal wallets, such as **hardware wallets** or software wallets, which provide greater control and security. Additionally, choosing exchanges with a strong track record of security, comprehensive insurance policies, and transparent operations is critical.

Exchanges themselves are also adopting more advanced security practices, such as **multi-signature** wallets, cold storage for the majority of funds, regular audits, and bug bounty programs to identify vulnerabilities. However, despite these efforts, no system is entirely foolproof, and users must remain vigilant to protect their assets.

In summary, while centralized exchanges provide convenience for trading and accessing cryptocurrencies, their centralized nature makes them prime targets for hackers. High-profile incidents like the Mt. Gox hack underscore the importance of both individual and institutional responsibility in safeguarding digital assets. By combining personal security measures with careful selection of reputable platforms, users can better navigate the risks associated with cryptocurrency exchanges.

Wallet Security: Wallet security is a crucial aspect of managing cryptocurrencies, as poorly secured wallets or the mismanagement of private keys can lead to the permanent loss of funds. Unlike traditional financial systems, where lost credentials can often be recovered through centralized support, cryptocurrencies rely on decentralized technology. This makes private keys the sole access point to a user's assets. If these keys are lost, stolen, or exposed, there is no way to retrieve the funds, underscoring the importance of robust security measures.

Second, users should enable **two-factor authentication (2FA)** on all accounts associated with their cryptocurrency activities, such as exchanges and software wallets. 2FA provides an additional layer of security by requiring a second verification step, such as a one-time code sent to a mobile device, making it more difficult for unauthorized users to access accounts.

Third, it is vital to avoid sharing private keys or seed phrases with anyone, regardless of the circumstances. Sharing this sensitive information, even inadvertently, can give malicious actors full access to funds. To ensure safety, private keys and recovery phrases should be stored in secure, offline locations, such as encrypted storage devices or physical safes.

Fourth, individuals must research projects and platforms thoroughly before investing or using them to store funds. This includes evaluating the platform's security features, reputation, and history of incidents such as hacks or fraud. Careful research can help users avoid falling victim to scams or using unreliable wallets and platforms.

Beyond these essential practices, understanding the differences between wallet types is key. Hot wallets, such as software wallets or browser-based wallets, are connected to the internet and offer convenience for frequent transactions. However, they are more vulnerable to hacking and phishing attacks. In contrast, **cold wallets**, such as **hardware wallets** or paper wallets, store private keys offline, providing a much higher level of security against online threats.

Additional protection can be achieved through **multi-signature (multi-sig) authentication**, which requires multiple parties or devices to approve a transaction. For example, a wallet might require two or three separate signatures before funds can be transferred, significantly reducing the risk of unauthorized access. Multi-sig wallets are especially beneficial for businesses or joint accounts where multiple stakeholders are involved.

While technology plays a significant role in securing funds, user behavior is equally critical. Common mistakes, such as clicking on phishing links, using weak passwords, or failing to update wallet software, can jeopardize even the most secure setups. Regular updates to wallet software often include patches for vulnerabilities, making them a necessary part of security maintenance.

In summary, protecting digital assets requires a combination of secure technology and responsible practices. By using hardware wallets for long-term storage, enabling 2FA, avoiding the sharing of private keys, and thoroughly researching projects and platforms, individuals can significantly reduce the risks associated with cryptocurrency ownership. As the cryptocurrency space continues to evolve, vigilance and informed decision-making remain essential for safeguarding digital wealth.

Volatility of Digital Markets: Lessons from Past Crashes

The cryptocurrency market is infamous for its volatility. While this creates opportunities for significant gains, it also introduces substantial risks for investors and businesses.

Market Fluctuations: Cryptocurrency markets are known for their extreme volatility, with prices capable of dramatic swings within hours or even minutes. A prime example is Bitcoin, which has experienced several notable cycles of booms and busts. In late 2017, Bitcoin reached an all-time high of nearly $20,000, driven by a surge of retail interest and speculative trading. However, by December 2018, the price had plummeted to around $3,000, marking a significant bear market and leaving many investors reeling.

The cryptocurrency market rebounded impressively in subsequent years, with Bitcoin soaring to over $60,000 by 2021. This surge was fueled by increasing institutional adoption, growing mainstream acceptance, and the rise of decentralized finance (DeFi) and non-fungible tokens (NFTs).

institutional adoption, growing mainstream acceptance, and the rise of decentralized finance (DeFi) and non-fungible tokens (NFTs). However, the market's volatility remained evident. Following its peak, Bitcoin experienced another significant correction, eventually dipping to around $14,000 during the crypto market downturn of 2022. This decline was influenced by macroeconomic uncertainty, regulatory concerns, and the collapse of major crypto platforms, which shook investor confidence.

Despite the setbacks, Bitcoin demonstrated resilience. By April 2024, the price surged to a new high of $70,000, driven by a renewed wave of institutional interest, technological advancements, and a broader recovery in the cryptocurrency market. The rise was further bolstered by increasing adoption in developing nations, where Bitcoin was embraced as a hedge against inflation and economic instability.

Entering 2025, the market reached a historic milestone. In January, Bitcoin surpassed $100,000 for the first time, marking a new all-time high during a remarkable bull run. This latest rally was attributed to several factors, including the halving event of 2024, which reduced Bitcoin's supply issuance, and the influx of traditional financial institutions offering crypto-related products. Additionally, global economic shifts and a weakening trust in fiat currencies further solidified Bitcoin's role as a store of value.

These dramatic price movements underscore the high-risk, high-reward nature of cryptocurrencies. For investors, understanding market dynamics is crucial. The volatility can present lucrative opportunities for those who time their investments effectively but can also lead to significant losses for those unprepared for sudden price swings. Factors such as regulatory developments, macroeconomic trends, technological innovations, and market sentiment all play a role in driving the market's fluctuations.

In conclusion, **Bitcoin's price history**—from its 2017 high of nearly $20,000 to the $3,000 low in 2018, the $14,000 dip in 2022, the $70,000 surge in 2024, and its recent rise to over $100,000 in 2025—illustrates the unpredictable yet transformative nature of the cryptocurrency market. As cryptocurrencies continue to gain traction globally, volatility will remain a defining characteristic, requiring investors to approach the market with caution, strategy, and a long-term perspective.

Understanding historical trends in the cryptocurrency market is crucial for navigating its highly volatile nature. Bitcoin's price history reveals a pattern of dramatic bull runs followed by sharp corrections, often referred to as "***flash crashes***". In the current bull run of 2025, we have already witnessed two significant spikes, with Bitcoin reaching an all-time high of over $100,000. This pattern strongly suggests the likelihood of an impending market correction, as has been the case in previous cycles. Such corrections, while potentially alarming, create significant opportunities for prepared investors. Setting strategic buy limit orders at lower price points can enable savvy participants to capitalize on sudden dips, acquiring Bitcoin and other assets at discounted prices. By analyzing historical trends and planning accordingly, investors can position themselves to turn market volatility into a profitable advantage, even in the face of a possible Bitcoin flash crash in 2025.

Emotional Investing: Emotional investing is a common pitfall in volatile markets like cryptocurrencies, where fear and greed often overshadow rational decision-making. These powerful emotions can drive investors to make impulsive choices that lead to poor timing and significant financial losses. For example, during market dips, fear of further losses may compel novice investors to panic-sell their holdings, locking in losses rather than waiting for a potential recovery. On the other hand, greed during bullish trends can push investors to over-invest at inflated prices, chasing gains and exposing themselves to higher risks if the market abruptly corrects.

The cyclical nature of the cryptocurrency market, characterized by sharp rises and equally steep declines, exacerbates emotional decision-making. **Fear of missing out** (**FOMO**) during a bull run often leads investors to buy assets at their peak, while **fear, uncertainty, and doubt** (**FUD**) during downturns cause them to sell at the bottom. This behavior not only erodes potential profits but can also undermine long-term investment strategies.

To counter emotional investing, it is essential to adopt disciplined and objective approaches. Setting clear investment goals, adhering to a predetermined strategy, and maintaining a diversified portfolio can help investors stay grounded during market fluctuations. For instance, using tools like **dollar-cost averaging** (**DCA**) allows investors to buy assets at regular intervals, reducing the impact of market **volatility** on their overall **cost basis**. Similarly, employing stop-loss orders and profit-taking strategies can help manage risks and secure gains without requiring constant emotional involvement.

Education also plays a key role in mitigating the effects of emotional investing. Understanding market cycles, the drivers of volatility, and historical trends can provide perspective and reduce the likelihood of impulsive reactions. Investors who recognize the inevitability of corrections and the opportunities they present are better equipped to navigate market swings with confidence.

In summary, while fear and greed are natural responses to the volatility of cryptocurrency markets, allowing these emotions to dictate investment decisions can lead to poor timing and significant losses. By staying informed, disciplined, and focused on long-term objectives, investors can minimize the impact of emotions and make more rational decisions, ultimately improving their chances of success in this high-risk, high-reward environment.

Lessons Learned: Diversification, dollar-cost averaging, and maintaining a long-term perspective are essential strategies for successful investing in the cryptocurrency market. Diversification involves spreading investments across multiple assets or sectors to reduce risk and avoid the potential pitfalls of overexposure to a single asset. By allocating funds across various cryptocurrencies, industries, or even asset classes, investors can mitigate the impact of price volatility in any one area. Dollar-cost averaging is another effective approach, where individuals invest a fixed amount at regular intervals, regardless of market conditions.

This strategy helps to smooth out the effects of market fluctuations and reduces the risk of making poorly timed investments. Additionally, adopting a long-term perspective is crucial in navigating the inherent volatility of cryptocurrencies. Rather than being overly focused on short-term price movements, investors should consider the broader potential of blockchain technology and its transformative impact on industries and economies. Together, these strategies provide a balanced and disciplined approach to managing the risks and opportunities of cryptocurrency investing.

Education, discipline, and a clear investment strategy are essential for mitigating the risks associated with market volatility. The digital era presents unparalleled opportunities for financial growth, but it is not without its challenges. Regulatory uncertainty, security vulnerabilities, market volatility, and environmental concerns are significant hurdles that must be addressed to ensure a smooth transition to blockchain-based systems.

By understanding these risks and adopting proactive strategies, individuals and institutions can navigate the complexities of the digital landscape with confidence. As this technology continues to evolve, staying informed, vigilant, and adaptable will be the keys to unlocking its full potential while minimizing exposure to its challenges.

CHAPTER 18

BUILDING A STRONG INVESTMENT FOUNDATION: ESTABLISH FINANCIAL GOALS AND OBJECTIVES

The True Value of Success: Who You Become in the Process

Jim Rohn's quote, "*The **greatest value** in life is not what you get, it is what you will **become***," underscores the idea that true success is not merely measured by material wealth, accolades, or external achievements, but by the **personal growth**, **character**, and **wisdom** gained along the journey. While financial success, career milestones, and personal accomplishments are valuable, they are only byproducts of a much deeper transformation—the evolution of a person's mindset, discipline, resilience, and abilities.

When pursuing goals, people often focus on what they will gain—a higher income, financial security, or career advancement. However, the most profound reward is the person they must become to achieve those things. To succeed, one must develop **self-discipline**, **perseverance**, **emotional intelligence**, and a strong **work ethic**. The habits and mindset required to achieve success are what truly shape an individual's future. A person who builds financial discipline will not only accumulate wealth but will also cultivate responsibility, patience, and foresight—qualities that extend beyond finances and influence all aspects of life.

This principle can be applied to any ambition, whether it be entrepreneurship, personal development, leadership, or fitness. The journey toward mastery in any field forces individuals to grow, adapt, and overcome challenges. Every setback teaches resilience, every risk strengthens courage, and every success reinforces self-confidence. Even if external **rewards** are lost, the **skills**, **knowledge**, and **mindset** gained remain, allowing a person to rebuild and thrive once again.

Ultimately, true fulfillment comes not just from what is acquired but from who a person becomes in the process. Those who focus on self-improvement, **learning**, and **character development** will find that success follows naturally. The real wealth in life is not just in possessions but in **wisdom**, **experiences**, and **personal transformation**, which create a lasting impact long after material success fades.

Building a Strong Investment Foundation: Establish Financial Goals and Objectives

Successful investing is not about luck or chasing quick gains—it is about following a disciplined and informed strategy that aligns with personal financial goals. By incorporating key investment principles such as diversification, long-term planning, risk management, and cost efficiency, individuals can create a well-balanced approach that maximizes returns while minimizing unnecessary risks. Understanding these fundamental concepts provides the foundation for financial growth, stability, and wealth accumulation over time.

Understanding the Value of Time: Investing for Financial Freedom

Time is the **one resource** that no amount of **money can buy**. It is finite and irreplaceable, making it one of the most valuable assets a person possesses. Understanding this fundamental truth is essential when it comes to financial planning and investing. The primary purpose of investing is not just to accumulate wealth, but to achieve **financial freedom**—the ability to let **money work** for an individual rather than constantly having to **work for money**.

Financial freedom provides the flexibility to make choices based on **passion** and **fulfillment** rather than financial necessity. Instead of being bound to a job solely for the income it generates, an individual can choose to work in a field they love, pursue entrepreneurial ventures, or even dedicate time to charitable causes and personal growth. It creates the opportunity to spend more time with family, travel, or engage in activities that bring joy and meaning to life.

Furthermore, financial independence offers security and peace of mind. It reduces **stress** related to job stability, unexpected expenses, or economic downturns. With a solid investment strategy and careful financial planning, an individual can build a future where they are in control of their time—choosing how, where, and with whom they spend it. In essence, wealth should not be viewed as the end goal but as a means to regain the most valuable commodity of all: time.

Developing a Wealth Mindset: Shifting the Way You Think About Money

As previously discussed, wealthy individuals approach money, investing, and financial growth with a fundamentally different mindset compared to those who struggle financially. Their perspective is shaped by an **abundance mentality**—one that sees money as a tool for creating opportunities rather than a scarce resource that must be constantly chased. This shift in thinking is a key factor in building lasting financial success.

Developing a **wealth mindset** requires unlearning negative beliefs and habits around money, such as the fear of scarcity, the idea that wealth is only for the privileged, or the belief that financial success is purely a matter of luck. Instead, it involves adopting a mindset rooted in financial education, long-term planning, and strategic decision-making. Wealthy individuals view money as something to be leveraged, invested, and grown over time, rather than something to be spent impulsively or hoarded out of fear.

This transformation in thinking does not happen overnight. It requires a commitment to continuous learning, surrounding oneself with financially successful role models, and embracing a proactive approach to wealth-building. In the chapters ahead, we will explore the core principles of the **wealth mindset** in greater detail—highlighting the importance of financial literacy, risk-taking, and adopting habits that foster long-term prosperity. By shifting the way one thinks about money, an individual can unlock new opportunities, break free from financial limitations, and ultimately build a future of **financial security** and **abundance**.

Setting Clear Financial Goals: The Foundation of Successful Investing

Establishing well-defined investment goals is a critical step in building long-term financial success. Without clear objectives, it becomes easy to make impulsive or misaligned investment decisions that may not serve an individual's broader financial aspirations. Taking the time to set specific, measurable, and realistic goals helps create a roadmap for financial growth and ensures that each investment decision is intentional and strategic.

Investment objectives will vary depending on personal circumstances and long-term ambitions. Some individuals may focus on building wealth for retirement, ensuring they have a stable and comfortable future without **financial stress**. Others may prioritize saving for major life milestones such as purchasing a home, funding a child's education, or starting a business. Some may seek financial independence, aiming to generate enough passive income to reduce their reliance on traditional employment.

Defining these goals also helps determine an individual's investment strategy, risk tolerance, and time horizon. For example, long-term goals, such as retirement planning, often allow for a more aggressive investment approach with higher-risk assets like stocks, as there is more time to recover from market fluctuations. Conversely, short-term goals, such as saving for a home within the next five years, may require a more conservative strategy, prioritizing stability and lower-risk investments.

By setting clear financial goals, an individual can make informed investment choices, stay focused on long-term success, and measure progress along the way. Whether aiming for financial security, wealth accumulation, or personal aspirations, having a well-defined vision will serve as a guiding force in the journey toward financial growth and stability.

Diversify Your Portfolio: Reducing Risk and Maximizing Growth

Diversification is one of the most important principles of successful investing, as it helps protect against market volatility while enhancing long-term financial growth. Rather than relying on a single asset or investment type, a well-diversified portfolio spreads investments across multiple asset classes, industries, and markets. This strategy reduces overall risk by ensuring that losses in one area can be balanced by gains in another, creating a more stable financial foundation.

A properly diversified portfolio includes a mix of different asset classes, such as **stocks**, which offer growth potential but can be volatile; **real estate**, which can generate passive income and long-term appreciation; **cryptocurrency**, which, while speculative, presents high-growth opportunities; **precious metals** like gold and silver, which act as a hedge against inflation; and **land**, which tends to appreciate over time and can serve as a valuable long-term investment. Within each asset class, further diversification can be achieved by investing in different sectors, geographic regions, and company sizes to minimize exposure to any single economic downturn.

The key to effective diversification is finding the right balance based on an individual's financial goals, risk tolerance, and investment timeline. Younger investors with a longer time horizon may opt for a more aggressive diversification strategy, allocating a larger portion of their portfolio to high-growth assets like stocks and real estate. Meanwhile, those approaching retirement may prefer a more conservative mix, with a stronger emphasis on stable investments such as bonds and dividend-paying stocks.

By diversifying across and within asset classes, investors can better withstand economic fluctuations, reduce overall risk, and improve the likelihood of achieving long-term financial success. A well-structured portfolio ensures that no single market event or downturn can jeopardize an individual's entire financial future, making it a fundamental practice for both beginner and seasoned investors alike.

Invest for the Long Term: The Power of Patience and Compounding

Successful investing is not about trying to perfectly time the market—it's about staying invested for the long haul. Many investors make the mistake of attempting to predict short-term market movements, often buying when prices are high and selling when markets decline due to fear. However, history has shown that time in the market is far more important than timing the market when it comes to building sustainable wealth.

Long-term investing allows individuals to benefit from compounding returns, where earnings on investments generate additional earnings over time. The longer an investment remains in the market, the greater the opportunity for exponential growth. Even during periods of market volatility, staying invested provides the ability to ride out downturns and take advantage of long-term upward trends. Over time, markets have historically recovered from short-term declines, rewarding patient investors who remain committed to their strategy.

Additionally, a **long-term approach** reduces the **emotional stress** associated with market fluctuations. Rather than reacting impulsively to daily or short-term price movements, a well-structured **investment plan** focused on long-term growth fosters discipline and confidence. This strategy also aligns well with financial goals such as retirement savings, wealth accumulation, and generational wealth building.

By maintaining a long-term perspective, investors can take advantage of the power of market cycles, **compounding growth**, and strategic reinvestment. Regardless of market conditions, a patient and disciplined approach to investing consistently outperforms short-term speculation, leading to greater financial stability and success in the years to come.

Understanding Risk and Reward: Balancing Growth and Stability in Investing

Every investment carries a certain level of risk, and understanding the relationship between risk and reward is crucial for making informed financial decisions. Generally, investments with the potential for higher returns also come with greater risk, while lower-risk investments tend to provide more stability but with modest growth. Striking the right balance between risk and reward requires evaluating both an individual's risk tolerance and investment horizon before selecting investment vehicles.

Risk tolerance refers to an individual's ability and willingness to endure market fluctuations and potential losses. Some investors are comfortable taking on high levels of risk in pursuit of significant gains, while others prioritize preserving capital and prefer safer, more predictable returns. Age, financial situation, experience, and personal temperament all influence how much risk an investor is willing to take. For instance, a younger investor with decades until retirement may have a higher risk tolerance, allowing them to invest more heavily in volatile assets like stocks or cryptocurrencies. Meanwhile, an investor nearing retirement may opt for lower-risk assets, such as bonds and dividend-paying stocks, to protect their wealth.

Investment horizon, or the length of time an investor plans to hold an investment before needing access to the funds, also plays a key role in risk assessment. Long-term investments, such as those for retirement, can typically withstand short-term market fluctuations and benefit from **compounding growth** over time. On the other hand, short-term investments, such as saving for a down payment on a home, require more stability and less exposure to high-risk assets to avoid significant losses before the funds are needed.

A well-diversified investment portfolio balances risk and reward by allocating funds across various asset classes, such as stocks, bonds, real estate, and commodities. By understanding one's risk tolerance and investment horizon, an individual can create a financial strategy that aligns with their goals, minimizing unnecessary risks while maximizing potential rewards.

Conduct Research: Making Informed Investment Decisions

Before committing to any investment, it is essential to conduct thorough research to ensure that decisions are based on solid data rather than speculation or emotion. A well-informed investor takes the time to understand an asset's fundamentals, historical performance, and future prospects, which can help mitigate risks and improve long-term financial outcomes.

Fundamental analysis involves examining an investment's intrinsic value by reviewing key financial metrics such as revenue, profit margins, debt levels, and earnings growth. For stocks, this means analyzing financial statements, such as balance sheets, income statements, and cash flow reports, to assess a company's stability and profitability. In real estate, this might include evaluating market demand, property appreciation potential, and rental income trends.

In addition to reviewing individual investments, it is also important to consider historical performance and broader market trends. While past performance does not guarantee future success, looking at how an investment has responded to different economic conditions can provide valuable insights into its resilience and risk factors. For example, understanding how a stock performed during previous recessions or bull markets can help set realistic expectations for future growth.

Economic indicators, such as interest rates, inflation rates, employment data, and GDP growth, also play a crucial role in investment decisions. These indicators can help predict market trends and identify the best times to buy or sell certain assets. Additionally, researching industry trends and technological advancements can uncover emerging investment opportunities in sectors with high growth potential, such as renewable energy, artificial intelligence, or biotechnology.

Beyond independent research, it can also be beneficial to seek insights from financial analysts, investment reports, and reputable sources such as earnings calls, company reports, and market analysis publications. Understanding multiple perspectives helps create a well-rounded investment strategy, minimizing the risks associated with uninformed decisions.

By conducting comprehensive research before investing, individuals can make more strategic, data-driven choices, avoid unnecessary losses, and position themselves for long-term financial success. Investing without proper research is like navigating without a map—understanding the landscape is key to making smart, profitable decisions.

Stay Informed: The Key to Smart and Strategic Investing

Successful investing requires more than just selecting assets and hoping for positive returns—it demands continuous learning and staying informed about financial news, market developments, and industry trends. The global economy is dynamic, with markets constantly influenced by factors such as interest rates, inflation, technological advancements, geopolitical events, and corporate earnings reports. Keeping up with these changes ensures that investment decisions remain timely, strategic, and well-informed.

To stay ahead, investors should regularly follow financial news sources such as Bloomberg, CNBC, The Wall Street Journal, and market analysis reports from reputable investment firms. Monitoring stock market indices, economic indicators, and Federal Reserve policies can provide valuable insights into market direction and potential risks. Additionally, staying informed about government regulations, tax policies, and monetary policies helps investors anticipate changes that may impact their portfolios.

Beyond macroeconomic trends, investors should also focus on industry-specific developments. Emerging technologies, consumer behavior shifts, and disruptions in key industries can create new investment opportunities or signal risks to existing holdings. For example, advancements in artificial intelligence, electric vehicles, and renewable energy have reshaped entire markets, presenting new areas for potential growth. Likewise, staying updated on company earnings reports, leadership changes, and competitive positioning can provide crucial insights into the future performance of individual stocks.

Networking with other investors, participating in financial forums, and listening to expert analyses through podcasts, webinars, and investment newsletters can further enhance an investor's understanding. Additionally, regularly reviewing and analyzing one's own investment portfolio ensures that it aligns with market conditions and personal financial goals.

Informed investors are better equipped to make strategic adjustments, manage risk, and capitalize on opportunities. By consistently staying engaged with financial news and market trends, individuals can maintain a proactive approach to investing, increasing their chances of long-term financial success.

Avoid Emotional Decision-Making: Staying Disciplined for Long-Term Success

One of the biggest challenges investors face is managing emotions when markets fluctuate. Fear, greed, and impatience can often lead to impulsive decisions that undermine long-term financial success. When markets decline, fear may drive an investor to panic-sell assets at a loss, while during market booms, greed may tempt them to chase overpriced investments with unrealistic expectations. However, reacting emotionally to short-term volatility can be one of the most damaging mistakes an investor can make.

To build wealth successfully, it is crucial to maintain discipline and focus on long-term investment strategies. Markets naturally experience cycles of growth and decline, and temporary downturns should not dictate an investor's overall financial plan. Instead of making **rash decisions** based on market noise, it is wise to adhere to a well-structured investment strategy that is built around personal financial goals, risk tolerance, and time horizon.

A key way to avoid emotional decision-making is to establish a clear investment plan with defined entry and exit strategies. Diversification, asset allocation, and periodic portfolio rebalancing help minimize risk and provide stability during market fluctuations. Additionally, maintaining a long-term perspective and understanding historical market trends can reinforce confidence—history has shown that markets tend to recover over time despite periods of volatility.

Another effective strategy is implementing automated investing, such as dollar-cost averaging, which involves consistently investing a fixed amount at regular intervals. This approach removes the temptation to time the market and reduces the impact of emotional reactions to short-term price swings.

Investors should also limit their exposure to market speculation, media hype, and social media-driven panic. While staying informed is important, reacting emotionally to daily headlines or market rumors can lead to poor financial decisions. Instead, consulting with financial advisors, reviewing data-driven research, and sticking to a long-term strategy can help maintain confidence and rational decision-making.

By avoiding emotional reactions and staying disciplined, investors can protect their wealth, reduce unnecessary losses, and maximize long-term growth opportunities. The key to financial success is not reacting to every market fluctuation, but remaining patient, informed, and committed to a strategic investment plan.

Minimize Costs: Maximizing Returns by Reducing Investment Expenses

While many investors focus on returns, one often-overlooked factor that can significantly impact long-term wealth accumulation is investment costs and fees. High fees can quietly erode profits over time, diminishing the benefits of **compounding** and reducing overall portfolio growth. Being mindful of these costs and selecting low-cost investment options whenever possible is essential for optimizing financial success.

Investment costs come in many forms, including management fees, expense ratios, trading commissions, and advisory fees. Actively managed mutual funds, for example, often charge higher expense ratios, which can eat into returns, especially over long-time horizons. In contrast, low-cost index funds and exchange-traded funds (ETFs) typically have lower fees while still offering strong market exposure and diversification. Over decades, even a difference of 0.5% in fees can translate into thousands—or even hundreds of thousands—of dollars in lost returns.

Another important consideration is transaction costs and commissions. Frequent buying and selling of investments can result in unnecessary fees, reducing net gains. Instead, adopting a long-term, buy-and-hold strategy helps minimize trading costs and allows investments to grow uninterrupted. Additionally, many brokerage firms now offer commission-free trading, making it easier to reduce expenses associated with buying and selling stocks, ETFs, and other assets.

For those using financial advisors, it is important to understand their fee structure. Some advisors charge a percentage of assets under management (AUM), while others work on a flat-fee or hourly basis. Comparing options and ensuring that advisory fees are reasonable relative to the services provided can help maximize net investment gains.

By proactively minimizing investment costs, individuals can keep more of their earnings working for them, enhancing long-term portfolio growth. Choosing low-cost funds, reducing trading frequency, and being aware of hidden fees are all key strategies to ensure that costs do not become a drag on financial success. Over time, keeping expenses low can make a substantial difference in building and preserving wealth.

Rebalance Your Portfolio: Maintaining Stability and Alignment with Your Goals

Over time, **market fluctuations** can cause an investment portfolio to drift away from its original asset allocation, potentially increasing risk or reducing growth potential. Rebalancing is the process of periodically reviewing and adjusting a portfolio to ensure it remains aligned with an individual's investment goals, risk tolerance, and time horizon. This disciplined approach helps maintain a well-structured investment strategy, preventing any single asset class from becoming overly dominant or underweighted.

As markets rise and fall, certain assets may appreciate significantly while others may decline. For example, if stocks perform exceptionally well over a period of time, they may end up comprising a larger percentage of a portfolio than originally intended, increasing overall risk exposure. Conversely, underperforming assets may shrink in proportion, causing the portfolio to become unbalanced. Rebalancing involves selling portions of overperforming assets and reallocating those funds into underweighted areas, restoring the portfolio to its intended allocation.

There are different approaches to rebalancing, including time-based rebalancing (e.g., quarterly, semi-annually, or annually) and threshold-based rebalancing (adjusting when asset allocations deviate by a certain percentage from the target). Some investors prefer automatic rebalancing through robo-advisors or retirement accounts, ensuring adjustments are made without emotional decision-making.

Rebalancing not only helps manage risk but also encourages buying low and selling high, a fundamental principle of successful investing. It prevents an investor from becoming too heavily exposed to a **single asset class** or market sector, reducing the impact of **volatility** and maintaining **long-term financial stability**.

By regularly reviewing and rebalancing their portfolio, investors can stay on track toward their financial goals, ensure that their investments reflect their risk tolerance, and optimize performance over time. Consistent rebalancing is a crucial part of disciplined, strategic investing that helps safeguard and grow wealth efficiently.

Seek Professional Guidance When Needed: Leveraging Expertise for Smarter Investing

Investing can be complex, and while independent research and financial education are valuable, there are times when seeking professional guidance can make a significant difference in financial success. A financial advisor or investment professional can provide personalized advice, helping individuals navigate important decisions, avoid costly mistakes, and develop a strategy tailored to their specific financial situation and long-term goals.

Professional guidance is particularly beneficial during major financial transitions, such as planning for retirement, managing a large inheritance, purchasing real estate, or adjusting investments due to market downturns. An advisor can help with asset allocation, tax-efficient investment strategies, estate planning, and risk management, ensuring that all aspects of an individual's financial plan work together seamlessly.

Additionally, investment professionals can offer objective insights and help prevent **emotional decision-making**. **Market volatility**, economic uncertainty, or sudden financial changes can lead to impulsive investment choices that may not align with a long-term strategy. A trusted advisor can provide data-driven recommendations, keeping investors focused on their goals rather than reacting to short-term market fluctuations.

When choosing a financial advisor, it is important to consider their qualifications, experience, and fee structure. Some advisors charge a percentage of assets under management (AUM), while others operate on a flat-fee or hourly basis. Understanding these differences ensures that investors find an advisor who aligns with their needs and provides value without excessive costs.

Ultimately, working with a professional can provide clarity, confidence, and strategic direction, making complex investment decisions more manageable. Whether consulting an advisor for occasional guidance or comprehensive financial planning, leveraging professional expertise can help individuals build, protect, and maximize their wealth effectively.

By adhering to these principles, investors can lay the groundwork for a structured and informed investment strategy tailored to their objectives, risk tolerance, and time horizon. A well-thought-out approach ensures resilience during market fluctuations and fosters confidence in long-term financial planning. As financial knowledge and experience grow, refining and adjusting strategies will further enhance investment success. In the end, a **disciplined**, well-researched investment plan is the key to achieving financial independence and long-term prosperity.

Establish Financial Goals and Objectives

The Power of Diligence in Building Wealth

Proverbs 10:4 states, "***Lazy** hands make for **poverty**, but **diligent** hands bring **wealth**.*" This verse highlights a fundamental truth about success and financial prosperity—**wealth** is not built by **chance** but through **consistent effort**, **discipline**, and **intentional action**.

To be diligent means to exhibit care, persistence, and a strong work ethic in one's responsibilities. A diligent person does not wait for opportunities to come to them; they actively seek ways to grow, improve, and create financial stability. Diligence involves being thorough, focused, and committed to long-term success, making it a key ingredient in wealth-building.

The journey to financial success begins with clear goals and a well-defined plan. It is not enough to simply desire wealth—one must be proactive in setting specific financial objectives and taking deliberate steps toward achieving them. This starts with outlining short-term and long-term financial milestones, such as:

- Saving for a home
- Planning for retirement
- Investing in education
- Launching a business
- Growing an investment portfolio

Each of these goals requires dedication, strategic planning, and persistence. It is important to not only set financial objectives but also to create a structured roadmap for achieving them. This might involve developing a savings strategy, learning about investments, budgeting effectively, and maintaining financial discipline.

Diligence in financial matters also means being mindful of daily habits and decisions. Small, consistent efforts—such as managing expenses wisely, avoiding unnecessary debt, and continuously increasing financial knowledge—compound over time to create lasting wealth.

Ultimately, the principle behind Proverbs 10:4 is that financial success is earned through steady, persistent effort. By applying diligence to money management, career growth, and investment strategies, individuals can build a secure and prosperous future, ensuring that their hard work today leads to financial stability and opportunities in the future.

The Power of Well-Designed Goals in Shaping Your Future

Jim Rohn's quote, from his book The Art of Exceptional Living, "*To design your future you must have well-designed goals. The harder you work on them the harder they pull*," highlights the transformative power of setting clear, meaningful goals and committing to them with dedication and perseverance. Goals are not just aspirations; they serve as guiding forces that shape decisions, fuel motivation, and create momentum. When structured with purpose and intention, well-designed goals become a magnetic pull, drawing individuals closer to the future they envision—even during challenging times.

Applying this principle begins with defining both short-term and long-term aspirations. Short-term goals, such as building an emergency fund, paying off debt, or advancing in a career, provide immediate direction and measurable progress. These milestones keep motivation high and create a foundation for greater achievements. Long-term goals, on the other hand, such as purchasing a home, achieving financial independence, or starting a successful business, serve as the ultimate vision for the future. While these may take years to accomplish, consistently working toward them strengthens resilience and determination.

The key to making goals effective and compelling is designing them in a way that inspires action. This involves setting **specific**, **measurable**,

achievable, **relevant**, and **time-bound (SMART) objectives**, ensuring that progress can be tracked and adjusted along the way. The more detailed and well-structured a goal is, the more tangible and powerful it becomes —constantly pulling an individual forward, even through setbacks and obstacles.

Life will inevitably present challenges, uncertainties, and setbacks, but well-designed goals serve as a constant source of motivation and clarity. When faced with difficulties, returning to these goals provides the mental and emotional strength needed to push forward. By continuously refining and working on personal and financial goals with persistence, individuals create their own future rather than leaving it to chance. Ultimately, the harder one works on their aspirations, the more those aspirations pull them toward a fulfilling, purpose-driven, and successful life.

Creating a Structured Roadmap for Your Aspirations and Goals

Achieving success in any area of life requires clear, well-defined goals that provide direction, motivation, and measurable progress. Establishing short-term, mid-term, and long-term goals ensures that every step taken today contributes to a larger vision for the future. By setting specific objectives in key areas such as finances, health, education, and family, individuals can maintain focus, track their progress, and create a structured path toward success.

1. Defining Short-Term Aspirations and Goals (1-2 Years)

Short-term goals lay the foundation for long-term success by focusing on immediate actions and measurable milestones. These goals typically cover a one-to-two-year timeframe and should be well-structured, actionable, and time-bound.

- **Financial Goals:** Start by developing a **30-60-90 day plan**, outlining key objectives for the next 30, 60, and 90 days, with clear milestones to track progress on a weekly and monthly basis. Extend these goals further, creating a structured roadmap for the next 12 months. Tools such as daily checklists, goal-tracking apps, or financial journals can help maintain focus and consistency. Set specific targets for savings, investments, and debt reduction, ensuring that each decision aligns

- with your overall financial growth. Without well-defined financial goals, building and maintaining wealth becomes significantly more difficult.

- **Health Goals:** Prioritizing health is essential for long-term success. Establish clear nutrition and fitness goals, breaking them down into daily, weekly, and monthly targets. Whether it's adopting a healthier diet, maintaining a consistent exercise routine, or improving mental well-being, creating realistic and achievable health objectives ensures continuous improvement. Small, daily habits—such as drinking more water, reducing processed foods, or committing to a regular workout—compound over time and lead to significant lifestyle improvements.

- **Education Goals:** Personal growth and skill development are lifelong pursuits. Identify key learning materials, courses, or books that align with your career and personal development aspirations. Create a structured plan, dedicating specific daily and weekly time slots for self-education. Whether it's taking online courses, reading books, or attending workshops, setting tangible education goals ensures consistent progress in personal and professional growth.

- **Family Goals:** Success is most fulfilling when shared with loved ones. Ensure that family remains a priority by including them in goal-setting and planning. Set specific family-oriented goals, such as scheduling regular quality time, family vacations, or shared financial objectives. Creating a balance between personal ambition and family commitments leads to stronger relationships and a more fulfilling life.

2. Defining Mid-Term Aspirations and Goals (2-5 Years)

Mid-term goals serve as a bridge between short-term achievements and long-term aspirations. These objectives typically cover a two-to-five-year timeframe, allowing individuals to build on early progress while working toward more substantial milestones.

- In the financial realm, mid-term goals may include saving for a home, starting a business, increasing investment contributions, or eliminating debt.
- Health goals may involve achieving a specific level of physical fitness,

- maintaining long-term dietary habits, or implementing stress-reduction techniques that contribute to overall well-being.
- Educational objectives could include earning a degree, mastering a new skill set, or obtaining a professional certification that enhances career opportunities.
- Family-focused goals may include planning for major life transitions, such as relocating, expanding the family, or securing financial stability for loved ones.

Mid-term goals should be regularly reviewed and adjusted based on progress and any changes in personal priorities or circumstances.

3. Defining Long-Term Aspirations and Goals (5-10 Years)

Long-term goals provide a vision for the future, shaping the life an individual ultimately wants to build. These objectives typically extend five to ten years into the future and require a strategic, patient, and disciplined approach.

- Financially, long-term goals may involve achieving financial independence, growing a diverse investment portfolio, reaching a retirement savings milestone, or building generational wealth.
- Health goals might include maintaining a sustainable fitness routine, adopting a long-term wellness plan, or ensuring lifelong health through preventive care.
- Educational aspirations could focus on career mastery, continuous learning, and expanding expertise in specialized fields.
- Family-related long-term goals may involve providing financial security for children, ensuring estate planning is in place, or planning for retirement with a partner.

Long-term goals require consistent commitment, adaptability, and long-range planning. By periodically reviewing and refining objectives, individuals can ensure steady progress toward their ultimate vision for success.

Final Thoughts: The Power of Goal-Setting in Achieving Success

The key to turning dreams into reality is to structure goals effectively, track progress consistently, and remain adaptable. By setting **short-term**, **mid-term**, and **long-term goals** in key areas of life—including finance, health, education, and family—individuals create a clear path toward personal and professional fulfillment.

Success is not achieved overnight, but through small, consistent actions, well-defined goals serve as a compass that guides every decision and effort. By working diligently toward each milestone, individuals design their future with intention, ensuring that every step taken today contributes to a more prosperous and fulfilling tomorrow.

The Power of Desire in Achieving Wealth

Another great quote from Jim Rohn's in his book The Art of Exceptional Living, "*If you don't have to be rich, you probably won't be driven to get rich*," speaks to the fundamental role that desire, and necessity play in achieving financial success. Wealth is not something that simply happens —it is created through ambition, persistence, and intentional action. Those who feel a deep personal need to achieve **financial freedom** are far more likely to pursue wealth with the focus, discipline, and determination required to attain it. On the other hand, individuals who view wealth as optional or unnecessary may lack the drive to make the sacrifices and strategic decisions necessary for financial prosperity.

This principle applies not only to financial success but to all areas of life. Whether in career advancement, entrepreneurship, personal growth, or physical fitness, the level of commitment and motivation often correlates with how deeply an individual feels the need to succeed. When the desire to become wealthy is rooted in a strong purpose—such as securing financial independence, providing a better future for one's family, or leaving a lasting legacy—it fuels the daily habits, mindset, and decisions that lead to wealth accumulation.

To apply this principle, individuals must identify why financial success is important to them. Is it to achieve freedom from a paycheck-to-paycheck lifestyle? To gain the ability to travel, pursue passions, or make a difference in the world? To build generational wealth and provide security for loved ones? When the need for wealth is deeply ingrained, it becomes a powerful motivator that drives action, discipline, and resilience through challenges.

Ultimately, success—whether financial or otherwise—does not come from passive wishing but from an unshakable internal drive. The more a person recognizes the necessity of achieving their goals, the more determined they become in making them a reality. As Jim Rohn suggests, those who deeply desire wealth and see it as a non-negotiable goal will be the ones who put in the effort, make the right choices, and ultimately achieve financial success.

The Importance of Setting Meaningful Financial Goals and a Strategic Investment Plan

A critical part of financial planning is setting clear, meaningful goals for savings and investments. Without a well-defined plan, financial success is left to chance. Take the time to ask yourself important questions: "*Am I being diligent in my preparation? Am I consistently scheduling time to work toward my financial goals?*" Achieving financial security and wealth requires more than just intention—it demands structured planning, commitment, and disciplined action. Simply thinking about financial success is not enough; writing down a concrete plan and executing it with consistency is what turns goals into reality.

One of the key elements of goal setting is establishing an investment strategy that aligns with personal risk tolerance, financial timeline, and specific milestones. Whether the objective is to build an emergency fund, save for a home, accumulate retirement wealth, or achieve financial independence, each investment decision should be strategically planned to match both short-term and long-term financial aspirations. By creating a structured investment strategy, individuals can effectively manage risk, optimize returns, and ensure steady financial growth over time.

However, setting financial goals is not a one-time event—it requires continuous evaluation and adjustment. Markets fluctuate, personal circumstances evolve, and new financial opportunities arise. As part of this financial journey, it is essential to regularly review and rebalance your investment portfolio to stay aligned with long-term objectives. This means adjusting allocations, reassessing risk tolerance, and ensuring that every investment decision still supports the overarching financial plan.

Ultimately, wealth-building is an intentional and ongoing process. By setting clear savings and investment goals, developing a solid investment strategy, and consistently reviewing progress, individuals can take full control of their financial future. Success does not happen by accident—it is the result of careful planning, strategic decision-making, and unwavering commitment to long-term financial well-being.

Guiding Questions for Setting Meaningful Financial Goals and Objectives

- Who are you today, and who do you aspire to become? Reflect on your current financial position, skills, and lifestyle, and envision the future version of yourself. What changes need to happen to bridge the gap between where you are now and where you want to be?
- What is your deeper purpose? What motivates and inspires you beyond financial gain? Identify the driving forces behind your goals—whether it's creating financial security for your family, making a meaningful impact in your community, or achieving personal fulfillment.
- What lifestyle do you envision, and how much wealth is required to sustain it? Define your ideal standard of living, including career aspirations, home ownership, investments, and long-term financial stability. Determine how much money is needed to fund and sustain this lifestyle.
- How does travel fit into your life plan? Do you aspire to travel frequently, and if so, will it be for leisure, business, or both? Where do you dream of going, and how often? Understanding these desires helps shape your financial roadmap.
- What causes, businesses, or projects do you want to support? If you are passionate about philanthropy, social impact, or business ownership, recognize that making a difference requires financial resources. Define how you want to contribute and what level of wealth will be necessary to support these endeavors.
- What skills or knowledge must you acquire to reach your goals? Consider the personal and professional development needed to achieve financial success. Whether it's mastering investment strategies, leadership skills, or entrepreneurial knowledge, identify the areas that require growth and create a plan to enhance your expertise.

By thoughtfully answering these questions, you can clarify your financial objectives, create a strategic plan, and develop the mindset needed to turn your vision into reality.

The Power of a Vision Board: Turning Financial Goals into Reality

Consider the use of a vision board, which is a powerful tool for visualizing and manifesting financial and life goals. By creating a physical or digital representation of aspirations—whether it's wealth accumulation, career success, travel, philanthropy, or personal development—a vision board serves as a daily reminder of what truly matters.

Visualization is a proven technique used by successful entrepreneurs, athletes, and leaders to stay focused and motivated. Seeing images, quotes, and symbols that represent financial independence, investment milestones, dream destinations, or business achievements reinforces the commitment to taking consistent action.

A vision board helps align thoughts with goals, making them feel more tangible and attainable. It also strengthens discipline and decision-making, keeping individuals focused on long-term success rather than being distracted by short-term temptations or setbacks. By placing the vision board in a visible location and reviewing it regularly, individuals can maintain clarity, stay inspired, and remain accountable to the financial future they are striving to create.

Pairing a Vision Board with a Detailed Financial Budget: Turning Dreams into Action

While a vision board serves as a powerful visual representation of financial aspirations, it must be accompanied by a detailed written financial budget to transform those dreams into actionable goals. Until goals are clearly defined and written down, they remain abstract ideas rather than concrete objectives. A well-structured financial budget outlines income, expenses, savings targets, investment contributions, and debt repayment plans, ensuring that every financial decision aligns with long-term goals.

This written plan provides clarity, direction, and accountability, helping individuals track progress and make adjustments as needed. By breaking down financial aspirations into specific milestones with realistic timelines, a budget helps prioritize goals—whether it's saving for a home, funding retirement, traveling the world, or starting a business. Reviewing both the vision board and financial budget regularly ensures that motivation stays high, spending habits remain aligned with priorities, and financial success is deliberate and strategic rather than left to chance. Combining visualization with structured financial planning creates a roadmap for achieving true financial freedom.

Achieving financial success requires more than just wishing for it—it demands clear goal-setting, strategic planning, and consistent action. A **vision board** serves as a daily reminder of what is truly important, keeping **motivation** high and **aspirations** within reach. However, without a detailed financial budget and a structured plan, these dreams remain intangible. By outlining specific financial goals, setting achievable milestones, and regularly reviewing both a vision board and budget, individuals can stay focused, disciplined, and proactive in building their desired future. Success is not a matter of chance but of intention and persistence—those who define their goals, create a plan, and take action will ultimately turn their financial dreams into reality.

CHAPTER 19

TAKING RESPONSIBILITY FOR YOUR PERSONAL FINANCES

Creating a personal **financial budget** is a crucial step toward achieving financial **stability** and **long-term wealth**. A well-planned budget serves as a **roadmap** for managing income, expenses, savings, and investments, ensuring that financial goals are met efficiently. Without a structured plan, it is easy to overspend, accumulate debt, or neglect important savings opportunities. By thoughtfully organizing financial resources, individuals and families can take control of their money, make informed spending decisions, and secure their future. In the following section, we will explore key strategies for building a comprehensive budget that prioritizes savings, minimizes unnecessary expenses, and incorporates smart investment practices.

1. **Creating a Personal Financial Budget**

A **well-structured budget** is the **foundation** of **financial** responsibility. Allocating funds toward a **savings category** and an **investment category** ensures that financial **stability** is prioritized. Setting aside money for future needs is crucial—consider it as paying oneself first. When an individual diverts money from savings to cover present-day expenses, they are, in effect, **robbing their future self**. It is essential to move beyond a casual approach to money management and treat it with the seriousness it demands. This is no longer a simple classroom exercise but a vital aspect of adult life that determines long-term financial security.

For individuals or families trying to save money and invest more, creating a comprehensive budget involves identifying essential and non-essential expenses. **Essential expenses** include housing costs (rent or mortgage payments), utilities, groceries, transportation, healthcare, and insurance. These are non-negotiable costs that must be accounted for before allocating funds to discretionary spending.

When seeking to optimize a budget for savings and investments, individuals should consider areas where spending can be minimized. Dining out, entertainment subscriptions, luxury purchases, and impulse shopping can often be adjusted or eliminated to free up more money for future financial growth. Additionally, small changes such as meal planning to reduce food waste, utilizing public transportation or carpooling to save on fuel, and negotiating lower rates on recurring expenses like internet and phone bills can create more opportunities to save.

Investing a portion of income should be a deliberate and recurring part of the budget. Automating transfers to a high-yield savings account, retirement funds, or brokerage accounts ensures that investing becomes a habit rather than an afterthought. Exploring tax-advantaged investment options such as an IRA or 401(k) can help maximize long-term savings while minimizing taxable income. Those looking to grow wealth should also consider diversifying investments across stocks, bonds, index funds, and real estate, depending on risk tolerance and financial goals.

By taking a structured approach to budgeting and prioritizing both savings and investments, individuals and families can build financial security, avoid unnecessary debt, and achieve long-term **financial independence**.

2. Sticking to the Budget

Merely creating a budget is not enough; it must be adhered to with discipline. Once funds are allocated to specific categories, deviating from those plans can result in financial instability. **Consistency is key**, and maintaining a steady commitment to financial goals ensures progress over time. Any deviation from the plan should be met with an immediate **review of expenditures** and necessary course correction.

To successfully stick to a budget, individuals should establish strong financial habits and routines. Setting up **automatic payments** for **recurring expenses** and savings contributions **helps remove** the temptation to **overspend**. Additionally, tracking daily expenses using financial apps or spreadsheets can provide a clear picture of spending patterns and help identify potential problem areas before they become significant setbacks.

Another effective strategy is practicing mindful spending. Before making a purchase, individuals should ask themselves whether it aligns with their financial goals and if it is truly necessary. Developing a habit of delayed gratification—waiting a day or two before making non-essential purchases—can help curb impulse spending and reinforce better financial discipline.

It is also important to anticipate and plan for irregular expenses, such as car repairs, medical bills, or holiday shopping. Setting aside a portion of income into an **emergency fund** can prevent these **unplanned costs** from **derailing** financial progress. Keeping financial goals visible, such as listing them on a bulletin board or using reminders on a phone, can also serve as motivation to stay on track. By maintaining discipline, tracking spending habits, and making necessary adjustments along the way, individuals can develop strong financial habits that lead to long-term financial security and success.

3. Categories of Spending in a Personal Financial Budget

A well-structured budget consists of various spending categories to help individuals allocate their income effectively. Below are examples of different categories of spending that should be considered:

Housing

- Rent/Mortgage Payments
- Property Taxes
- Homeowners or Renters Insurance
- Home Maintenance and Repairs
- HOA Fees
- Lawn or Gardening Services

Healthcare

- Health Insurance Premiums
- Medical and Dental Expenses
- Prescription Medications
- Vision Care
- Mental Health Services
- Medical and Dental Discretionary fund (savings)

Utilities

- Electricity
- Water and Sewer
- Gas
- Trash Collection
- Internet and Cable
- Phone Services

Food

- Groceries
- Dining Out
- Coffee and Snacks
- Meal Delivery Services
- Vitamins and supplements

Transportation

- Car Payments
- Fuel and Gas
- Auto Insurance
- Public Transportation
- Ride-Sharing Services
- Vehicle Maintenance and Repairs

Personal Expenses

- Clothing and Shoes
- Cleaning and household supplies
- Haircuts, Grooming, Hair Maintenance, and Nails
- Hobbies and Leisure Activities
- Gym Memberships

Education and Self-Improvement

- Child Daycare or After-School Programs
- Tuition and School Fees
- Books and Learning Materials
- Online Courses and Certifications
- Conferences and Workshops

Debt Repayment

- Credit Card Payments
- Student Loans
- Personal Loans
- Car Loans
- Mortgage Payments

Savings and Investments

- Emergency Fund Contributions
- Retirement Savings (401(k), IRA, Roth IRA)
- Stock Market Investments
- Cryptocurrency Investments
- College Fund (529 Plan)

Insurance

- Health Insurance
- Life Insurance
- Auto Insurance
- Homeowners or Renters Insurance
- Disability Insurance

Entertainment and Leisure

- Movies and Concerts
- Streaming Services Subscriptions (e.g., Netflix, Prime, Hulu, HBO, Magazines, Apps, etc.)
- Sports and Outdoor Activities
- Vacations and Travel
- Gaming and Recreational Activities

Miscellaneous Expenses

- Pet Expenses
- Gifts and Celebrations
- Emergency and Unexpected Costs

Charitable Giving and Donations

- Religious Tithing
- Non-Profit Donations
- Crowdfunding Contributions

4. Plan Ahead To Keep From Being Caught In A Jam

Now while I could go through each of these points with specific examples, here below are a few things to consider in the following categories of spending:

Transportation: A person's transportation costs will vary based on their specific situation. This may include expenses such as car payment and auto insurance or, alternatively, costs for ride-sharing services and public transportation. For those who own a vehicle, budgeting for regular maintenance and potential repairs is essential. To better prepare for these expenses, it can be helpful to research and estimate the costs of common maintenance items for your specific vehicle—or the one you plan to purchase. This will give you a clearer understanding of how much you should allocate annually for unexpected automotive expenses, helping you avoid financial surprises.

- **Oil Changes** - Typically needed every 3,000-7,500 miles, depending on your vehicle and oil type.
- **Tire Rotations and Balancing** - Helps ensure even wear and extends the life of your tires (usually every 5,000-7,500 miles).
- **Brake Inspections and Replacements** - Includes brake pads, rotors, and fluid checks (brake pads usually last 30,000-70,000 miles).
- **Air Filter Replacement** - Both engine and cabin air filters should be replaced periodically for efficiency and air quality.
- **Fluid Checks and Top-offs** - Transmission fluid, coolant (antifreeze), power steering fluid, and brake fluid all require periodic checks and refills.
- **New Tires** - Plan for replacements every 25,000-60,000 miles, depending on driving habits and tire quality.
- **Wheel Alignment** - Keeps tires wearing evenly and ensures proper handling, often needed after hitting potholes or replacing tires.
- **Battery Replacement** - Most car batteries last between 3-5 years; regular testing can prevent unexpected failures.

- **Spark Plug Replacement** – Essential for engine performance, typically replaced between 30,000–100,000 miles depending on the vehicle.
- **Headlight, Brake Light, and Turn Signal Bulb Replacements** – Regular checks ensure visibility and compliance with road safety laws.
- **Timing Belt or Chain Replacement** – Failure can cause major engine damage; replacement intervals vary by manufacturer, typically 60,000–100,000 miles.
- **Transmission Service** – Fluid replacement or flushes are necessary to maintain smooth shifting and prolong the life of the transmission.
- **Coolant System Flush** – Helps prevent overheating and engine damage, usually recommended every 30,000–50,000 miles.
- **Fuel System Cleaning** – Includes fuel injector cleaning and replacing the fuel filter for better performance and efficiency.

Having a warranty on a newer vehicle can be incredibly valuable, especially as a car approaches the 100,000-mile mark. It is important for an individual to be aware of when their maintenance warranty is set to expire and to seriously consider extending it. Allowing a warranty to lapse can lead to significant out-of-pocket expenses just as a vehicle reaches the stage where costly repairs are more likely to arise. Extended warranties are often timed perfectly to cover major maintenance and unexpected repairs, making them a worthwhile investment.

Unfortunately for me, I allowed my warranty to lapse and did not purchase an extended warranty. Within the last six months, my vehicle required a combination of necessary maintenance for the 100,000-mile milestone and unexpected repairs totaling approximately $18,000. These included a blown head gasket, transmission replacement, motor mount replacement, new tires, coolant line replacements, front and rear shocks, and brake pad replacements. At times, it felt as though an entirely new vehicle was being rebuilt. While it would have been possible to purchase a used car for the same amount, I had worked hard to purchase and fully pay off this vehicle—a 2018 Chevy Tahoe—within two years of purchase, making the investment in repairs the preferable option.

Planning ahead for vehicle maintenance, warranty extensions, and potential repairs can save a significant amount of money in the long run. Whether keeping an existing vehicle on the road or upgrading to a newer one, factoring in maintenance costs and warranty coverage is a critical part of responsible vehicle ownership.

Healthcare: For most employees, health and dental insurance premiums are automatically deducted from their paychecks, eliminating the need to set aside funds for these expenses. However, for those who work as independent contractors or are self-employed, this is not the case. If you fall into this category, you are responsible for researching, selecting, and enrolling in a suitable insurance policy, as well as making premium payments independently. This can be a significant financial commitment, so careful planning is necessary to ensure coverage without straining your budget.

Beyond standard health and dental insurance, it's also important to consider other wellness-related expenses. Mental health services, for example, are a crucial aspect of overall well-being and may require additional budgeting. This can include costs for personal coaching, regular visits with a therapist or psychiatrist, meditation classes, or even massage therapy for stress relief and relaxation. While some of these services may be covered under certain health plans, others may need to be paid for out-of-pocket, making it essential to factor them into your financial plan.

In addition to building an emergency fund, setting aside money specifically for medical co-pays, prescription costs, or unforeseen out-of-pocket medical expenses is a wise financial strategy. As people age, healthcare expenses tend to rise, whether due to more frequent doctor visits, specialist consultations, or ongoing treatments. Proactively planning for these costs can help alleviate financial stress and ensure continued access to necessary care without disruption.

Miscellaneous Expenses: Again, speaking from personal experience here, it is important to consider the costs of owning a pet before making commitments to becoming a pet owner. Pet medical expenses are not cheap and if you do have a pet, it might be worth looking into pet medical insurance. Because you never know when your pet is going to eat a crayon, a tennis ball, or something else that will require a life saving surgery that could cost anywhere between $5,000 - $7,000.

An unexpected complication that arose when we got our dog spayed, (due to a lack of sufficient oxygen during surgery), caused brain damage and resulted in our dog now having epilepsy. This requires a very special diet, monthly medications that cost on average $120 per month, annual check-ups with blood work that cost on average $500, as well as other unexpected health issues that arise from time-to-time that have resulted in varying costs over the years.

In addition, it is important to consider allocating funds towards an 'Emergency Fund' to help cover any unexpected costs that may arise, because they will. By categorizing spending effectively, individuals can gain better control over their finances, identify areas where they can cut costs, and allocate funds to achieve financial goals more efficiently. A well-balanced budget allows for financial security and stability while ensuring essential and discretionary spending are well-managed.

5. Reducing and Eliminating Needless or Frivolous Spending

One of the biggest impediments to financial growth is frivolous spending. Unnecessary expenditures, such as impulsive shopping, frequent dining out, or expensive entertainment, can quickly add up. Identifying and eliminating such spending habits allows for more money to be directed toward savings and investments. Thoughtful spending is the first step toward long-term financial security.

To effectively reduce frivolous spending, individuals should start by assessing their purchasing habits. This can be achieved by **reviewing bank statements**, tracking daily expenses, and categorizing purchases into needs versus wants. Identifying patterns in unnecessary spending can provide valuable insight into where adjustments can be made.

Creating a spending plan that prioritizes necessities and long-term goals over short-term gratification is essential. Strategies such as implementing a **24-hour** or **30-day rule** for **non-essential purchases** can help curb impulse spending. By delaying purchases, individuals may find that their initial desire for an item diminishes over time, saving money in the process.

Another useful approach is establishing a set allowance for discretionary spending each month. Setting a reasonable limit for non-essential items ensures that indulgences do not derail financial goals while still allowing for occasional enjoyment. Using cash instead of credit or debit cards for discretionary purchases can also help maintain control over spending, as physically handing over cash tends to make individuals more conscious of their purchases.

Seeking cost-effective alternatives to expensive habits can also lead to significant savings. For example, preparing meals at home instead of dining out, borrowing books instead of purchasing new ones, or taking advantage of free recreational activities rather than costly **entertainment** options can all help reduce expenses. Additionally, canceling unused subscriptions, negotiating better rates on recurring bills, and utilizing discount programs can contribute to long-term savings.

Financial accountability is another powerful tool for curbing unnecessary spending. Sharing financial goals with a trusted friend, partner, or mentor can provide encouragement and reinforcement. Joining budgeting groups or online communities focused on frugal living can also offer inspiration and support in maintaining financial discipline.

By consistently evaluating and adjusting spending habits, individuals can redirect funds toward meaningful financial goals, such as building an emergency fund, investing for the future, and achieving **financial independence**. Through mindful spending and intentional financial decisions, long-term financial security can become a reality.

6. Identifying Areas to Cut or Reduce Spending

Achieving financial goals may require making hard decisions and getting creative with expenditure reductions. Cutting unnecessary expenses, such as subscription services that are rarely used, choosing to prepare meals at home instead of dining out frequently, and opting for cost-effective alternatives for daily habits like coffee purchases, can significantly impact overall financial health. Adjusting these spending patterns may be challenging at first, but the rewards of financial stability far outweigh the initial inconvenience.

To start, individuals should conduct a thorough **review** of their expenses to determine where **reductions** can be made. This may include canceling unused gym memberships, switching to generic brands for groceries and household products, or carpooling to reduce fuel costs. Additionally, negotiating better rates on recurring bills such as insurance, phone plans, or internet services can yield substantial savings over time.

Another way to **cut spending** is by adopting a minimalist approach to lifestyle choices. Prioritizing needs over wants and avoiding impulse purchases can help reduce financial strain. Consider second-hand shopping for clothing, furniture, or electronics instead of purchasing brand-new items at full price. Utilizing community resources such as public libraries, local events, and free recreational activities can also provide **entertainment** without unnecessary expenses.

For those who frequently eat out, meal prepping and batch cooking can help minimize food costs while also promoting healthier eating habits. Planning meals in advance, taking advantage of grocery store discounts, and using coupons can significantly reduce grocery expenses. Additionally, avoiding food waste by properly storing perishables and repurposing leftovers can further contribute to financial savings. By making these conscious adjustments and developing a strategic approach to spending, individuals can free up more resources to allocate toward savings and investments, ultimately paving the way for long-term financial success and security.

7. Identifying Problem Areas

Financial pitfalls often stem from a **lack of awareness**. If an individual struggles with using **financial tools** such as **Excel**, it is imperative to learn them to gain better control over personal finances. If there is an overreliance on credit cards to get by each month, it signals a deeper issue with budgeting and cash flow management. Identifying problem areas such as overspending on unnecessary luxuries, eating out excessively, or indulging in habits like alcohol consumption can pave the way for meaningful financial reform. Self-awareness is a crucial step toward financial improvement.

To effectively identify problem areas, individuals should conduct a thorough review of their financial statements, categorizing expenses and identifying patterns of overspending. Recognizing triggers that lead to excessive spending—such as stress, emotional shopping, or peer influence—can help address underlying behavioral habits.

Another key consideration is evaluating financial literacy and skills. If difficulty in understanding and managing personal finances is an issue, seeking educational resources, such as online courses, books, or financial advisors, can provide valuable insights. Additionally, utilizing financial management tools, such as budgeting apps or spreadsheets, can help create a clearer picture of spending habits.

Individuals should also assess debt levels and their reliance on credit cards. If monthly expenses consistently exceed income, this may indicate a need for lifestyle adjustments. Exploring alternative ways to meet financial obligations, such as increasing income through a side hustle or cutting unnecessary expenses, can be an effective solution.

By regularly evaluating financial habits, learning necessary financial skills, and making informed adjustments, individuals can take meaningful steps toward improving their financial health and achieving long-term stability.

8. Brainstorming Alternatives to Problem Areas

After identifying financial problem areas, the next step is to develop alternatives to reduce reliance on credit or unnecessary expenses. If credit cards are being used as a crutch, it may be necessary to cut back on discretionary spending or seek additional income sources. Finding cost-effective alternatives, such as brewing coffee at home instead of buying expensive lattes, carpooling instead of using personal vehicles daily, or switching to a more affordable phone plan, can create significant savings over time. A proactive approach to addressing these issues leads to financial freedom.

Additionally, individuals can explore side hustles or freelance opportunities to supplement their income. Selling unused household items, taking on remote gigs, or monetizing a skill such as tutoring or graphic design can provide extra financial cushion.

For those struggling with housing costs, considering a roommate or downsizing to a more affordable home can significantly cut expenses. Exploring public transportation options, biking, or negotiating car insurance rates can also contribute to overall savings.

Meal planning and bulk shopping can further stretch a budget. Preparing meals at home rather than dining out, taking advantage of grocery store discounts, and utilizing cash-back or rewards programs can all help reduce food costs.

Seeking community resources, such as local food banks, financial counseling services, or free educational workshops, can provide additional support in managing expenses. By continuously evaluating and refining **financial strategies**, individuals can develop **sustainable habits** that lead to **financial independence** and **stability**.

9. Creating Focused and Specific Monthly Goals

Goal setting plays a vital role in financial responsibility. Establishing clear and specific financial goals, such as allocating $100 from each paycheck towards investments or setting aside **$150** for savings each month, ensures accountability. These **goals** should be **realistic**, **achievable**, and **measurable** to track progress effectively. Incremental **financial discipline** will eventually lead to substantial financial growth.

To enhance the effectiveness of financial goal setting, individuals should break down larger financial objectives into smaller, manageable steps. Instead of a vague resolution to "*save more money*," setting a goal to reduce dining-out expenses by $50 each month or increasing investment contributions by 5% per quarter creates a concrete, actionable plan.

Additionally, categorizing financial goals into short-term, mid-term, and long-term objectives allows for better organization and prioritization. Short-term goals may include saving for a vacation or an emergency fund, while mid-term goals could focus on purchasing a home or paying off debt. Long-term objectives, such as retirement planning and wealth accumulation, should be factored into monthly savings and investment strategies.

Tracking progress is essential to maintaining financial accountability.

Using budgeting apps, financial journals, or spreadsheets to monitor progress toward goals ensures that individuals remain committed to their financial strategies. Regularly reviewing and adjusting goals based on financial performance can also provide the flexibility needed to accommodate unexpected expenses or changes in income.

Setting monthly financial challenges, such as a "***no-spend week***" or increasing contributions to a savings account by an additional percentage, can serve as motivation while reinforcing positive money habits. Rewarding oneself for reaching a milestone—such as a small treat after paying off a credit card balance—can help maintain enthusiasm and drive toward larger financial achievements.

Examples of Focused and Specific Monthly Goals:

1. Savings Goals:

- **Short-term:** Save $200 this month for an emergency fund.
- **Mid-term:** Build a $1,500 emergency fund over the next six months.
- **Long-term:** Establish a $10,000 emergency savings account within three years.

2. Cryptocurrency Investment Goals:

- **Short-term:** Invest $250 this month into specific cryptocurrencies that have been identified for your phase 1 investment strategy. Be proactive in setting sell limit orders for each of these cryptocurrencies.
- **Mid-term:** Increase cryptocurrencies investments holdings by graphing your investments, and trading these currencies when profitable, then buying back in at the next dip. Learning how to trade by taking small profits more frequently, rather than HODL-ing long term. Research and invest in one new altcoin each quarter.
- **Long-term:** Identify your long-term holding cryptocurrencies and continue to buy back into these assets when the prices dip. Grow and diversify cryptocurrency assets that can create generational wealth over the next five years.

3. Debt Reduction Goals:

- **Short-term:** Apply for credit cards offering zero percent interest for the next 12 months and transfer balances of highest interest credit

- card debt each month, until this debt is paid-off.
- **Mid-term:** Reduce outstanding loan balances or credit cards by $200 per month within a year. Other options include using a percentage of cryptocurrency profits to reduce overall debts.
- **Long-term:** Pay off all student loans within 10 years.

4. **Spending Reduction Goals:**
- **Short-term:** Limit dining out to $100 this month. Itemize and track all entertainment subscriptions and reduce by 50%.
- **Mid-term:** Reduce overall entertainment expenses by 20% within six months.
- **Long-term:** Cut discretionary spending in half over the next five years.

5. **Side Income and Additional Revenue Goals:**
- **Short-term:** Earn an extra $200 this month through a freelance job.
- **Mid-term:** Build a side business generating $500 per month within a year.
- **Long-term:** Achieve financial independence through multiple investments that will generate passive income streams.

By setting clear, actionable, and measurable financial goals each month, individuals can cultivate disciplined financial habits that pave the way for greater financial stability and long-term success.

10. Conducting Regular Performance Reviews

Reviewing past financial performance is essential in determining success and areas that need improvement. Assessing the previous month's expenditures compared to the budgeted amounts can highlight areas of success and areas requiring adjustment. If a goal was missed, understanding the reasons behind it is necessary to avoid making the same mistake in the future. If there is an opportunity to catch up on missed goals in the next month, it should be pursued. However, if catching up is not feasible, persistence in working toward those goals remains crucial.

A structured performance review involves categorizing spending, analyzing financial trends, and identifying specific patterns that may hinder progress. Using financial tracking tools or spreadsheets can provide a clear overview of income, savings, and expenditures. This process allows individuals to pinpoint problem areas, recognize progress, and make data-driven decisions to enhance financial health.

In addition to tracking past spending, individuals should reassess their financial goals regularly. Life circumstances, such as job changes, unexpected expenses, or new financial opportunities, may necessitate adjustments to a financial plan. Conducting **quarterly** or **annual** financial reviews can help align **long-term aspirations** with current financial strategies.

Furthermore, **accountability** plays a key role in **financial performance reviews**. Engaging in discussions with a financial advisor, trusted friend, or accountability partner can offer valuable insights and keep individuals motivated. Joining financial communities or budgeting groups can also provide external support and encouragement.

To ensure continuous improvement, individuals should set new financial challenges based on their review findings. If an area of overspending is identified, creating a specific action plan—such as limiting discretionary spending by 20%—can foster better financial habits. Similarly, if savings goals are consistently being met, increasing contribution percentages to investments or retirement accounts may be a beneficial next step.

In summary, conducting regular **financial performance reviews** is a vital step toward achieving long-term financial success. By systematically assessing spending patterns, tracking progress, and adjusting goals when necessary, individuals can maintain financial stability and work toward independence. Performance reviews not only highlight successes but also provide opportunities to **refine strategies** and develop better **financial habits**. Consistency, discipline, and adaptability in financial management contribute to a sustainable and secure financial future.

CHAPTER 20

VISION FOR THE FUTURE

As the world teeters on the edge of a financial and technological revolution, the coming decade promises transformative changes that will redefine commerce, ownership, and identity. At the heart of this evolution lies blockchain technology—an innovation that fosters decentralization, transparency, and efficiency in an increasingly interconnected global economy. The impact of these advancements will extend far beyond financial markets, influencing governance, supply chains, healthcare, and personal identity management. Understanding these shifts and preparing for the new digital landscape is crucial for individuals, businesses, and institutions alike.

This chapter explores key predictions for the future of finance and technology, the profound impact of blockchain, and strategies for adapting to and thriving in this new era of digital transformation.

Predictions for the Next Decade in Finance and Technology

The rapid acceleration of technological and financial innovation will reshape industries and redefine the way individuals and organizations interact with money, assets, and data. Blockchain, **artificial intelligence (AI)**, and decentralized systems will drive this shift, fostering a more secure, accessible, and efficient financial ecosystem. Below are some of the most significant trends expected to shape the next ten years:

1. Widespread Adoption of Blockchain Technology

Blockchain is set to become the foundation of global financial systems, providing a secure, immutable, and transparent ledger for transactions. Governments, financial institutions, and multinational corporations will integrate blockchain into their operations to enhance efficiency, reduce costs, and eliminate intermediaries. As a result, financial transactions will become faster, more secure, and less reliant on traditional banking infrastructure. Supply chain management, healthcare records, and identity verification will also benefit from blockchain's ability to provide verifiable and tamper-proof data.

2. Central Bank Digital Currencies (CBDCs) and the Future of Money

Central banks worldwide are actively exploring and developing CBDCs as a digital extension of traditional fiat currencies. These blockchain-based digital currencies will facilitate real-time transactions with enhanced security, improved traceability, and reduced costs for cross-border payments. While CBDCs offer efficiency and financial inclusion benefits, they also introduce concerns about government oversight, privacy, and potential restrictions on financial autonomy. The balance between regulation and personal financial freedom will be a crucial topic in the coming years.

3. The Expansion of Decentralized Finance (DeFi)

DeFi is set to disrupt traditional financial institutions by providing open, permissionless access to banking, lending, and trading services. By leveraging smart contracts on blockchain networks, DeFi platforms will enable users to conduct financial transactions without relying on centralized intermediaries like banks. This shift will empower underbanked populations, increase financial inclusion, and create a more resilient global financial system. However, the sector will also face regulatory scrutiny, security challenges, and the need for user education to ensure responsible adoption.

4. Tokenization of Real-World Assets

The tokenization of tangible and intangible assets will revolutionize investment and ownership structures. Real estate, art, intellectual property, and commodities will be represented as digital tokens on blockchain networks, allowing for fractional ownership and increased liquidity. This shift will democratize access to traditionally exclusive investment opportunities, enabling individuals and businesses to diversify their portfolios and participate in previously inaccessible markets. As regulatory frameworks evolve, tokenization will reshape industries by unlocking new economic possibilities.

5. Artificial Intelligence and Blockchain Integration

The convergence of AI and blockchain technology will enhance automation, security, and data-driven decision-making. AI-powered smart contracts will revolutionize business processes by executing agreements autonomously based on predefined conditions, reducing the need for human intervention. Blockchain's decentralized nature will also improve AI transparency and prevent data manipulation, ensuring more ethical and accountable AI applications. This integration will lead to advancements in predictive analytics, fraud prevention, and algorithm-driven financial strategies, further optimizing global economic systems.

Preparing for the Future

As these technological advancements unfold, individuals and businesses must take proactive steps to adapt and capitalize on emerging opportunities. Education and awareness will be crucial in navigating the complexities of blockchain, DeFi, and AI-driven systems. Investors should explore diversified portfolios that include tokenized assets, cryptocurrency, and blockchain-based solutions. Meanwhile, regulatory frameworks will need to strike a balance between fostering innovation and ensuring consumer protection.

The next decade presents an unprecedented opportunity to reshape global finance and technology. By staying informed and embracing these innovations, individuals and organizations can position themselves at the forefront of this digital revolution, contributing to a more inclusive, efficient, and decentralized future.

How Blockchain Will Redefine Ownership, Identity, and Commerce

The decentralized and immutable nature of blockchain technology is set to revolutionize fundamental aspects of society, including ownership, identity, and commerce. By eliminating the need for centralized intermediaries and providing secure, transparent, and verifiable records, blockchain is reshaping how individuals and businesses interact with assets, personal data, and economic transactions. This transformation will empower individuals with greater control, security, and efficiency in their financial and personal dealings.

1. Ownership: A New Era of Digital Asset Control

Blockchain introduces a groundbreaking model for asset ownership, shifting reliance away from traditional institutions toward decentralized, transparent, and verifiable digital records. Through tokenization, physical and digital assets—including real estate, fine art, intellectual property, and even commodities—can be represented as blockchain-based tokens.

One of the most significant benefits of tokenization is fractional ownership, which allows multiple individuals to hold shares in high-value assets. This innovation lowers financial barriers to entry, making investment opportunities more accessible and increasing liquidity in traditionally illiquid markets. Additionally, the immutable nature of blockchain ensures that ownership records cannot be altered or tampered with, reducing disputes and streamlining the transfer of assets without the need for intermediaries.

2. Identity: Self-Sovereign and Secure Digital Identities

Decentralized identity solutions on the blockchain are redefining how individuals manage and protect their personal data. Traditional identity systems rely on centralized entities—such as governments, banks, and corporations—that control and store sensitive information, making it vulnerable to breaches, identity theft, and misuse.

Blockchain-based self-sovereign identities (SSIs) give individuals direct control over their digital identities, allowing them to authenticate themselves without relying on third parties. Through cryptographic verification, users can prove their credentials—such as age, citizenship, or qualifications—without exposing unnecessary personal details. This reduces the risk of identity theft, enhances privacy in digital interactions, and streamlines access to services such as banking, healthcare, and online platforms. As blockchain adoption grows, decentralized identity systems will become a cornerstone of secure, user-controlled digital identity management.

3. Commerce: Trustless Transactions and Transparent Supply Chains

The integration of blockchain into commerce will redefine how businesses and consumers engage in transactions, fostering trust, efficiency, and transparency. By eliminating intermediaries, blockchain enables peer-to-peer transactions where parties can exchange goods, services, and payments securely without requiring third-party validation.

Smart contracts—self-executing agreements encoded on the blockchain—will further streamline commercial processes by automating contractual obligations. These digital agreements execute predefined terms without human intervention, reducing costs, preventing disputes, and ensuring transparency.

Beyond financial transactions, blockchain will enhance supply chain transparency by allowing consumers to track the journey of products from origin to final destination. With blockchain-based supply chains, businesses can provide verifiable proof of authenticity, ethical sourcing, and sustainability practices. This level of transparency will empower consumers to make informed purchasing decisions and hold corporations accountable for ethical business practices.

Preparing for a More Decentralized and Interconnected World

As blockchain adoption accelerates, individuals, businesses, and governments must prepare for a future driven by decentralization and digital connectivity. Proactively embracing new technologies, acquiring relevant knowledge, and adapting to an evolving financial landscape will be crucial for success in this new era.

1. Cultivate Blockchain Literacy

Understanding the core principles of blockchain technology is essential for individuals and businesses looking to navigate the decentralized world effectively. Educational initiatives, online courses, and industry resources can provide valuable insights into blockchain's applications, risks, and opportunities. As blockchain continues to shape industries beyond finance—including healthcare, logistics, and governance—staying informed will be key to capitalizing on its potential.

2. Embrace Digital Asset Adoption

The emergence of digital assets—ranging from cryptocurrencies and **non-fungible tokens (NFTs)** to tokenized investments—presents new opportunities for wealth creation and financial diversification. Businesses and investors should explore how blockchain-based assets can enhance their portfolios and create new revenue streams. Companies, in particular, can integrate digital payment solutions, leverage NFTs for brand engagement, and explore blockchain-based business models to stay ahead in the evolving economy.

3. Prioritize Cybersecurity and Digital Asset Protection

As blockchain ecosystems expand, cybersecurity risks will grow alongside them. Individuals and organizations must implement robust security measures, such as secure digital wallets, multi-factor authentication, and private key management, to safeguard their assets and personal data. Understanding and mitigating risks associated with smart contracts, DeFi platforms, and **decentralized applications (dApps)** will be critical to preventing fraud, hacking, and loss of funds.

4. Develop a Collaborative and Adaptive Mindset

The decentralized world emphasizes cooperation, open-source development, and global connectivity. Unlike traditional industries that rely on competition and proprietary systems, blockchain thrives on collaboration and interoperability. Businesses, developers, and policymakers must foster partnerships and contribute to blockchain ecosystems to unlock the full potential of this technology. By engaging with decentralized communities and staying adaptable to regulatory changes, stakeholders can actively shape the future of blockchain adoption.

In conclusion, the next decade will fundamentally redefine how society perceives and engages with ownership, identity, and commerce. Blockchain technology is at the core of this transformation, enabling a decentralized, transparent, and secure digital economy. Individuals and businesses will gain unprecedented autonomy, while financial systems, supply chains, and identity management will undergo revolutionary changes.

By embracing innovation, investing in education, and preparing for the decentralized future, society can harness the immense potential of blockchain to build a more inclusive, efficient, and equitable global economy. The shift toward decentralization is not just a technological advancement—it is a paradigm shift that will shape the way we interact, transact, and secure our digital lives in the years to come.

The Future Growth of Kingdom-Based Businesses

As the world stands on the precipice of a financial shift, an unprecedented opportunity is emerging for **Kingdom-minded entrepreneurs**—those who seek to **build businesses** rooted in biblical principles and led by **Christian values**. This coming wealth transfer, **driven** in part by **innovations** in cryptocurrency, digital assets, and other financial markets, is poised to reposition God's people as leaders in commerce, influence, and economic stewardship.

For centuries, economic systems have been controlled by secular institutions and traditional financial structures. However, as decentralization disrupts existing power dynamics, a new wave of Christian entrepreneurs and business leaders will rise—establishing Kingdom-based businesses that prioritize integrity, generosity, and the advancement of God's purposes on Earth. This chapter explores the significance of this shift, the characteristics of Kingdom-minded enterprises, and strategies for stewarding the coming wealth transfer to establish businesses that glorify God and impact the world.

The Coming Wealth Transfer and Its Kingdom Implications

Throughout biblical history, God has orchestrated wealth transfers to position His people for influence and provision. From the Israelites receiving gold and silver upon their Exodus from Egypt (Exodus 12:35-36) to Joseph managing Egypt's resources during a time of famine (Genesis 41), Scripture is filled with examples of divine economic shifts that benefit God's people and His purposes.

Today, a similar shift is on the horizon. The emergence of cryptocurrency, decentralized finance (DeFi), and digital assets is disrupting traditional financial systems, creating opportunities for wealth to be redistributed. Those who are prepared—spiritually, strategically, and financially—will be positioned to steward these resources for the advancement of God's Kingdom. This wealth transfer is not merely about financial gain but about positioning Christian leaders to establish businesses that reflect God's righteousness, justice, and abundance.

The Characteristics of Kingdom-Based Businesses

Kingdom-based businesses differ from secular enterprises because they are founded on biblical values and operate with a higher purpose: to honor God and serve others. As Christian entrepreneurs step into greater financial influence, their businesses will become catalysts for cultural transformation, ethical commerce, and widespread generosity.

1. Christ-Centered Leadership

The success of Kingdom-based businesses begins with leaders who prioritize their relationship with God and lead with humility, wisdom, and integrity. These entrepreneurs understand that their business is not solely for personal gain but a tool for advancing God's will. They seek divine guidance in decision-making, treat employees and customers with love and respect, and build organizations that reflect godly principles.

2. Ethical and Transparent Practices

In a world where corruption and greed often define business, **Kingdom-minded** entrepreneurs will set a new standard for honesty, fairness, and ethical dealings. With blockchain technology offering greater **transparency** in financial transactions, **Christian businesses** will lead in promoting **accountability**, fair wages, and ethical supply chains. They will reject exploitative practices and instead foster a culture of trust and responsibility.

3. Wealth as a Tool for Kingdom Impact

Rather than hoarding wealth, **Kingdom-based businesses** will channel resources into missions, humanitarian efforts, and community transformation. This aligns with biblical teachings on generosity: "*Command them to do good, to be rich in good deeds, and to be generous and willing to share.*" (1 Timothy 6:18). Profits will be reinvested into Kingdom initiatives, helping fund ministries, support Christian education, and empower underprivileged communities.

4. Marketplace Ministry and Discipleship

Beyond financial success, these businesses will serve as platforms for evangelism, discipleship, and spiritual growth. Employees will experience a workplace culture infused with biblical values, prayer, and mentorship. Through ethical commerce and community involvement, these businesses will influence society, demonstrating that faith and business excellence can coexist.

5. Innovation and Industry Leadership

Kingdom entrepreneurs will not just participate in existing markets but lead in **innovation—developing** groundbreaking **solutions** in technology, finance, healthcare, and education. With divine wisdom, they will create products and services that solve real-world problems while upholding biblical values. Blockchain technology, for example, will provide new opportunities for Christian businesses to build decentralized, trustworthy systems that benefit communities globally.

Stewarding the Wealth Transfer for Kingdom Purposes

As this economic shift unfolds, it is essential for Christian business leaders to be prepared. Without wisdom and proper stewardship, wealth can easily become a distraction or a burden. Here are key steps to ensuring that this wealth transfer leads to sustainable, God-honoring business growth:

1. Develop a Kingdom Mindset Toward Wealth

Christian entrepreneurs must break free from any limiting beliefs about wealth and embrace a biblical perspective—understanding that wealth is a resource entrusted by God for His purposes. They must resist the love of money while using financial resources to advance the Gospel, support their communities, and create opportunities for others.

2. Invest in Financial and Business Education

As new financial systems emerge, it is crucial for **Kingdom-minded individuals** to gain **knowledge** about blockchain, cryptocurrency, and decentralized **finance**. Those who understand these innovations will be best positioned to leverage them for God's purposes. **Business education**, leadership development, and strategic planning will also be vital in ensuring that Kingdom businesses thrive and remain sustainable.

3. Build Networks of Kingdom Entrepreneurs

Collaboration among **Christian business leaders** will be essential in this new era. By forming alliances, sharing knowledge, and supporting one another, **Kingdom entrepreneurs** can strengthen their influence and create ecosystems of ethical commerce. Christian investment groups, business mentorship programs, and faith-driven incubators will play a crucial role in fostering this movement.

4. Prioritize Philanthropy and Community Impact

Kingdom-based businesses must be committed to **giving back**—funding missions, supporting **Christian education**, and **empowering local economies**. By adopting a model of radical generosity, these businesses will become a force for good, demonstrating God's love through **tangible action**.

5. Seek God's Guidance in Every Decision

At the heart of every Kingdom enterprise must be a deep reliance on God. Through prayer, fasting, and **seeking divine wisdom**, Christian business leaders will receive supernatural strategies, creative solutions, and discernment to navigate economic changes. The Holy Spirit will guide them in making decisions that align with God's will, ensuring that their businesses remain in His favor and purpose.

A New Era of Kingdom Influence

In conclusion, the financial landscape is shifting, and a historic wealth transfer is on the horizon. This moment presents a divine opportunity for Christian entrepreneurs to rise as industry leaders, shaping commerce, technology, and society with biblical values. By embracing ethical business practices, stewarding wealth wisely, and using their influence for God's glory, these Kingdom-minded leaders will pave the way for a new era of faith-driven innovation.

As this movement unfolds, it will not be about individuals merely acquiring wealth—it will be about positioning God's people to impact nations, uplift communities, and fund the expansion of His Kingdom on Earth. Those who prepare their hearts, equip themselves with knowledge, and commit to walking in obedience will be at the forefront of this divine shift. The future of Kingdom-based businesses is not just about economic success—it is about fulfilling God's calling to be salt and light in the marketplace, ushering in a new age of righteousness, prosperity, and influence.

CHAPTER 21

THE IMPORTANCE OF SAFE AND RELIABLE STORAGE FOR YOUR CRYPTOCURRENCY ASSETS

As the world of digital finance continues to expand, the safe and reliable storage of cryptocurrency assets has become one of the most critical aspects of managing wealth in the digital age. With increasing **cyber threats**, **exchange hacks**, and **phishing scams**, securing your crypto holdings is not just an option—it's a necessity. Unlike traditional financial systems where banks protect your funds, cryptocurrency ownership means taking full responsibility for safeguarding your private keys and assets.

One of the best ways to protect your digital wealth is by using a cold wallet—a hardware wallet that stores your **private keys offline**, making it virtually immune to online hacking attempts. Whether you are an investor holding long-term positions or actively managing your portfolio, choosing the right cold wallet can make all the difference in keeping your assets secure. Below, we explore some of the most widely used and highly trusted **cold wallets**, detailing their features, advantages, and potential drawbacks to help you make an informed decision.

Top Cold Wallets for Secure Cryptocurrency Storage:

1. Ledger Nano X

The Ledger Nano X is a highly secure cold wallet designed for offline storage of cryptocurrencies. As the flagship model of Ledger's hardware wallets, it offers Bluetooth connectivity, enabling users to manage their assets on the go via a mobile device while maintaining the security of cold storage. The Nano X supports over 5,500 cryptocurrencies, making it one of the most versatile hardware wallets available.

Built with Secure Element (SE) technology, the Ledger Nano X ensures that private keys never leave the device, protecting assets from online threats such as hacks, malware, and phishing attacks. It integrates with the Ledger Live app, allowing users to manage their portfolios, stake assets, and even use decentralized applications (dApps) securely. With its larger storage capacity, the Nano X can accommodate multiple apps for different cryptocurrencies, making it a great choice for serious investors with diverse portfolios.

✔ **Pros:**

- **High security** – Uses Secure Element (SE) chip technology for robust protection.
- **Bluetooth-enabled** – Allows mobile management via iOS and Android.
- **Supports 5,500+ cryptocurrencies** – Compatible with a wide range of assets.
- **Large storage capacity** – Can hold more apps compared to older Ledger models.
- **Staking capabilities** – Allows earning rewards on supported cryptocurrencies.
- **User-friendly** – Works with the Ledger Live app for easy asset management.

✖ **Cons:**

- **Higher price point** – More expensive than other hardware wallets like the Ledger Nano S Plus.
- **Bluetooth may pose security risks** – While convenient, some users prefer wired-only wallets for extra safety.
- **Not fully open-source** – Some elements of Ledger's firmware remain proprietary, raising concerns for transparency-focused users.
- **Requires Ledger Live for full functionality** – While it supports third-party wallets, the best experience is with Ledger's own software.

The Ledger Nano X is a premium cold wallet ideal for users who need a secure, mobile-friendly, and versatile storage solution for their cryptocurrency assets. While more expensive than some alternatives, its Bluetooth connectivity, large storage capacity, and extensive coin support make it an excellent choice for serious investors and traders. However, those concerned about Bluetooth security or seeking a lower-cost alternative may prefer the Ledger Nano S Plus.

2. Ledger Nano S Plus

The Ledger Nano S Plus is a secure and affordable cold storage wallet designed for cryptocurrency investors who want to safely store their digital assets offline. As an upgraded version of the original Ledger Nano S, the Nano S Plus offers more storage capacity and supports over 5,500 cryptocurrencies, making it a versatile choice for managing multiple assets.

Unlike the Ledger Nano X, the Nano S Plus does not have Bluetooth connectivity, meaning it requires a **USB-C connection** to a computer or mobile device for asset management. This makes it a more secure option for those who prefer a wired-only connection, eliminating any potential Bluetooth-related security concerns. While it lacks the portability of the Nano X, it still integrates seamlessly with the Ledger Live app, enabling users to buy, sell, stake, and manage their cryptocurrencies with ease.

Differences Between the Ledger Nano S Plus and Ledger Nano X

- **Connectivity:** The Nano X supports Bluetooth, allowing mobile device access without cables, while the Nano S Plus requires a USB-C connection.
- **Storage Capacity:** The Nano X has a larger memory, allowing more apps to be installed simultaneously. The Nano S Plus has expanded storage compared to the original Nano S but still holds fewer apps than the Nano X.
- **Price:** The Nano S Plus is more affordable, making it a great entry-level hardware wallet, while the Nano X is more expensive due to its added features.
- **Portability:** The Nano X is designed for mobile use, whereas the Nano S Plus is better suited for desktop use with a **USB connection**.

✔ **Pros:**

- **High security –** Uses Secure Element (SE) chip for robust protection.
- **Affordable** – Lower cost compared to the Nano X, making it ideal for budget-conscious users.
- **Supports 5,500+ cryptocurrencies** – Compatible with a vast range of assets.
- **Wired-only connection** – No Bluetooth, eliminating wireless security risks.
- **Expanded storage** – Can hold more apps compared to the original Nano S.

✕ Cons:

- **No Bluetooth** – Must be connected via **USB-C**, making it less portable than the Nano X.
- **Less storage than Nano X** – Can install fewer apps at the same time.
- **Requires Ledger Live for optimal use** – While compatible with third-party wallets, the best experience comes from Ledger's own software.

The Ledger Nano S Plus is an excellent cold storage wallet for those who want high security, affordability, and support for multiple cryptocurrencies. While it lacks Bluetooth connectivity and the expanded storage capacity of the Nano X, it eliminates potential wireless security risks, making it a solid choice for long-term crypto holders who prefer a wired-only connection. If you need mobile access and greater storage, the Nano X may be the better option, but for budget-conscious users looking for a secure and reliable hardware wallet, the Nano S Plus is a great investment.

3. Tangem Wallet

The Tangem Wallet is a **smartcard-based cold wallet** designed for secure and convenient cryptocurrency storage. Unlike traditional hardware wallets that require USB connections or Bluetooth, Tangem uses **Near Field Communication** (**NFC**) technology, allowing users to manage their crypto assets simply by tapping the card against their smartphone. Each Tangem wallet is self-contained, does not require a battery, and has no cables, making it a lightweight and portable solution for storing private keys securely.

Tangem wallets are known for their tamper-proof security, as the private key is generated inside the card and cannot be extracted, ensuring that users retain full control of their funds. The wallet supports multiple cryptocurrencies and integrates seamlessly with mobile devices, providing an easy-to-use and highly secure storage method.

✓ **Pros:**

- **Ultra-portable & durable** – The credit card-sized design makes it easy to

carry in a wallet.
- **No cables or battery needed** – Works with NFC on smartphones.
- **Tamper-proof security** – Private keys cannot be extracted, preventing hacking attempts.
- **User-friendly** – Simple tap-to-use feature makes it great for beginners.
- **Multi-currency support** – Supports various cryptocurrencies, making it a versatile option.
- **Affordable** – Cost-effective compared to traditional hardware wallets.

✕ **Cons:**

- **Limited ecosystem** – Does not support as many coins as Ledger or Trezor.
- **No recovery seed** – If lost or damaged, funds could be inaccessible unless a backup is made with multiple cards.
- **Requires a smartphone** – Since it relies on NFC, it cannot be used with computers or non-mobile devices.
- **Dependence on the Tangem app** – Although the wallet is secure, users must trust the Tangem ecosystem for continued functionality.

The Tangem Wallet is an innovative, highly secure, and beginner-friendly cold storage solution, especially for users looking for portability and ease of use. However, its lack of a **recovery seed** and limited coin support may make it less suitable for advanced crypto users or those managing diverse portfolios. It is an ideal choice for those seeking a simple, on-the-go storage option without the complexity of traditional hardware wallets.

4. Trezor Model T

The Trezor Model T is a premium cold storage wallet designed for secure and convenient management of cryptocurrency assets. As the flagship model of Trezor's hardware wallets, it offers advanced security features, including a touchscreen interface, which makes it easier to navigate compared to traditional button-based wallets. The Model T supports over 1,000 cryptocurrencies, including Bitcoin (BTC), Ethereum (ETH), and many altcoins, providing a versatile solution for crypto investors.

One of the standout features of the Trezor Model T is its **open-source firmware**, allowing the crypto community to audit and verify its security, ensuring full transparency. Unlike the Ledger series, which uses a **proprietary Secure Element (SE) chip**, Trezor prioritizes fully open-source security. The Model T also integrates with the Trezor Suite software, providing users with an intuitive platform to buy, sell, stake, and manage their assets securely.

✓ **Pros:**

- **Touchscreen interface** – Makes navigation easier compared to button-based hardware wallets.
- **High security** – Private keys never leave the device, ensuring protection from hacks and malware.
- **Supports 1,000+ cryptocurrencies** – Compatible with many major digital assets.
- **Open-source firmware** – Allows the community to verify security, ensuring transparency.
- **No Bluetooth connectivity** – Eliminates wireless security risks.
- **Backup and recovery features** – Offers Shamir Backup, an advanced security feature for splitting **recovery seeds**.

✕ **Cons:**

- **Higher price point** – More expensive than the Trezor One and some competing wallets like Ledger Nano X.
- **Lacks support for some coins** – While it supports many cryptocurrencies, some newer altcoins are not yet integrated.
- **No Secure Element (SE) chip** – Unlike Ledger wallets, Trezor does not use a proprietary security chip, which some users consider a

- disadvantage.
- **Requires a wired connection** – No Bluetooth support, meaning users must connect via USB-C.

The Trezor Model T is an excellent cold wallet for users who want top-tier security, a user-friendly touchscreen interface, and full transparency with open-source firmware. While it lacks Bluetooth connectivity and uses a different security model than Ledger, it is trusted by many in the crypto community for its strong security measures and ease of use. Its higher price may be a downside for some, but for those looking for a reliable, feature-rich, and open-source hardware wallet, the Trezor Model T is a top choice.

5. Trezor One

The Trezor One is a secure and affordable cold wallet designed for offline storage of cryptocurrency assets. As the first-ever hardware wallet developed by Trezor, it has established itself as a trusted option for crypto investors looking for a simple yet highly secure solution. It supports over 1,000 cryptocurrencies, including Bitcoin (BTC), Ethereum (ETH), and many ERC-20 tokens.

The Trezor One follows a wired-only security model, meaning it must be connected via USB to a computer or smartphone for transactions and management. It uses open-source firmware, allowing the community to audit its security and verify its trustworthiness. The device integrates with Trezor Suite, a user-friendly software platform that enables users to buy, sell, stake, and manage their assets safely.

Differences Between Trezor One and Trezor Model T

- **User Interface:** The Trezor One uses physical buttons for navigation, whereas the Trezor Model T has a touchscreen, offering a more intuitive user experience.
- **Security Features:** Both use open-source firmware, but the Model T offers Shamir Backup, which allows for multi-share recovery protection.
- **Supported Cryptocurrencies:** While both support over 1,000 assets, the Trezor One lacks support for newer coins, such as XRP, Monero (XMR), and some other altcoins.

- **Connectivity:** Both wallets require USB connection, as neither supports Bluetooth.
- **Price:** The Trezor One is significantly more affordable than the Trezor Model T, making it a great entry-level option.

✓ **Pros:**

- **Affordable** – Lower cost compared to the Trezor Model T and Ledger Nano X.
- **High security** – Keeps private keys offline and protected from hacking.
- **Open-source firmware** – Fully auditable, ensuring transparency.
- **Supports 1,000+ cryptocurrencies** – Works with major coins and ERC-20 tokens.
- **No Bluetooth connectivity** – Wired-only security reduces wireless risks.

✕ **Cons:**

- **No touchscreen** – Uses physical buttons for navigation, which may feel outdated for some users.
- **Lacks support for certain coins** – Does not support XRP, Monero (XMR), and some newer altcoins.
- **No Secure Element (SE) chip** – Unlike Ledger wallets, it does not use a proprietary security chip.
- **Requires a wired connection** – No Bluetooth means must connect via USB, which may be less convenient for mobile users.

The Trezor One is an excellent entry-level cold storage wallet for those who want a secure, reliable, and budget-friendly option for protecting their cryptocurrency assets. While it lacks the advanced features of the Trezor Model T, such as a touchscreen and wider coin support, it remains one of the most trusted and widely used hardware wallets in the crypto community. For those seeking enhanced functionality and a touchscreen experience, the Model T is the better choice, but for users who prioritize affordability and security, the Trezor One is a solid investment.

6. Ellipal Titan

The Ellipal Titan is a highly secure, air-gapped cold storage wallet designed to provide maximum protection against online threats, hacks, and malware attacks. Unlike traditional hardware wallets that rely on USB or Bluetooth connections, the Ellipal Titan operates entirely offline, using QR code scanning for transactions. This air-gapped security model ensures that the private keys never come into contact with an internet-connected device, making it immune to remote hacking attempts.

Built with a rugged, tamper-resistant metal design, the Ellipal Titan is not only highly secure but also physically durable, protecting against external damage and tampering. It supports multiple cryptocurrencies, including Bitcoin (BTC), Ethereum (ETH), XRP, Litecoin (LTC), and more than 10,000 digital assets. The device integrates with the Ellipal mobile app, which enables users to manage their crypto portfolio, sign transactions, and interact with decentralized applications (dApps) using QR codes.

✓ **Pros:**

- **Air-gapped security** – No USB, Bluetooth, or Wi-Fi connectivity, making it immune to remote hacks.
- **Tamper-proof design** – Built with a rugged metal body, resistant to physical damage and unauthorized access.
- **Supports 10,000+ cryptocurrencies** – Compatible with a vast range of digital assets.
- **QR code-based transactions** – Provides a simple and secure way to sign transactions offline.
- **Large touchscreen** – Intuitive interface, making it easy to navigate and use.
- **Integrated with Ellipal mobile app** – Allows for seamless asset management without compromising security.

✗ **Cons:**

- **Bulkier design** – Larger and heavier compared to Ledger and Trezor wallets, making it less portable.
- **Higher price point** – More expensive than many traditional hardware wallets.
- **Requires mobile app** – Users must rely on the Ellipal app for transaction management.

- **No Bluetooth or USB support** – While this enhances security, it limits connectivity options, making it less convenient for some users.
- **Limited third-party integrations** – Unlike Ledger and Trezor, Ellipal does not integrate with many external wallets or dApps.

The Ellipal Titan is an ideal hardware wallet for those who prioritize maximum security and offline protection. Its air-gapped design ensures that private keys never touch the internet, making it one of the most secure cold wallets available. However, its bulkier size, reliance on the mobile app, and higher price point may not be ideal for everyone. If security and durability are your top priorities, the Ellipal Titan is a great investment, but if you need a more portable or third-party-integrated wallet, alternatives like Ledger Nano X or Trezor Model T may be better suited.

7. KeepKey

The KeepKey Wallet is a simple yet secure cold storage wallet designed for safely managing and storing cryptocurrency assets offline. Known for its sleek and durable design, KeepKey provides a user-friendly interface with a large OLED display, making transaction verification and management easy. It is designed to work seamlessly with ShapeShift, a built-in exchange feature that allows users to swap cryptocurrencies directly from the wallet without needing to use a third-party service.

KeepKey supports major cryptocurrencies, including Bitcoin (BTC), Ethereum (ETH), Litecoin (LTC), and other ERC-20 tokens, making it a solid choice for users with diverse portfolios. It offers USB connectivity, meaning it must be connected to a computer to authorize transactions, ensuring that private keys never touch the internet and remain secure from online threats.

✔ **Pros:**

- **Sleek design** – Features a premium metal casing and a large OLED screen for easy transaction verification.
- **High security** – Keeps private keys offline, protecting against malware and hacking attempts.
- **User-friendly interface** – Simple to set up and navigate, making it great for beginners.

- **Built-in ShapeShift exchange** – Allows users to swap assets directly from the wallet.
- **Affordable** – Priced lower than many other hardware wallets like Ledger Nano X or Trezor Model T.

✕ Cons:

- **Limited coin support** – Does not support as many cryptocurrencies as Ledger or Trezor wallets.
- **No Bluetooth or mobile connectivity** – Requires a USB connection, making it less convenient for mobile users.
- **Lack of frequent firmware updates** – Compared to competitors like Ledger and Trezor, KeepKey receives fewer software upgrades.
- **Not open-source** – Some users prefer open-source wallets for greater transparency and security audits.
- **ShapeShift reliance** – While integration is useful, users are dependent on ShapeShift for full functionality.

The KeepKey Wallet is an excellent choice for beginners and long-term holders who want a secure, affordable, and easy-to-use cold wallet. Its sleek design, large screen, and built-in exchange functionality make it stand out. However, its limited coin support, lack of Bluetooth/mobile access, and infrequent updates may make it less appealing for advanced traders or users who manage a diverse portfolio. If simplicity and security are your priorities, KeepKey is a great option, but for broader coin support and mobile connectivity, Ledger or Trezor wallets may be better suited.

8. CoolWallet Pro

The CoolWallet Pro is a credit card-sized cold storage wallet designed for secure, on-the-go cryptocurrency management. Unlike traditional hardware wallets that require USB connections, the CoolWallet Pro is Bluetooth-enabled, allowing users to connect wirelessly to their smartphones while keeping their private keys securely offline. It offers a sleek, waterproof, and tamper-resistant design, making it one of the most portable and durable cold wallets available.

CoolWallet Pro supports staking, NFT storage, and DeFi integration, making it an excellent choice for users who want more than just cold storage. It is compatible with multiple cryptocurrencies, including Bitcoin (BTC), Ethereum (ETH), Binance Coin (BNB), Polkadot (DOT), and several ERC-20 tokens. The wallet pairs with the CoolBitX app, providing a seamless way to buy, sell, swap, and stake cryptocurrencies while keeping private keys securely offline.

✔ **Pros:**

- **Ultra-portable** – Slim, credit card-sized design, easy to carry in a wallet.
- **Bluetooth-enabled** – Allows wireless connection to iOS and Android devices.
- **Supports staking** – Enables earning passive income on supported coins.
- **DeFi and NFT support** – Works with decentralized applications and NFT storage.
- **Waterproof and tamper-resistant** – Built for durability and security.
- **User-friendly** – Simple mobile app integration for easy transaction management.

✖ **Cons:**

- **Limited storage capacity** – Cannot store as many assets as Ledger or Trezor wallets.
- **Bluetooth connectivity may pose security risks** – Some users prefer wired-only cold wallets for added security.
- **Not fully open-source** – Firmware security is not community-audited like Trezor.
- **Higher price point** – More expensive than entry-level cold wallets like Ledger Nano S Plus.
- **Requires the CoolBitX app** – Users must rely on the app for full functionality, making it dependent on third-party software.

The CoolWallet Pro is an ideal cold wallet for crypto users who need mobility, staking, and DeFi functionality while maintaining offline security. Its compact design, wireless connectivity, and staking features make it a great choice for active traders and investors. However, its limited storage, Bluetooth security concerns, and reliance on the

CoolBitX app may make it less appealing for those prioritizing maximum security. If portability and flexibility are your top priorities, the CoolWallet Pro is a strong option, but for advanced security and open-source verification, Ledger or Trezor wallets may be better suited.

9. SafePal S1

The SafePal S1 is a highly secure, air-gapped hardware wallet designed to store and manage cryptocurrencies completely offline. Unlike traditional cold wallets that rely on USB or Bluetooth connections, the SafePal S1 uses QR code scanning to sign transactions, ensuring that private keys never come into contact with an internet-connected device. This eliminates hacking risks and enhances overall security.

Developed with Binance's backing, the SafePal S1 supports over 10,000 cryptocurrencies, including Bitcoin (BTC), Ethereum (ETH), Binance Coin (BNB), and multiple ERC-20, BEP-2, and BEP-20 tokens. It integrates with the SafePal mobile app, allowing users to buy, sell, swap, and stake assets securely. The device also features a self-destruct mechanism, which wipes all data if physical tampering is detected, providing an additional layer of protection.

✓ **Pros:**

- **Air-gapped security** – No USB, Bluetooth, or Wi-Fi connectivity, making it immune to remote hacks.
- **Supports 10,000+ cryptocurrencies** – Compatible with a vast range of digital assets.
- **Affordable** – Lower price compared to Ledger and Trezor wallets.
- **Self-destruct feature** – Erases private keys if unauthorized tampering is detected.
- **Portable and compact** – Lightweight and easy to carry, making it great for everyday use.
- **Integrated with the SafePal app** – Enables buying, swapping, staking, and NFT storage.

✗ **Cons:**

- **Less user-friendly for beginners** – The QR code-based system may

- feel less intuitive than Bluetooth or USB wallets.
- **Requires mobile app for full functionality** – Users must rely on the SafePal app to manage assets.
- **No direct desktop support** – Unlike Ledger and Trezor, SafePal S1 is primarily mobile-focused.
- **Limited third-party wallet integrations** – Does not support as many external applications as Ledger or Trezor.

The SafePal S1 is an excellent choice for users who prioritize security and affordability. Its air-gapped design, wide crypto support, and self-destruct feature make it one of the most secure hardware wallets available. However, its reliance on QR codes and mobile app integration may make it less convenient for beginners or those who prefer desktop-based management. If security and cost-effectiveness are your top concerns, the SafePal S1 is a solid investment, but if ease of use and desktop compatibility are priorities, Ledger or Trezor wallets may be a better fit.

10. NGRAVE ZERO

The NGRAVE ZERO is one of the most secure hardware wallets on the market, offering EAL7-certified security, the highest level of security certification available for cold storage devices. Designed for absolute offline storage, the NGRAVE ZERO operates entirely air-gapped, meaning it has no USB, Bluetooth, NFC, Wi-Fi, or other forms of connectivity that could expose it to cyber threats. Instead, it relies on QR code scanning to sign transactions, ensuring that private keys never interact with online devices.

With a large touchscreen display, open-source cryptographic algorithms, and advanced **biometric security**, the NGRAVE ZERO is built for serious crypto investors who prioritize maximum protection for their assets. It also integrates with the NGRAVE LIQUID app, allowing users to manage their portfolios without compromising the cold storage security model.

✓ Pros:

- **Highest security certification (EAL7)** – More secure than Ledger, Trezor, or any other hardware wallet.

- **Completely air-gapped** – No USB, Bluetooth, NFC, or Wi-Fi connectivity, eliminating all remote hacking risks.
- **Advanced biometric security** – Includes fingerprint authentication for added protection.
- **Large touchscreen interface** – User-friendly and intuitive compared to traditional button-based wallets.
- **Open-source cryptographic algorithms** – Enhances transparency and trustworthiness.
- **Supports QR code-based transactions** – Ensures secure offline signing of transactions.

✕ **Cons:**

- **Expensive** – One of the most costly hardware wallets due to its high security standards.
- **Limited coin support** – Does not support as many cryptocurrencies as Ledger or Trezor.
- **Larger than most hardware wallets** – Bulkier than devices like the Ledger Nano X or SafePal S1.
- **Requires the NGRAVE LIQUID app** – Portfolio management depends on the app, though private keys remain secure.
- **Limited third-party integrations** – Unlike Ledger and Trezor, it does not support many external wallets or DeFi platforms.

The NGRAVE ZERO is the best option for those who prioritize absolute security over convenience. With EAL7-certified protection, air-gapped design, and biometric authentication, it is virtually unhackable, making it ideal for users storing large amounts of cryptocurrency for the long term. However, its high price, bulkier size, and limited ecosystem may not suit everyday traders or those looking for broad crypto support. If top-tier security is your priority, the NGRAVE ZERO is unmatched, but if you need a more flexible, cost-effective, and widely integrated wallet, options like Ledger or Trezor may be more suitable.

11. BitBox02

The BitBox02 is a compact, open-source hardware wallet designed for secure cryptocurrency storage and easy usability. Developed by Shift Crypto, it is known for its high-security standards, minimalist design, and user-friendly interface. Unlike traditional hardware wallets with physical buttons, the BitBox02 features touch-sensitive slide controls, allowing for smooth navigation and transaction signing.

The wallet comes in two versions:

- **BitBox02 Multi-Edition** – Supports Bitcoin (BTC), Ethereum (ETH), Litecoin (LTC), and ERC-20 tokens.
- **BitBox02 Bitcoin-Only Edition** – Designed exclusively for Bitcoin maximalists, removing unnecessary code to enhance security for Bitcoin storage.

It integrates with the BitBoxApp, providing users with a seamless experience for managing, buying, and selling cryptocurrencies. With microSD card backup functionality, the BitBox02 makes wallet recovery simple and efficient.

✓ **Pros:**

- **Compact and lightweight** – Small, easy to carry, and highly portable.
- **Open-source firmware** – Allows for transparency and security audits.
- **Touch-sensitive controls** – Intuitive slide gestures for navigation.
- **MicroSD card backup** – Easy and secure wallet recovery option.
- **No physical buttons** – Minimizes mechanical failure risks.
- **USB-C compatibility** – Plug-and-play functionality with modern devices.
- **Bitcoin-only version available** – Optimized security for Bitcoin maximalists.

✕ **Cons:**

- **Limited cryptocurrency support** – Supports fewer coins than Ledger and Trezor.
- **No Bluetooth or mobile app support** – Requires a USB-C connection, making it less convenient for mobile users.
- **Touch controls may take time to adjust** – Some users may prefer physical buttons for navigation.
- **Not widely integrated with third-party wallets** – Works best within its own BitBox ecosystem.

The BitBox02 is an excellent choice for security-conscious users who prefer an open-source, minimalist, and easy-to-use cold wallet. Its compact design, microSD backup, and transparent firmware make it a trusted option for long-term crypto storage. However, its limited coin support, lack of Bluetooth, and reliance on USB-C may not be ideal for those managing a diverse portfolio or requiring mobile connectivity. If you are a Bitcoin maximalist or prefer a streamlined crypto experience, the BitBox02 is a great investment, but for broader asset support and mobile-friendly features, a Ledger or Trezor wallet may be better suited.

12. Coldcard Wallet

The Coldcard Wallet is a high-security, Bitcoin-only hardware wallet designed for advanced Bitcoin users who prioritize maximum security and offline storage. Developed by Coinkite, it is one of the most secure cold wallets available, featuring air-gapped transactions, advanced encryption, and **multi-signature** support. Unlike traditional hardware wallets, the Coldcard Wallet allows users to sign transactions completely offline using a microSD card, ensuring that private keys never touch an internet-connected device.

Built with a secure element (SE) chip, the Coldcard Wallet provides strong encryption and tamper-proof protection. It is an ideal choice for Bitcoin maximalists, tamper-proof protection. It is an ideal choice for Bitcoin maximalists, as it only supports Bitcoin (BTC) and does not store any other cryptocurrencies. The wallet is fully open-source, allowing the Bitcoin community to audit and verify its security.

✔ **Pros:**

- **Bitcoin-only design** – Optimized for Bitcoin maximalists with no unnecessary code or altcoin support.
- **Air-gapped security** – Allows for offline transaction signing using a microSD card, keeping private keys completely offline.
- **Open-source firmware** – Transparent and community-audited security.
- **Secure element (SE) chip** – Advanced encryption and tamper-resistant hardware.
- **Multi-signature support** – Compatible with multi-sig Bitcoin wallets for extra security.

- **Built-in keypad** - Allows users to enter PIN codes and passwords directly on the device, reducing the risk of keylogging attacks.

✕ **Cons:**

- **Bitcoin-only** - Does not support Ethereum, altcoins, or NFTs, making it unsuitable for users managing diverse crypto portfolios.
- **Steep learning curve** - Best for advanced users; not as beginner-friendly as Ledger or Trezor wallets.
- **No Bluetooth or mobile support** - Requires USB or microSD card for transactions, which some may find less convenient.
- **Bulky design** - Larger than most hardware wallets, making it less portable.
- **Higher price point** - More expensive than basic Bitcoin wallets, though justified by its security features.

The Coldcard Wallet is the ultimate choice for Bitcoin maximalists and security-focused users who want the highest level of protection for their BTC holdings. Its air-gapped design, multi-signature support, and open-source firmware make it one of the most trusted and secure Bitcoin wallets available. However, its lack of altcoin support, complex interface, and reliance on USB/microSD transactions make it less ideal for beginners or users managing multiple cryptocurrencies. If Bitcoin security is your top priority, the Coldcard Wallet is an unmatched choice, but if you need support for various cryptocurrencies and easier usability, a Ledger or Trezor wallet may be more suitable.

13. D'Cent Biometric Wallet

The D'Cent Biometric Wallet is a next-generation cold storage wallet that features biometric fingerprint authentication, enhancing both security and user convenience. Unlike traditional hardware wallets that rely solely on PIN codes and passwords, the D'Cent wallet integrates fingerprint recognition to provide a faster and more secure way to access and authorize transactions. The wallet supports multiple cryptocurrencies, including Bitcoin (BTC), Ethereum (ETH), XRP, Litecoin (LTC), ERC-20 tokens, and more. It connects via Bluetooth to a mobile device, allowing users to buy, sell, swap, and manage assets through the D'Cent mobile app. Additionally, its built-in OLED display makes transaction verification easy, while its sleek and lightweight design makes it a portable alternative to bulkier cold wallets.

✓ **Pros:**

- **Biometric fingerprint authentication** - Enhances security and speeds up wallet access.
- **Supports multiple cryptocurrencies** - Works with BTC, ETH, XRP, ERC-20 tokens, and more.
- **Bluetooth connectivity** - Enables wireless transactions via mobile devices.
- **User-friendly design** - Simple setup with an intuitive OLED display.
- **Affordable** - Lower price point than some premium wallets like Ledger Nano X and Trezor Model T.
- **Secure element (SE) chip** - Protects private keys from hacking attempts.

✕ **Cons:**

- **Bluetooth security concerns** - While convenient, wireless connectivity introduces potential vulnerabilities.
- **No desktop support** - Only works with mobile devices, making it less versatile than Ledger or Trezor wallets.
- **Limited third-party integrations** - Not as widely supported as Ledger or Trezor in external wallets and dApps.
- **Fingerprint sensor may not appeal to all users** - Some prefer PIN-based access for privacy reasons.
- **Less storage than Ledger Nano X** - Can hold fewer cryptocurrency apps at the same time.

The D'Cent Biometric Wallet is an excellent choice for users who value both security and convenience, offering biometric authentication and Bluetooth connectivity for seamless mobile transactions. Its support for multiple cryptocurrencies, user-friendly interface, and affordability make it a strong competitor in the hardware wallet market. However, its lack of desktop support, Bluetooth-related security concerns, and limited third-party integrations may make it less appealing to advanced users. If biometric security and mobile convenience are your priorities, the D'Cent Wallet is a great investment, but for broader compatibility and enhanced storage, Ledger or Trezor wallets may be better options.

14. Cobo Vault (Keystone Pro)

The Cobo Vault (Keystone Pro) is a high-security, air-gapped cold storage wallet designed for maximum protection against cyber threats and unauthorized access. This tamper-proof hardware wallet is completely air-gapped, meaning it has no USB, Bluetooth, Wi-Fi, or NFC connectivity, reducing the risk of hacking. Instead, transactions are signed using QR code scanning, ensuring that private keys never come into contact with an online device.

Built with military-grade security, the Keystone Pro features a self-destruct mechanism that wipes all data if it detects tampering. Its large touchscreen display provides an intuitive user experience, making transaction management seamless. The wallet supports Bitcoin (BTC), Ethereum (ETH), XRP, Litecoin (LTC), ERC-20 tokens, and more, making it a strong choice for serious investors looking for long-term crypto security.

✓ **Pros:**

- **Air-gapped security** – No USB, Bluetooth, Wi-Fi, or NFC, ensuring protection from cyber attacks.
- **Tamper-proof self-destruct mechanism** – If physical tampering is detected, the device erases all data automatically.
- **Large touchscreen display** – Makes transaction verification and navigation simple and user-friendly.
- **QR code-based transactions** – Keeps private keys offline, enhancing security.
- Supports multiple cryptocurrencies – Works with BTC, ETH, XRP, LTC, ERC-20 tokens, and more.
- **Open-source firmware** – Allows for community audits and enhanced transparency.

✗ **Cons:**

- **Higher price point** – More expensive than many standard hardware wallets like Ledger Nano S Plus.
- **Bulkier design** – Larger and heavier compared to Ledger and Trezor wallets, making it less portable.

- **No direct desktop or mobile connectivity** – Requires QR code scanning, which may feel inconvenient for some users.
- **Limited third-party integrations** – Not as widely supported in external wallet applications compared to Ledger or Trezor.
- **Requires Keystone companion app for full functionality** – Users must rely on Keystone's ecosystem for complete asset management.

The Cobo Vault (Keystone Pro) is an ideal choice for users who prioritize absolute security and air-gapped cold storage. Its tamper-proof design, large touchscreen, and QR code transaction system make it one of the most secure hardware wallets available. However, its higher price, bulkier size, and reliance on QR code transactions may not appeal to casual users or those who prefer a more compact solution. If security is your top concern, the Keystone Pro is an excellent investment, but for portability and ease of use, a Ledger or Trezor wallet may be a better option.

15. Arculus Key Card

The Arculus Key Card is a next-generation, NFC-enabled cold storage wallet that provides a secure and convenient way to store cryptocurrencies offline. Unlike traditional hardware wallets that rely on USB or Bluetooth connections, the Arculus wallet functions as a credit card-sized key card, allowing users to access their funds via NFC (Near Field Communication) by tapping the card on their smartphone using the Arculus mobile app.

Designed for ease of use and portability, the Arculus wallet supports Bitcoin (BTC), Ethereum (ETH), Litecoin (LTC), XRP, and multiple ERC-20 tokens. It uses a 3-factor authentication system that includes the key card, biometric authentication (fingerprint or face recognition), and a PIN code, ensuring a high level of security. The wallet also boasts no cables, no batteries, and no reliance on external servers, making it an easy-to-carry and durable solution for secure crypto storage.

✔ **Pros:**

- **Ultra-portable** – Credit card-sized design, making it easy to carry in a wallet.
- **NFC-enabled** – Allows wireless authentication via tap-to-access on a smartphone.

- **3-factor authentication** – Combines biometric authentication, PIN code, and NFC key card for enhanced security.
- **No cables or batteries** – Unlike traditional hardware wallets, it requires no charging or wired connections.
- **Supports multiple cryptocurrencies** – Works with BTC, ETH, LTC, XRP, and ERC-20 tokens.
- **User-friendly mobile app** – Provides a seamless and intuitive crypto management experience.

✕ Cons:

- **Limited coin support** – Supports fewer assets than Ledger or Trezor wallets.
- **Requires a smartphone** – No desktop or USB support, which may be inconvenient for some users.
- **NFC security concerns** – Wireless transactions may pose potential vulnerabilities if proper precautions are not taken.
- **Dependence on the Arculus app** – Users must rely on the Arculus mobile app for managing their assets.
- **No staking or DeFi integrations** – Unlike Ledger or Trezor, the Arculus wallet does not support staking or decentralized applications (dApps).

The Arculus Key Card Wallet is an excellent choice for users who prioritize portability, ease of use, and NFC-based convenience. Its credit card-sized design and 3-factor authentication system provide a secure yet seamless experience for crypto storage. However, its limited coin support, smartphone dependency, and lack of staking or DeFi features may not appeal to advanced users. If you want a simple, ultra-portable cold wallet, the Arculus Key Card is a strong option, but if you need broader asset support, desktop compatibility, and staking capabilities, a Ledger or Trezor wallet may be a better choice.

The Benefits of Using Cold Wallets

Cold wallets are considered the gold standard for storing large amounts of cryptocurrency securely. Here's why:

✓ **Security** – Because they remain offline, they are immune to hacking attempts, malware, and phishing scams.

✓ **Full Control** - Users have complete ownership of their private keys, unlike keeping assets on an exchange.
✓ **Long-Term Storage** - Ideal for HODLers (long-term investors) who do not need frequent access to their funds.

Choosing the right cold wallet depends on your individual needs, budget, and the cryptocurrencies you plan to store. Whether you prioritize maximum security, portability, or staking capabilities, there is a cold wallet suited to every type of investor. In an era of increasing cyber threats, securing your crypto assets is no longer optional—it's essential.

CHAPTER 22

LEVELING THE SEVEN MOUNTAINS OF INFLUENCE

In Revelation 17-18, Mystery Babylon and the Harlot (Great Prostitute) represent a **corrupt** global system that influences the world through false **religion**, political control, and economic power. These chapters describe their rise to power, global influence, and ultimate destruction as part of God's judgment.

The Harlot (Revelation 17):

The Harlot, described in Revelation 17, is a symbolic figure representing a **corrupt religious system** that wields global influence, wealth, and power while leading nations into **spiritual adultery**. She is called "*the great prostitute who sits on many waters*," indicating her **widespread control over peoples, multitudes, nations**, and languages (Revelation 17:1-15). Additionally, she is said to sit on **seven mountains** (Revelation 17:9), which many interpret as a reference to a prominent city known for its seven hills—historically associated with Rome, I have come to some see it as a broader symbolic reference to the seven mountains of influence which encompasses every arena of daily living.

She is clothed in purple and scarlet, adorned with gold, precious stones, and pearls, symbolizing wealth, prestige, and religious authority (Revelation 17:4). The golden cup in her hand, filled with abominations and the filthiness of her fornication, suggests she is engaged in spiritual corruption—promoting false worship while appearing righteous (Revelation 17:4). She is drunk with the blood of the saints and martyrs of

Jesus (Revelation 17:6), meaning she is responsible for persecuting true believers.

The Harlot is riding the Beast (Revelation 17:3), indicating that she is not only a religious system but a governmental one as well, and closely allied with the Antichrist's kingdom, using political power to spread her influence. However, she is ultimately betrayed and destroyed by the Beast and his ten kings (Revelation 17:16-17), showing that her power is temporary, and the Antichrist will replace her with direct Satanic worship. Many scholars and theologians believe the Harlot represents a compromised religious institution that gains global dominance in the end times, possibly an apostate Christian church or a one-world religious system that aligns with political powers for control. Her characteristics—global reach, immense wealth, religious influence, political connections, spiritual deception, persecution of true believers, and ultimate destruction—suggest she is a counterfeit faith system that opposes God's truth in favor of worldly power.

Mystery Babylon (Revelation 18):

Mystery Babylon, referred to in Revelation 17:5 as "*Babylon the Great, the Mother of Harlots and Abominations of the Earth*," symbolizes a powerful global system that influences the world through economic, political, and religious control. This entity is described as one that deceives nations, leading them into spiritual corruption, moral decay, and economic exploitation. As a center of great wealth and trade, Mystery Babylon wields immense financial influence, yet it is also marked by greed, oppression, and unrighteousness, exploiting both people and resources for its own gain. However, despite its apparent strength and global dominance, Babylon's fall is swift and catastrophic, as God's judgment destroys it in one hour (Revelation 18:10). The sudden collapse of this corrupt system causes merchants, kings, and nations to mourn, recognizing that the source of their wealth and power has vanished. This destruction signifies the end of corrupt world systems and the righteous judgment of God, paving the way for the establishment of His eternal kingdom.

Now while we are anticipating the collapse of the old financial system and transition into a new digital financial system, it is unlikely that we are at the time yet to see "***The Fall of Babylon***". The fall of Babylon, both historically and prophetically, has long served as a symbol of the collapse of a great empire due to **corruption**, **idolatry**, and **moral decay**. Throughout history, Babylon represented not only a physical city but a system of power that seeks to control, manipulate, and dominate societies. In today's world that system of power has transcended borders and is now a global network that encompasses all seven mountains of influence. What has been spoken prophetically, is that The Lord is about to "*Level the playing field,*" and this involves "*Leveling the Seven Mountains of Influence*" and the subsequent plundering of Egypt.

In summary, Mystery Babylon will be discussed in further detail in later books of this series, and as we know from the bible is depicted as a dominant global force, exerting control over nations through politics, religion, and commerce. It holds significant influence over world leaders, economic systems, and spiritual affairs, deceiving nations into following its corrupt ways. However, its power is not only based on wealth and influence but also on corruption and persecution. Both the Harlot and Babylon play a role in misleading the world, promoting false worship and oppressing God's people, leading to widespread spiritual deception and moral decay. Despite its apparent strength, Babylon's fate is sealed. The very system it aligns with—the Antichrist's empire—eventually turns against the Harlot, destroying her in a calculated betrayal (Revelation 17:16). Soon after, God executes final judgment on Babylon, bringing about its swift and complete destruction (Revelation 18:10). This event marks the end of corrupt human rule and paves the way for Christ's eternal kingdom to be established. In Revelation 19, Babylon's fall is followed by the triumphant return of Jesus Christ, who reigns in righteousness, ensuring that God's justice and sovereignty prevail over all earthly kingdoms.

The Seven Mountains of Influence and Their Role in Society

In modern times, the concept of Mystery Babylon can be linked to the "*Seven Mountains of Influence*"—areas that shape culture and dictate the direction of a civilization. Understanding how these mountains contribute to societal shifts provides insight into how Babylon's downfall will manifest.

The Seven Mountains of Influence refer to seven key spheres that shape human civilization:

- **Religion** – The spiritual and moral foundation of a society, including churches, faith-based organizations, and religious institutions.
- **Family** – The structure of family life, including marriage, parenting, and generational legacy.
- **Education** – School, universities, and the shaping of minds through curriculum, teachers and academic institutions.
- **Government** – Political leadership, law making and justice systems that influence policies and national direction.
- **Media** – News outlets, social media, television, and other communication platforms that shape public opinion and information.
- **Art & Entertainment** – Movies, music, theater, sports, and other cultural expressions that influence societal values and creativity.
- **Business & Economy** – Commerce, finance, entrepreneurship, banking, and wealth creation that impact economic stability.

Each of these domains holds immense power over society, influencing beliefs, behaviors, and values. When corruption infiltrates these areas, it leads to moral decay, economic instability, and cultural degradation—echoing the downfall of ancient Babylon.

1. Religion: The Corruption of Spiritual Foundations

Religion serves as the moral compass of society, guiding individuals in ethics, spirituality, and their connection to the divine. However, when religious institutions become corrupted, their influence shifts from moral guidance to manipulation and control. Instead of promoting truth, righteousness, and a genuine relationship with God, these institutions often pursue power, wealth, and influence, leading people into spiritual deception rather than enlightenment. This pattern of religious corruption is not new; throughout history, Babylon's downfall was marked by spiritual apostasy, where false gods, idolatry, and occult practices replaced genuine worship.

Similarly, in modern times, many religious institutions, secret societies, and global organizations have been accused of aligning with dark forces, engaging in hidden rituals, deception, and control under the guise of faith. Organizations and religious institutions such as the Freemasons, the Illuminati, and the Beni Jesuits have long been rumored to operate behind the scenes, wielding influence over governments, economies, and religious systems. These groups, often associated with esoteric knowledge and secret rituals, are believed by some to be working toward a **New World Order**, where faith is weaponized to control the masses rather than liberate them.

The **Freemasons**, for example, have deep historical ties to religion, politics, and architecture, with their symbols appearing in government institutions and religious buildings. While many claim the organization is merely a fraternal order, others argue that its higher degrees are steeped in occult knowledge, drawing from ancient pagan and Egyptian mystery schools. The **Illuminati**, allegedly founded to infiltrate institutions of power, has been linked to elite figures, financial institutions, and cultural influencers, with some believing they seek to reshape global religion into a single, controlled belief system.

The **Beni Jesuits**, a sect often associated with hidden knowledge, political intrigue, and manipulation, have historically played roles in religious reformations, world conflicts, and education systems. Their influence within the Catholic Church and beyond has been a topic of controversy, with some believing they are the shadow hand behind major religious and geopolitical shifts. Meanwhile, pagan and satanic influences have crept into mainstream culture, infiltrating entertainment, politics, and even certain religious circles, where hidden rituals and sacrifices are said to occur in secrecy.

The resurgence of **Satanic** and **Pagan** worship, often disguised as spiritual enlightenment, self-empowerment, and mystical traditions, mirrors the idolatry and moral decay seen in ancient Babylon. From the ritualistic sacrifices of ancient cults to modern-day ceremonies that glorify darkness, self-worship, and secret knowledge, these practices have corrupted true faith and drawn many away from God's light. Witchcraft, blood sacrifices, and occult symbolism have increasingly become mainstream, influencing media, politics, and religious structures in ways that subtly normalize rebellion against God.

The **New Age Movement** has experienced significant growth in recent decades, emerging as a spiritual but non-religious belief system that blends Eastern mysticism, occult practices, and esoteric knowledge with modern philosophies on self-empowerment, consciousness expansion, and cosmic enlightenment. At its core, the New Age religion rejects traditional doctrines of sin, salvation, and the sovereignty of God, instead emphasizing personal divinity, spiritual awakening, and interconnected energy fields that supposedly influence reality.

Many adherents of this movement believe in the existence of aliens, life on other planets, and an intergalactic council that oversees world affairs from a higher plane. However, they claim that these beings—often referred to as "*ascended masters*" or "*enlightened extraterrestrials*"—have chosen not to interfere in human development at this time. In their teachings, Jesus is not seen as the Son of God, but rather an alien being born to a virgin, sent to deliver wisdom and show humanity how to evolve spiritually, rather than to provide redemption through His sacrifice.

Many in the New Age movement also engage in tarot card reading, astrology, and divination, practices that are strictly condemned in the Bible (Deuteronomy 18:10-12, Leviticus 19:31) as deceptive and demonic. Tragically, many lukewarm Christians—those who profess faith but lack a firm biblical foundation—have been drawn into New Age teachings, deceived by its promises of hidden wisdom, enlightenment, and universal love. Without discernment, they are led astray from the truth of Scripture, exchanging the Gospel of Jesus Christ for mystical experiences, self-worship, and occult practices, further fulfilling the prophecy of 2 Timothy 4:3-4, which warns that in the last days, many will turn away from sound doctrine and embrace myths and deceptions.

As these forces continue to shape religious institutions, the reckoning foretold in biblical prophecy may not be far off. Just as Babylon was judged for its idolatry and spiritual corruption, modern institutions that prioritize status over substance, power over faith, and deception over truth may soon face divine judgment. The rise of false prophets, deceptive doctrines, and counterfeit spirituality warns that the battle between good and evil is intensifying, requiring discernment and unwavering faith from those who seek the true path of righteousness.

2. Government: The Rise of Oppressive Rule

The governance of a nation determines its stability, prosperity, and moral compass, yet throughout history, corruption, greed, and the lust for power have led to the downfall of great empires. When leaders become self-serving, oppressive, and deceitful, the foundations of a nation begin to erode, making way for chaos, division, and eventual collapse. Babylon fell not simply because of its military conquests or political strength, but because of its arrogance, moral decay, and disregard for divine principles. Likewise, modern governments that embrace corruption, implement unjust policies, and oppress their people are setting themselves on a path toward destruction and divine judgment.

In today's world, the exposure of corruption among political leaders and government institutions is increasing, revealing scandals, deceit, and unlawful practices that have been hidden for years. High-ranking officials and elite figures, once untouchable, are now facing public scrutiny, criminal investigations, and legal consequences as their dark dealings come to light. The abuse of power, manipulation of elections, financial fraud, human rights violations, and cover-ups have shown that many governments are not acting in the best interest of their citizens, but rather in favor of globalist agendas, corporate elites, and personal gain. In many cases, these governments are actively working against the very people they were entrusted to serve, enforcing policies that destroy economies, restrict freedoms, and compromise national sovereignty.

However, just as Babylon fell under God's judgment, the corrupt structures of today's political systems are being shaken. The Lord is leveling the mountain of governmental influence, exposing wicked rulers and dismantling their strongholds of deception. As more truth is brought to light, the world will witness the unraveling of deep-seated corruption, forcing nations to choose between righteousness and continued rebellion. Those who repent and turn back to just governance may find restoration, but those who persist in deception and oppression will face inevitable collapse. Proverbs 29:2 reminds us, "*When the righteous are in authority, the people rejoice; but when the wicked rule, the people groan.*" In these times of exposure and reckoning, the call for justice, accountability, and godly leadership grows louder, heralding a new era where the nations will no longer be ruled by deception, but by truth and righteousness under God's sovereign hand.

3. Family: The Erosion of Foundational Values

Family is the bedrock of civilization, serving as the foundation upon which societies are built and sustained. When the institution of the family is weakened, the moral, social, and spiritual fabric of a nation begins to unravel. Strong families create stability, discipline, and a sense of belonging, but when these structures are compromised, entire communities suffer. Babylon's decadence and moral corruption played a major role in its downfall, as excess, self-indulgence, and moral relativism replaced discipline, faith, and strong family bonds. Today, history is repeating itself, as modern society wages an all-out war on the family unit, leading to the fragmentation of communities, identity confusion, and widespread social decline.

One of the greatest attacks on family today is the push for gender confusion and the erasure of traditional roles through transgender ideology and radical LGBTQ+ agendas. The idea that biological sex is fluid and subjective is being aggressively pushed on children, families, and the education system, leading to widespread confusion about gender, identity, and purpose. Many schools now teach gender ideology without parental consent, promoting hormone treatments, puberty blockers, and even surgeries for minors who are too young to understand the lifelong consequences of these decisions. This movement, which claims to advocate for tolerance and inclusion, has instead resulted in the breakdown of identity, mental health crises, and a direct attack on God's design for humanity (Genesis 1:27). Instead of reinforcing the God-ordained structure of male and female, society is encouraging gender dysphoria, distortion of truth, and rebellion against nature itself.

Additionally, the sanctity of marriage is being systematically devalued and redefined. Marriage, once seen as a sacred covenant between one man and one woman under God, is now viewed as temporary, optional, or unnecessary. The rise of divorce, cohabitation, and casual relationships has made commitment and faithfulness seem outdated, leading to an increase in single-parent households and broken homes. Meanwhile, fornication is widely celebrated, with hook-up culture, pornography, and sexual promiscuity being normalized, further corrupting the purity and significance of intimate relationships. As a result, children grow up in unstable environments, lacking the firm moral and emotional foundation that a strong, God-centered family provides.

Another major assault on the family is abortion, which has led to the devaluation of human life and the destruction of millions of unborn children. Instead of embracing motherhood as a blessing, abortion is marketed as empowerment, deceiving women into believing that sacrificing their child is necessary for freedom and success. This culture of death and convenience disregards God's command to "*be fruitful and multiply*" (Genesis 1:28) and instead promotes selfishness, irresponsibility, and moral numbness. Governments, corporations, and media giants actively push pro-abortion propaganda, while pro-life voices are silenced, showing how deep the war against family and life itself has become.

The family is also under attack through the erosion of parental rights. Governments and activists are increasingly working to remove parental authority, dictating what children should be taught about gender, sex, morality, and even faith. Laws are being passed that allow minors to make life-altering decisions without parental consent, undermining the God-given role of parents as protectors and guides. As the state seeks to replace parents as the primary influence in children's lives, the family structure continues to weaken, setting the stage for greater societal control and manipulation.

If these assaults on the family continue unchecked, the very foundation of civilization will collapse, just as it did in Babylon. A society that rejects God's design for family, marriage, and life will inevitably descend into chaos, confusion, and moral depravity. However, there is still hope. Those who uphold biblical family values must stand firm, raise their children in truth, and resist the deception of the age. The restoration of the family begins with a return to God's Word, the strengthening of marriages, the protection of parental authority, and the rejection of cultural lies that seek to destroy the home. Only by rebuilding strong, God-centered families can society be preserved from total moral and spiritual collapse.

4. Education: Indoctrination Over Truth

Education shapes the minds of future generations, influencing not only what individuals believe but also how they interact with society, government, and the economy. However, when truth is replaced by propaganda, and critical thinking is suppressed in favor of ideological agendas, entire civilizations become vulnerable to manipulation and deception. Babylon thrived on knowledge and advancement, yet it ultimately collapsed when wisdom was abandoned in favor of corruption, control, and deceit. Similarly, in today's world, the educational system has become less about empowering individuals with knowledge and more about programming them to fit within a controlled societal framework.

A critical flaw in modern education is the Babylonian system's agenda to train up workers rather than teach civilians how to create wealth or true independence. The structure of education has been designed not to foster financial literacy, creativity, or innovation, but to produce obedient employees who serve corporate and governmental interests. The system conditions people to work for wages rather than understand wealth-building principles, keeping them trapped in cycles of debt, taxation, and economic dependency. Instead of promoting entrepreneurship, sovereignty, and self-sufficiency, education funnels people into government-approved career paths, reinforcing the modern slave system where people are dependent on their employers and the state. Babylon's influence can be seen in how nations rely on this model to sustain their economic structures, ensuring that the elite class remains wealthy while the masses struggle to survive.

Beyond financial deception, history itself has been rewritten to fit specific narratives, leaving out key events, ancient knowledge, and alternative perspectives that challenge the mainstream agenda. Many historical records have been sanitized, altered, or outright omitted to present a linear story that upholds governmental, economic, and religious power structures. There are glaring gaps in history education, particularly concerning ancient civilizations, lost technologies, and suppressed knowledge. The public has been deliberately kept unaware of breakthroughs in ancient engineering, medicine, and even free energy, ensuring that technological advancements benefiting humanity remain inaccessible while corporations and governments profit from controlled, monetized energy systems. The suppression of Nikola Tesla's discoveries on free energy is one example of how revolutionary knowledge has been buried to maintain economic control over global resources. Instead of fostering curiosity about the true capabilities of past civilizations, modern education indoctrinates students with a carefully curated version of history that prevents them from questioning the narratives fed to them.

Another deceptive layer of the Babylonian education system is the manipulation of science and knowledge about the earth, space, and the universe. Institutions like NASA, an independent agency of the U.S. federal government, have played a key role in shaping public perceptions about the nature of space, planetary existence, and cosmic phenomena. While NASA presents itself as a pioneer of space exploration, many believe it operates under an agenda of misinformation and controlled disclosure, ensuring that the true nature of the cosmos and our own planet remains obscured from public knowledge. There are numerous inconsistencies, altered images, and classified discoveries that have raised suspicions about what is truly being hidden from the masses. If the true nature of space, ancient technologies, or extraterrestrial knowledge were to be fully revealed, it could destabilize modern power structures, forcing people to rethink their beliefs about science, energy, and existence itself.

Thus, the Babylonian education system functions not as a tool for enlightenment, but as a mechanism of control. By suppressing critical thinking, financial independence, hidden history, and technological advancements, it ensures that people remain subservient to the structures of power rather than liberating themselves through knowledge and truth. As society continues to awaken to these manipulations, it is crucial to seek knowledge outside of traditional education, challenge the narratives imposed upon us, and embrace wisdom that leads to true freedom rather than enslavement to deception.

5. Media: The Manipulation of Information

Media holds the power to inform, educate, and shape public perception, but when it falls into the hands of corrupt institutions and self-serving elites, it becomes a tool for mass manipulation and control. In an ideal world, journalism and media would serve as watchdogs of democracy, exposing corruption and holding power accountable. However, today's mainstream media is largely owned and controlled by a select few corporations that dictate the narrative, silence dissenting voices, and push government propaganda to maintain their own influence and agendas. Instead of serving the public interest, news outlets, television programs, movies, and social media platforms have become tools of indoctrination, designed to manipulate emotions, distort reality, and enforce ideological conformity. Just as Babylon's rulers used propaganda and deception to maintain their grip on power, modern societies have perfected the art of misinformation, using media to suppress truth, create division, and manufacture consent for oppressive policies.

One of the most glaring examples of media corruption is the blatant partnership between governments and major news networks to control public perception. Corporate media outlets no longer function as independent entities; they are instead mouthpieces for political parties, globalist organizations, and powerful elites. Through carefully crafted narratives, they push agendas that benefit the ruling class, whether it be fear-mongering, war propaganda, economic manipulation, or the erosion of civil liberties. The COVID-19 pandemic, for example, exposed the coordinated effort between governments, tech giants, and mainstream news outlets to control discourse, silence dissenting opinions, and punish those who questioned the official narrative. Meanwhile, real investigative journalism is censored, demonetized, or deplatformed under the guise of "*fact-checking*" and "*misinformation control*," effectively creating an information monopoly that suppresses alternative viewpoints.

Because of the glaring dishonesty of mainstream media, there has been a rise in independent journalism—a movement driven by individuals who seek to expose hidden truths and counter the propaganda machine. These independent journalists, often working outside corporate sponsorship, rely on direct audience support and decentralized platforms to share information that the mainstream suppresses. Their reporting often uncovers corruption in governments, corporate greed, false flag operations, and media lies, making them targets for censorship, demonization, and even legal persecution. The need for uncensored, independent media has never been greater, as people recognize that truth is being systematically hidden from the public by legacy media corporations, tech giants, and government agencies.

Beyond the news, television, movies, music, and social media have also been weaponized to push political agendas and accelerate moral decay. Hollywood and the entertainment industry, once considered creative and artistic platforms, have become propaganda arms for ideologies that undermine traditional values, attack faith, and normalize perversion. The family unit, which is the foundation of a stable society, is a primary target. Through constant exposure to LGBTQ+ ideologies, transgenderism, hypersexualization, and anti-family messaging, media works to reshape societal norms and desensitize audiences, particularly children, to what was once considered immoral or unnatural. Cartoons, TV shows, and even children's programming now actively promote gender confusion, radical social theories, and the breakdown of traditional marriage. The goal is clear: to erode the biblical understanding of family, confuse young minds, and create a society that prioritizes self-indulgence over righteousness.

Social media has also become a weapon of control, ensuring that only certain narratives are amplified while dissenting voices are buried through shadow bans, algorithmic suppression, and outright censorship. The same platforms that claim to support "*free speech*" and "*open dialogue*" have been exposed as gatekeepers of information, ensuring that only government-approved messaging is seen by the masses. Meanwhile, these platforms also serve as tools of social engineering, promoting degeneracy, vanity, and division while discouraging critical thinking, faith, and traditional values.

Much like Babylon of old, modern media is being used to control, deceive, and lead society further from truth and righteousness. However, as more people awaken to the lies and manipulation, the demand for real, unfiltered truth continues to grow. Independent journalists, alternative media platforms, and truth-seekers are beginning to break through the carefully curated illusions, exposing the deep corruption and hidden agendas behind the world's most powerful institutions. The battle for truth is ongoing, but as light shines into darkness, deception will eventually be exposed and Babylon's propaganda empire will crumble under the weight of its own lies.

6. Arts & Entertainment: The Normalization of Moral Decay

The arts and entertainment industries serve as powerful reflections of a society's culture and values. When used righteously, they inspire, uplift, and communicate truth. However, when they become tools for glorifying violence, immorality, and decadence, they accelerate the spiritual and moral decline of entire civilizations. Babylon was infamous for its opulence, indulgence, and depravity, and its cultural decay played a major role in its ultimate downfall. Likewise, today's entertainment industry—particularly Hollywood, the music industry, and social media influencers—has become saturated with hedonism, perversion, and empty spectacle, leading society further away from truth and morality. A culture obsessed with self-indulgence, hypersexuality, and fame often finds itself on the brink of collapse, just as past civilizations that embraced similar excesses eventually crumbled.

One of the deepest, darkest secrets of the entertainment world is its longstanding involvement in corruption, abuse, and hidden sexual crimes. In recent years, major sex trafficking and child exploitation scandals have exposed the underbelly of Hollywood, the music industry, and elite circles. The Epstein trial shed light on a global network of powerful figures engaged in human trafficking, child exploitation, and blackmail operations. The P. Diddy allegations, as well as multiple testimonies from former industry insiders, have further confirmed that the entertainment industry is rife with abuse, cover-ups, and sexual exploitation, particularly targeting young and vulnerable individuals seeking success. Victims are often lured into the industry with promises of fame and fortune, only to be groomed, exploited, and silenced by those in power.

Hollywood, music labels, and major media conglomerates have actively protected predators and suppressed information about rampant sexual abuse, pedophilia, and human trafficking within their ranks. High-profile cases like Harvey Weinstein's conviction, the Jeffrey Epstein flight logs, and the Ghislaine Maxwell trial have pulled back the curtain on the depravity among the elites, but many believe these exposures are just the tip of the iceberg. The music industry is also deeply implicated, with countless stories emerging of artists being trafficked, manipulated, or forced into compromising situations in exchange for contracts, promotions, or protection from blacklisting.

Beyond these crimes, entertainment as a whole has become a weaponized tool for mass indoctrination, normalizing sexual perversion, violence, drug abuse, and rebellion against God. Music videos, films, and award shows are increasingly filled with satanic imagery, occult symbolism, and sexual exploitation, conditioning audiences—especially the youth—to accept immorality as entertainment. Artists who refuse to participate in these agendas are often silenced, blacklisted, or mysteriously eliminated, reinforcing the tight grip of powerful elites over the industry.

As society becomes increasingly obsessed with fame, fortune, and the pursuit of pleasure, the warnings from Babylon's downfall grow ever more relevant. A civilization that prioritizes spectacle over substance, lust over love, and deception over truth will inevitably self-destruct. However, as the corruption of the entertainment industry continues to be exposed, there is an awakening among those seeking righteousness and truth. More people are turning away from mainstream media, rejecting industry idols, and seeking alternative sources of art and entertainment that honor God rather than glorify sin. The collapse of Babylon's culture serves as a warning that a society built on deception, corruption, and indulgence cannot stand—and the same fate awaits modern-day institutions that follow its path.

7. Business & Economy: The Consequences of Greed

A strong economy is the backbone of a thriving civilization, providing stability, opportunity, and prosperity. However, when greed, fraud, and corruption infiltrate financial institutions, economies become unstable, manipulated, and vulnerable to collapse. Babylon was once an economic powerhouse, yet its reliance on exploitation, excess, and dishonest gain ultimately led to its downfall. Similarly, modern financial systems are now showing the cracks of unchecked greed, with major scandals, market manipulations, and corporate fraud coming to light, exposing the depth of corruption in both traditional and digital financial markets. When profit is prioritized over integrity, economies become fragile, leading to crises, recessions, and the collapse of industries, ultimately plunging nations into economic chaos and uncertainty.

In recent years, some of the biggest financial scandals in history have been exposed, revealing systemic fraud and manipulation at the highest levels of banking, investment, and digital markets. The collapse of major financial institutions and the reckless behavior of corporations have triggered widespread economic instability. The 2008 financial crisis, largely caused by predatory lending and banking fraud, showed how unchecked greed led to the collapse of global markets, forcing governments to bail out banks while ordinary citizens lost homes, jobs, and savings. More recently, the FTX cryptocurrency collapse, led by Sam Bankman-Fried, exposed how a multi-billion dollar Ponzi scheme was allowed to flourish under false promises of financial security and innovation. Investors were duped, billions vanished overnight, and regulatory agencies failed to intervene until the damage was irreversible.

Beyond individual scandals, the manipulation of financial markets—both stock and cryptocurrency—has become a widespread issue, with corporate elites, hedge funds, and governments orchestrating schemes that unfairly benefit the powerful at the expense of everyday investors. The GameStop short squeeze scandal of 2021 revealed how Wall Street hedge funds and institutional investors manipulate stock prices, creating artificial volatility to maintain control over markets. Retail investors who attempted to challenge the system were met with trading restrictions and financial retaliation, exposing the deep-rooted corruption within financial institutions. The same tactics of manipulation, insider trading, and market rigging continue in cryptocurrency markets, where pump-and-dump schemes, exchange fraud, and hidden government intervention make it increasingly difficult for honest investors to build wealth.

Additionally, central banks and government-controlled monetary policies have played a massive role in devaluing national currencies and pushing economies toward artificial boom-and-bust cycles. The endless printing of money, skyrocketing inflation, and unsustainable debt accumulation have placed many nations on the brink of economic collapse. The U.S. national debt has exceeded unsustainable levels, while inflation continues to erode purchasing power. The creation of **Central Bank Digital Currencies (CBDCs)** is now being positioned as a solution to financial instability, but in reality, it represents an even **greater level** of **government control** over personal finances, allowing for monitoring, restrictions, and the potential loss of financial freedom.

Just as Babylon's economic structure eventually crumbled under the weight of its own corruption, today's global financial system is on the verge of major upheaval. The exposure of deep-seated fraud, institutional manipulation, and reckless financial policies signals that the current economic system cannot sustain itself indefinitely. As more individuals awaken to the deception and exploitation embedded within these institutions, alternative financial models are emerging—from decentralized finance (DeFi) to independent economic networks that seek to return to ethical, transparent financial practices. The question remains: Will society correct course and establish financial systems rooted in integrity, or will the Babylonian model of greed and exploitation bring about yet another catastrophic collapse? History has shown that when wealth is built on deception rather than honesty, the collapse is inevitable.

The Future: Leveling the Seven Mountains of Influence

The modern world mirrors ancient Babylon, as corruption, greed, and moral decay have infiltrated every major sphere of influence. The Seven Mountains of Influence—Religion, Government, Education, Media, Arts & Entertainment, Family, and Business—have been compromised, leading societies into deception, lawlessness, and moral decline. Babylon's downfall serves as a warning—when nations and cultures prioritize materialism, power, and corruption over truth, justice, and morality, destruction is inevitable. However, just as Babylon fell, so too will the current systems built on deception, making way for a new era of kingdom-minded leadership. The jungle of chaos grows when the garden of righteousness is neglected, but in the wake of Babylon's fall, God's people will have the opportunity to reclaim and rebuild.

The Rise of Kingdom Builders

As corrupt systems crumble, a divine opportunity is arising for God's children to step into leadership and establish new foundations of righteousness. With the leveling of the Seven Mountains, there will be vacancies in leadership, governance, and influence—and those who are prepared will have the chance to build something better, rooted in kingdom principles. This is not a moment of despair, but a divine transition, where new institutions, businesses, and communities can emerge, reflecting integrity, truth, and justice. Those with the wisdom to discern the times will find themselves in key positions of influence, pioneering new economic models, educational systems, media platforms, and governing structures that align with God's righteousness.

A Kingdom-Driven Revival in Each Mountain

- **Religion** – The fall of corrupt religious institutions will pave the way for a return to true biblical Christianity, where authentic worship, holiness, and truth replace compromise, false doctrines, and self-serving leadership. God will raise up faithful shepherds, revivalists, and reformers who will guide His people into a renewed understanding of His Word.
- **Government** – As corrupt leaders and institutions are exposed, there will be an opening for righteous governance based on justice, truth, and servant leadership. God-fearing leaders will have the opportunity to restore law, order, and freedom, ensuring governments serve the people rather than control them.
- **Education** – The exposure of indoctrination, historical deception, and academic corruption will lead to a restructuring of education systems that truly empower people with knowledge, wisdom, and discernment. New schools, universities, and apprenticeship programs will arise that equip future generations with real skills, entrepreneurial mindsets, and biblical values rather than ideological programming.
- **Media** – The collapse of corporate-controlled propaganda machines will create a vacuum for independent, truth-based journalism and media platforms that inform rather than manipulate. God's people will step into this space, using media to spread truth, expose deception, and bring righteous narratives back into the public sphere.
- **Arts & Entertainment** – The exposure of Hollywood's corruption and the music industry's exploitation will lead to the rise of a new generation of kingdom creatives—musicians, filmmakers, writers, and artists who will reclaim the arts for God's glory. Authentic, inspirational, and morally sound storytelling will return, replacing the darkness that once dominated entertainment.
- **Family** – The destruction of anti-family agendas (transgenderism, LGBTQ+ indoctrination, abortion, and the breakdown of parental rights) will allow for a renewed focus on biblical family values. Christian marriages, strong fatherhood, and motherhood, along with new systems of child development and parenting resources, will flourish.
- **Business & Economy** – As global financial corruption is exposed and collapses, new kingdom-based economic systems will emerge. Entrepreneurs, business owners, and financial leaders will build wealth ethically, ensuring that commerce, banking, and trade operate in a way that serves humanity rather than enslaving it. Decentralized

- financial models, ethical trade, and wealth redistribution based on godly principles will replace the old system of manipulation and exploitation.

A Call to Action: Preparing for the Shift

In a world teetering on the edge, the question remains: Will history repeat itself, or will society heed the warnings of the past? The answer lies in whether God's people will rise to the occasion—preparing themselves to step into positions of influence and leadership when needed. This is not the time for fear but for preparation, strategy, and bold action. God is calling kingdom-minded individuals to train, build, and position themselves for this coming transition. Those who are faithful, discerning, and willing to lead will be the ones who inherit the responsibility of restoring these mountains and ushering in a new era of righteousness and truth.

As The Lord levels the playing field, the Kingdom of God will rise, but only those who are ready and willing to act will be part of the rebuilding. The future belongs to those who align with God's truth and step boldly into the positions He has prepared for them. Will you be among them?

CHAPTER 23

THE RED SEA MOMENT

Throughout biblical history, God has demonstrated His sovereign power by delivering His people from bondage, oppression, and systems of control. One of the most dramatic and awe-inspiring moments of divine intervention occurred when God parted the Red Sea, allowing the Israelites to escape from Egypt and cross into their destiny, while their enemies—Pharaoh and his army—were swallowed by the returning waters. This moment was not just an act of deliverance but also a divine separation, a supernatural wealth transfer, and a final judgment upon the oppressors.

Plundering the Land Before Departure

Before the Israelites left Egypt, God commanded them to ask their Egyptian neighbors for **silver**, **gold**, and fine clothing (Exodus 12:35-36). This was not merely an act of economic redistribution but a divinely orchestrated wealth transfer. The riches that had been hoarded through the oppression of God's people were now being restored to those who had endured hard labor and injustice. Likewise, in today's world, systems of oppression—whether financial, governmental, or corporate—have hoarded wealth and resources, but in God's appointed time, these riches will be released to His faithful remnant. The plundering of Egypt was not theft; it was repayment.

The prophetic parallel for today suggests that as God's people are being prepared for their exodus from spiritual Egypt (the world's corrupted systems), they will receive supernatural provision, opportunities, and influence that will fund their journey into the Promised Land. This will be a sudden, unexpected shift that will leave the wicked reeling, unprepared for the divine restructuring that is about to unfold.

A Modern Wealth Transfer: Plundering the Markets

As in the days of the Exodus, a modern-day financial shift is imminent, where the wealth of the wicked will be transferred to the righteous. The Lord has prophetically spoken about a planned "*glitch*" in the system, a moment when the corrupt elite attempt to manipulate financial markets to their advantage. However, just as Pharaoh's army was swallowed up by the Red Sea in pursuit of the Israelites, this event will likely backfire on the wicked, creating an unprecedented opportunity for God's people to buy up assets at a fraction of their current value.

There is a coordinated effort among global elites to engineer a market collapse—both in stocks and cryptocurrency markets—with the goal of consolidating wealth into the hands of a few. By artificially crashing the markets, they plan to purchase assets at record lows, increase their control, and reset the global financial order. However, in a divine reversal, this scheme will open the door for God's remnant to step into the greatest financial opportunity of a generation.

As institutions and corporations crumble under the weight of their own corruption, those who have been spiritually prepared and financially discerning will be positioned to acquire wealth, land, businesses, and investments at significantly reduced prices. The Lord is calling His people to be ready—to watch, discern, and move when the moment arises. Just as Joseph stored grain in Egypt during the years of plenty, so too must the faithful be wise stewards, prepared to act when this wealth transfer occurs.

Gods people will need to strengthen their relationship with Him, and ability to hear His instruction. The enemy and monitoring spirits are aware of God's plans and are preparing for such events. They do not want God's people or common folks to benefit from the events that are coming. One evidence of this is Coinbase, on February 13th, 2025, they systematically cancelled all buy and sell limit orders that had a large profit margin. Now their platform will not allow you to set a buy or sell limit order greater than (3x) the current price which is significantly different than what the platform previously would allow. This means that if this is one of the exchanges being utilized for cryptocurrency trading, one will need to be on the platform live to take advantage of key events like a "***flash crash***" of "***flash spike***". The Lord has also instructed to pay attention to any urgings that are received to get up in the middle of the night, or check the markets, as this could be Him instructing to take action.

Spiritual Egypt Will Pursue, Seeking to Reclaim Their Wealth

The wealth transfer and the departure of God's people will not go unnoticed by those operating in wickedness. Just as Pharaoh and his army realized they had lost their entire labor force and their wealth, the modern-day oppressors–whether financial elites, corrupt leaders, or compromised institutions–will attempt to regain control. This could manifest as economic warfare, legal entrapments, or outright financial reclamation. However, just as in the Exodus account, this pursuit will lead them into a trap of their own making.

Remember the phrase, "*not your keys, not your crypto*". It means, if you are not the owner of the private keys of where your cryptocurrency is being stored than you are not the custodian of that cryptocurrency. If you have your cryptocurrency on an exchange like Coinbase or Kraken, then these exchanges have ownership of the private keys and are the custodian. If there is a "*Glitch*" in the system, or a coordinated event that occurs with unintended consequences, then we may see a situation where these exchanges will try to reverse orders that have been placed. They may also try to prevent large quantities assets or funds from being moved off the exchange, or from processing the selling of this crypto when the price points recover. Such activities might also trigger red flags in the system resulting in an automatic lock-out from your exchange account. Be aware of this and make sure you do not get caught in these traps. In the event that buy limit orders are filled or able to purchase cryptocurrency during one of these crash events, my plan is to move it off these exchanges as soon as possible and before the price points revalue or the exchange has time to reverse trade activities that they did not intend to happen. This will require diligence, staying alert and quick action. In the days that follow the crash it will be important to safely store your crypto and keep it in your possession, and cold storage devices like the ones previously mentioned in this book are the safest means of doing that.

The enemy will undoubtedly underestimate God's plan, believing that they can recover their wealth, influence, and power by chasing after those who received that wealth. Their arrogance and unwillingness to submit to divine order will lead them into a trap they cannot escape. As they pursue, God will create a path of divine escape for His people—a Red Sea Moment—in which the righteous will cross over, and those who pursue with wicked intent will be caught in their own downfall.

The Crossing Over: Entering the Promise

For God's people, the Red Sea Moment signifies a transition from oppression to promise, from survival to abundance, and from **bondage** to **freedom**. Just as the Israelites walked on dry ground, those who trust in the Lord will be led supernaturally into places of safety, prosperity, and purpose. This moment is not just about leaving Egypt (the old systems) behind, but about stepping into a covenant promise—a land where God's righteousness and justice reign.

As this exodus takes place, the world will witness the hand of God moving in unprecedented ways. Just as the waters of the Red Sea were held back until every Israelite had crossed, so too will the Lord ensure that His remnant is fully prepared and positioned before allowing judgment to fall upon the oppressors. This is not just a moment of escape —it is a divine transition into a new era.

The Final Judgment of Egypt: The Wicked Caught in the Trap

Once God's people have safely crossed over, the Red Sea will close over those who pursue them. The wicked who serve Egypt, blinded by their hunger for power and wealth, will find themselves trapped in a **judgment** of their own making. Just as Pharaoh and his army were swallowed by the sea, so too will corrupt systems, unrighteous rulers, and oppressive structures collapse under the weight of divine justice.

This Red Sea Moment will be both **deliverance** and **judgment**—blessing for the righteous, and destruction for the unrepentant. What the enemy meant for harm will backfire, ensuring that those who sought to enslave, deceive, and oppress are removed from positions of influence. The same forces that once held dominion over God's people will be utterly dismantled, ensuring that the cycle of oppression is broken once and for all.

A Call to Prepare for the Crossing

As this Red Sea Moment approaches, those who are attuned to the voice of God must prepare. Just as the Israelites had to be ready to move when the time came, we too must be spiritually, mentally, and financially prepared for the transition ahead. This is not a time for complacency—it is a time for alignment, strategy, and faith. God is calling His people out of Egypt and to become leaders, pioneers, and builders in this new season.

Key Steps to Prepare for the Red Sea Moment:

- **Strengthen your relationship with God**—Seek wisdom, discernment, and divine direction. Prepare your hearts to ensure you are focused on seeking a true relationship with God and not just for personal gain or attaining wealth.
- **Detach from corrupted systems**—If God is calling you out of spiritual Egypt, a compromised environment, be willing to leave.
- **Steward resources wisely**—The wealth transfer is coming; be ready to handle it with integrity.
- **Develop your kingdom assignment**—Whether in business, governance, media, education, or ministry, position yourself to build in the Promised Land.
- **Stand firm in faith**—When the enemy pursues, do not fear; trust that God has already set the trap for their downfall.

Conclusion: A New Era Awaits

The Red Sea Moment is coming, and it will mark the final separation of the righteous and the wicked. It will be the greatest shift of our time, as God's people transition into a season of dominion and influence, while the oppressors face their inevitable reckoning. The call is clear—prepare to cross over, stand firm in faith, and embrace the divine destiny that awaits. Just as the Israelites walked into freedom and promise, so too will God's remnant step into a new era where His kingdom principles govern, and His people thrive.

The waters are parting. The exodus is near. The promise is at hand. Will you be ready and have the faith to step into it?

CHAPTER 24

PREPARING YOUR HEART POSTURE FOR THE COMING WEALTH TRANSFER

Throughout Scripture, we see examples of God shifting resources from the hands of the unrighteous into the hands of His people. However, before we can receive and steward this wealth properly, we must first prepare our hearts. If our **heart posture** is not aligned with God's will, the very **wealth** that is meant to be a blessing can become a burden or even a **stumbling block** in our relationship with God.

Sudden wealth can be a dangerous trap for those who lack a strong foundation in the Word of God or who do not have the right heart posture toward His Kingdom. Without **spiritual maturity** and a deep-rooted dependence on God, **wealth** can easily become an **idol**, leading people away from their faith. The Bible warns that the **love of money** is a root of all kinds of **evil** (1 Timothy 6:10), and many who gain riches without a heart anchored in Christ become consumed by greed, pride, or self-indulgence. Instead of using their wealth to serve God's purposes, they may drift into worldly temptations, compromise their values, or develop a false sense of security in their material possessions rather than in God. Proverbs 30:8-9 cautions against **both poverty** and **excessive wealth**, emphasizing the danger of **forgetting** the **Lord** in times of abundance. Without a heart postured in humility, stewardship, and obedience, sudden wealth can lead a person to destruction rather than destiny, causing them to miss the true purpose for which God entrusts His resources.

1. Humility: A Heart That Recognizes God as the Source

"But remember the Lord your God, for it is he who gives you the ability to produce wealth, and so confirms his covenant, which he swore to your ancestors, as it is today."
– Deuteronomy 8:18 (NIV)

One of the greatest dangers of wealth is pride. When people experience financial abundance, it becomes easy to believe that their success is solely the result of their hard work, intelligence, or strategic decisions. While diligence and wise stewardship are important, the Bible makes it clear that it is ultimately God who gives us the ability to produce wealth (Deuteronomy 8:18). When we forget this truth, pride creeps in, leading us to rely on our own understanding rather than acknowledging the Lord in all our ways (Proverbs 3:5-6).

"Humility is the fear of the Lord; its wages are riches and honor and life." – Proverbs 22:4 (NIV)

True humility in the area of wealth begins with recognizing that everything we have—our skills, opportunities, and even the breath in our lungs—is a gift from God. He is the one who opens doors of favor, orchestrates divine connections, and blesses the work of our hands. When we fail to acknowledge Him as our source, we risk falling into self-sufficiency, which distances us from God and makes us vulnerable to spiritual downfall. This is why Scripture repeatedly warns against arrogance that comes with prosperity. James 4:6 reminds us that "*God opposes the proud but gives grace to the humble.*" If we desire to be recipients of God's wealth transfer, we must cultivate a posture of humility that acknowledges His sovereignty over our finances.

A humble heart not only recognizes God as the source but also remains dependent on Him even as wealth increases. The danger lies in becoming so comfortable in financial abundance that we no longer seek God as we once did in times of need. Many people who start with good intentions in their faith journey stray when financial success dulls their sense of dependence on God. This is why Proverbs 30:8-9 wisely prays, "*Give me neither poverty nor riches, but give me only my daily bread. Otherwise, I may have too much and disown you and say, 'Who is the Lord?'*"

To maintain a heart of humility, we must continually practice gratitude and generosity. When we openly acknowledge that our wealth belongs to God, we become better stewards, using it to advance His Kingdom rather than indulging in selfish ambitions. Humility also means being teachable —recognizing that no matter how much wealth we acquire, we still need God's wisdom to manage it effectively. Wealth without humility leads to destruction, but wealth stewarded with a humble heart becomes a tool for fulfilling God's purposes on the earth. Therefore, as we prepare for the coming wealth transfer, let us position our hearts in humility, giving God the glory for all that He entrusts to us and remaining faithful stewards of His blessings.

2. Stewardship: A Heart That Manages Resources Wisely

God is not just looking for people He can bless—He is looking for faithful stewards who will manage wealth according to His Kingdom principles. Stewardship is more than just handling money; it is a mindset and a responsibility that requires diligence, discipline, and a heart that seeks to glorify God with resources rather than squander them on selfish desires. When God entrusts wealth to His people, He expects them to use it wisely, not just for personal gain but for advancing His Kingdom, supporting the needy, and fulfilling His divine purposes on the earth.

A few months back, the Lord gave me a dream on the airplane and just prior to landing in Scotland as I was flying there for a work meeting. In my dream, Jesus instructed me to tithe into a certain individual, I was made to know in the dream that even though this person had been following His instructions faithfully and has been steadily investing over the past several years, they did not have the amount of funds that would be needed for the next stages of the wealth transfer. I did not know it then, but he was alluding to the crash that is coming. When I asked the Lord how much of a tithe I should send to this person, he gave me a specific amount, it was clear and audible to me. In my dream, I know I was to send this dollar amount in the Shiba Inu holdings that I had acquired. It was not a small amount, but at the time was about 7% of the total crypto that I had accumulated. Before waking up from this dream from, quite literally, the plane landing is:

"Whoever can be trusted with very little can also be trusted with much, and whoever is dishonest with very little will also be dishonest with much. So if you have not been trustworthy in handling worldly wealth, who will trust you with true riches?" — Luke 16:10-11 (NIV)

Jesus then asked me, "*What difference does it make that I ask you to send this amount to (this person) now, or if I should have you send the equivalent of what this will become after the Wealth Transfer.*" Which in my spirit I was made to know would be worth hundreds of millions of dollars. The answer from me, was that "*there would be no difference.*" I was made to know that not only was this a testing of obedience for me, but it would also be a testing for this individual that I was tithing into. I also had a knowing that in the future, there will be situations where the Lord will be speaking to me regarding specific causes, charities, businesses, events, communities and the like, that he will be providing instruction on the funds I am to provide for these causes. This will be the same for many of God's children and it is important to prepare now by becoming more sensitive for the Holy Ghost in order to properly hear His instructions when the time comes.

The Bible teaches that everything we have belongs to God, and we are merely managers of His resources. Psalm 24:1 states, "*The earth is the Lord's, and everything in it, the world, and all who live in it.*" When we understand that wealth is not our own but a tool given by God, we approach financial blessings with a greater sense of accountability. Jesus reinforces this principle in the Parable of the Talents (Matthew 25:14-30), where the servants who wisely managed what was given to them were rewarded, while the one who acted carelessly lost everything. This parable illustrates that God expects us to multiply what He places in our hands and use it in ways that align with His will.

"The plans of the diligent lead to profit as surely as haste leads to poverty." – Proverbs 21:5 (NIV)

Stewardship requires wisdom and self-control. Without financial discipline, wealth can be wasted on impulsive desires, temporary pleasures, or unwise investments that do not yield lasting fruit. Proverbs 21:20 warns, "*The wise store up choice food and olive oil, but fools gulp theirs down.*" This verse highlights the importance of managing resources with foresight, setting aside for the future, and avoiding reckless spending. True stewards recognize that financial prosperity comes with responsibility—responsibility to give, invest wisely, and avoid debt traps that lead to bondage.

Another crucial aspect of stewardship is generosity. When God blesses us, it is not only for our own benefit but so that we can be a blessing to others. 2 Corinthians 9:10-11 says, "*Now he who supplies seed to the sower and bread for food will also supply and increase your store of seed and will enlarge the harvest of your righteousness. You will be enriched in every way so that you can be generous on every occasion.*" A good steward understands that giving is an essential part of financial management. **Tithing**, supporting ministries, helping the poor, and funding Kingdom initiatives are all ways we demonstrate faithfulness in our financial stewardship.

Additionally, good stewardship involves seeking God's wisdom in financial decisions. Before making significant purchases, investments, or business ventures, we must seek the Lord's guidance through prayer and godly counsel. Proverbs 3:9-10 instructs, "*Honor the Lord with your wealth, with the first fruits of all your crops; then your barns will be filled to overflowing, and your vats will brim over with new wine.*" Honoring God with our finances includes prioritizing Him in our financial decisions, trusting that as we put Him first, He will take care of our needs and bless the work of our hands.

A heart of stewardship is one that understands that wealth is a tool, not a treasure. Those who mismanage finances, hoard selfishly, or allow money to control their lives will find that riches can quickly fade away. However, those who approach wealth with a Kingdom mindset, using it as a means to fulfill God's purposes, will experience divine increase and long-term fruitfulness. As we prepare for the coming wealth transfer, let us cultivate a heart of stewardship—managing God's resources wisely, sowing into His Kingdom, and remaining faithful to His calling in every financial decision we make.

As we prepare for the coming wealth transfer, it is essential to cultivate a heart of stewardship. This means developing financial wisdom, practicing discipline, avoiding wastefulness, living within our means, embracing generosity, and seeking God's guidance in all financial decisions. Wealth is a tool that can be used for either good or destruction, and only those who approach it with humility and responsibility will be able to sustain and multiply it for God's glory. The true reward of stewardship is not just financial abundance but the privilege of partnering with God in His Kingdom work, ensuring that His resources are used to fulfill His purposes on the earth.

3. Generosity: A Heart That Gives Freely

God does not bless us so we can hoard wealth but so we can be a blessing to others. The coming wealth transfer is not just about personal abundance—it is about funding Kingdom work, helping the needy, and advancing the Gospel. A heart that is prepared for wealth is a heart that is willing to give generously, recognizing that resources are entrusted to us for a greater purpose beyond ourselves.

Generosity is a central principle of God's economy. The world operates on a mindset of accumulation—seeking to gain more, store more, and secure wealth for self-preservation. However, God's Kingdom operates on a different principle: the more we give, the more we receive (Luke 6:38). This is not just about financial giving; it is about having an open heart that willingly shares resources, time, and energy to uplift others and expand the reach of God's work. When we understand that wealth is a tool rather than an end goal, we begin to see money not as something to control but as something to steward for Kingdom purposes.

Generosity is a form of worship and an expression of faith. When we give freely, we acknowledge that God is our provider and that He will continue to supply all our needs. Many people struggle with giving because they fear lack, but biblical generosity is rooted in trust—trust that God is able to multiply what we sow and take care of us abundantly. 2 Corinthians 9:6-7 reminds us that giving should not be done reluctantly or under pressure, but with a cheerful heart, because God delights in those who give willingly and joyfully. True generosity is not transactional; it is transformational. It changes not only the lives of those who receive but also the heart of the giver, making them more like Christ, who gave everything for us.

The Bible also teaches that generosity leads to prosperity. Proverbs 11:25 states, "*A generous person will prosper; whoever refreshes others will be refreshed.*" This verse highlights a powerful Kingdom principle—when we give, we open ourselves up to divine provision and increase. God's system of multiplication does not operate through greed but through generosity. When He finds people who are faithful givers, He entrusts them with even more resources because He knows they will use it wisely for His purposes. This is why many of the greatest financial blessings come to those who are intentional about supporting the work of God, helping the less fortunate, and ensuring that His Gospel reaches the ends of the earth.

Generosity is also a test of the heart. Jesus said in Matthew 6:21, "*For where your treasure is, there your heart will be also.*" If our hearts are attached to wealth more than they are to God, we will struggle to give freely. But when our hearts are postured correctly, we see money as a means to glorify God rather than as a source of security or status. A generous person understands that wealth is temporary, but the impact of giving can be eternal. Sowing into ministries, supporting missionaries, providing for the poor, and investing in causes that align with God's heart are ways we ensure that our wealth serves a higher purpose.

Furthermore, generosity should be a lifestyle, not just an occasional act. Many people wait until they have an abundance before they start giving, but God calls us to be generous with what we have now. The widow in Mark 12:41-44 gave only two small coins, yet Jesus praised her above all the wealthy people because she gave sacrificially and with a heart of faith. True generosity is not about the amount but about the heart behind the giving. It is about being willing to release what God has given us, knowing that He is faithful to supply more when we need it.

As we prepare for the coming wealth transfer, we must cultivate a generous heart. This means not only giving from our abundance but also being faithful with what we have now. If we are not generous with little, we will not be generous with much. God is looking for people He can trust with resources—those who will use their wealth to build His Kingdom, serve others, and bring glory to His name.

Prayer for a Generous Heart:

"*Lord, I thank You for every resource You have placed in my hands. Help me to cultivate a heart of generosity, to give freely and cheerfully, knowing that You are my ultimate provider. Teach me to see wealth as a tool for Your Kingdom and not just for personal gain. May I always be willing to bless others, support Your work, and advance the Gospel. Let my giving be a reflection of Your love and an act of worship unto You. In Jesus' name, Amen.*"

Generosity is a key principle in preparing for financial increase. The more we align our hearts with God's purposes, the more He entrusts us with resources to be used for His glory. If we desire to be part of the wealth transfer, we must be willing to let go, sow generously, and trust God as our ultimate source of provision.

4. Faithfulness: A Heart That Stays Committed to God

Wealth should never replace our dependence on God. Many people start with a strong faith but drift away when material abundance brings comfort, ease, and a false sense of security. While wealth itself is not inherently evil, the love of money can become a snare that pulls people away from their relationship with God. The Bible warns in 1 Timothy 6:10, "*For the love of money is a root of all kinds of evil. Some people, eager for money, have wandered from the faith and pierced themselves with many griefs.*" This verse highlights the dangers of placing financial gain above spiritual devotion. When money becomes the focus, it slowly takes the place of God, leading to compromised values, spiritual complacency, and, ultimately, separation from Him.

Faithfulness means that our trust and commitment to God remain unshaken, whether in seasons of plenty or scarcity. A faithful heart does not allow wealth to dictate its level of devotion. In Matthew 6:24, Jesus makes it clear that we cannot serve both God and money; one will always take precedence over the other. If we desire to be part of the coming wealth transfer, we must prove that our love for God surpasses our love for material gain. God is looking for people whose hearts are fully devoted to Him—those who will remain steadfast in worship, prayer, and obedience regardless of their financial status.

One of the most significant tests of faithfulness is how we **handle increase**. It is easy to depend on God in times of need, but what happens when all our needs are met, and we experience financial overflow? Many people unintentionally drift away from prayer, church, and spiritual disciplines when they no longer feel desperate for God's provision. They begin to trust in their wealth rather than in God, forgetting that it was He who provided for them in the first place. This is why Deuteronomy 8:18 reminds us, "*But remember the Lord your God, for it is he who gives you the ability to produce wealth.*"

To cultivate faithfulness, we must develop habits that keep us grounded in God's presence, no matter how much wealth we attain. This includes maintaining a lifestyle of worship, consistent prayer, generosity, and obedience to His Word. It also means keeping a spirit of humility, recognizing that everything we have belongs to God and should be used for His purposes. Proverbs 30:8-9 expresses this balance well: "*Give me neither poverty nor riches, but give me only my daily bread. Otherwise, I may have too much and disown you and say, 'Who is the Lord?'*"

Faithfulness also requires integrity in financial matters. When God blesses us with wealth, we must commit to handling it righteously—paying debts, conducting honest business, treating employees fairly, and avoiding corruption. Many people compromise their faith when money is involved, justifying unethical decisions in the pursuit of greater profits. But a truly faithful heart refuses to cut corners or engage in dishonest gain, trusting that God's way leads to lasting prosperity. Proverbs 28:20 says, "*A faithful person will be richly blessed, but one eager to get rich will not go unpunished.*"

Finally, faithfulness is tested through our ability to remain generous and obedient to God's direction. God does not just bless us for our own benefit

—He blesses us to be a blessing. If we withhold generosity and fail to use our wealth for Kingdom purposes, we show that our trust is in money rather than in God. Luke 16:10–11 states, "*Whoever can be trusted with very little can also be trusted with much, and whoever is dishonest with very little will also be dishonest with much. So if you have not been trustworthy in handling worldly wealth, who will trust you with true riches?*" This verse teaches that how we manage our current resources determines whether God can entrust us with greater responsibility.

As we prepare for the wealth transfer, we must ask ourselves:

- Will I remain faithful to God when I have more than enough?
- Will I continue to seek Him just as fervently in abundance as I did in lack?
- Will I honor Him with my financial decisions, or will I allow wealth to lead me away from Him?

The answer to these questions determines whether we are truly prepared to receive and sustain wealth in a way that glorifies God. Faithfulness is not about the amount of money we have; it is about our commitment to God, no matter our financial situation. When He sees that our hearts are steadfast and unmovable in devotion, He can confidently entrust us with greater resources, knowing that they will be used for His Kingdom rather than for selfish gain.

Prayer for a Faithful Heart:

"*Lord, I declare that my heart belongs to You above all else. No matter what level of wealth I attain, I choose to remain faithful to You, trusting in Your provision and not in material riches. Keep my heart pure, my motives aligned with Your will, and my devotion unwavering. May I never allow wealth to pull me away from You, but instead, let it be a tool to serve You and advance Your Kingdom. In Jesus' name, Amen.*"

A heart of faithfulness is a heart that is ready for God's blessings. If we desire to be part of the coming wealth transfer, we must demonstrate that our commitment to God is greater than our desire for riches. Only then can we truly handle wealth in a way that honors and glorifies Him.

5. Righteousness: A Heart That Aligns with God's Will

God transfers wealth into the hands of those who walk in righteousness. While the world often promotes the idea of obtaining wealth through any means necessary—whether through deception, manipulation, or selfish ambition—the Kingdom of God operates differently. True wealth that comes from God is not just about financial abundance; it is about being positioned to receive and sustain His blessings in a way that aligns with His will. A righteous heart is the key to long-term, God-ordained prosperity.

Righteousness is not just about morality—it is about living in alignment with God's ways, obeying His commands, and making decisions based on His principles rather than the world's standards. This includes integrity, honesty, generosity, and a heart that seeks justice and fairness in all dealings. Proverbs 13:22 confirms that "*A good person leaves an inheritance for their children's children, but a sinner's wealth is stored up for the righteous.*" This verse reveals two critical truths: First, righteousness leads to generational blessing, and second, wealth that is accumulated unrighteously will eventually be transferred to those who are aligned with God.

One of the biggest tests of righteousness in the area of wealth is how we obtain, manage, and distribute financial resources. Many people compromise their integrity for money, engaging in **dishonest** business practices, cutting ethical corners, or prioritizing profit over people. However, the Bible makes it clear that **God** does **not bless** wealth gained through **unrighteous** means. Proverbs 10:22 states, "*The blessing of the Lord brings wealth, without painful toil for it.*" This implies that there is a difference between wealth obtained through God's blessing and wealth obtained through human striving, deceit, or oppression. The latter comes with burdens, stress, and instability, while the former is established in peace and sustainability.

Walking in righteousness also means trusting in God's provision rather than resorting to ungodly means to gain financial security. Psalm 37:25-26 declares, "*I was young and now I am old, yet I have never seen the righteous forsaken or their children begging bread. They are always generous and lend freely; their children will be a blessing.*" This verse reassures us that when we live righteously, God provides—not just for us but for future generations. It also highlights that righteousness produces a spirit of generosity, reinforcing the principle that wealth in the hands of the righteous is meant to be shared and used for the benefit of others.

A heart that aligns with God's will also operates in obedience and humility. Some people seek wealth purely for personal gain, status, or selfish desires, but those who seek God's Kingdom first will find that provision is a natural result of their alignment with His will. Matthew 6:33 states, "*But seek first his **kingdom** and his **righteousness**, and all these things will be given to you as well.*" This means that when we prioritize God's ways and pursue righteousness, He takes care of everything we need—including financial blessings.

Additionally, righteousness demands that we honor God with our wealth. This means being faithful in giving (**tithing**, offerings, and helping those in need), handling finances ethically, and ensuring that our wealth is used to glorify God rather than fueling selfish ambitions. Proverbs 3:9-10 instructs, "*Honor the Lord with your wealth, with the first fruits of all your crops; then your barns will be filled to overflowing, and your vats will brim over with new wine.*" When we honor God in our financial matters, we position ourselves for supernatural increase.

The coming wealth transfer is not simply about shifting money from one group to another—it is about positioning righteous individuals to steward resources that will advance God's Kingdom. If we desire to be recipients of this divine shift, we must ensure that our lives reflect integrity, holiness, and a commitment to godly principles. Wealth in the hands of the unrighteous leads to corruption, but wealth in the hands of the righteous leads to transformation.

Practical Steps to Walk in Righteousness for the Wealth Transfer:

- **Commit to honesty and integrity:** Never compromise biblical principles for financial gain. Conduct business with fairness and transparency.
- **Remain generous and open-handed:** Use wealth to bless others, fund Kingdom work, and support those in need.
- **Seek God's direction in financial decisions:** Avoid chasing wealth for personal gain; instead, ask God how He wants to use you as a vessel for provision.

- **Avoid greed and covetousness:** Never allow money to become an idol; instead, keep God as your first priority.
- **Live with a long-term, generational mindset:** Righteousness produces wealth that lasts for generations, not just temporary riches.

Prayer for Righteous Stewardship:

"Lord, I desire to live a life that aligns with Your will. Purify my heart so that I may walk in righteousness, integrity, and honesty in all areas of my life, including my finances. Help me to manage wealth in a way that honors You and advances Your Kingdom. May my hands be open to give, my heart be set on obedience, and my trust remain in You, not in riches. Position me to be a recipient of Your divine wealth transfer so that I may glorify You with all that You entrust to me. In Jesus' name, Amen."

A heart of righteousness is a heart that God can trust with wealth. As we prepare for the financial shift that is coming, let us ensure that our lives reflect God's character so that when the wealth transfer happens, we are ready to handle it with wisdom, integrity, and a Kingdom-minded purpose.

6. Obedience: A Heart That Follows God's Instructions

When wealth comes, we must be sensitive to God's voice regarding how to use it. God's blessings always come with divine purpose—some will be called to invest, some to give, some to build, and others to steward in unique ways. The key to sustaining and multiplying the wealth God entrusts to us is obedience. Without obedience, wealth can easily become mismanaged, wasted, or used for self-serving purposes rather than for advancing God's Kingdom. Preparing our hearts requires developing a lifestyle of obedience now, so that when the wealth comes, we can move in alignment with God's plan and not be swayed by human reasoning or selfish desires.

Obedience is not just about avoiding sin—it is about actively seeking God's will and following His specific instructions. Isaiah 1:19 declares, "*If you are willing and obedient, you will eat the good things of the land.*" This scripture reveals that obedience leads to abundance. However, obedience must be willing, not forced—God is looking for people who joyfully submit to His guidance, trusting that His ways are higher and better than our own (Isaiah 55:8-9).

Obedience Requires Trust in God's Plan

Many times, God's instructions regarding wealth may not make sense in the natural. He may ask us to give sacrificially, invest in something that doesn't seem logical, or take steps of faith that require complete dependence on Him. Abraham's obedience is a prime example—when God told him to sacrifice Isaac (Genesis 22), it seemed contradictory to the promise of descendants as numerous as the stars. However, Abraham obeyed without hesitation, and God provided a ram in place of Isaac, rewarding Abraham's faithfulness with a covenant blessing. Likewise, when we obey God's financial instructions, we position ourselves for supernatural provision and multiplication.

A heart of obedience is one that is surrendered to God's timing and methods. Some people miss divine wealth opportunities because they are too impatient to wait for God's leading, or they reject what He is instructing because it does not align with their personal preferences. But true obedience means trusting God even when we don't fully understand His plan. The widow at Zarephath (1 Kings 17:8-16) is an example of this—when Elijah asked her to use her last bit of flour and oil to make bread for him first, it seemed unreasonable. Yet, because she obeyed the prophetic instruction, her supply never ran out, and she and her household were sustained through the famine.

Obedience Leads to Kingdom Advancement

When we obey God's instructions regarding wealth, it leads to Kingdom advancement. Some will be called to fund ministries, plant churches, support missionaries, or create businesses that provide employment and resources for communities. Others will be called to invest in land, real estate, media, or other industries that influence society for God's glory. Whatever the specific assignment, obedience ensures that wealth is directed towards God's agenda rather than personal ambition.

A great example is Joseph in Egypt (Genesis 41:28-49). God gave him divine insight to store grain during seven years of plenty so that Egypt and surrounding nations would survive the coming famine. His obedience to God's revelation positioned him to be a distributor of resources in a time of crisis. Likewise, many believers today will be entrusted with wealth not for personal luxury alone, but to be Joseph-like distributors for Kingdom purposes.

Disobedience Leads to Loss

Just as obedience brings increase, disobedience can cause loss. Saul, Israel's first king, is a sobering example—he lost his kingship because he chose to partially obey God's command (1 Samuel 15). Many people forfeit financial blessings because they refuse to follow God's voice completely. Whether through greed, fear, procrastination, or disobedience, failing to obey divine instructions can block the full manifestation of God's provision.

Preparing Our Hearts for Wealth Through Daily Obedience

We must train our hearts to obey God now before wealth comes. If we are not obedient with little, we will not be obedient with much (Luke 16:10). This includes:

- **Obeying in Small Matters:** Faithfully **tithing**, **giving**, and stewarding finances wisely now prepares us for greater responsibilities later.
- **Seeking God's Direction in Financial Decisions:** Instead of relying solely on human wisdom, we should pray and seek His guidance before making financial moves.
- **Remaining Open to Unconventional Instructions:** God's ways are not always predictable. He may ask us to give when it seems unreasonable or invest in something that requires faith.
- **Resisting the Temptation of Self-Reliance:** As wealth increases, we must ensure that we are still depending on God, not just our financial security.
- **Keeping a Kingdom Mindset:** Our wealth should align with God's purposes, not just personal gain.

Prayer for an Obedient Heart:

"*Lord, I surrender my finances to You. Help me to develop a heart of obedience so that when You bless me with wealth, I will steward it according to Your will. Let me never trust in riches, but only in You. Give me wisdom to recognize Your instructions and the courage to follow them, even when they don't make sense. Position me to be a vessel for Kingdom wealth and an instrument of blessing. In Jesus' name, Amen."*

Obedience is the foundation for sustaining the Wealth Transfer. God is not looking for people who only desire riches; He is looking for those who will steward them according to His divine purpose. If we desire to receive financial increase, we must cultivate a lifestyle of daily obedience, ensuring that our wealth will be used for His glory and the expansion of His Kingdom.

A Warning: Heed the Lord's Call to Prepare Your Heart

The Lord is issuing a clear warning in this hour: Prepare your heart, for the wealth transfer is not just a blessing—it is a test. Those who claim to love God yet secretly harbor selfish ambition, greed, and an unhealthy fixation on personal gain are in dangerous territory. The deception of wealth is that it can make one feel secure, powerful, and even justified in their ways, but if the heart is not truly surrendered to God, that same wealth can become a snare leading to spiritual downfall.

Some may receive financial blessings for a time, experiencing the overflow of the wealth transfer, yet without a heart that is truly postured toward God, they will lack the discernment to steward it properly. The enemy is waiting to exploit those who receive increase but have not submitted their desires to the Lord. They may celebrate their financial breakthrough, but what happens when God gives further instructions that require faith, obedience, and sacrifice? If their heart is fixed on their wealth instead of on Him, they will either resist His voice or become deaf to it altogether. They will move forward in their own wisdom, leaning on their riches rather than on God, and what was meant to be a blessing will become a stumbling block.

This is the final test. The Lord is weighing hearts in this season to see who is truly faithful and who is only after His hand, not His heart. Will you cling to your wealth, or will you remain anchored in the Kingdom of God? Will you trust in your riches, or will you continue trusting in the One who gave them to you? Those who pass this test—who keep their hearts pure and their ears open to God's voice—will not only receive wealth but will also receive the divine strategy to protect, multiply, and use it for Kingdom advancement. But those who fail, who refuse to surrender their attachment to money, will soon find that what they received was temporary, fleeting, and vulnerable to loss.

This is your warning: Do not let wealth become your god. Do not fail this test. Keep your heart positioned in humility, obedience, and righteousness, so that when the Lord speaks, you will hear and move accordingly. For only those who prove faithful in this hour will be entrusted with true, enduring riches that will not only bless them but will also establish God's purposes for generations to come. Choose wisely.

Conclusion: Aligning Our Hearts for the Shift

The coming wealth transfer is not just about financial increase—it is about Kingdom advancement. God is positioning His people to be conduits of His resources so that His purposes can be fulfilled on the earth. If we desire to be a part of this movement, we must start by preparing our hearts.

We must embrace humility, stewardship, generosity, faithfulness, righteousness, and obedience. When our hearts are in the right posture, we will not only receive wealth but also manage it in a way that brings glory to God and expands His Kingdom.

Prayer for Preparation:

"Lord, I recognize that all wealth and provision come from You. Prepare my heart to steward Your blessings wisely. Keep me humble, faithful, and obedient. Help me to be generous and align my desires with Your will. May I never love money more than I love You. I trust You to position me for Your divine wealth transfer and to use me as a vessel for Your Kingdom purposes. In Jesus' name, Amen."

CHAPTER 25

CONCLUSION: NAVIGATING THE FINANCIAL FUTURE WITH CONFIDENCE

The Great Wealth Transfer is not just a financial shift; it is a transformative moment in history that will redefine how individuals, businesses, and governments interact with money, assets, and technology. This movement from traditional financial systems to a digital, decentralized economy carries profound implications for global wealth, accessibility, and opportunity. Understanding the significance of this transition and preparing for it is no longer optional—it is essential.

Recap: The Significance of the Great Wealth Transfer

At the heart of the Great Wealth Transfer lies the migration from fiat-based systems to blockchain-powered digital assets. This shift offers unprecedented opportunities for financial inclusion, wealth creation, and technological innovation. It challenges outdated models of centralization and opacity, replacing them with decentralization, transparency, and efficiency.

Throughout this book, we have explored the foundations of this transition, from the origins of blockchain technology to its practical applications in cryptocurrencies, decentralized finance (DeFi), and tokenized assets. Each chapter has underscored the transformative potential of these innovations and the need for individuals to adapt to a rapidly changing financial landscape.

The opportunities within this wealth transfer are immense, but they are reserved for those who are willing to take proactive steps to understand, embrace, and leverage the changes. The wealth generated during this era will not only redefine personal and corporate fortunes but will also reshape industries and economies for decades to come.

The Urgency of Taking Action Now

Timing is critical in any major economic shift, and the Great Wealth Transfer is no exception. The early adopters of blockchain technology and digital assets are already witnessing substantial benefits, while those who delay risk being left behind.

The urgency stems from several key factors:

- **Accelerating Adoption:** Governments, businesses, and institutions are integrating blockchain and digital assets at an increasing pace. This mainstream adoption signals that the window for entering this market early is closing.
- **Technological Advancements:** Innovations such as smart contracts, decentralized applications, and tokenized assets are rapidly transforming the financial ecosystem, creating opportunities that demand immediate attention.
- **Global Competition:** As the wealth transfer unfolds, individuals and nations are positioning themselves to lead in the new economy. Delaying action could mean forfeiting a competitive edge.

By taking action now—whether through financial education, strategic investments, or building a diversified portfolio—individuals can position themselves to thrive during this period of immense change.

Embracing Change and Staying Informed

Change is often accompanied by uncertainty, but it also brings opportunity. Embracing change requires a shift in mindset, a willingness to learn, and the courage to take calculated risks. Staying informed is equally vital; knowledge of trends, emerging technologies, and market dynamics will empower individuals to make sound decisions.

Here are key strategies to navigate this evolving landscape:

- **Continuous Learning:** Stay updated on advancements in blockchain technology, cryptocurrency markets, and decentralized finance.
- **Engagement:** Join communities, attend seminars, and follow thought leaders to gain insights and connect with others navigating the same journey.
- **Adaptability:** Be prepared to pivot as the financial landscape evolves, leveraging new tools and opportunities as they arise.

Final Thoughts: Navigating the Future with Confidence and Purpose

The Great Wealth Transfer is more than an economic event—it is an opportunity to reshape the future of wealth, access, and opportunity. It will be the event that will enable God's children to rebuild the world and establish God's kingdom on this earth. For those willing to embrace change, invest in knowledge, and take calculated steps, this transition represents a pathway to financial freedom and empowerment.

As the new financial system emerges, it will challenge traditional ways of thinking about money, investments, and opportunities. Those who navigate this era with confidence and purpose will not only build personal and generational wealth but also contribute to a global economy that is more inclusive, transparent, and resilient.

This journey begins with a single step—educating oneself, embracing innovation, and taking action. The future of finance belongs to those who are prepared to seize it. With the right mindset, tools, and strategies, navigating the Great Wealth Transfer can be a transformative experience, paving the way for a prosperous and purpose-driven life.

REFERENCES

Allen Iverson

- TalkSport. (2023, January 15). I blew $200 million on jewelry, cars, and nights out – now I'm a millionaire again and working with Shaquille O'Neal. Retrieved January 7, 2025, from https://talksport.com/basketball/2085310/allen-iverson-net-worth-reebok-shaquille-oneal/

Mike Tyson

- The Scottish Sun. (2023, February 20). How Mike Tyson blew $400m with reckless spending on mansions, fast cars, women, drugs, pet tigers and $2.2m bath tub. Retrieved January 7, 2025, from https://www.thescottishsun.co.uk/sport/13852770/mike-tyson-mansions-cars-women-drugs-tigers-fortune/
- The Scottish Sun. (2023, January 10). Mike Tyson admits he used to blow through $5 million in a couple of days ahead of money-spinning Jake Paul fight. Retrieved January 7, 2025, from https://www.thescottishsun.co.uk/sport/13594985/mike-tyson-money-jake-paul-fight/

Nicolas Cage

- MarketWatch. (2018, January 26). Why Nicolas Cage blowing more than $100 million is an essential money lesson for us all. Retrieved January 7, 2025, from https://www.marketwatch.com/story/why-nicolas-cage-blowing-more-than-100-million-is-an-essential-money-lesson-for-us-all-2018-01-26

Multiple Celebrities

- Living.alot.com. (n.d.). Celebrities who wasted their wealth. Retrieved January 7, 2025, from https://living.alot.com/entertainment/celebrities-who-wasted-their-wealth--22073
- AARP. (2012, December 12). Celebrities who went broke. Retrieved January 7, 2025, from https://www.aarp.org/money/credit-loans-debt/info-12-2012/celebrities-who-went-broke-slideshow.html
- AOL. (n.d.). 18 celebrities who lost their fortunes. Retrieved January 7, 2025, from https://www.aol.com/18-celebrities-lost-190000965.html

LeBron James (Athlete):

- Investopedia. (2023, October). LeBron James Net Worth. Retrieved from https://www.investopedia.com/lebron-james-billionaire-7497709
- Sportskeeda. (2023). 5 major investments contributing to LeBron James' billionaire portfolio. Retrieved from https://www.sportskeeda.com/basketball/5-major-investments-contributing-lebron-james-billionaire-portfolio

Rihanna (Musician and Entrepreneur):

- Investopedia. (2024, October). Rihanna's Net Worth—and How She Made Her Billions. Retrieved from https://www.investopedia.com/rihanna-net-worth-7108308
- Forbes. (2024). Rihanna. Retrieved from https://www.forbes.com/profile/rihanna/

Oprah Winfrey (Media Mogul):

- Forbes. (2024). Oprah Winfrey. Retrieved from https://www.forbes.com/profile/oprah-winfrey/
- Investopedia. (2023, November). Oprah Winfrey's Net Worth. Retrieved from https://www.investopedia.com/oprah-winfrey-net-worth-7503456

Ashton Kutcher (Actor and Tech Investor):

- CNBC. (2019, September 24). Ashton Kutcher's tech investments have a promising track record. Retrieved from https://www.cnbc.com/2019/09/24/ashton-kutchers-tech-investments-have-a-promising-track-record.html

REFERENCES

- Forbes. (2016, March 23). Ashton Kutcher's Investment Portfolio: What He Owns. Retrieved from https://www.forbes.com/sites/ryanmac/2016/03/23/ashton-kutchers-investment-portfolio-what-he-owns/

Beyoncé and Jay-Z (Musicians and Entrepreneurs):

- Forbes. (2023). America's Richest Self-Made Women: Beyoncé. Retrieved from https://www.forbes.com/profile/beyonce-knowles/
- Forbes. (2023). Jay-Z. Retrieved from https://www.forbes.com/profile/jay-z/

Jeff Bezos (Tech Mogul and Entrepreneur):

- Forbes. (2023). Jeff Bezos. Retrieved from https://www.forbes.com/profile/jeff-bezos/
- Investopedia. (2023, November). Jeff Bezos' Net Worth. Retrieved from https://www.investopedia.com/jeff-bezos-net-worth-5177218

Sara Blakely (Entrepreneur):

- Forbes. (2023). Sara Blakely. Retrieved from https://www.forbes.com/profile/sara-blakely/
- Investopedia. (2023, November). Sara Blakely's Net Worth. Retrieved from https://www.investopedia.com/sara-blakely-net-worth-5186573

George Clooney (Actor and Businessman):

- Forbes. (2018, July 16). George Clooney Tops Forbes' Highest-Paid Actors List With $239 Million. Retrieved from https://www.forbes.com/sites/natalierobehmed/2018/07/16/george-clooney-tops-forbes-highest-paid-actors-list-with-239-million/
- CNBC. (2017, June 21). George Clooney just sold his tequila business for up to $1 billion. Retrieved from https://www.cnbc.com/2017/06/21/george-clooney-sells-casamigos-tequila-for-up-to-1-billion.html

Elon Musk (Tech Mogul and Entrepreneur):

- Forbes. (2023). Elon Musk. Retrieved from https://www.forbes.com/profile/elon-musk/
- Investopedia. (2023, November). Elon Musk's Net Worth. Retrieved from https://www.investopedia.com/elon-musk-net-worth-5177243

Reese Witherspoon (Actress and Producer):

- Forbes. (2021, August 2). Reese Witherspoon Sells Hello Sunshine For $900 Million To Media Company Backed By Blackstone. Retrieved from https://www.forbes.com/sites/maddieberg/2021/08/02/reese-witherspoon-sells-hello-sunshine-for-900-million-to-media-company-backed-by-blackstone/
- Investopedia. (2023, November). Reese Witherspoon's Net Worth. Retrieved from https://www.investopedia.com/reese-witherspoon-net-worth-5186574

Agenda 2030 References:

- Ajay Banga. (2023). How Ajay Banga Plans to Transform the World Bank for a Climate-Changed Future. Retrieved January 7, 2025, from https://time.com/7172525/ajay-banga-world-bank-climate/
- Carnegie Endowment for International Peace. (2024). Tomorrow's Global Financial Architecture: A Reform Plan for People and Planet. Retrieved January 7, 2025, from https://carnegieendowment.org/research/2024/04/tomorrows-global-financial-architecture-a-reform-plan-for-people-and-planet

REFERENCES

- Financial News London. (2024). Gary Gensler tells UK to set firm T+1 transition deadline. Retrieved January 7, 2025, from https://www.fnlondon.com/articles/gary-gensler-tells-uk-to-set-firm-t-1-transition-deadline-94d3dbc8
- Financial Stability Board. (2024). FSB Sets Out 2024 Work Programme. Retrieved January 7, 2025, from https://www.fsb.org/2024/01/fsb-sets-out-2024-work-programme/
- FT.com. (2024). EU targets shorter settlement times to align with global standards. Retrieved January 7, 2025, from https://www.ft.com/content/26436fcf-8971-4e79-b3e2-81aa1594aefc
- Global Solutions Initiative. (2023). Reforming the Global Financial Architecture to Drive a Resilient Net-Zero Transition. Retrieved January 7, 2025, from https://www.global-solutions-initiative.org/wp-content/uploads/2023/12/T20_PB_TF5_11_Reforming_the_Global_Financial_Architecture_to_Drive_a_Resilient_Net-Zero_Transition.pdf
- Le Monde. (2024). COP29: The need to reform the global financial architecture has become even clearer. Retrieved January 7, 2025, from https://www.lemonde.fr/en/opinion/article/2024/10/18/cop29-the-need-to-reform-the-global-financial-architecture-has-become-even-clearer_6729782_23.html
- Reuters. (2024). Policy Watch: At COP29 and G20, leaders face calls to direct more finance to Global South. Retrieved January 7, 2025, from https://www.reuters.com/sustainability/cop/policy-watch-cop29-g20-leaders-face-calls-direct-more-finance-global-south-2024-11-19/
- United Nations Environment Programme Finance Initiative (UNEP FI). (2023). 30 Years of UNEP Finance Initiative: Transforming the Financial Industry. Retrieved January 7, 2025, from https://www.unepfi.org/news/timeline/
- United Nations. (2018). UN Secretary-General's Strategy for Financing the 2030 Agenda. Retrieved January 7, 2025, from https://www.un.org/sustainabledevelopment/sg-finance-strategy/
- Atlantic Council. (n.d.). Central bank digital currency tracker. Retrieved January 7, 2025, from https://www.atlanticcouncil.org/cbdctracker
- Investopedia. (n.d.). Countries developing central bank digital currency (CBDC). Retrieved January 7, 2025, from https://www.investopedia.com/countries-developing-central-bank-digital-currency-cbdc-5221005
- Reuters. (2024, June 25). India digital currency transactions slump after reaching initial c.bank target, sources say. Retrieved January 7, 2025, from https://www.reuters.com/technology/india-digital-currency-transactions-slump-after-reaching-initial-cbank-target-2024-06-25
- Reuters. (2024, July 1). Bahamas to regulate banks to offer cbank digital currency. Retrieved January 7, 2025, from https://www.reuters.com/technology/bahamas-regulate-banks-offer-cbank-digital-currency-2024-07-01
- Reuters. (2024, September 17). Central bank digital currency momentum growing, study shows. Retrieved January 7, 2025, from https://www.reuters.com/markets/currencies/central-bank-digital-currency-momentum-growing-study-shows-2024-09-17
- Wikipedia. (n.d.). Central bank digital currency. Retrieved January 7, 2025, from https://en.wikipedia.org/wiki/Central_bank_digital_currency
- World Economic Forum. (n.d.). What are central bank digital currencies? Advantages and risks. Retrieved January 7, 2025, from https://www.weforum.org/stories/2023/10/what-are-central-bank-digital-currencies-advantages-risks
- Citi, JPMorgan, and SIX finally see big business in blockchain. Financial News London. Available at: https://www.fnlondon.com/articles/citi-jpmorgan-and-six-finally-see-big-business-in-blockchain-0ee70621. Accessed January 7, 2025.
- Société Générale se suma a los bancos europeos que se abren paso "con cautela" a las criptomonedas. Cinco Días. Available at: https://cincodias.elpais.com/criptoactivos/2024-09-25/societe-generale-se-suma-a-los-bancos-europeos-que-se-abren-paso-con-cautela-a-las-criptomonedas.html. Accessed January 7, 2025.

REFERENCES

- The big boys want in on crypto, too. The Verge. Available at: https://www.theverge.com/2024/10/3/24261453/paypal-visa-blockchain-stablecoins. Accessed January 7, 2025.
- How banks will mint their own stablecoins. The Financial Brand. Available at: https://thefinancialbrand.com/news/cryptocurrency-banking/how-banks-will-mint-their-own-stablecoins-129207. Accessed January 7, 2025.
- The world of corporate stablecoins: What to expect in the years ahead. BeInCrypto. Available at: https://beincrypto.com/the-world-of-corporate-stablecoins-what-to-expect-in-the-years-ahead. Accessed January 7, 2025.

References for ISO 20022 Cryptocurrencies:

- Cryptonews. (n.d.). ISO 20022 compliant cryptocurrencies and their role in global finance. Retrieved January 7, 2025, from https://cryptonews.com/cryptocurrency/iso-20022-crypto
- Ripple. (n.d.). Ripple and ISO 20022: Driving innovation in financial messaging. Retrieved January 7, 2025, from https://ripple.com
- Algorand Foundation. (n.d.). Algorand's unique advantages in global financial systems. Retrieved January 7, 2025, from https://algorand.foundation
- Stellar Development Foundation. (n.d.). Building bridges between traditional finance and blockchain. Retrieved January 7, 2025, from https://stellar.org
- Quant Network. (n.d.). Quant's Overledger and ISO 20022 compliance. Retrieved January 7, 2025, from https://quant.network
- IOTA Foundation. (n.d.). IOTA: Distributed ledger technology for IoT and finance. Retrieved January 7, 2025, from https://iota.org
- Hedera Hashgraph. (n.d.). Hedera: Decentralized finance and enterprise-grade applications. Retrieved January 7, 2025, from https://hedera.com
- XinFin. (n.d.). XDC Network's approach to hybrid blockchain for trade finance. Retrieved January 7, 2025, from https://xinfin.org

Made in the USA
Long Beach, CA
27 February 2025

ISBN: 9798895905586

www.ingramcontent.com/pod-product-compliance
Lightning Source LLC
LaVergne TN
LVHW052222200926
848481LV00001B/187